THE BEST OF THE BEST

the best of the best

BECOMING ELITE at an AMERICAN BOARDING SCHOOL

Rubén A. Gaztambide-Fernández

HARVARD UNIVERSITY PRESS

Cambridge, Massachusetts | London, England

2009

Library of Congress Cataloging-in-Publication Data
Gaztambide-Fernández, Rubén A., 1971–
The best of the best: becoming elite at an American boarding
school/Rubén A. Gaztambide-Fernández.
p.   cm.
Includes bibliographical references and index.
ISBN 978-0-674-03568-3 (alk. paper)
1. Boarding schools—United States—Case studies.
2. Elite (Social sciences)—Education—United States—Case studies.   I. Title.
LC4941.G39   2009
373.2'220973—dc22   2009018307

A mis amores
Bonnie, Mercedes, y Alejandro

CONTENTS

THE BEST OF THE BEST

INTRODUCTION

This is a book about privilege. It examines the educational experiences of a group of students at an elite boarding school in the United States, and documents the cultural practices through which they internalize elite status and convince themselves that they deserve what they get. This is also a book about difference. It considers the experiences of students from diverse sociocultural backgrounds, and explores how race, class, and gender shape the process of becoming elite and the internal hierarchies of elite status.

The experiences and the particular context that are the focus of this book are rarely the subject of educational research or public debates about education. While much has been said about the predicaments of students who are "left behind" by a system that is sorely underfunded, few have ventured into a world in which abundance, opportunity, and success are defining characteristics. Yet "studying up" is crucial for understanding the dynamics of an educational system in which elite schools are an important piece of the puzzle. Studying the experiences of students in the most privileged educational settings sheds light on the social and cultural dynamics that shape inequality across the educational system.[1]

In this book, I seek to illustrate how elite status is continually produced through cultural practices that yield particular ways of being in and understanding the world—what academics call "subjectivities"—at one elite boarding school. What interests me is what actually happens day to day at an elite boarding school, and how the students who benefit from the abundance of resources and opportunities that such a school provides make sense of their experience. How does such abundance shape the ed-

ucational experiences of these students and the identifications they construct as members of such a small and privileged group? Are they, as Ross
Gregory Douthat suggests about his fellow Harvard graduates, "a privileged class of talented students [sitting] atop the world, flush with pride
in their own accomplishments, secure in the knowledge that they rule
because they *deserve* to rule, because they are the *best*"?[2] And if this is
the case, how do they come to internalize such entitlements?

In this introduction, I offer some background for the work presented
in this book and introduce the rarefied world of an elite boarding school
that I will call the "Weston School." I describe how the research began,
introduce the methodology, and offer a brief discussion of the theoretical concepts that inform my analysis. Academic readers will not find in
this book a thorough discussion of theoretical concepts or substantive
engagement with analytic problems. Readers who would like to pursue
topics in depth can consult the works cited in the notes. Other readers
may choose to skip all or some of the sections of this introduction, depending on their interests and background.

ENTERING

The campus of the Weston School appears as a surprise, as I drive into
the charmingly old-fashioned New England town of Weston. The venerable, austerely elegant Weston Hall faces the angular and contemporary
Alumni Library, both buildings framed by cautiously manicured lawns.
Since I'm an outsider, used to the hustle of northeastern cities, Weston
feels spacious and quiet to me; its wealth is immediately evident in the
ornate countenance of its brick and stone structures. The campus extends
over several hundred acres of green fields and wooded areas, which blend
with the surrounding town across boundaries that are imperceptible to
an outsider.[3]

Today, on my first visit to the Weston School, a teacher meets me at a
small café off campus to discuss the details of a research project that
a group of faculty and students are initiating. We sit with our espresso
drinks at a small round table by a window, to talk about the research and
exchange ideas about how to study a school's culture. The teacher seems
eager and relaxed in her blue jeans and black cowboy boots, as we discuss the intricacies of ethnographic research. After an extended conversation, she escorts me to the campus, walking up a straight path that cuts
diagonally across one of the lawns and between several tall buildings.

The redbrick structures remind me of textile mills I've seen in other New England towns. While factory work could not be further from what actually happens at Weston, I have few other ways to make sense of the space, which feels confusing and unfamiliar.

We enter one of the buildings through a back door and quickly turn down a marble staircase to the basement and into a classroom, where I am greeted by the smiles and handshakes of other teachers and a few students. In the middle of the room is a large wooden table displaying an enormous English dictionary next to a copy of Dostoyevsky's *Crime and Punishment*. Everyone takes a seat at the table, and as the conversation begins I revert to the comfort of academic language about research on schools and schooling. The committee is curious about my own experience living and working for two years at a smaller and less well-known boarding school for young artists, and I eagerly join the insider banter about life at a boarding school. Despite my discomfort in such an affluent school, being able to "talk shop" about boarding schools while engaging in academic discussions about education seems to legitimate my presence. I feel increasingly at ease as I chat with everyone around the table.

During the meeting, the members of the group tell me that they are interested in learning more about the research methodology of portraiture, first developed by Sara Lawrence-Lightfoot, as a possible way to explore the school's culture.[4] Their interest is informed mainly by the work of Theodore Sizer, Elliot Eisner, and Michael Apple, and their development of Philip Jackson's notion of the "hidden curriculum."[5] Their aim is to produce a document that they can use to engage the entire school community in reflecting on the implicit dimensions of their school's curriculum. Their vision is similar to Gerald Grant's idea: hire an anthropologist "who could pass for a teenager, [and] turn him or her loose in the school for several months with the aim of writing a portrait of the moral life of the community."[6] While it is obvious to the committee that I, a thirty-year-old doctoral student, can hardly pass for a teenager, I have to explain the ethical dimensions of performing such work and challenge some of their assumptions about the "fly on the wall" conception of qualitative research.

After several subsequent meetings, I was hired as a guest researcher to collect the data and write the research portrait.

My initial entry into Weston hinged on my willingness to do work for, and under the auspices of, the school itself. Weston's invitation was also premised on my own status as a graduate student at Harvard University, where many Weston teachers had obtained their own degrees and for which they had great respect and admiration. From the very beginning of my work, several faculty members who had done graduate work at Harvard encouraged me to consider expanding the research I was doing on their behalf, and suggested that I make it the focus of my dissertation. As educators, they were familiar with educational research and often expressed their eagerness for learning more about their school—whether positive or negative—with the hopes of improving their work. That they could relate to me as a graduate student and understood the value of this kind of research, both for them and for other educators, was key in their willingness to allow me to continue doing research at the school after I was no longer a consultant.

The unique opportunity to do research at an elite boarding school was intriguing to me for scholarly as well as personal reasons. I knew that the Weston School was one of the most prestigious institutions of its type. During my brief stint as an admissions officer at a smaller boarding school, I had visited three other elite boarding schools, and had been stunned by the sheer abundance of resources and disoriented by the patrician character of the spaces.

At the same time, there were aspects of elite boarding schools that reminded me of my own schooling. Before coming to the United States in 1989, I had attended the University of Puerto Rico's laboratory high school, which—like Weston—required an entrance exam and an application. Much like Weston, the school attracted students with high grades and achievement test scores, yet its public status and urban location imposed tight limits on the resources available. The students sat at old desks made of metal and veneered particle-board, the classroom walls sported water stains and cracking paint, and the lab equipment was discolored from decades of use. Still, as students of the esteemed "UHS," we were considered extremely privileged by the standards of most other public schools in Puerto Rico.[7]

In retrospect, I realized that my own experiences as a graduate student at what is perhaps the most prestigious of universities also motivated me to do this work. Often it is easier to understand ourselves through the experiences of others, and the more I examined how the students at Weston made sense of their experience at an elite institution, the more I understood about my own.

Still, after seven years as a graduate student at Harvard I find the abundance of a place like Weston daunting. After more than two years of fieldwork, entering Weston remains an out-of-the-ordinary event. Though I can navigate the campus paths with ease, greet students and adults alike with comfort, and eat in the dining hall without having to wear a visitor badge, each visit continues to remind me of my outsider status. I am not, nor will I ever be, a Westonian.

So it was that I arrived at the Weston School to assist these teachers in studying the school's culture and the "hidden curriculum" of the students' life outside the classroom. Despite all the prior negotiations and conversations, on the first day of fieldwork, October 30, 2002, I felt the weight of my own ambivalence about the complex ethnographic task I was undertaking. The following excerpt from my fieldnotes on the first day of observation at the school points to some of my own preoccupations with how I did or did not want to be perceived and my own hesitations about embarking on the fieldwork:

> I sit in the middle of the blue-gray carpeted square room, hesitant to enter this space, self-conscious and ambivalent about what I'm about to do. Where do I start? This is a space I'm rather unfamiliar with. Although I lived at [another boarding school], I am aware that Weston is the epitome of elite education and . . . I'm not sure where to enter without the protection and legitimacy that walking around with [faculty members] allows me. I'm hungry, but mostly I'm timid [and] feeling rather unprepared: What will I ask? How will the students respond to me? "Hi, my name is Ru-BEN." How will I pronounce my name? Will I give in to the English version, or will I assert my identity in this context? I have to make a decision, a symbolic decision. Do I insist that people call me Ru-BEN or do I slip into the culture easier if I allow RU-ben to become my name while I'm here?
>
> The green pines outside the window of my studio are the only trees that remain green in the fall. . . . I step out. It is very cold, and I want to go back inside.

THE FIVE E'S OF ELITE SCHOOLING

From October through December 2002, I visited Weston two to four days every week, usually spending the night at a faculty house. During that time, I conducted close to fifty formal and informal interviews with anyone who was willing to speak with me: students in every grade, faculty members, kitchen staff, administrators, alumni, and a few parents. I sought to observe many different contexts, deliberately exploring as much of the large campus as I could. I traveled in buses to sports events, cheered at pep rallies, attended faculty and student meetings, socialized with staff members, went on admissions tours, hung out in dorm lobbies after curfew, danced at semiformals, and ate with students as well as faculty in the dining hall until I, too, started to complain about the food. I attended two to five classes in every academic department, as well as several formal ceremonies.

During my first year of research, I learned that being a Westonian encompasses individual characteristics (such as being smart, showing a commitment to learning and hard work, tolerating difference) and a range of educational experiences (including seminar-style classes, classical languages, and college-level courses) that the school provides. These experiences encourage a collective sense of entitlement to the privileges of a Weston education and allow students to envision themselves assuming leadership roles and positions of power. In many ways, this exploratory research confirmed the analysis of previous scholars on the role of elite boarding schools in the formation of the power elite.[8] Building on this work and drawing on the data I collected and analyzed during that first year of research, I began to develop a model of the interrelated processes that contribute to how students come to see themselves as Westonians—a model that I call *the five E's of elite schooling:* exclusion, engagement, excellence, entitlement, and envisioning.

Students at the Weston School are carefully selected from hundreds of applicants through a complex admissions process that involves standardized tests, essays, recommendations, and often interviews. While the explicit purpose of the admissions process is to choose who will be allowed inside, the implicit purpose is to *exclude* and to provide a rationale for such exclusions. Once admitted and enrolled, students *engage* a plethora of learning opportunities in a wide range of academic, athletic, and artistic disciplines that rival those available at many small liberal arts colleges. As students develop their talents and demonstrate their *excellence,* they confirm their *entitlement* to the privilege of a Weston education. At the end of their Weston careers, students *envision* themselves in other equally elite spaces, pursuing challenging careers and assuming leadership roles.

Like most previous research on elite schooling, my initial inquiry left unanswered just how students make sense of these experiences, and it raised questions regarding the way they negotiate cultural boundaries in the process of becoming Westonians. My research suggested that the cultural dynamics of race, class, and gender shape the experiences of all students and the multiple meanings associated with being a Westonian. Indeed, I learned that not all students experience the five *e*'s of elite schooling the same way. The significance of elite schooling as a social process, in fact, seemed to be most evident in the particularities of how different students experienced the process differently.

With this in mind and with the school's permission, I returned to Weston the following year to continue the research independently.[9] I wanted to better understand the process of becoming Westonian, and to examine the contextually specific ways in which students enact different versions of what it means to be a Westonian. I was curious about whether and how students from different sociocultural backgrounds identified as Westonians, and how their identification with other social categories of race, class, and gender shaped the way they negotiated cultural boundaries and the various means they used to construct Westonian identifications of their own. These are questions that previous scholars who have studied the education of the elite have left unaddressed and that informed my work for a second year at Weston.

Given my own ambivalence about elite schooling, throughout this process I strove to remain skeptical of my conclusions and descriptions of the setting and the people within it, and to maintain an open mind and a perceptive ear. I have highlighted the ways in which the experiences I describe both confirmed and challenged my preconceptions, by making the familiar strange and the strange familiar. Whenever I saw or heard things that resonated with my preconceptions, I asked why; and when they did not resonate, I also asked why.[10]

Building on the data previously collected, during the second year I continued the "deep hanging out" that characterizes ethnographic research and that I had started a year earlier.[11] This time, I identified particularly salient contexts in which students enacted their Westonian identifications, and observed how social distinctions emerged and shaped interactions in specific contexts. I also developed a set of new data-collection strategies, including a survey of the senior class, in-depth narrative interview protocols, and three different focus group activities. I adapted these new strategies as the work evolved, to accommodate my emerging understandings. I also developed several strategies for analyzing these data, including giving students opportunities to challenge my emerging analysis and to contribute their own views as "sociologists" of their own experience.

In the process of doing this research, I encountered a group of students who eagerly joined me in this exploration and whom I learned to appreciate and respect a great deal. The thirty-six seniors who agreed to participate in the in-depth interviews and focus groups, in particular, challenged me to continue asking difficult questions and to avoid assuming I had a grasp of the complexity of their experience. These students represented a cross-section of the senior class, came from a wide range of social and cultural backgrounds, and identified themselves in many different ways across categories of race, class, gender, and sexuality. While most were boarding students, some commuted from home every day. Participants varied as to the number of years they had been at Weston, which I learned was an important distinction; students differentiated themselves as "four-year," "three-year," or "two-year" seniors, depending on what year they arrived at Weston. They also varied in the extent of financial support they received from the school. Some students were active and held leadership positions in artistic activities, and others were varsity athletes, including two team captains. Participating students also identified with different social spaces and claimed membership in a range of friendship groups. Readers who wish to know more about the research should consult the appendix, which contains a more detailed discussion of the methodology and the participants.

Throughout this book, I will use the words of these thirty-six participants to show how I came to understand their experiences. The descriptions of the students are incomplete, and in some cases deliberately inaccurate, as they have been altered with fictional details in order to preserve privacy and confidentiality. I suspect that some of the participants may not agree with the way I represent them, yet I hope they will see some reflection in these pages of their experience at the Weston School. With the same eagerness and excitement they demonstrated in sharing their lives with me and challenging my thinking while I was with them, I hope they will engage with the work presented here and I trust that they will continue to challenge my conclusions.

THE CULTURAL PRACTICE OF ELITE IDENTIFICATION

The Weston School, founded more than a century ago, is one of the most prestigious independent boarding schools in the United States. Every year, its graduating seniors are admitted to some of the most selective colleges and universities, and many prominent politicians, celebrated literary authors, and illustrious academics and intellectuals are among the school's alumni. My choice to stay at the Weston School for another year of research and to dedicate the time and effort that ethnographic research demands to this particular educational context was driven by my broader interest in the role of schools in the reproduction of social inequality. I was interested specifically in the particularities of the relationship between school culture and processes of identification within a resource-rich educational context. To make sense of this process and to sharpen my analysis, I drew insight and theoretical guidance from a wide range of mainly sociological and anthropological works.

Beyond Social Reproduction

Studies of elite schools have tended to focus primarily on understanding their role in *social reproduction*.[12] There is little doubt among scholars that all schools play a fundamental role in reproducing social-class structures and, more specifically, that schools like Weston are crucial for the reproduction of the upper class. This reproduction, they argue, is the outcome of a set of implicit mechanisms through which social-class status is transferred from one generation to another over time. For instance, practices such as legacy admissions (giving preference in admission to the children of alumni, particularly those who are large donors) simply yet compellingly suggest that certain social mechanisms are designed solely to ensure that those who have access to elite institutions maintain and consolidate that access, thus reproducing a stratified social order. Like colleges and universities, elite boarding schools justify legacy practices as an issue of loyalty and financial savvy. Yet we rarely ask how sustaining loyal alumni may be undemocratic, or what social logic undergirds legacy as a smart financial practice. Indeed, legacy practices have rarely been challenged publicly, even though it is the oldest and most commonly practiced form of affirmative action on behalf of wealthy elites.[13]

Elite boarding schools are also implicated in social reproduction by the fact that they exemplify the gross inequality in the distribution of resources and educational opportunities throughout society as a whole. In 2008, 16,043 students—roughly 0.10 percent of the more than 16 million secondary school students in the United States—enrolled in schools that could be categorized as elite boarding schools. While the U.S. public spent an average of $8,701 per pupil in 2005, elite boarding schools spent more than $46,000 per pupil.[14] In 2008, the average charge for tuition and fees for a (boarding) student at an elite boarding school was $41,744.[15] To the extent that class is a social category defined by money, elite boarding schools are clearly an example of how the sheer ability to pay for the kind of education an elite boarding school can provide enhances the prospect of future economic success for the very small portion of the population that has the luxury of attending them.

Of course, not all students who attend an elite boarding school come from wealthy families. Some scholars question the significance of social class in understanding inequality, pointing out that the fact that not all Westonians come from upper-class families is proof that the United States is an increasingly classless society.[16] They would argue that the permeability of class boundaries is evidence that economic status is less significant than other forms of stratification in determining an individual's life chances. While this may be the case in relation to specific individual experiences, the very existence of elite boarding schools underscores the persistence of class in a capitalist society in which educational experience is qualitatively different across the class divide. Indeed, there should be no doubt that remarkable investments are made every year in the education of a few, while the large majority of students are drastically shortchanged in a public school system that remains sorely underfunded.[17]

While social reproduction theory offers a powerful explanation of the persistence of inequality, it also suggests a rather linear process through which economic resources are transferred from one generation to another. Legacy admissions, for instance, might be better described simply as a form of reproduction through which parents pass their social status to their offspring.[18] Authenticating the transfer of social and economic resources from one generation to another is certainly an important function of elite schooling. Yet ensuring that *all* students who gain access to an elite boarding school, regardless of their social-class origins, learn to justify and internalize that they deserve the privileges of an elite education implies a more complex process. This is especially so when such a process requires some students to dissociate from previous experiences and status markers that might be in conflict with the elite status that an elite boarding school confers on them.[19]

In other words, admitting students who come from upper-class families is not enough; *all* Weston students must learn how to be part of this elite status group, particularly those who do not come from upper-class backgrounds. On the one hand, for students who come from upper-class families, schools like Weston simply underscore what they have already begun to internalize and learn before they are admitted. White middle- and working-class students and most students of color, on the other hand, are inducted through what one student described as "assimilation" into the elite. In fact, rather than diversifying the elite, students at the Weston School construct a narrow identification as elite students; it is the students who change, not the elite or the role of an affluent class in a capitalist society. Social reproduction theory cannot fully address how *all* students who attend an elite boarding school experience the process of becoming elite.

Status Groups and Symbolic Boundaries

This book is not about whether attendance at an elite boarding school guarantees wealth or upper-class status. Indeed, it is important here to distinguish between social class and elite status. The former is directly related to economic resources, while the latter refers to the hierarchical standing of what Max Weber calls "status groups." Status groups are defined only in part by their economic resources. For Weber, status groups are formed around status signals and behaviors that symbolically limit who can access membership in such groups.[20] Status hierarchies are not simply reproduced through the transference of economic resources, but also of the symbolic materials and subjective dispositions that are required to demonstrate membership in particular status groups. In other words, having access to economic resources alone does not give a person elite status; rather, the ability to demonstrate particular behaviors, dispositions, knowledge, and aesthetic choices is essential in order to assert particular kinds of status-group membership. These symbolic resources are the meaning-full materials, behaviors, and preferences that individuals mobilize in order to communicate a particular way of being, including membership in particular groups and affiliations with specific social categories.

Accordingly, my aim is to illustrate the cultural practices through which different students come to identify as Westonians as an elite status group, and to internalize their entitlement to the privileges (including the economic privileges) of an elite education. This process implies the formation of symbolic boundaries that not only define who is and who is not a Westonian, but also differentiate between different kinds of Westo-

nians and the hierarchies implied in such distinctions: what cultural sociologists call "boundary work."[21] Symbolic boundaries define the behaviors and identifications acceptable for individuals within specific contexts,
and play an important role in how individuals identify with and differentiate themselves from other groups.[22] Thus, this book examines how
students mobilize symbolic resources to construct and enact elite identifications, and the role such constructions and enactments play in how
they negotiate other symbolic boundaries within the context of one elite
boarding school.

Processes of Identification

In opposition to the view that identity is a unified and stable set of
characteristics, behaviors, or beliefs that "belong" to an individual or a
group,[23] sociologists and cultural theorists have argued that individuals
do not have a single and coherent identity, but a repertoire of identities
that they enact in particular social or cultural contexts.[24] Identities do
not manifest in coherent or consistent ways, but vary according to particular interactions and the requirements of particular situations.[25] This
view of identity as performance points toward a definition of identity
as something people *do*, rather than something people *are* or something
people *have*.[26] Throughout this book, I refer to the practices through
which identity claims (or identifications) are made—either by individuals
or groups, about themselves or about others—as *processes of identification*. Identification is the process through which social entities (individuals or groups) identify and/or are identified with various categories and
labels. This approach to processes of identification recognizes that institutions are powerful identifiers, and, furthermore, that institutions provide the necessary resources and the legitimation that enable certain identifications to have social and political consequences.[27]

Studying cultural practices among young people, especially in public
schools, has been central to our understanding of student agency and the
role of schools as institutions where students learn their "proper" place
in the social structure.[28] By and large, this work has focused on whether
and how students who identify (or are identified) with marginalized
groups at times resist, other times reproduce, and often redefine the repertoires of identification available to them.[29] Most of this research has
centered on urban and other public schools, mainly because educators
are concerned about the way processes of identification closely relate to

the reproduction of social inequality in schools. Thus, theories of youth identification and cultural practice tend to rest on antagonistic views of the relationship between schools and students. As such, they do little to help us understand how students who benefit the most from the current arrangements of schools experience their education. In what ways do the cultural practices of students who identify positively with schools contribute to the reproduction of inequality?[30] This question is further complicated when students are "positioned" in a context of economic affluence, abundant resources, and expanding opportunities, such as an elite boarding school.[31] How do students who are selected to enter such an elite context make meaning of their own subjective positions as "elite students"? How are race, class, and gender implicated (both explicitly and implicitly) in the process through which students come to identify as academically elite?

Accounting for the way processes of identification are negotiated in elite schools, where presumably students have much to gain by reproducing the boundaries that structure their identification, provides a fuller and more complex view of schools as institutions of social and cultural reproduction. Furthermore, comparing how students from different sociocultural backgrounds identify as students of an elite school would inform the view of the dynamic "boundary work" involved in the relationship between cultural practice and social reproduction.

The Discourse of Distinction

The analytic premise of this book is that when individuals tell stories about their experience, they construct and enact particular versions of how they understand themselves and their social context.[32] In other words, every story someone tells contains what Jerome Bruner calls a "delineation of the Self as part of the story."[33] The ability to claim an identification as a Westonian depends on the students' ability to know the sets of ideas and beliefs that shape experience at the school. These ways of understanding experience are what cultural theorists call a "discourse," and in this book I offer the notion of a *discourse of distinction* to refer to the particular ideas and ways of understanding experience that students draw upon to make sense of their experience at Weston and construct Westonian identifications.

The word "distinction" has two general meanings: one associated with difference, discrimination, and division; the other associated with ranking and quality, with honor and excellence. The first of ten definitions provided by the *Oxford English Dictionary* is an example of the former: "The action of dividing or fact of being divided; division, partition; separation." The second definition suggests the latter: "One of the parts into which a whole is divided; a division, section; a class, category. Class (in relation to status); rank, grade of the first distinction: of the highest rank; highly distinguished."[34] In what follows, I will illustrate how students at the Weston School convince themselves that they deserve the privilege of attending an elite boarding school by virtue of their respective distinctions. As a particular elite identification, Westonians are distinguished— or, as the *OED* specifies, they experience "the condition or fact of being distinguished or of distinguishing oneself; excellence or eminence that distinguishes from others; honourable preeminence; elevation of character, rank, or quality; a distinguishing excellence."[35]

Reflecting broader dynamics of social exclusion, the discourse of distinction delimits who is authorized to assume particular roles in the discursive space. As such, it bears on the range of meanings and the organization of the experiences that students can have.[36] This discourse of distinction provides students with a particular way of making sense of their experiences as Weston students, by providing the "patchwork of thoughts, words, objects, events, actions, and interactions" that makes up their experience.[37] It informs how students identify as members of a special group that is distinguished in both kind and status from most other students in the United States. Discourse is the logic that underlies not just how individuals communicate through language and other symbols, but how statements and representations, whether symbolic or more narrowly linguistic, relate to one another and to the sociohistorical context in which they are uttered.[38] In this sense, I draw my use of the concept of discourse from the traditions of critical discourse analysis, particularly those that focus primarily on the relationships between language as a social practice, institutions, and the broader sociohistorical context surrounding those practices and institutions.[39]

The discourse of distinction is one of the underlying formations that organize the culture of the Weston School as an elite boarding school.[40] This discourse frames the production of stories through which students enact (and justify) their elite status. It is "embodied" in Weston's particular institutional logic (including its curriculum and pedagogy), in the patterns of social behaviors and arrangements, and in the rituals around which students develop a sense of collective identification. It is in appropriating the discourse of distinction that students inherit—if unequally—the knowledge and the power that their status as elite students grants them. The discourse of distinction premises (but doesn't predetermine) how students experience their elite schooling; it is in the "daily practices and lived activities" of the students themselves that the discourse is constituted and mediated.[41]

At the center of this book, then, is a *cultural* explanation of elite identification, but not one that holds culture to be merely the "distinctive attitudes, values and predispositions, and the resulting behavior" of the members of a particular (and essentialized) group.[42] Rather, I take culture to be an analytic tool for describing how particular subjectivities are achieved in a given context, and how "webs of meaning" are produced to sustain the status arrangements implied in such subjective positions.[43] It is discourse, not culture, that delimits subjective positions through ideologies, spatial arrangements, and rituals that thicken how individuals understand their "positioning" and, therefore, how they behave.[44] Not only is such a dynamic view of culture more accurate, but, as many critical social theorists have argued, it opens up the possibility that social and cultural analysis might "create plans for escape."[45] Understanding the symbolic processes through which specific classes are produced at the level of cultural practice underscores how these processes continue to perpetuate gross inequality in a class-stratified society.[46] But it also points to the open-ended nature of the way status hierarchies are produced—and suggests the possibility that we might choose otherwise.

This book illustrates how becoming elite at the Weston School involves the remaking of the way students understand themselves in light of their particular educational experiences. This remaking of the self is premised on an overarching *discourse of distinction,* and articulated through processes of identification that manifest through narratives and in cultural practices. Each of the chapters in this book illustrates how the construction of elite identifications unfolds through different dimensions of students' educational experience, and how students craft an image of themselves as Westonians that implies "distinction" in both senses of the term.

There are three dimensions of the discourse of distinction that are central to this book, and that provide the framework around which it is organized: ideology, space, and ritual. These three aspects of discourse manifest through what I will define as the "three spheres of experience": the sphere of work, the social sphere, and the sphere of intimacy. Drawing on Erving Goffman's notion of the "total institution," in Chapter 1 I define these spheres of experience and build on Goffman's work to make the framework more relevant to the particular context of elite boarding schools.[47] Chapters 2 and 3 are primarily concerned with ideology, and the ways in which ideologies are implicit in the taken-for-granted assumptions students make about their experience. In Chapter 2, I describe how students make sense of their admission to Weston, and how they experience the inherently exclusive nature of that process as they begin to internalize their particular Westonian identifications. Chapter 3 explores how the ideology of meritocracy informs the way students make sense of the demands that the official school curriculum puts on them as students.

Chapter 4 focuses on the experiences of students in the social sphere and the relationship between the social boundaries students construct to distinguish various kinds of Westonians and how these are arranged in space. The experience of bonding in the sphere of intimacy is the focus of Chapter 5, where I describe different rituals through which the discourse of distinction is enacted and the sense of entitlement to a Westonian identification is "thickened."[48] In Chapter 6, I look across the spheres of experience to highlight how elite distinctions are unequally distributed among students and, specifically, how social processes of race, class, and gender influence—and to some extent limit—how students identify as Westonians. In the last chapter, I return to the five *e*'s of elite schooling, paying special attention to how the first four—exclusion, engagement, excellence, and entitlement—set the stage for the fifth: envisioning. To illustrate this last aspect of the process of becoming elite, I describe how students talk about their college prospects and the kinds of professional careers they envision for themselves.

"READING PRACTICES"

In the basement of the Weston modern-languages building, only the dim light from half-a-dozen lamps and a little sunlight leaking through dirty ground-floor windows illuminate the pages of Tennessee Williams' play *A Streetcar Named Desire* during a mid-morning English class. The walls are decorated with political posters, cartoon clips, and photographs; the large brown eyes of Kurtz, from Conrad's *Heart of Darkness*, watch over the conversation from a picture on the wall that seems about to fall. The teacher pays close attention to the students as they converse; she says little, asking questions that focus on particular sections or themes. Frustrated with the ambiguity of the text, one student asks: "Do we have to decide if he raped her?" From her seat, the teacher challenges him: "We have to ask why Williams leaves it ambiguous," moving beyond the "facts" of the story and asking the students for interpretations of authorial intent.

The students carry on, conversing with one another and taking turns without raising hands as they attempt to shed light on the text through their collective understanding, and bringing their own ideals about love and sex to bear on their interpretation of the scene. The teacher offers guidance: "Can we look at the word choice here?" The students argue over the use of the word "love," and giggle as they search for "voluptuous" in the large old dictionary lying in the middle of the seminar table. "Is this love? Are they husband and wife? Why is it not love?" The teacher pushes on, challenging students to move beyond their own emerging conceptions of gender and sex relations. As an audience, the students make meaning of the play in the darkness of the seminar room. "We are all constantly constructing meanings," explains a student, recognizing that her own understanding of love is only one way of interpreting the scene—and the class comes to an end.

This book is primarily descriptive; the argument evolves mainly through the details of life at the school and the words I have borrowed from the students. While I offer my own interpretations of these words and details, their meaning is surely open-ended. Most of us who study the culture of schools agree that there are many possible interpretations of a single event. Each person "reads" events and spaces according to particular perspectives and through specific lenses. Of course, as with every story, the teller is central to the telling. My assumptions and predilections, my own ways of looking and listening, my own interpretive and descriptive lenses shape the ways in which I describe the spaces and the participants. It may be, for instance, that diversity is a prominent theme in this book because I, as a Puerto Rican, am listening for this theme, or because the participants are speaking to diversity in view of how they identified me.

Like the students around the table, I invite you, Reader, to bring your own lenses and different "routes of reading" to the descriptions and the quotes in this book and to interpret them through your own perspective.[49] I invite you to engage with this text through multiple "reading practices"; to search for yourself as reader, to examine your own assumptions, and to find the ways in which looking into this context might reflect back something new about how you identify yourself.

1

TOTALLY ELITE

In Holden Caulfield's privileged world of adolescent angst, prep schools are "full of phonies" who study endlessly just so they can buy a "goddam Cadillac some day" and where "everybody sticks together in these dirty little goddam cliques."[1] J. D. Salinger's character moves from one boarding school to another, mightily resisting the transition to manhood while fantasizing about sex with girls from his elite Manhattan circles and dreaming of becoming "the catcher in the rye." From her midwestern middle-class home, Lee Fiora, in Curtis Sittenfeld's *Prep,* has a different view of elite boarding schools, which is fashioned after admissions catalogues with images "of teenagers in wool sweaters singing hymns in the chapel, gripping lacrosse sticks, intently regarding a math equation written across a chalkboard."[2] Though Lee finds this "glossiness" replaced by the rude reality of class privilege and masculine domination, she ultimately cherishes the imperfections of life in her prep school "bubble." Other imperfections drive the evolution of the friendship between Gene and Finny in John Knowles's *A Separate Peace* and between John and Owen in John Irving's *A Prayer for Owen Meany.*[3] Both of these friendships are encapsulated within a world of privileged and blissful isolation, where the cruelty of the world outside intrudes as subtle, but omnipresent, and ultimately tragic.

Elite boarding schools also provide the necessary background in the narratives of popular movies like *Dead Poets Society* and *School Ties.*[4] In the film *O,* a version of Shakespeare's *Othello,* the main character is a young black athlete named Odin who finds himself in a quagmire of jealousy and betrayal at an all-white elite boarding school.[5] Shakespeare's drama about sex, class, and race is rearticulated in a modern-day boarding school, which provides the perfect setting for such a restaging. Indeed, elite boarding schools are a preferred context among Hollywood directors and literary authors as a setting not only for depicting adolescent angst but also for playing out dramas about all kinds of social conflict.[6] Yet as audience and readers, we rely on the drama to tell us something about a setting that most of us hardly know.

When David Greene arrives at St. Matthews, the fictional elite boarding school in the film *School Ties,* he is stunned at the sight of the lush green campus and its elegant redbrick buildings. On arrival day, families frolic on the grass with their golden retrievers, while boys toss footballs and play volleyball without taking off their neckties. Fathers look relaxed in their blue blazers, white Oxfords, and beige khakis, while mothers stroll about in their pastel dresses and hats. The crisp blue sky and early-fall foliage frame the scene in the background, as boys pass the marble columns on their way in and out of the dormitories, carrying cellos, wooden trunks, and bicycles, or ably spinning a tennis racket. Stunned, Green exclaims, "Jesus, this is a high school?!" as bells peal from the chapel tower.

Richard Barbieri, former executive director of the Independent School Association of Massachusetts, opens his description of the various forms of "independent education" with a complaint about the "consistent and narrow" images "ingested" by American audiences about the typical boarding school—depicted as a "male institution [that] is populated by jacketed-and-tied youths who exhibit varying degrees of arrogance over or rebelliousness toward their privileged state. Moving across playing fields, classrooms where literature or history are discussed in small groups, and dormitory bull sessions or illicit nighttime escapes, these young men rehearse for war or Wall Street, or for opposition to the cultural values of the American upper class."[7] Most nonpublic schools would not fit the stereotype of the exclusive private boarding school portrayed in novels and movies. Yet such prestigious and highly selective educational institutions do exist, and they continue to provide elaborate educational experiences that would seem extravagant and highly privileged by the standards of most public schools in the United States. So what exactly is an elite boarding school?

Schools in the United States are either public or private. Private schools are typically identified as either "denominational" or "independent." The former—which outnumber the latter—are most often established with the purpose of integrating religion into the curriculum and are characterized by their affiliation with the religious organizations that fund them. Some elite boarding schools, though technically denominational, belong to the "independent" category. Independent schools, in turn, can be classified as either "day" or "boarding." Here the easy distinctions end. Determining what makes some boarding schools "elite," on the one hand, and what significance residential space has for elite schooling, on the other, is more complicated.[8]

Fictional representations of elite boarding schools are not directly concerned with accurate definition, yet the authors rely on the audience's ability to recognize the setting as a particular kind of school for a particular kind of student. Meanwhile, academic authors who write about elite boarding schools tend to tackle definition with either contempt or respect. The latter go out of their way to stress that each school is unique and offer multiple disclaimers about the dangers of assuming common characteristics. These academics work hard to avoid, and even argue against, characterizing these schools as "elitist."[9] Scholars whose primary aim is to demonstrate the role of elite boarding schools in the reproduction of an elite class simply define them primarily in terms of their demographics. In their resolve to mount a critique of elite schooling, these authors usually fail to note significant differences. A third group of authors ignore distinctions between elite and other private schools, as they argue for the importance of choice alternatives in the marketization of education.[10]

While recognizing that elite boarding schools vary in meaningful ways, I want to offer a working definition to develop what sociologist Max Weber calls an "ideal type." For Weber, ideal types are not to be taken as an evaluative representation of the "best kind" of any social entity. Rather, ideal types are abstractions drawn from reality in order to illustrate a particular social phenomenon.[11] The descriptions in this chapter are not meant as indictments, assessments, or endorsements of elite boarding schools. My purpose is to introduce the reader to the particular context of this research by highlighting those aspects that elite boarding schools like the Weston School share.[12] To illustrate these characteristics, I will draw on scholarly works, personal and autobiographical accounts, and works of fiction, including films, that may portray elite boarding schools stereotypically yet reflect actual features that are important for their definition.

This book investigates how students at the Weston School understand

what it means to be Westonians and how they come to identify themselves as such. This identification process requires a remaking of the self
in light of particular experiences within the distinct institutional context
that the term "elite boarding school" specifies. While a term like "prep
schools" may be more familiar, it is also more vague, as it can reference
many different kinds of private and even some public schools. The term
"elite boarding school" points directly to the fundamental role that both
the residential aspect and the elite status of a school like Weston play in
shaping students' educational experience and how they understand their
privilege. As with any boarding school, the particular ways in which the
Weston School encompasses multiple dimensions of students' lives are
central to how identifications are achieved.[13] As an elite institution, however, the Weston School provides the necessary cultural, social, political,
and historical context to construct specifically elite identifications premised on material abundance and social status. In other words, being a
Westonian is premised on the encompassing character of a residential
school, as well as on its character as an elite institution, and both aspects
are intimately related to each other. Therefore, I will describe elite boarding schools in terms of, first, how they constitute a particular kind of "total institution," and second, the characteristics that mark each school as
an elite institution.[14]

"TOTAL INSTITUTIONS"

On my very first visit to the Weston School, I joined a group of teachers
and students who were exploring various alternatives for doing an in-
tramural study of the school's culture and its "hidden curriculum"—the
lessons learned in school that are not officially part of the curriculum.[15]
After a good hour discussing the advantages and possibilities of ethnographic research for the kinds of work they wanted to do, some of the
teachers expressed interest in my previous experience living and working
at a lesser-known boarding school. As the conversation evolved, I found
myself highlighting shared experiences and drawing on my prior knowledge to establish a shared identification and legitimacy as a colleague. As
we started to wrap up our session and gather our things, one veteran
teacher asked me somewhat nonchalantly whether I was familiar with
the term "total institution" and whether I thought schools like Weston fit
the definition; I fumbled for an answer. I knew the term and believed that
it was somewhat relevant to all schools, particularly boarding schools.

Yet, aware of its association with prisons and mental institutions, I tried to reassure my hosts by downplaying the comparison.

The conventional wisdom among scholars has been to assert that a boarding school of any kind is, by definition, what sociologist Erving Goffman describes as a "total institution."[16] Goffman himself lists boarding schools as belonging to a particular kind of total institution that enables "inmates" to pursue a particular focused task—such as academic study—or particular kinds of work.[17] Goffman implies that the primary purpose of boarding schools (or at least of their institutional arrangements) is to fulfill the "manifest function" of providing an education. Most authors assume that the concept accurately and appropriately captures the important dimensions of this particular type of school. But does it? And if so, what specific characteristics of an elite boarding school might underlie the process of achieving elite identifications?

The principal characteristic of total institutions is that all "aspects of life are conducted in the same place and under the same single authority."[18] Generally, total institutions comprise a large group of people who share a predetermined set of characteristics or goals. They spend most of their time in one another's presence; they are treated alike and expected to engage in the same activities. Life in a total institution is bound by rules and relatively tight schedules that are imposed from above. How individuals enter, how they are treated, and how their life is organized and regulated all follow a rational plan designed to fulfill the goals of the institution.[19] It should be easy to see how elite boarding schools (and perhaps schools in general) fit the concept of a total institution. Students are selected through predefined criteria; they spend most of their daily life in one another's company; they all follow the same rules; their days are tightly scheduled; and they come together with the explicit shared goal of obtaining an elite education.

Yet the force of Goffman's argument lies largely in the dramatic character of his examples, which are drawn primarily from mental hospitals, prisons, and concentration camps.[20] While he emphasizes that total institutions vary widely, his analytic focus on these particularly stigmatized institutions raises questions (and nervous eyebrows) about the applicability of his framework to educational institutions like elite boarding schools. For instance, students in elite boarding schools presumably chose to be there and could, at any moment, choose to leave. Indeed, Goffman's discussion pays little attention to the difference between total institutions where inmates choose to enter and leave, and those where they are forced to enter and stay.

The association of the term "total institution" with prisons and mental hospitals also conjures up images of mistreatment, restricted freedom, and complete control over individuals' bodies. Goffman's discussion of "rituals of mortification," "loss of identity equipment," and "contaminations of the self" seems rhetorically constructed to offer a staunch critique of specific kinds of total institutions. As such, the assumptions Goffman makes about the character of total institutions might seem too drastic and the examples he offers too tangential, at least in relation to what one might observe at an elite boarding school. When he does offer illustrations of life at boarding schools, he draws primarily from the bitter autobiographical accounts of authors like George Orwell.[21]

Yet Goffman's analysis need not be restricted to institutions that stigmatize their inmates. For instance, he argues that within total institutions, "the outside world is used as a point of reference to demonstrate the desirability of life in the inside, and the usual tension between the two worlds is markedly reduced."[22] This is certainly part of how students construct an identification as Westonians: by drawing a boundary between the "Weston bubble" and the "real world." In one of the few places where Goffman actually mentions elite boarding schools, he notes that where the identification and status conferred by the institutional affiliation are favorable, "jubilant official reunions, announcing pride in one's school, can be expected."[23] While this is indeed accurate, the value of Goffman's work for an analysis of the experiences of students at an elite boarding school seems elusive. At first glance, it appears more likely that elite boarding schools like Weston simply "approach Goffman's prototype."[24]

On my initial visit to Weston, I was too new and too busy "managing" my own presentation to attend to the details that may or may not constitute Weston as a total institution.[25] At the beginning of my research, the more I learned about the experiences of students at Weston, the less Goffman's framework seemed applicable in any significant way. The boundaries of the bubble seemed too permeable, the rules too negotiable, and the students too satisfied to enable me to draw a parallel between the school and a prison or a concentration camp, even when a few students were pointing me in that direction.

It wasn't until well into the second year of my fieldwork that I perceived a theme that would lead me back to Goffman. Students often repeated the idea that in order to succeed at Weston they had to choose two of the three aspects of their life at the school: they could be really good at their work, they could have a great social life, or they could get some sleep. Initially, I understood these comments as part of the general notion that schools like Weston are very demanding places, where students have to make sacrifices in order to succeed in what I was beginning to understand as the "culture of excellence." But the theme continued to emerge as I began to code interviews; and when I reread Goffman's essay, his discussion of the "central feature" of a total institution stood out from the page: "A basic social arrangement in modern society is that the individual tends to *sleep, play,* and *work* in different places, with different co-participants, under different authorities, and without an over-all rational plan. The central feature of total institutions can be described as a breakdown of the barriers ordinarily separating these three spheres of life."[26] Goffman's words directly echoed how students described their experience. His use of mental hospitals and prisons notwithstanding, Goffman's basic definition of total institutions is that they are more encompassing than other (nontotal) institutions. If nothing else, elite boarding schools share with prisons and mental hospitals their encompassing character and the fact that students sleep, play, and work in the same institutional space.

Yet Goffman's concept does not directly yield a framework for understanding the particular institutional context of an elite boarding school. For instance, not all students at an elite boarding school sleep in the same building, and day students (who go home to sleep) are part of the fabric of the school and also claim an identification as Westonians. Additionally, unlike the inmates of prisons and mental hospitals, students are willing participants who, to varying degrees, have chosen to enter the institution and can, presumably, choose to leave. Most of Goffman's discussion assumes that inmates are unwilling participants who must be closely monitored by a staff that works to convince the inmates that they belong in this place.[27] Nonetheless, Goffman's discussion does offer insights into the processes through which the institution shapes how inmates come to think of themselves and accept an institutional identification.

Goffman argues that by desegregating the various spheres of experience, the total institution achieves relative control over the subjective experiences of inmates. The encompassing tendencies of elite boarding schools are clear when students talk about having to choose between working, socializing, and sleeping in order to succeed at Weston. Yet when I listened to their stories, their narratives suggested a more nuanced distinction. As students talked about what it meant to be a Westonian, they rarely (if ever) told stories about sleeping; though they often (and readily) told stories about experiences with other Westonians that were neither work nor play but that may be better characterized as *intimacy*. In fact, it became clear from their narratives that "socializing" involved two distinct types of experience: one comprised public behaviors and relations that were open to the scrutiny of others (often but not always involving social play); the other entailed intimate relations that were enclosed within "private" spaces, most typically in students' dormitories (where, as it happened, they also slept).

On the basis of this distinction, and building on Goffman, I suggest that elite boarding schools can be described as "total" in the sense that they encompass three *spheres of experience* that are central to how students develop an identification with the institution: the sphere of work, the sphere of social interactions, and the sphere of intimacy. This way of understanding the schools' encompassing character allows the analysis to include, for instance, how it is that day students (who do not sleep at the school) also experience a sense of bonding as Westonians. Indeed, shifting from simple "sleep" to an analysis of the role that intimacy plays in the construction of elite identification is crucial. Additionally, a focus on intimacy opens the analysis to a consideration of ritualistic as well as "regressive" behaviors that are important in how students describe bonding with other students.[28]

As an institution, the Weston School provides students with a sense of collective identification. But it is through these experiences of intimacy— those "little kookie things," as one student said—that students create deeper bonds with other Westonians. The sharing of apparently innocuous moments of intimacy and the engagement in private rituals strengthens the bonds that students make with one another and promotes the "closure" of Westonians as an elite status group. This closure is particularly crucial for the conferring of elite status that makes elite boarding schools distinct from most other total institutions. Indeed, it is their character as particularly *elite* institutions that provides the necessary context and resources for the production of elite identifications.[29]

DEFINING ELITE BOARDING SCHOOLS

Authors whose primary aim is to demonstrate the role of elite boarding schools in the reproduction of an elite class simply define them in terms of the social-class status of the populations they serve. Most of these arguments are based on analyses of documents like the *Social Register* and *Who's Who,* but authors typically say little about what makes these boarding schools *elite*.[30] Even when their analysis points to the characteristics that elite boarding schools have in common and how these characteristics help explain their social role, authors tend to rely on an apparent consensus about which schools are the most elite or have the most "snob appeal."[31] Though the vagueness of such descriptions may have been adequate at a time when being listed in the *Social Register* mattered, the contemporary character of elite status in the United States requires a different approach.[32]

To call these schools "elite" is to indicate that they are accorded high status among social groups that have the power to make such judgments and with which, presumably, these schools "correspond" as educational institutions.[33] My goal in this chapter is not to explain the social, historical, and cultural processes that lead to the identification of these schools as elite, but to articulate what makes them recognizable as elite boarding schools. To that end, I will specify their eliteness along five constitutive characteristics. I will describe how the schools are:

1. typologically elite, by virtue of their identification as "independent schools";
2. scholastically elite, by virtue of the extensive and sophisticated curriculum they offer;
3. historically elite, by virtue of the role that elite social networks have played in their historical development;
4. demographically elite, by virtue of the population that attends elite boarding schools; and
5. geographically elite, by virtue of their physical character and location.

While the elite status of a school in any of these particular dimensions may be open to debate, it is the particular conjunction of these five traits that makes a school an *elite* boarding school.[34] Furthermore, each dimention is important for understanding how elite identifications are achieved within this institutional context.

Typologically Elite

The first characteristic common to all elite boarding schools is that they identify as "independent" schools. This independent status is critical for how elite boarding schools function and what they are able to accomplish. Pearl Kane, head of the Klingenstein Center for Independent School Leadership at Columbia Teachers College, defines independent schools according to six basic traits: self-governance, self-support, self-defined curriculum, self-selected students, self-selected faculty, and small size. The vast majority of the roughly one thousand schools that identify as independent are by no means elite. It is crucial, therefore, that we establish how elite boarding schools stand out from other independent schools by describing them in terms of the six characteristics outlined by Kane.[35]

Since the early days of the academies, independent schools have always been self-governing, and thus self-supporting. They received government charters but little or no public funding, which meant that they were not accountable to local officials.[36] This also meant that they were responsible for sustaining themselves, either by charging tuition or by raising funds from private supporters. Today, the typical independent school is governed by a self-perpetuating board of trustees that is in charge of hiring the school's director and overseeing the general management of school finances and infrastructure. Boards of trustees are usually made up of alumni, large donors, and other community leaders identified by the school and enlisted to fulfill particular advising or funding roles.

Unlike most independent schools, elite boarding schools have endowments that could be the envy of most liberal arts colleges. The wealthiest schools have reported endowments around the billion-dollar mark, and some have held individual fundraising campaigns that yielded revenues exceeding the total endowment of most other schools.[37] While most elite boarding schools still depend on tuition to keep up with the large expense of providing a scholastically elite education, some of the wealthiest schools are considering a plan—following the examples of Harvard and Princeton—to provide need-blind admission.[38]

Independent schools have also always had relative autonomy to define their curriculum. I say "relative" because, while academies were not mandated to offer state-sanctioned curricula, they nonetheless had to respond to the pressures of their constituents—mainly from parents and colleges—in defining the content and pedagogy of their courses. Indeed, the *raison d'être* of the early academies was to provide the curriculum that those who could pay for an education wanted; and as such, it was driven by the needs and interests of potential "clients," many of whom were the children of merchants and business owners.[39] Most elite boarding schools still offer a curriculum that in many ways mirrors that of the early academies, at least in their attempts to combine a "classical" and an "English" curriculum. Early Americans who found wealth in the colonies promoted a classical model focusing on instruction in Latin and Greek as the core of the curriculum.[40] Elite boarding schools continue to offer an extensive curriculum that often rivals that of small liberal arts colleges.

Because they are self-governed, independent schools also have the freedom to select their students and have broad flexibility to select their teachers; independent schools are self-selected communities, and both implicit and explicit criteria play an important role in defining who is included and, by extension, who is excluded. Elite boarding schools, however, have room to be far more selective on both counts than the large majority of independent schools. They tend to have a larger selection pool, and as their financial resources expand, their ability to attract qualified students regardless of their need is also increasing.[41]

The last characteristic of independent schools is that they are small. This again is part of the long history of the academies. Early schools held classes in private homes, and even those that had their own buildings were small by today's standards. Elite boarding schools tend to be large in comparison to most independent and other boarding schools, ranging from roughly 350 students to just over 1,000, with an average of roughly 500.[42] Even the bigger schools are dwarfed by many public schools, whose enrollment can reach several thousand. Elite schools also differ from most independent schools (and most public schools) in another, perhaps more important way: their physical size.[43] Their sprawling campuses, resulting from decades of land acquisition in rural settings, are a determining factor not only in the schools' overall wealth but in their character as *geographically elite* institutions.

Elite boarding schools, then, are unlike most independent schools in the abundance of their resources and their ability to construct the kinds of communities they want to be by carefully selecting who is allowed in and who is not.[44] The independence, wealth, selectivity, and range of opportunities that characterize elite boarding schools are crucial in the process by which students construct elite identifications and internalize their privilege.

Scholastically Elite

Schools like Weston afford their students a spectacular array of opportunities to explore various interests, engage in unique pursuits, and find a "bubble" or "niche" in which to demonstrate their abilities. This is part of the promise that Weston and its peer schools make to their students, and what attracts many of those students (and their parents) to the school in the first place. A welcoming statement from Weston's headmaster tells students that they "are fortunate to attend a school that offers hundreds of courses and many choices." "Don't be afraid to challenge yourself," she invites students, "and especially to develop new skills and areas of knowledge. . . . [You] will encounter areas of inquiry . . . which are unavailable to most high school students." She urges Westonians to "enjoy the richness of these offerings and make the most of them."

The explicit aim of this wide range of opportunities and challenges is, according to the mission statement of a similar school, "to educate young people—intellectually, aesthetically, socially, physically, and morally—so that they become responsible, contributing citizens, and fulfilled human beings." At another elite boarding school, the mission is to "foster the life of the mind, . . . promote fitness and health, . . . [and] nurture integrity, empathy, and kindness." Most elite boarding schools have very similar mission statements. "Dare to be True" is the motto of another school, which claims to "cultivate in its students a passion for learning and a respect of others. Embracing diversity and the pursuit of excellence create a community in which individuals develop competence, confidence and character." To accomplish these goals, elite boarding schools have sophisticated courses of study, and students are able to choose from a wide range of offerings in many disciplines. Once admitted to an elite boarding school, students embrace—albeit to varying degrees—the expectation that they will take full advantage of the school's offerings and strive to be, as one student put it, "the best of the best."

Elite boarding schools like Weston have a plethora of academic departments: Classical Languages, which usually include both Latin and Greek; Modern Languages, including English and many other foreign languages, from French and Spanish to Russian and Chinese; Mathematics; Science; Computer Science; Religion; and History and Social Sciences, which often include courses in anthropology, economics, and psychology, among others. The academic program is described in the Weston course catalogue as paralleling that of a four-year college, and the offerings would be the envy of any small liberal arts college, including courses in (to name just a few) cultural anthropology, Greek and Latin (multiple levels, with five advanced courses), and macroeconomics; courses on Shakespeare, Faulkner, Hemingway, Nabokov, and themes ranging from existentialism to contemporary Spanish theater; courses entitled "Colonial America," "Capitalism and Its Critics," "The Contemporary Middle-East," "Advanced Statistics and Probability"; advanced courses in linear algebra and differential equations; and several courses in French literature, from the sixteenth through the twentieth century.

Elite boarding schools are also characterized by a Socratic approach to pedagogy that is rare in other schools.[45] This is so not because other educators do not value this approach to teaching, but because teaching at elite boarding schools is premised on two implicit assumptions: first, that the great majority of classes are small, and, second, that the students who come into the classroom have been preselected through the admissions process. Unlike the vast majority of public schools, elite boarding schools can afford a low student-to-teacher ratio that typically hovers between five and eight students per teacher. Unlike the vast majority of public schools,[46] these students (and teachers) have been carefully preselected through an elaborate process of exclusion to ensure that they are not only able but eager to engage in the seminar style of teaching that has become "the central classroom metaphor of the boarding school."[47] Thus, wealth and exclusion are the basis for the kinds of learning and teaching experiences students have and for the kinds of "intimacy" necessary for such experiences.[48]

Yet elite boarding schools are scholastically elite because they offer not only a wide range of academic offerings, but also a great variety of opportunities in areas like athletics, the arts, and extracurricular (or co-curricular) activities.[49] Overall, the "official curriculum" of schools like Weston comprises four domains, in which all students, to some extent or another, must engage. These domains are the academic, the athletic, the artistic, and the extracurricular.

Sports are a centerpiece of the nonacademic culture at elite boarding schools, and there are long-standing traditions that revolve around sports—traditions such as pep rallies, and rivalries with particular schools. All elite boarding school students must go through some sort of physical education program, and many engage in sports through interscholastic athletics. The range of sports opportunities at elite boarding schools can be daunting, including the full gamut of interscholastic sports —field hockey, crew, squash, wrestling, ice hockey, tennis, cycling, water polo, swimming and diving, lacrosse, ultimate frisbee, and many others. Elite boarding schools have athletic facilities that mirror those of college campuses. They often have multiple gymnasiums; some dedicate more than a hundred acres of land to fields for lacrosse, soccer, and field hockey; most have football stadiums. Some schools have lavish boathouses for crew and sailing equipment, multiple hockey rinks and basketball courts, and state-of-the-art facilities dedicated to one or two sports. Many have two swimming pools (one for diving and one for laps), climbing walls, row after row of tennis courts, well-equipped weight rooms with dedicated sports science and physical therapy centers. Some schools abut rivers broad enough for "straightaway" sections dedicated to crew practice, have hills steep enough for skiing practice, and own land extensive enough for playing golf.

Elite boarding schools also provide an astonishing range of artistic opportunities, and students are often required to participate in artistic endeavors at some point. Schools offer courses and training in music, theater, and the visual arts. With the advent of coeducation, many elite boarding schools have dedicated resources to dance training and dance facilities. Some schools have rehearsal halls for large ensembles (such as a symphony orchestra, choir, and concert band), private lesson rooms with grand pianos, and rows of soundproof practice studios. Courses in the visual arts usually include ceramics, painting, drawing, sculpture, photography, printmaking, architecture, and digital design. Elite boarding schools have ceramic studios, photography workshops, digital-imaging labs, and art galleries, where work by students as well as by internationally renowned contemporary artists is often displayed. The schools usually have more than one theater—at least one main stage and smaller, black-box theaters—with full lofts, wardrobe and scenery shops, and professional stage equipment. Courses often include all aspects of the theater arts, from production to acting, including stagecraft, directing, and filmmaking. Even many high schools that specialize in the arts do not have nearly the resources and facilities that elite boarding schools provide for their students.[50]

Last, the extensive catalogue of student groups, clubs, and other extracurricular activities at elite boarding schools "is nearly endless."[51] Extracurricular activities can be categorized generally into three types: student leadership organizations that typically require some sort of selection process (examples are student council, dorm proctors, disciplinary committee, student newspaper), service and volunteerism organizations (the yearbook, social services volunteering), and affinity groups (organized around religious or spiritual interests, political affiliations or activism, ethnic or cultural backgrounds, topical areas, sexual preferences).

Some large comprehensive public schools likewise have extensive cur-ricular offerings, particularly elite public schools.[52] Yet what makes elite boarding schools scholastically elite is not only the range, but also the phenomenal quality of their facilities, some of which rival those of pro-fessional sports clubs and professional arts organizations. In addition, the particular approach to pedagogy that characterizes an elite boarding school education is often found only in Advanced Placement and other high-track courses in traditional public schools.[53] Of course, not all stu-dents experience these high-level seminars in the same way. Seminar ta-bles are not neutral spaces. Indeed, they can become competitive arenas where race, class, and gender have a bearing on the outcome of the fight over the last word.

Historically Elite

Historical accounts of the emergence and evolution of elite boarding schools in the United Sates are sparse. The handful of educational histori-ans who have studied the way schools like Weston developed are divided on whether their elite status was the cause or the consequence of their evolution, and on whether elite boarding schools emerged for the express purpose of consolidating an upper class.[54]

The first American boarding schools emerged as part of the wide pro-liferation of the "academies" prior to the Revolutionary War and through the early part of the nineteenth century. The early settlers of the Brit-ish colonies in North America had profound faith in the human capac-ity for "betterment"; more important, they believed that such betterment could be accomplished through organized and institutionalized school-ing. Despite their optimism about organized schooling, they were weary of spending their limited financial resources on such collective ventures. While growing states established Latin grammar schools, most individu-als, particularly those in isolated and rural areas, opposed the financial burden that such initiatives would have put on their taxes. As a result, the first academies were most often the ventures of individuals, typically with the support of new merchants and industry owners who wanted to provide an education for their children. While local governments often provided some support through land donations or money, their main in-volvement was in providing state charters that would give official institu-tional standing to the new academies but no economic commitments.[55]

Early colonists were also ambivalent about academic and intellectual activities, which they associated with the classed society against which they were defining themselves and the new nation. At the same time, they were aware that education could serve two important roles: preparing all citizens for civic participation, while identifying a professional and political elite that would lead the development of the nation. Although they were ambivalent about the classic curriculum that was the model of early academies, the colonists also acknowledged the symbolic power of such skills and retained the belief that these were important for distinguishing a learned class. Still, they wanted the early academies to do more than just teach the classics. Academies were expected to teach an overwhelming number of courses in a wide range of subjects and specialties, from Latin and religion to surveying and penmanship. This enormous range eventually proved to be a major factor in their demise.[56]

The combination of limited financial resources and the demand for a comprehensive curriculum eventually undermined the viability of independent academies. The rise of publicly funded comprehensive high schools after 1850 rendered the smaller academies financially and educationally impractical. By the time of the Civil War, the thousands of academies that had developed during the eighteenth century had virtually disappeared. Yet not all academies were created equal, and some of them, mostly in New England, were endowed early in their histories with large financial resources. Theodore Sizer, in his history of the academies, suggests that the "well-known New England academies in particular survived by altering their character and student body [and] becoming socially or academically exclusive."[57] Yet it is unlikely that many of the thousands of academies that existed in the early nineteenth century could suddenly have decided to become socially or academically exclusive. Rather, those schools that already had a base of wealthy alumni, associations with elite universities, and connections with the emerging mercantile, industrial, and financial elite were the ones that survived the decline of the academies. Many of today's elite boarding schools were founded as the older academies were closing down, and those that existed prior to 1850 underwent substantial reconfiguration during this time, responding to the desires and needs of the elites that supported them.[58]

According to James McLachlan, both surviving and new elite academies had close ties to the elite circles of the time, particularly those associated with the Boston Brahmins.[59] The members of this New England–based elite had a vested interest in developing their own schools parallel to, but a cut above, the schools that emerged both prior to and during the expansion of public schools.[60] The central role that wealthy families in Boston (and later New York) played in the reinvigoration of old boarding schools and the establishment of new ones provides a clue as to whether elite boarding schools developed in line with the consolidation of an American aristocracy.

If the first historical antecedents of elite boarding schools were the early colonial academies, the second model consisted of the British "public" schools.[61] The men responsible for promoting and establishing elite boarding schools during the second half of the nineteenth century admired and were closely familiar with the schools responsible for educating the British aristocracy. They were keenly aware of the role that these cloistered environments played in consolidating ties among the British elite and were well versed in the curriculum that these schools provided.[62] While the early academies suffered from their ambivalence about their role in promoting class distinctions, elite boarding schools embraced that role with enthusiasm.[63]

This enthusiasm, however, is not obvious, and historians of elite boarding schools are often circumspect regarding the role of elite boarding schools in promoting class distinctions. For instance, James McLachlan, in his book *American Boarding Schools,* goes to great lengths to argue that these schools "have consciously educated their students to avoid, abjure, and despise most of what are traditionally thought to be aristocratic or upper-class values and styles of life. They have worked instead to *prevent* the development of aristocratic attitudes."[64] Instead, McLachlan asserts without any sense of irony that elite boarding schools served the necessarily elitist function of educating the true *aristoi:* "Since there can be only a few of the 'best' at any one time, the concept of the American gentleman has been of necessity elitist."[65] From this perspective, the historical foundations of the elite boarding schools rested on the terrain of the meritocracy, where the most capable were to be taken to the "school in the garden" to be nurtured intellectually and culturally.

Yet the expansion of private elite boarding schools alongside the public education system was not premised, as this view would suggest, on their ability to identify those few students with the raw material to become leaders of the meritocracy. On the contrary, their histories suggest that it was their ability to bring together the children of old and new wealthy families from geographically distant financial centers that ensured their survival. Elite boarding schools consolidated at a time when the fortunes of the old New England elites were decreasing in value and when new wealth was emerging, particularly with the development of the banking industry in New York City. These new elites, however, lacked the cultural dispositions and refinements necessary to distinguish themselves symbolically and justify their rise, qualities that the old elites had in abundance. Elite boarding schools served the important function of consolidating the old and the new aristocracies. While the new aristocracy provided the economic capital to protect the old from the imminent decline of their fortunes, the members of the old aristocracy provided the necessary terms for defining the credentials that would entitle any elite boarding school graduate to their presumably hard-earned privileges.[66]

As millions of new immigrants arrived in the United States, overwhelming the rapidly expanding public school system, elite boarding schools became even more significant for ensuring that the children of the elites were properly educated among their own. Schools like Weston share a history that points to an expansion, along with the public school system, that is premised on their elite status. These schools have experienced all kinds of difficult histories, and questions about their legitimacy have always been raised.[67] In every instance, they have survived these challenges through a combination of charismatic leadership, the support of wealthy alumni, and their associations with elite colleges, which played a role in their establishment and their development from the very beginning.[68]

Demographically Elite

Today, the majority of the students who attend elite boarding schools are still the children of the very wealthy. The face of wealth in the United States has changed a great deal from the days of the Boston Brahmins and the robber barons, and one cannot measure the eliteness of a school on the basis of how many of its families are listed in the *Social Register*. Nonetheless, more than two-thirds of the families that send their children to elite boarding schools can afford the considerable cost of attendance, which according to one estimate would place them in the top 4 percent of the income distribution.[69] While this does not automatically place a family among the most elite groups in U.S. society, it cannot be denied that such wealth is indicative of the extreme disparity between the very few families that can afford an elite boarding school education and the rest of the U.S. population.[70]

Yet in the past thirty years, elite boarding schools have changed the face of their student bodies a great deal and have expended substantial resources to recruit, enroll, and graduate a more diverse student body.[71] Since the early 1970s, most elite boarding schools have become coeducational, and the number of their students who identify racially as other than white has increased. More recently, their attention has shifted to the goal of attracting more socioeconomic diversity, by raising the necessary funds to admit all qualified students regardless of their financial need. These efforts alone, of course, do not and probably cannot change the social and cultural conditions that determine who arrives at the admissions office of an elite boarding school in the first place, or change prospective students' ability to produce the sort of application materials that would render them qualified.[72] Notwithstanding important changes, then, students at elite boarding schools remain by and large the children of the very wealthy.[73]

Students at elite boarding schools have also demonstrated high levels of academic achievement and scholastic aptitude through standardized forms of measurement. Students admitted into elite boarding schools typically rank above the eightieth percentile on the Secondary School Admissions Test (SSAT), and in 2008 their average scores on the Scholastic Aptitude Test (SAT) was close to 2,000.[74] These are the standard indicators that elite boarding schools use to determine the academic aptitude of their students, and while the value of the indicators may be contested, they are an important status marker. In addition, the large majority of elite boarding school graduates apply and are accepted to four-year colleges, often the most prestigious and selective colleges. Princeton, Harvard, Columbia, Georgetown, New York University, the University of Virginia, and the University of California at Berkeley are typically listed among those accepting the largest number of students from any given school.

Of course, just because a school has an impressive record of sending students to elite colleges, has a high SAT average, or can say that two-thirds of its families have greater financial resources than the vast majority of the U.S. population does not mean it is an elite boarding school. Many schools (even some elite public schools) meet these criteria and perhaps even some of the criteria I described earlier. Elite boarding schools, however, have more. Their beautiful and extensive pastoral settings are a physical manifestation of their eliteness and provide the "total" institutional setting for the construction of elite identifications.

Geographically Elite

When filmmakers choose elite boarding schools as a setting, they typically set the scene with images of pristine campuses, including spacious green fields surrounded by large trees usually dressed in New England's colorful fall foliage. Redbrick and stone buildings with marble columns, archways covered in ivy, golden domes and tall steeples, crystal-clear lakes, and cloudless skies usually form the backdrop. The campus of the Weston School extends over hundreds of acres, encompassing wooded areas, brooks, meadows, and playing fields. The landscape is dotted with buildings where students pursue their academic, athletic, artistic, and extracurricular activities—buildings that range from quaint colonial homes to modern poured-concrete structures.

In the film *Dead Poets Society*, the boundlessness of the geographic space is central to the story. Nature imposes no limits on the boys' intellectual curiosity, as they escape at night through dense fog and into thick forest, to find the "old Indian cave" where they will reconvene their secret society of poets. As they venture to the edges of their school's physical space, their own personal and intellectual space expands, and they begin to challenge the limits set by their teachers and parents. Their metaphoric run into the dark woods comes to a tragic end when the "four pillars" of their elite education—Tradition, Honor, Discipline, and Excellence—come tumbling down on their poetic parade. The adults and the traditions and expectations of the institution set limits on the otherwise unbounded range of possibility.

The immense rural space is also a crucial element of the story in the novel *A Separate Peace*, by John Knowles. It is in the green fields of Devon that Finny invents "blitzball," and it is at the edges of the campus that he encourages the other boys to jump from the fateful tree and into the river. The importance of the campus terrain is also highlighted in nonfictional accounts of life at an elite boarding school. Lorene Cary, in her autobiographical narrative, describes venturing into the woods only to find herself stumbling over tree logs and crashing into streams through thin ice. Standing at the edge of the "safety barrier" by her school's pond and contemplating the invisible dangers of the black ice that lies before her, Cary contrasts the chapels, jutting through the snow "vigilant, haunted, and holy," with the dangerous woods behind her.[75]

The rural character of elite boarding schools is immediately evident to anyone who visits them or browses through their admissions catalogues or websites, which are filled with images of rolling fields, barn-like buildings, country views, lakes and rivers, and colonial houses. What is not obvious is how important this geographic context is for the very definition of the institutions, and indeed for the experiences of students as they form elite identifications. Unlike the cloistered environment of most total institutions, at elite boarding schools space is so open and extensive that one cannot immediately see how much it matters.[76]

Most elite boarding schools are located in the Northeast, particularly in New England.[77] While the academies were a national movement that spread into the Midwest and the frontier, schools that survived were almost all in New England. Each early academy was "fundamentally a rural institution, a school uniquely appropriate for a population thinly spread."[78] The large campuses of elite boarding schools are generally located in rural areas isolated from cities.[79] These schools had the luxury of being more exclusive than their nonboarding counterparts because they could draw from a larger pool of applicants who could pay the high tuitions; day schools were limited to nearby communities.[80] The pastoral campuses and venerable architecture of elite boarding schools are reminders of their historical reliance on wealth and abundance.

While other scholars have noted the importance of architecture and space in shaping the curriculum at elite boarding schools, they have tended to assume that these schemes work subliminally on all students equally.[81] In fact, however, space is a highly contested dimension of student experience, and students spend an enormous amount of energy negotiating, arranging, and staking claims over the space. Elite boarding schools are premised on the almost unlimited abundance of a particular kind of pastoral landscape associated with elite status and wealth—a landscape that is based on a "romanticized vision of pre-industrial England" and whose aesthetics played an important part in the way new elites in Britain's colonies materialized their sense of eliteness.[82] This pastoral landscape becomes an important symbol and a crucial assumption in how the meritocracy is organized: when there are no limits to space, everyone can find a niche in which they can claim their own elite distinctions.

The elite status of elite boarding schools, then, is constituted at the point where their autonomy to define themselves as independent schools intersects with the scholastic opportunities and experiences they offer, their historical trajectories, the wealth and scholastic aptitude of their students, and the sumptuousness of their geographic setting. These five characteristics make elite boarding schools a particular kind of total institution: one in which a carefully selected group of students takes advantage of a broad range of opportunities within a context of abundance defined historically and institutionally as elite. How students come to justify this privilege and identify themselves as deserving members of this elite institution is the focus of the rest of this book.

ELITE BOARDING SCHOOLS TODAY

Films and literary works set in elite boarding schools often take place in a distant past, sometimes as a flashback from the perspective of a lead character. This may be because many of these portrayals are at least loosely based on the author's experience. Furthermore, many of these stories generate their dramatic energy by pitting individual needs and desires against the constraints of what is often portrayed as an antiquated and staunchly conservative educational institution. Setting the stories in the past allows the author to highlight—even to stereotype—the old and stringent character of an imagined boarding school, while enabling the audience to avoid thinking about the contemporary context of elite boarding schools.

In the film *The Emperor's Club,* a teacher named William Hundert reminisces about his experiences and his relationships with a group of students in the 1970s. The fictional St. Benedict's Academy is a school for boys, and with one exception the students in Hundert's past are all white. At the end of the film, as an older Hundert begins his introduction to his course on Western civilization, the class is strikingly different: it now includes girls, as well as several black and Asian students. But although the faces in Hundert's class have changed, the room itself looks exactly the same, adorned with busts and images of Socrates, Aristotle, Augustus, Plato, and Cicero, figures whom Hundert describes as "giants of history, men of profound character, men whose accomplishments surpassed their own lifetime and survive even in our own. Their story is our story." The camera pans out of the classroom, and the film ends with a bird's-eye view of a grassy quadrangle, crisscrossed with walkways, surrounded by blossoming apple trees, pines, and carefully pruned greenery, and edged by the façades of elegantly stoic stone buildings.

While the schools' physical character remains the same, their official curriculum has expanded beyond Western civilization and Latin. Today, course catalogues are sprinkled with offerings like "African History," "Afro-American Experience in the United States," "Latin American Literature," and other area studies. Almost all elite boarding schools today have equal numbers of male and female students, and they are increasingly open to sexual diversity. Elite boarding schools remain officially committed to changing the profile of their student populations to reflect the multicultural society in which the schools are embedded. In espousing these changes and continued commitments, the schools parallel and typically follow the lead of the elite colleges and universities where they seek to place their graduates.[83] Indeed, the changing landscape of higher education and the broader social, political, and cultural context in the United States have brought tremendous pressures to bear on elite boarding schools.

The schools have weathered these pressures well. Not unlike elite colleges and universities, they are experiencing increases in the numbers of applicants and, overall, are becoming wealthier. This means, presumably, that they have greater ability now than ever before to become more diverse and to offer a broader and more diverse curriculum. Yet we know very little about what this diversification looks like and what it has actually meant for the experiences of the students. What do students say about what it is like to attend an elite boarding school today? How do they negotiate the increasing diversity of the student body? And how do they make sense of the privileges afforded to them in these unique and rarefied educational contexts? These are the questions that I address in this book, with the hope that it will inform a broader dialogue about the role and purpose of elite boarding schools in the twenty-first century.

2

GETTING IN

The golden steeple and ornate towers of the Weston School chapel welcome prospective students who are arriving on campus for the first time. As newcomers and their families drive past the green expanse of the main campus, the imposing façades of the buildings might seem intimidating to anyone who is not expecting the college-like appearance of the school. In the fall, brilliantly colored trees line the road to the admissions office. The receptionist at the front desk greets visitors with a warm smile. Sitting behind her computer, she guards the entrance to a large hallway and staircase filled with school memorabilia in glass cabinets, introducing visitors to Weston's rich traditions and famous alumni.

On the second floor are three waiting rooms, bright with the sunlight that streams through the bay windows and adorned with oriental rugs and antique lamps. Families review admissions materials or page through picture books illustrating the school's long history. The rooms display images associated with the school: photos of students in classrooms, on playing fields, and in dormitories; oil portraits of former faculty members. The couches are large and cushy, the kind in which one might find easy comfort while reading one of the books scattered on the coffee tables, all written by Weston graduates. In a meeting room near the back, the portrait of an African American former coach hangs among eleven others of white men and one white woman, as if hoping to balance the otherwise starkly Anglo American atmosphere of the space.

This first Saturday in December is particularly cold, even by New England standards, and I've decided to join an admissions tour, as I often did during the early days of my fieldwork. The office is full of prospective students and their families, who are completing information forms and reading promotional materials. A snowstorm has kept several families from making the journey, and the receptionist is busy handling cancellations and rescheduling appointments. The deep snow blanketing the campus seems bucolic and romantic from the inside. Several Weston students have gathered by the front desk, ready to lead tours. They are well dressed, aware that they're emissaries for the school. The receptionist offers them coffee and hot chocolate, to fortify them against the wind and below-freezing temperatures outside. I ask Emily, one of the tour guides, if I can tag along, and she introduces me to a visiting family.

The father of the family shakes my hand and introduces himself: "Gardiner, '75"—his last name and the year of his Weston graduation. He explains that the tour is mostly for the benefit of his daughter, who is applying to enter the tenth grade. As Emily introduces me, I assure the family that I am not part of the admissions staff and explain my purpose. As we walk along the snowy path toward the library, the father inquires about my work. Seeking to legitimize my presence and anxious to set a comfortable tone, I answer: "I teach sociology at Harvard," exaggerating my role as a teaching fellow for a Sociology of Education course. He quickly responds with a list of Westonians affiliated with Harvard. I smile back, admitting that I recognize none of the names.[1]

Emily leads the family into the magnificent library, a building that would be the envy of any small liberal arts college. She describes the online resources for research and the excellent periodicals collection in the reading room. I'm in awe of the abundance of resources that the library gives access to, most of which I didn't know existed until I became a graduate student. The prospective student's light-blue eyes are wide with wonder, and she seems overwhelmed by the vision of herself doing archival research. Emily explains that first-year students spend a great deal of time learning to use these resources, but this seems to raise the mother's concern about her daughter applying as a tenth-grader: "Will she be at a disadvantage?" Emily's response is measured. "Nothing happens in ninth grade that will cut you out," she reassures the family as we enter the older part of the building, which is now used for special events. The young prospect strays away from her mother, looking around at the marble staircase and the large windows. The old marble walls seem to spark more curiosity and inspire more comfort than the gray cement of the newer part of the library. We ascend the wraparound marble stairs, and I notice that the lacing on one of the girl's knee-high black boots has come undone. I caution her, worried that she might fall, and she answers, frustrated, "I can't figure out how to!" I'm surprised by her response, and even more by her mother's exclamation: "She still needs me!" The mother leans down and ties the teenager's boots.

"WESTON IS NOT FOR EVERYBODY"

No one arrives at the admissions office of an elite boarding school by accident.[2] Every arrival at Weston is the result of a unique and often convoluted path, and every student has a different story to tell. For some, Weston is part of a particular family experience with elite boarding schools, via parents, grandparents, or siblings, a place where they are expected or at least encouraged to arrive via a road already traveled. For others, the long journey to an elite boarding school takes place on an untraveled road, and is unexpected, perhaps even serendipitous. All the students I spoke with indicated that the story of their arrival at the school was an important part of how they identified as Westonians and how they drew boundaries between themselves and non-Westonians. Such stories also point toward the social and cultural complexities of the way students arrive at an elite boarding school.

Weston's admissions brochure defines the student body for potential applicants and their parents. "We seek to enroll students who combine proven academic ability, intellectual curiosity, and tenacity with decency and good character, . . . who welcome the challenges and opportunities provided by a strong academic program within a diverse community." The school makes a great effort to attract students from across the United States and around the globe. In the atrium that leads to the Student Center, a map of the country and another of the world are pierced with hundreds of colored pins marking students' hometowns. On the U.S. map, there are so many pins in New England and the New York City region that some seem ready to fall. There are smaller clusters around Los Angeles, San Francisco, Chicago, and Washington, D.C. Yet vast areas of the map are unmarked. There is also a skewed distribution on the world map, with most pins grouped in the United States, Western Europe, Korea, Japan, and Hong Kong.

Elite boarding schools like Weston often take pride in the fact that their students come from many different places and diverse backgrounds; the schools like to highlight their own efforts to be inclusive and diverse. Yet as institutions that have complete jurisdiction over whom they admit, and given the very particular characteristics they seek in students, elite boarding schools are by definition exclusionary. Indeed, in the highly selective context of a prestigious elite boarding school like Weston, exclusion is the primary task of the admissions office. The selectivity of an elite boarding school is crucial to the way students who are admitted begin to identify themselves as an elite.

Students are not privy to the admissions process, yet they speculate a great deal about it and have much to say about those aspects of the process that they do get to see. For instance, Westonians are skeptical about how the school promotes itself, and readily offer criticism of the school's recruitment and promotion materials. At the same time, they accept the school's self-description as at least a good generalization or a partial truth. As one of them said during a focus group in which the students cynically criticized the admissions brochure, "Basically, all, most of the stuff in it is objectively, like, fairly true, but the way it's presented is, well, very deceiving." Another described the brochure as "idealized," but all the students in the group agreed that it "accurately" described Westonians. Indeed, by the end of their senior year, students have internalized the school's characterizations as their own, and are using the language of the brochure to describe themselves and their fellow Westonians.

"I knew that Weston was supposed to be, like, the best school and take the best applicants," explained one student as he pondered his own admission. Weston's reputation, and its descriptions of itself and its students in admissions materials, influence the way students begin to identify themselves as Westonians. Prospective students must see themselves reflected in the wording of the brochure, at least to some extent, before they decide to invest the time and energy required to apply. When I asked students about admission to Weston, they described feeling "as if it was sort of a matching process" in which admissions officers would try to determine whether a student would "fit in well" at the school. The notion that "Weston is not for everybody" was repeated like a mantra by various members of the school community during my two years there. To be sure, asking students about the admissions process can hardly illuminate what actually happens behind the closed doors of the admissions committee room (to which no student has access).[3] Yet students have a lot to say about how they experienced the process, and what they say reveals a great deal about how they begin to construct identifications as students of an elite boarding school.

Becoming a student entails three critical steps. First, students must somehow know or come to find out that there is such a thing as an elite boarding school and that Weston is one of the most prestigious. This typically involves what sociologists call "social capital": networks, relationships, institutional ties, or other kinds of "connections."[4] Second, students—and usually, though not always, their parents—must decide to undertake the process of application. This decision usually requires that applicants begin, at least in some measure, to identify themselves as prospective Westonians, usually on the basis of the school's descriptions of itself and its students. Last, students—and usually, though not always, their parents—must be able to put together all of the myriad elements required for application, a process that can be as complex as applying to college.

Once admitted to Weston, students are never told directly why they were accepted, but they do a great deal of speculating. The mysteriousness of the admissions process is critical to the way students make sense of what it means to be a Westonian and, more important, to the way they begin to see themselves as such. It is the initial step toward internalizing the notion that, while "Weston is not for everybody," it is certainly for them.

Discovering Weston

Arriving at Weston "was really, like, the best thing that's happened to me," says Greta Dunst, a senior who has been at Weston for four years and is heavily involved in public service through school clubs. She is an avid flautist and has a busy performance schedule as a member of several ensembles. As a day student, she drives a short distance to the school and goes home after her day's activities, often late at night, at the end of rehearsals and club meetings. When I ask Greta how she found out about Weston, her round pink cheeks lift with a big smile. She tells her story of how she came to think of herself as a Westonian, beginning with a comment about how "lonely" and "just fed up" she was with her public middle school. "I was really dying to get out of that whole scene." Greta describes herself as a "bookworm nerd person" who wanted to be in a place where others appreciated her interest in social issues and good literature. Greta's parents both work for social services organizations in the area, and she used to pass the campus on her way to middle school. "I just remember being in total awe," she recalls, noting that she "didn't really think of myself ever coming here."

Unfamiliar with the world of elite boarding schools, she derived her ideas about such schools primarily from novels. When a classmate brought a pamphlet about Weston to school, Greta "went through the whole thing and was absolutely in love. . . . I don't really know what I would have done if I hadn't gotten into Weston, because I was so unhappy at my other school." She notes that while her parents were supportive, "we didn't think it was going to happen, for financial reasons." Ultimately, with financial aid from the school, "it worked out, and that was a big surprise."

Like Greta, Charlene Rodreau describes her junior high school as "ridiculously easy." "I like work and challenges and things like that," she says, as her large silver hoop earrings dangle on either side of her face, framed by the red bandanna that wraps her long black cornrow braids. But unlike Greta, Charlene grew up in a large urban center, far from the rural tranquillity of an elite boarding school. She remembers teasing a close friend whose parents had enrolled her in one of the minority recruitment programs that place students in elite boarding schools. "Oh, yeah, because your parents don't want you," she remembers joking, noting that she "didn't really know much about the whole boarding school, or anything about that." Her friend turned the joke on Charlene:

> As soon as I heard "boarding school," I just—that was usually associated with your parents giving you away. So, it was kind of like, kind of like a reform [school]—that's what I would think. And so me and all my friends also, we would kid about it until [my friend] got mad. And so she went to her mom and said, "You know, Charlene is really interested in the whole private school thing." And her mom, was like, "Really?" So her mom called my mom, 'cause we were all really close, since I knew her since the sixth grade. And then, so, my mom heard about it and she was like, "Oh, really?" And then, that's how I started. That's how I started the whole process. So, I mean, like, before that, I didn't know, I didn't even know about, like, private school, let alone Weston.

In addition to helping students of color prepare for the SSAT, select schools, and complete admissions materials, programs such as A Better Chance (ABC), Prep for Prep, and Prep 9 offer students of color a supplementary academic program. Typically, students attend classes after school and on Saturdays, and they receive focused preparation and orientation for applying to elite boarding schools and other preparatory schools.[5] School visits are a key element in helping students select schools and prepare for the admissions process. Most students, in fact, talked about their campus visit as a crucial part of beginning to see themselves as Westonians. "I really liked the campus," says Charlene, "I don't know why. I just—I think I most liked the trees, . . . because we came around fall time and so, you know, there was all the—the trees were turning colors, the leaves were turning colors, and it was very pretty." Minority recruitment programs usually arrange for prospective students to stay with other students of color who come from the same program. "They were really nice to us, and they introduced us to their friends, and it was just— it was just really nice. We just stayed here for a weekend, and I liked it. . . . I just thought it would be more challenging work here, and I thought it would be fun to come. And that's how I started really getting into it." Charlene and Greta present their arrival at Weston as serendipitous. They both say they were discontented with their schooling experience, but not fully aware of the alternative that elite boarding schools might provide.

Other students, however, describe boarding schools almost as destiny, or an assumed part of their upbringing. Frances Sackler, for instance, describes spending the summers at her family's summer home surrounded by students from other elite boarding schools. When I ask Frances about her decision to come to Weston, she stares at me for a moment, as if I'm asking her an obvious or perhaps a trick question. She pauses briefly, adjusts her light-blue and purple hat knitted with pink hearts and the letters of her name, and pushes her long blond hair off her shoulders. "Um, in my family, my brother and sister both went to boarding school, . . . [and] my mom went to boarding school. So its just kind of a natural thing for me to look at boarding schools. And I knew I wanted to, um, go to a larger place, because I went to a very small private school where there were forty kids in my grade. Um, so I looked at [four different schools], and, um, it basically came down to Weston and, um, [another elite boarding school]. And I chose Weston." Frances explains that she "knew a lot of the people" at the other school that offered her admission, but she "wanted to go to a place where I didn't know anyone, where it was just going to be a whole—a totally new experience."

Frank Maxwell embraces the prep school dress code. Today he is wearing a black-and-red necktie, a light-blue long-sleeved Oxford shirt, and brown corduroys. His jet-black hair is a bit disheveled, and behind his glasses his thick black eyebrows stand out against his fair complexion. Frank claims that the decision to come to Weston was entirely his own. "Mine completely," he underscores. "As I remember it, it's just one morning I woke up and decided I wanted to apply." At first, it might seem as if Frank's arrival at Weston was serendipitous as well. Not so. The son of a Weston alum, Frank recalls coming to visit the school as a child, for one of his father's reunions, and finding the place "magical": "I don't know. I mean, there's something about this place in the spring where just the brick and the grass and the [*pause*]. I don't know [*pause*]. The way it looks. I mean, that's how—that's what first got me thinking about [applying], and then after that I read into it a little and then I really realized, 'This is something I wanna do.' So it was kind of, that childhood interest led into research that made me decide it would be a good idea." As Frank reveals the amount of information he had prior to applying to Weston, it becomes evident that it was not just something he decided to do upon waking up one morning. Unlike Greta and Charlene, Frank was not escaping his local public school, which he had attended since kindergarten and which he describes as "excellent" and comparable academically to Weston. Despite access to excellent public schooling and his apprehension about moving away from his parents, Frank decided—perhaps largely on his own—that attending Weston was a good idea.

Most students, in fact, describe attending Weston as something they pursued to some extent independently of their parents. Paradoxically, when I asked students why they thought others came to Weston, they often talked about the pressures and parental expectations that they thought drove students to apply—but they didn't ascribe such pressure to their own parents. It is quite possible, in fact, that by the time students are ready to leave Weston and have internalized the Westonian identification, they are more likely to see the admissions process as being self-driven. Whatever the extent to which parents were involved in the admissions process, by the time I interviewed students in their senior year, they were generally convinced that it was they—not their parents—who made the decision and who initiated the process of becoming a Westonian.[6] This is, of course, part of what it means to be a Westonian: self-directed, independent, and hardworking.

For some students, the process of constructing a Westonian identification may begin when they're just a gleam in the eye of a Weston alum; for others, the idea emerges later with a suggestion from a teacher, a memory from a parent, or the random sighting of a mailed brochure headed for the wastebasket. Many students learn about Weston through their relatives—uncles or grandparents, or siblings who may be current students. Social networks, in fact, are at the heart of how students learn about and decide to apply to Weston. Whether the intermediaries were friends, cousins, teachers, or other extended relations, all students describe some kind of social connection leading them to Weston.

For students from backgrounds with weaker ties to the world of elite schools, the role of social networks in discovering Weston is less significant and the decision to apply depends a lot more on chance. For William Mueller, a student from a southern professional family who describes himself as "Caucasian," the process began with a visit from a recruiter to his local public magnet school. "We had class one day, and, uh, instead of having class, it turned out we were going to have a, um, I guess a seminar, because a student from my school had gone [to Weston] eighteen years before I'd, I'd even applied. . . . I was kind of precocious. . . . It was just kind of on a whim." Will says that most of his ideas about elite boarding schools came from movies like *School Ties,* and that his home friends, who call him "Weston boy" and who share little of his academic curiosity, still don't know much about what actually happens in places like Weston.

For students like Charlene and most of the students of color from inner cities, recruitment programs like ABC and Prep for Prep are the only path toward an elite boarding school, and learning about these programs typically takes places through word of mouth and social networking. Regardless of how students learn about Weston, in order to consider applying, they (in conjunction with their parents) must consider whether they see themselves as the kind of student that the school cultivates and has a reputation for admitting. Yet knowledge about schools like Weston does not necessarily translate into an application, and certainly not into an admission.[7]

Being admitted to Weston is the first indication many students receive that they are worthy of the distinctions such admission implies. Although the process by which they think of themselves as Westonian may begin earlier, the acceptance letter is the first substantive indication to students that they have the qualities of a Westonian. Admission letters are individually tailored for each new admit, highlighting the particular interests and strengths the student brings to the school and positioning the student as distinct among a group of equally distinguished new Westonians. Julie Lasky, a four-year senior and the youngest of four siblings who have all attended Weston, remembers: "After you've been admitted, they send you a letter [with] brief descriptions of three different people. And it is very specific. . . . It's essentially to describe the diversity and also the, you know, excellent nature of the students you're gonna be attending school with. You're always included, but they do it in such a way that it's, like, sort of anonymous." With this letter, the admissions office quickly establishes students' emerging identification as Westonians by telling them they are part of a "diverse" and "excellent" group of students—and of course the newly admitted student is "always included."[8] The process of identifying as a Westonian, which begins with the decision to apply, is now reinforced by the school not only with the act of admitting the student, but with a letter that "anonymously" identifies the student as part of a diverse population of excellent students.

"There's Always Something That Makes Us Special"

At the end of her middle school years in public school, Sandi Li was seeking "something more challenging." Although several relatives had attended another elite boarding school, she says that in her midwestern suburban town, boarding schools were "for, like, the kids who are not really good, who have, you know, uh, just done bad things." One of her relatives, however, encouraged her to apply, and gave Sandi a list of schools she "should definitely apply to," including Weston. She was admitted at some, rejected at others, and waitlisted at Weston. When she received the notice that she was off the waitlist and admitted to the school, the choice seemed obvious:

> My parents had sort of the mentality that, like—I don't know if this is, like, necessarily a good thing, but—since the only, like, good boarding schools they've ever heard of were, like, Weston and [other elite boarding schools], they were—I guess in the end they, they didn't tell me this, but this is what I'm assuming—they were sort of like, "If you get into one of those schools, you can go. If you don't get into those schools, then you're just staying home and going to public school." . . . Um, because I come from a pretty good district. Um, so, then when I got into Weston, my, my parents were still a little bit wary, but I think my sister talked to them and, um, I called my cousin, and he was like, "Oh, definitely go," you know, "Weston is great." So that's sort of how I ended up here.

Sandi is "heavily involved in several activities" at Weston, including publications, sports, and painting. She arrived at both of our interviews dressed in Weston athletic apparel, sweating from a workout or from playing squash, with her hair pulled up tight into a pony tail, and her slightly tanned face still perspiring. Sandi says she is Asian American, but notes in her survey response: "I tend not to associate myself with that very often."

As a student tour guide, Sandi gets to meet many new applicants and their families. When I ask her what she thinks the admissions office is looking for, she starts by saying, "It seems really random to me sometimes." I inquire further. "For the most part, you get a lot of, like, outstanding kids. Like, you have, well, ok, there's only one Damien." She laughs, and I comment on the fact that almost everyone uses Damien, a student who has won several international science awards, as an example of how smart some Weston students can be. "There are people like him, too—like, a slightly lesser degree, you know? [People] who are very, very smart, um, or like, very, very athletic, or very just, like, well-rounded." I ask Sandi why she thought she was admitted, and she reminds me that she was actually waitlisted. She offers her view of why she was not admitted immediately:

> I don't think that I had a spark. Like, on paper, I looked pretty good. Like, I had, I had like—just like everyone else when they come here—I had like, all A's at home in middle school, like, I ran track, and I ice skated, and I, like, played piano, had a flute, and, like, just did a lot of things and had, like, all those random awards or whatever that you get in middle school that aren't really a big deal at all, like, I had that all on paper. But I don't think that, like, I was that interesting of a person, like, I, I don't even know if I'm that interesting now. But, like, it's just, like, I—that might be one thing, one of the things that they are looking for in students.

Still uncertain about why she was admitted, she offers examples of some of her closest friends, who, she says, "all have just, like, interesting little, like, twists about them"—but she remains vague about just what that means. "I don't know how to describe it exactly, but it's just, like, something about their personality that makes you think, 'Wow, this person is really special.' And I think actually that's probably what they look for. And that's why it seems random."

The air of mystery and apparent randomness that surrounds the ad-

missions decision is important because it leaves unspoken the myriad social and cultural processes involved in actually being admitted. It enables
students to ignore, or at least downplay, how their previous privileges
and experiences helped them to become students at Weston. This is important in the process by which they begin to identify as Westonians and
come to believe they deserve the privileges and opportunities that the
school provides. Because students are never certain why they were admitted, they are left to speculate on the basis of what the school says about
whom it admits, and on the basis of their own self-comparison with other
students. As Will Mueller explains: "I think everybody probably wonders, 'cause there's a—there's a degree of humility a lot of times. You
don't see that many arrogant kids. And so you always wonder, 'Well, I'm
not that smart. Why am I here?'"

In pondering their own admission, students typically talk about grades
and SSAT scores as the most important criteria. "Obviously they look for
high academic record," says Frances Sackler, and most other students
agree. As accepted metrics of a student's academic status, grades and
SSAT scores are the clearest indication that students deserve to be admitted. As Sandi notes, her grades were part of what made her look good
"on paper": "Just like everyone else when they come here, I had, like, all
A's at home in middle school." Will Mueller—who wonders why he was
accepted, since he was not "that smart"—later in our interview offers
that he "did have really good grades." "I actually took them out a while
ago and looked at them, and I was surprised how they were all high 90s
and things like that." He then clarifies why grades are not necessarily an
indication of smartness: "I never really actually worked in, in middle
school. But I think that's the case in most kids at Weston. They always
kind of skate through middle school, and then they get here, and, just,
frightened and terrified." Other students echoed this idea. It served as an
important way for them to draw a boundary between the academic demands of Weston and those of other schools, particularly public schools.

"Public school wasn't exactly entirely rigorous," says Sabrina Macy as
she laughs about her previous experience. The only child of parents who
have already retired from highly successful business careers, Sabrina lives
in an affluent New England suburb and vacations with her family in one
of the most exclusive oceanfront towns on the northeastern seacoast.
Sabrina's long auburn curls seem to bounce as she exclaims, "I had never
gotten an A-minus! It was—all my grades were A's for like four or five
years. Um, so I guess I had that going for me."

Though grades may be a weak measure of intelligence, students' scores on the SSAT confirm their sense that they are, in fact, smart. "I tested in the ninety-fifth percentile on the SSATs. I had ninety-eighth percentile for verbal and I think ninety-first percentile for math, so I tested really well," says Deborah Mirabelli, who came from a small private Catholic school where she had to work hard for her good grades. Even when students try to downplay the role of standard measures, they acknowledge its importance. "I know they don't place that much emphasis on SSATs, which is the standardized test for high school," explains Matthew Briggs, "but you gotta—you gotta score strong on them, you know? You gotta be competitive with the rest of the applicants." Ramón Pérez speculates about why these metrics are important in terms of what Weston expects from its students: "Weston, um, I guess, supplies you with a certain amount of work, and I guess the admissions office has evaluated that amount and decided what it takes to actually do it, and what SSAT scores people should have, what's a good range, what grades they should've been getting in, uh, junior high, how easy that should have been for them. And, um, and then they pick people that have relatively high, um, grades in junior high and a relatively high, um, SSAT score. I guess." Ramón has to "guess" about how the admissions office determines "what's a good range" in these metrics because he, like all other students, knows that good grades and a high SSAT score are not a guarantee and most certainly not a requirement of admission.

Students speculate about the many other criteria that they suspect play a role in the admissions process. They have a range of theories, for instance, about whether and how legacy status, wealth, and financial need have a bearing on admissions. Patricia Sanders, whose grandfathers—on both sides—attended Weston, says that she was accepted because she "did really well academically," and she adds, "I'm sure, uh, that my grandparents' coming here helped, you know. . . . I'm not gonna pretend like that wasn't a factor at all." "You could have gotten in because your family owns a building here, or because you're that wealthy that you're going to definitely ensure that the school will get a lot of money in the future," says Radhika Chaudari, a day student who receives financial aid from the school. She suspects that "if you're on financial aid, it means you must have been really smart."

Students also mention athletic ability as a criterion, and they speculate about how important it is to the school to field winning teams. They're uncertain about how athletic ability relates to academic achievement in the admissions process. In the absence of any clear indication that they were admitted because of their academic achievements, students are likely to claim that they were admitted because they were, as Sandi puts it, "well-rounded."

Ken Ellerly remembers going as a kid to his father's alma mater, another elite boarding school, and thinking, "Wow! I really love this school. Boarding school is awesome!" With the enthusiastic support of his family, Ken looked at several options and ultimately chose Weston "because I thought it had the best academics and it, um, I liked the fact that it's still kind of, was, what I thought, adhering more to its traditions." Neither a stellar athlete nor an academic genius, Ken says he was just "a well-rounded kid, who, I mean, I did a lot of things before I came here. I mean, I played sports, I, you know, was heavy in the clarinet. . . . And so I think they just saw me as a well-rounded kid who would do well here."

Students explain the importance of being "well-rounded" in terms of the expectation that they should take advantage of the many opportunities available at Weston. "There were a lot of things that I wanted to do that I just couldn't do at home," says Kevin Bausch, "and that I knew I'd be able to do at Weston." While not technically a legacy student, Kevin is related through his father's second marriage to four generations of Weston alumni. "It would be your Utopia," he remembers his relatives describing Weston to him, "and you would really love it there. I took their word for it." Kevin is both an athlete and an artist, and he remembers being "blown away by all the groups and activities that were offered" at Weston. "It was really impressive to me," he adds, drawing a comparison to his previous public school. "It was unlike anything that we had at my other school, pages and pages of student-run organizations and all those things. It just was very intriguing to me." Kevin believes his interest in all these extracurricular activities was an important part of his admission to Weston. "I think they look for people who are going to really take advantage of what they have to offer. And not just in the classroom, but like, outside the classroom as well. Because such a big part of what goes on here is what happens outside the classroom. . . . So I think they really stress that as well, which people at first might not realize. I think a lot of people are really wrapped up in the, like, 'Oh, I need to be, like, a straight-A student,' and all that, but at the same time, I think they care a lot about the other things as well."

While the school doesn't explicitly state how academic achievement, athletic ability, and economic wealth are taken into account in the admissions process, these criteria make compelling points of speculation and comparison because they are presumed to matter in some measurable amount. Even the idea of being "well-rounded" is assumed to be related to the extent to which students are involved in various activities. Establishing some sort of metric for determining how they compare to each other becomes one important way for them to make sense of their own admission and start to understand themselves as Westonians entitled to the privileges that the school provides.[9] Yet as students are quick to point out, such metrics don't always appear to add up to what students imagine should be required for admission, often in their own cases. "I didn't do too well on [the SSAT], so I don't know," says Alex Crosby, who suspects it was the interview that made the difference. "To be honest, I really have no clue what they focus on." When metrics fail as an explanation, students embrace the official language the school uses to describe its students, which is often part of the reason they chose to apply on the first place. Intellectual curiosity and desire to learn, self-motivation and enthusiasm, character and virtue, uniqueness and personality, are some of the intangible criteria that students assume play a central role in admission. While a student may look "pretty good" on paper, as Sandi says about her own application, it is the "spark" of these intangibles that, according to the students, yields an admission.

"I think they look for—for people who have a particular passion for something," says Roland Carter, who also came to Weston from an urban school through a minority recruitment program. Roland is tall and elegant, always dressed neatly in carefully pressed Oxford shirts, dress slacks, and clean leather shoes. He explains that what attracted him to Weston were the many "opportunities for you to break out of the mold" and to take risks. "I think I always had the—the idea that I might push the envelope," he adds, noting the extent of his experiences as a student leader prior to coming to Weston, as well as his strong spiritual commitment. Other students also described what they thought made them "unique" as applicants, and most of them noted the importance of having "something interesting about you." Matthew Briggs explains: "I mean, something that's not, 'I have straight A's,' 'I have a 1600,' or whatever, you know. I mean, I guess if you were that smart you'd probably get in, but something that sets you apart from, you know, several thousand other fairly bright, fairly competitive people. . . . So, something else about you that is really going to intrigue them." Echoing Matthew's words, Kevin Bausch says he "thought they were just looking for, like, obviously a strong student, but also someone who has something to offer that's, you know, unique in a sense." Laura Miller, a day student from a nearby town, talks about the importance of prior experiences in the admissions process. She puts it succinctly: "There's always something that makes us special."

The individualism implied in the idea that every student has "something particular, something that's really unique," as Ken Ellerly puts it, runs counter to the other criteria students describe as playing a role in admission, most of which underscore similarity rather than difference. This is important because it stresses individualism as an ideal: it tells students that although they are *like* all other Westonians (they are smart, enthusiastic, and well-rounded), their uniqueness is what ultimately gains them admission. Weston students identify with "distinction," in both senses of the term. They are, following the *OED,* "distinguished by excellence" in that they are smart and motivated to succeed at a place like Weston; and they are distinguished in the "condition or fact of being distinct or different," meaning that they differ from one another in significant ways and have had "distinguishing" experiences.

Once at Weston, students can identify with the idea that they are collectively distinct from other students (especially public school students), and can focus on what makes them distinct from one another as individuals. They believe, in fact, that they are expected to contribute their "different perspectives" to the classroom and to pursue their "unique" talents through the broad range of opportunities the school provides. This is most evident when students talk about the importance of actively participating in classroom discussions. For Frances Sackler, this focus on participation is part of what sets Weston apart from the other elite boarding schools that most of her friends and family attend. "Weston is a place that, um, fosters talking, fosters discussion. So they probably look for kids who, um, even as eighth graders were able to express their ideas, and talk, and be passionate about things, and not just kind of sit there."[10]

"I think they want someone who is not going to really hold back," says Jack Mitchell, underscoring the importance of participation in the Weston classroom. Before his admissions tour, Weston's was just one brochure among many that arrived in the mail after Jack participated in a summer program for talented youth. "I was getting a lot of information all the time, . . . and [the Weston brochure] was just kind of sitting there on top of the wastebasket in the living room." Rummaging through brochures and online information, Jack selected a handful of elite boarding schools and applied to four of the most widely known. "I didn't care one way or the other. I was like, fun, go, see places I haven't been before, and get out of class." In the process of touring the school and observing classes in action, Jack concluded, "I desperately want to come here." He says it was the classroom discussion "that desperately appealed to me," and he contrasts his experience at his local public school with what he saw at Weston:

> [I was] someone who would just sit in the back of, like, classes and just really not pay attention, or just have one channel open, and the other channel was kind of reading or doing whatever. And I was doing well in class, you know, better than a lot of people, without any effort. I would just argue with people if they were saying something that was wrong, which was a lot of the time. And basically, just whenever possible, I would try and get into a discussion with the teacher. . . . My history class, for example—I hated the class, but the teacher was intelligent, so I was able to learn through a discussion that made my day better for a half an hour. It seemed like it was like that [at Weston] all the time.

Jack remembers talking to the admissions officer at Weston, and describing his interest in learning through dialogue: "I feel that I always have things to say, and if I don't have things to say, I'm interested in what someone else has to say. I'll ask some questions about it, you know, [that] would be a catalyst for conversation." The ability and the desire to participate in classroom discussions is one of the centerpieces of what students describe as essential for being admitted to the school, and often one of the first things they mention when speaking about what it means to be a Westonian.

"The personality of a Westonian is to argue things, you know, in a mental way," says Terrence Wilson, another student from the South who identifies specifically as a "black American" and who came to Weston through a minority recruitment program. He says that being a Westonian means "to express your opinion about something and be serious about it, especially within the classroom." Terrence describes the instances when he finds "the Westonian coming out of me . . . when I am in a discussion, because . . . we are taught to discuss things and search for the meaning behind things, or try to find logic in different things."

BECOMING WESTONIANS

"I think the admissions office definitely looks for people who will get their hands messy," explains Annie Kasper. Annie arrived at Weston with the reluctant guidance of her mother, who graduated from Weston with one of the first group of female students in the early 1970s. "She had a very different experience," Annie says about her mother, who brought Annie to the campus for an alumni reunion. "I actually saw Weston's campus, um, and really liked it. I mean, I just really liked the academic setting." The seminar classrooms were especially appealing to Annie. "The idea of being able to have a conversation in class, and have that being the central role, um, like, of, um, of the classroom. And that kind of interaction really intrigues me, so I was really drawn to that." After our interview, Annie insists that I go with her to one of her favorite classes, a course on the Beat poets.

The instructor, Mr. Lauria, is close to retirement, and is widely respected by the students, who often describe him as contrasting with most other Weston teachers because of his frank and unapologetic style. He welcomes me to the class and invites me to sit at the table next to Annie. The classroom is relatively plain compared to others I've seen, but it feels elegant, with a carved wood mantel framing an old fireplace. There are only a few posters on the walls, including a copy of Gottfried Helnwein's clichéd watercolor *Boulevard of Broken Dreams* (with Marilyn Monroe, Humphrey Bogart, James Dean, and Elvis Presley sitting sadly around an otherwise empty bar), plus a photo of E. E. Cummings and another of Bud Cort in *Why Shoot the Teacher?* The large bay windows look out on one of the quadrangles, and the room is flooded with sunlight. There are two blackboards, one at the front of the room and one at the back, where a student has left a message for Mr. Lauria: "I stopped by wondering if we needed to talk."

The students sit around the table with their copies of *The Portable Beat Reader,* and Mr. Lauria tells them that today they will be reading a "bad" poem by Alan Ginsberg. He jokes that there are "baad" poems (stretching the a and lowering his tone), and then there are just bad poems. "This one is *baad,* even if you sung it," he says, and the students chuckle. Once the students find "The Sunflower Sutra" in their books, Mr. Lauria tells them they are to go around the circle reading the poem out loud. "*Ru*-ben, you are going to read, too," he informs me, and I freeze. None of the teachers in the dozens of classes I have visited so far has asked me to participate in this way, and I'm an immediate nervous wreck. I worry that I'll stumble over a word, or deliver the lines the wrong way. Will I pronounce the words correctly? Will they understand me? Will they like the way I read? I think about one of the students at the table whom I interviewed earlier—he told me that he had a reading disorder. I wonder if he's as nervous as I am.

My turn comes quickly, and I deliver the lines unremarkably, reading from Annie's copy of the book: "The oily water on the river mirrored the red sky, sun sank on top of final Frisco peaks, no fish in that stream, no hermit in those mounts, just ourselves rheumy-eyed and hungover like old bums on the riverbank, tired and wily." The students take their turns going around the table until we finish the poem. Without any prompting from the teacher, the discussion begins immediately. One student offers that poems like this "sound better" than they read, and they talk about the difference between hearing and reading. They discuss how the Beat poets approached their writing, and debate the merits of working from first drafts. Mr. Lauria offers some insights about how these poets approached their writing and makes connections to jazz, inviting the students to extend their thoughts. "Go ahead, tell me some other things." A student comments on the relationship between insanity and the color yellow, making a connection to something he has heard about new mothers going crazy. I jump in to clarify his reference to Charlotte Perkins Gilman's story *The Yellow Wallpaper*, and Mr. Lauria thanks me for my contribution. The conversation continues around the table, but Mr. Lauria offers little more, simply listening and cracking a joke every once in a while, as the students move from Ginsberg to *Miami Vice*, and from *Sesame Street* to MTV, drawing connections with Ginsberg's imagery and the musicality of his work.

Being admitted to Weston is only the beginning of the students' journey toward becoming Westonians. They must take advantage of the range of opportunities the school provides, in order to demonstrate that they are the "best applicants" at the "best school" and in the process internalize the fact that they are Westonians. As they approach the end of their time at Weston, seniors reminisce about their arrival at the school in ways that may or may not reflect the actual experience. Yet these stories say a lot about what it means to be a Westonian.

Victor Martínez didn't always want to be a part of Weston. In fact, he says he didn't even "know what boarding school was, really," until "I actually started the application process and I started visiting schools." Victor describes his large urban public middle school as "the worst school in the district." He says that as "one of the top students," he was selected by the principal to participate in a selective program that placed students in elite boarding schools:

I think your want to become a part of Weston comes through your, um, your learning about Weston, what Weston actually is. And then after being, being at Weston and going through things, and meeting people, I think your mentality changes it, and if you didn't wanna come originally, that quickly erases. And so when someone asks you, um, about the admissions process, you say, "Well, I think I've always been a part of Weston, I've always wanted to be a part of Weston." . . . So I think that's exactly what happens. Some people actually come here not wanting to go. They dread it. They talk—well, even throughout the year, sometimes people just dread Weston, they hate it. But if you ask them after they graduate, "What do you think about Weston?" you know they'll tell you, you know, "I didn't regret it." So there's something about, you know, just the experience.

Indeed, the stories students tell about their experience of being at Weston are the best indication of how they come to identify as Westonians and of how Westonian identifications are constructed and enacted. It may seem obvious to say that all students speak about the experience of being at Weston as the sine qua non of being a Westonian. Yet the obviousness of the statement hides its significance. The nuances of the stories they tell, and the relationship between what they say about their experience and what actually happens at the school, enable us to understand how elite identifications take shape. While having a "common experience" ultimately defines how students become part of the "Weston family," it is the kinships, internal hierarchies, dining room exclusions, and sibling rivalries that illuminate the complex processes forming an elite social class. Experiences in classrooms like Mr. Lauria's are, of course, crucial to the way students become Westonians. These are part of the academic experience that lies at the heart of a school like Weston.

3

BEING SMART, WORKING HARD

White marble steps and ivy-covered Ionic columns lead to the front entrance of Weston Hall, the school's main academic building. Over the portico, a long row of Latin words in capital letters reminds me of other elite boarding schools I've visited and of the oldest structures in Harvard Yard. I immediately feel inept as I write the words in my fieldnotes, trying to decide if some of the V's are actually U's and wondering whether I will find a translation. I push open one of the heavy wooden doors and pass into a foyer. The polished luster of the hardwood floor accents the contrast between the dark oak floorboards and the lighter sycamore inlays. The air feels hot and dry, but my attention turns to the dirt on my shoes. Except for the imprint of my sneakers, there isn't a speck of dirt. More Latin words are inscribed along the walls, and the school shield is carved into the marble over the archway. At the end of the hall there's a memorial wall with lists of names carved in stone, honoring Westonians who have fallen while serving in the armed forces.

As I walk into the lobby, the soles of my shoes feel slippery on the polished floor, and I wonder why I feel so uncomfortable amid such neat opulence. The lobby is luxurious yet classical in its spacious simplicity. I climb a wide marble staircase and notice a small wooden door marked with a word I can actually read ("JANITOR"), next to a balcony with wall-to-wall French doors. I continue to climb one of the side stairwells and notice that the handrails are carved into the spotless white marble walls. The stairs, scuffed and worn by decades of shoes, echo like tympani with every step I take. As I reach the second floor, I notice paint peeling from the wall in a corner. The speck of disrepair reminds me for the first time that I'm in a school building.

An archway leads to the school's oldest library room, now known as the "Old Library" and used exclusively by the Classics and Religion departments. The room is utterly silent. One student sits in front of a mountain of books he has pulled off the shelf. I enter, apprehensive yet curious, noting the book-filled wooden shelves lining the room. The hardwood floor creaks, and I feel self-conscious as the student notices my presence. His name is Steve Hart, and he sits alone at the end of a long table, translating ancient poems into English. He explains that he likes to study in this room because it is always quiet and because it has all the classics and religion books he needs. Displaying my ignorance about the study of classical languages, I ask him if the discussions are in Greek. He chuckles. "The class is taught in English. Ah, you can't really speak—it's ancient Greek, so you don't speak."

Steve's brown hair is shaggy, and his otherwise pale face is strewn with red acne. He describes himself as "very WASPy," adding that his "whole family went to Princeton." Before coming to Weston, Steve attended what he describes as a "pretty good private school" in a large eastern city from which "many people go to boarding schools." There he began to study Latin and to develop many of the academic skills necessary in order for students to succeed at Weston. He explains that he is "pretty serious" about the classics, and as a junior he is already in his fifth year of Latin and the second of Greek. I ask Steve why he likes the classics so much, and he says simply, "The teachers are the best in the Classics Department." He compares this to his experience in English classes, where "there's a lot of time spent understanding what is going on in the material and not as much time spent debating it." Once students make it into advanced courses in Latin and Greek, "they understand the material right away" and they "are able to just debate the whole time," Steve explains. "You understand the literature a lot better, and it becomes more like an English class, except without having to explain to people who do not understand."

Curious about the distinction, I ask Steve whether he thinks the difference has to do with the nature of the class, the text, or the teaching. He replies that it is partly the class, but underscores that his Latin "teacher is pretty smart, and we are just able to go to a pretty high level with it, ah, pretty quickly." Later in the conversation, Steve summarizes the distinction between the classics and English hierarchically. "I think the only reason why I really like [the classics] more than I like anything else is just because the people—like, the teachers here are so much better, and the people in my classes are so smart."

"English class," Steve acknowledges, "gets better as you get older because it becomes more of a—sort of an inborn skill in people." The idea that a skill *becomes* inborn is a paradox. Does Steve think about his own academic abilities—his capacity to understand, critique, and debate a text with his peers—as a predetermined "inborn" skill, or as a skill that "becomes" ingrained over time and with experience? This paradox is also evident when Steve describes how his prior private schooling prepared him to succeed at Weston: "I was sort of lucky to have a lot of those skills already, and it was a really important jumping-off point. . . . It made it a much easier transition to already know what an expository essay is, how to write a thesis, how to write a five-paragraph essay. You know, it's innate now for me because I've been doing it now for five years."

If a skill is inborn or an ability is innate, it usually means that an individual is born with at least the predisposition to develop and refine such skills and abilities. But Steve describes a process by which certain skills and abilities *become* inborn and innate, metaphorically suggesting that some skills can become so polished as to appear biologically endowed. The paradox implicit in the metaphor is somewhat clarified as Steve downplays the role of his background in the differences he experienced:

> I don't think it was a huge difference. . . . There were three kids who came from my [same year] to the school, and, ah, one of the other kids and I have done really well, and the other kid has barely—just not been able to use what he had learned. . . . So I think it's a combination of being able to understand what a thesis is and what writing is, um, and being able to think on your feet and draw conclusions about stuff. So I mean, it helped to be able to know what it was before I came, but I think, um, there are also people who were able to work really quickly, and pick that up.

Steve believes that even if some skills and abilities can become innate or inborn, there must be individual differences that determine how innate or inborn they become and that are independent of a person's background or prior education. I ask Steve whether there are other things that he feels have "become innate." He describes the "universal" teaching method at Weston and what all students must learn to "survive" in that system:

> The entire school is built around talking about it around the table. And in order to survive in that system, you have to be able to have a thesis and, ah, support it with evidence. Because otherwise there are, you know, twelve other people who are just waiting for you to, um, mess up. And I guess some people think that that's too much a cutthroat method of teaching, but I think it's the best way to sort of conclude what the best thesis is. Because if everyone is trying to make their own thesis, and then you bring in the whole together, then that makes it really interesting.

Steve describes the classroom as a competitive space in which "survival" depends on the ability to make a good argument without "messing up." In order to manage this potentially "cutthroat" learning environment, Steve says, students have to be "able to separate the different parts of your, like, into sort of bubbles. . . . Each class is a different bubble."

> Most of the people who come here are, if they are not all-around really good, they are very good in one aspect of their academics, or their sports, or whatever, and they are not so good in the other parts. So in my math class there are people who are awful at math, but then you go to English class, and they'll kick my ass in the discussion. . . . So it's like, you have to understand that everyone has a different thing that they are working on in each class. . . . I think, for the competitiveness, it sort of transferred into more of a—just a desire to be good at whatever I am doing. And not necessarily be better than anyone, but just to do it as well as I can.

The way Steve talks about his academic experiences at Weston is filled with the underlying tensions and ideological assumptions of meritocracy: from the tension between the innate and the learned, to the competitive process of finding a "bubble" in which to "kick ass," to defining what it means to be smart or "the best."[1] How do Westonians describe work? How does their understanding of work relate to notions of being smart, working hard, and being the best in some particular domain? Just as Steve suggests a hierarchical view in which the classics are better than English, students always articulate the sphere of work hierarchically. In large part, becoming Westonian is about "finding a niche" in that hierarchy and about working hard to do it "as well as I can."

Seeing themselves as smart and hardworking, Westonians begin to convince themselves that they deserve the privileges of a Weston education; at the same time, they fail to recognize any other advantages and the privileges that may have led them to Weston in the first place. Indeed, notions of merit and hard work play a critical role in how students at this elite boarding school avoid questions of privilege and unequal access.[2]

"EVERYONE HERE IS SMART"

A torrential downpour has delayed my arrival at the Weston train station, and I have to run to the school amid thunder and lightning. Drenched and weary, I arrive at Ms. Crawford's religion class. She has invited me to sit in and observe as the students contrast different philosophical proofs of the existence of God, including Blaise Pascal's wager, William Paley's watchmaker analogy, and Saint Anselm's ontological argument. Before the class begins, Armando, a Latino student whom I've seen in several other classes, sits down next to me and asks where I'm from. As we discover that we're both Puerto Rican, Aspeth, a pretty girl with long, straight blond hair and bright blue eyes, and wearing a pink-and-lavender sweater, arrives with a coffee mug and pauses by the door, staring at Armando without saying a word. Armando turns to look at her and says, "Oh!" as he moves to the next seat. Although seats are not assigned, Aspeth has clearly laid claim to this spot, and Armando is quick to acquiesce to her quiet reclamation. Aspeth sits down. "My world collapsed!" she says, with her hand to her heart, and she smiles.

The class begins with students sharing their findings from a small homework task in which they were to ask people in their dorms whether they believed in God, and if so, why. They share examples, ranging from individuals' upbringing to echoes of Anselm ("There has to be something greater than me") and Paley ("Look at the world—something made it!"). The teacher asks Armando if he did the assignment, and there is laughter when he says yes. Liona, a Muslim student, says she is more receptive to religion at Weston than she is at home, where her mother insists that she practice her religion and go to mosque regularly. The conversation moves from the distinction between religion and spirituality, and the relationship between religion and ethnicity, to questions about the role of religion in adulthood and childrearing. Ms. Crawford, a middle-aged woman with a background in the clergy, says little, asking pointed questions to challenge the students or redirecting the discussion whenever one student seems to take over. I'm drawn into the conversation, and begin to forget that I'm just observing and to write down some of my thoughts on the notion of God. The students are clearly engaged and thoughtful, as they consider the role of fear and the impossibility of neutrality in discussing the existence of God. They pursue different lines of argument, and they arrive at a vexing question: "Can I conceive of the possibility that my religion might be wrong?"

During my time at Weston, I have had many opportunities to observe students engage in discussions around the seminar table in many different classes. I have always been impressed with students' ability to engage in difficult conversations, to challenge one another's ideas, and to engage in lively discussions. Sometimes, their insightful comments and questions clearly illustrate their academic inclinations and abilities. "You have to realize that when you come here, everyone here is smart, and stuff," explains a first-year student while walking down a marble corridor in Weston Hall. "You need to see yourself in the same level as everyone else." Students often note that "Weston is not for everybody"—and the way they engage in classroom discussions and demonstrate their academic skills is crucial to their ability to justify that Weston *is* for them.

Being "Smart"

When I ask students to describe their fellow Westonians, phrases like "unbelievably smart kids," "all the kids in Weston are really smart," and "people are very bright" are typical. One student puts it succinctly: "We are all here 'cause we're smart." There are, however, at least two ways of being smart at Weston. One way is to appear naturally talented, and the other is to be driven to reach high levels of academic achievement through dedication and hard work. Ramón Pérez is a four-year student who came to Weston through a demanding minority recruitment program, but he is not fond of working too hard. He puts the distinction this way: "Some people, um, do a lot of work, and when you do work, you get good grades. . . . But some people don't do any work, and still get good grades."

Scott Jaffee has been at Weston for two years, since transferring from another boarding school. He makes a distinction similar to Ramón's, but adds a layer of complexity: "Working hard can mean really focusing on schoolwork. . . . Working hard can mean you just happen to have really good genes." While for Ramón being "naturally" smart is about being able to get good grades without much work, for Scott it is about being "genetically" prepared for hard work. For both Ramón and Scott, there is something "innate" about academic achievement, whether it is the ability to work hard or to do well without hard work. Either way, the ability to demonstrate smartness is crucial in order for students to justify that they can identify as Westonians; otherwise, it would contradict the meritocratic assumptions that underlie the discourse of distinction.

Weston is "a very *unique* place, in the sense that you have a group of kids who are *extremely* high-powered, um, academically," explains senior Annie Kasper, asserting that this is "both a reputation and a reality."[3] Annie is a "three-year senior" from the Southwest who came to Weston as a sophomore and who identifies as white. She explains what being a student at Weston means, to her mind: "The number-one thing . . . that I think of, in being a Westonian, is, um, the academics. Um, and being—being smart. . . . And so, what does it mean to be a Westonian? It means, um, that you're, like, a high-achieving, um, rigorously smart person who is pushing, um, who isn't necessarily pushing the boundaries, but pushing forward towards, towards a greater goal. . . . That's definitely what it means to be a Westonian."

The phrase "rigorously smart person" captures well the connection between being smart and working hard, which are intertwined in students' descriptions of themselves as exceptional.[4] By linking the idea of being smart with the notion of hard work, students can describe themselves as smart without feeling that they are claiming to be better than others. Hence, one of the most salient ways in which students distinguish themselves from non-Westonians is by claiming that they, unlike most students their age, study hard six days a week and value academic work.[5]

"There are some universal things about Weston students—that, to get in, just about everyone is pretty driven, is pretty hardworking, and is pretty bright," explains Matthew Briggs, a day student from a nearby town. Matthew is a New Englander who describes himself as a "third-generation immigrant" of Italian and Irish descent, and a Roman Catholic. He is proud to be the first person in his family to attend an elite boarding school. Even wearing shorts, Matthew is well groomed, with white socks pulled tight around his well-defined calf muscles, and his short black hair carefully combed. Matthew discovered Weston through the encouragement of a middle school teacher, who assured him that the school would provide him with the necessary financial aid were he accepted. Hesitant about the unknown world of this prestigious (and expensive) private school, Matthew attended an open house with his mother. He recalls two aspects of the visit that made a strong impression on him: the stark difference between the physical space of Weston and that of his public middle school, and the demanding schedule that organizes students' work. "I remember there was a student panel, and they were talking about how you deal with going to classes from eight in the morning until six at night, six days a week, and I just about fell out of my chair. I'm like, 'What do you mean six days a week!' Saturday morning is, you know, that's when I go play soccer. And this is, this is not a school day! Um, I—I think the open house itself was on a Saturday. I'm like, 'Wait, you have classes today!? What!?' I was just *shocked*." I ask Matthew whether being smart at Weston means something different from what it meant at his previous school. He draws the boundary by accentuating how the competitive learning environment promotes respect for "being smart":

> I think it definitely does mean something different. . . . Um, at Weston there's—people definitely place a very high value on being smart, and you do have a lot of respect for people who can beat you, um, you know, people who manage to pull, you know, really good grades. . . . It might be because we all sort of—we're here because we are good at academics, and we do sort of value it, more so than in a normal high school, where some people are—you know, if you're good at math you're the geek in the class.

"At my old school, academically I was bored," says Kevin Bausch. "I wasn't really doing much, and I was getting good grades. I mean, I didn't feel challenged at all," he adds, echoing the sense that Weston is an exceptional place. An avid singer and swimmer, Kevin describes himself as coming from "white suburbia" and wanting to be with different kinds of students "who I knew would be on the same page as me in terms of their pursuit of, you know, like, academic excellence." For students like Kevin, being admitted to Weston reinforces an identification with students who are smart, hardworking, and driven to learn. It entitles them to leave behind what they describe as the boredom of public school. Indeed, the boundary between public school and Weston is one that all Westonians are quick to draw as they construct identifications as smart and hard-working students.

"I knew I didn't want to go to the public high school, so I was either gonna go to [a local parochial school], or I wanted to go here," says Jennifer Cooper, a day student who was determined "big time" to leave the school system in her small city. Jennifer, who claims a Middle Eastern background but identifies as white, suspects that this is also "why a lot of people come to Weston, 'cause they get really bored with their [public school]." She also comments that the transition from public school to Weston was not easy. "I was really overwhelmed . . . about how smart people were." She believes that for students "coming out of public school [who] think they're great," the intensity of the learning experience at Weston can be overwhelming.

Matthew Briggs, who likewise feels that he is no longer the best, connects this feeling with the highly demanding Weston environment:

> If you really put your mind to it, you could be the best [in] most things in middle school. At Weston, you put your mind to it, and you go, "Pass!" And, and you just—you're amazed that, you know, I won't be the best at this. . . . Um, so you—you really get quite a shock of, you know, wow, there are all these other people who are at least as good if not significantly better than I am. Um, and after a while you sort of start to appreciate that, because you have all these really interesting people to meet and to learn from. But at first it's just sort of, "Oh, my God!"

Terrence Wilson came to Weston from a southern city, where, according to him, few people know about schools like Weston. Terrence identifies as a "southern black" and describes his home community as working class and middle class. He also describes feeling "not so smart" once he was at Weston:

> I guess, like, when coming here, I thought, "Well, maybe I'm not smart." . . . I think it's 'cause also here, is, is—everyone strives around you, and so you're not able to become, um, distinct. Like, you're not able to distinguish yourself among the group that you're, you're in. . . . You have prodigies here, you have people who are doing wonderful, and I'm—and I'm

here, and I'm struggling, you know, I'm struggling a lot, and it's like, well . . . I guess I'm not really [*chuckles*] even smart, you know. . . . "Smart" seemed to mean being, uh, above, above your peers, in, in distinguishing yourself among the group. And me not being able to do that, it felt as if, you know, I'm really just an average Joe.

Though Terrence feels inadequate at Weston, when he goes home he is "kind of seen differently. I'm kind of seen as like a, you know, very smart, talented guy, you know." Terrence's distinction as a smart person is reinforced by people at home who still think of him as smart and who "put it in a different perspective" for him. Yet he still rejects an identification as smart and feels that he is just "a regular person," but "a regular person who has ambitions and who has—who has goals, um, to do something. . . . I guess I will call myself smart, in that I know that I want to get something in life." Terrence reasserts a distinction as smart only by identifying as someone who works hard, rather than someone who's more intelligent. Indeed, while most students readily described Westonians as smart, they were hesitant and often ambivalent about claiming that they were smart themselves. By contrast, they were always ready to claim that they worked hard.

Alex Crosby was not sure she wanted to go to boarding school when she first visited her mother's alma mater, another elite boarding school much like Weston. Alex describes her mother as "one of four black girls" from a large urban area who attended an elite boarding school "during the civil rights movement." She describes her mother's reluctance to talk about her experience in boarding school, yet her narrative about discovering Weston begins with a visit to her mother's high school, where a friend noted Alex's exceptional academic record and encouraged her to apply elsewhere. Alex discovered Weston by searching the Internet and made an immediate connection: "To be honest, I think the reason why I decided to apply to Weston was because of the library. I really was a reader, and so the idea of having [a larger] school library at my disposal really—I really liked that idea."

Rather than directly identifying herself as a smart person, Alex establishes this indirectly by having someone else in the story note her academic record, and then makes a personal connection between her self-description as a "reader" and the image Weston presents as an academic institution. She also downplays the role of her mother's social networks by stressing that she did not attend her mother's school, while highlighting her own academic record and her interest in books. After four years at Weston, she describes her experience with some confidence and assertiveness, underscoring the notion of hard work but with a hint of humor regarding the idea of being smart: "I think that what's been, like, the most challenging is just adapting to being here, being around some of the smartest people that you're ever gonna meet—some of the dumbest people you're ever gonna meet [*we laugh*]—um, in an environment that, it is competitive and it is—you wanna be the best that you can be."

Her joke about the "dumbest people" is suggestive of how Westonians go about identifying as "smart" and as "hard workers." First, it implies a hierarchy through the notion that not all Westonians are equally smart. Second, for Alex to claim that Westonian students are *all* the "smartest people" would imply that she is herself one of those people. By suggesting that some students are not so smart after all, and that there is a range, she may be trying to reposition herself as being among "smart people" but not the smartest of them. This ambivalence is also present in Alex's comments on what she believes her parents and their friends think about her being a Weston student: "It validates the fact that I'm supposedly smart."

Students' reluctance to identify themselves as smart (at least directly) while readily claiming to be hard workers is part of how they articulate the tension between being the same while being different—a tension that is at the center of the discourse of distinction. For Will Mueller, "there is a degree of humility a lot of times." Will compares himself to students at Weston "who are really, really smart" and who are "really hyper-intelligent." He offers the example of a student whom he considers "a genius at math," while he himself "can't even add, basically." He adds, "You always wonder, 'Well, I'm not that smart. Why am I here?'" Yet Will finds other, less direct ways of presenting himself as a smart person. His response to the first item on the questionnaire, where I ask students to describe themselves, is a good example: "My name is William D. Mueller. I am a four-year senior at Weston on near-full financial aid. At Weston, I live in Grove Hall, and as of [last] fall term I have a 3.29 GPA. I am from [a large southern city] and heard about Weston from the Director of Financial Aid . . . after he gave a talk at my public magnet school. The first time I visited Weston was the day before school restarted. I have learned to love it."

In lieu of describing himself as "smart," Will notes that he comes from a magnet school (a school devoted to specific programs involving selective admission) and that he has a 3.29 GPA, or grade point average.[6] As a "white/Caucasian" student, as Will describes himself on the questionnaire, being on financial aid is also a marker of distinction. Being white eliminates the possibility that a student has been admitted for reasons of "diversity," while being "poor" and from the South presumably eliminates the possibility that a student is admitted because of his or her wealth—or, worse, for being a legacy student. At the same time, by noting that he qualifies for full financial aid, Will underscores the one dimension of his class status that would suggest he got to Weston because he is smart. Yet he explains later in the interview that both of his parents are lawyers working for nonprofit organizations in the South. Absent from his narrative is any suggestion of how his parents' own educational attainment and their access to information and resources may have played a role in his prior success and eventual arrival at Weston.[7]

Another reason Will avoids claiming to be smart relates to the "hidden injuries" of upward mobility and the ways being smart is classed.[8] "At home," says Will, "people tell me I'm smart . . . and things like that." He explains how he feels about this:

> I don't like to believe it, because as soon as I believe that and—that means I'm, I guess, above average, or I'm not, like, the norm. And that's really disturbing to think about . . . because then that means, well, you're, you're somehow different, maybe, maybe better than someone. . . . [*pause*] I don't like knowing that, like, I, I could be smarter than somebody else. I, I just don't. And so I think a lot of, a lot of kids here understand that [*pause*] the emotions of someone looking at them, and saying, "Wow, they're smarter than I am. They must be better than I am." 'Cause I've seen it at home, and it really upsets—it upsets me.

I ask Will how he has experienced this at home, and he talks about telling his friends that he was admitted to an Ivy League school—an event that, he says, "was a big shock for me." He describes being asked,

> "Where are you going to college?" and I'd say, "Ivy University," and they'd just kind of look at me. And that would be the end of the conversation. . . . It assumes, I mean, there's

still—even though it's, it's been so many years since the schools have changed—there's still the sense that it's somehow all white, male, rich people running around, talking about "Daddy's, uh, trust fund." I mean it's, it's just upsetting to know that there are some people who think that. I had an ex-girlfriend who broke up with me because she said I was too smart for her, I mean, you know?

Will's narrative suggests that his ambivalence about being "smart" is bound up with anxiety about upward mobility and a reluctance to be seen as a wealthy person—an important connection that I will explore in some depth later in this book. It is also suggestive of how the concept of being smart is closely associated with wealth and privilege, which helps explain why students are reluctant to identify as smart. According to Will, his friends assume that attending Weston and being accepted to an Ivy League school can mean only two things: that he is a white male with a trust fund, or that he is "an intellectual giant, which I don't—I don't believe at all." Either way, he feels that he is perceived as "condescending":

> I used to constantly worry . . . that I'd say something. . . . Like, sometimes I'd use, I guess, big words, and people would say, "Oh, come on!" But I actually use those words. I mean, I don't . . . and I know that might be arrogant on my part, to say that I can't—but it, it does, like, it does play in your mind, and that's why . . . at least I feel that way—that most kids here don't want to be seen as smart, or above average. Which is why it's nice to be in a group of people who are all on your level.

Thus, while not wanting to be distinguished as "smart," Will nonetheless is glad to find himself among students who are on his "level," and who won't, presumably, be put off by his use of "big words." Ironically, using "big words" around the seminar table at Weston can sometimes be seen as an attempt to seem overly smart, or what students call a "seminar hijacker." Hijackers "are people who just dominate the class, and just talk nonstop. Any simple question, they just jump right off, . . . shut other people down," says one student during an informal gathering in a dorm common area.

Terrence Wilson describes hijackers as the extreme of what he defines as the "personality" of Westonians, who have strong opinions which they are expected to put forth and defend.

> You also can't be so opinionated that you are a seminar hi-jacker. . . . I've had some classmates who are extremely bright, but they can debate with themselves. I mean, they can say something and say the opposing point of view right after it, and everyone else is sort of sitting there like, "We'd like to talk, but we can't get past you!" Um, and that, that's just as bad for a class, because then the rest of the class doesn't really get involved, because of one person's opinions and [*pause*] you really have to be careful.

"I'd say a class wouldn't be a class without, like, a seminar hijacker. You know, like, one without one, um, usually is really dull," says Victor Martínez, who describes a hijacker as "someone who doesn't really leave room for, uh, other people to speak. They're—they always have a re-sponse to everything. . . . They're just people who are really aggressive at the table, . . . and if you left it up to them, they'd talk all class." The son of immigrants from Latin America, Victor admits that "in the past I've been sort of a Spanish-seminar hijacker, because, like, I'm, you know, it's my language, you know. I'm fluent." He explains that sometimes "students are hesitant, to talk, to speak, and so I get a little antsy, a little frustrated and so I just go ahead and answer it." Still, like most students, Victor draws a line and distances himself from the idea of being a seminar hi-jacker. "I've been in situations where people just don't shut up, and I don't wanna be that kind of person." He offers his view of what consti-tutes adequate participation in the seminar: "I'll just lay back and just be patient, wait for other people to actually join in and stuff like that. And that's what it's about. It's about, you know, contributing, but make sure that you're not—you don't contribute to the point where you're gonna annoy everyone, including the teacher." Demonstrating smartness around the seminar table, then, is a measured affair—one that requires a student to know how to articulate ideas without seeming aggressive or conceited. Thus, there are constraints around how smartness can be demonstrated, in part because students are anxious to be *seen* as smart without *acting* smart.[9]

Emily Lau, a day student who has been at the school for four years, says that the pressure to "be the best" can often work against the goal of the seminar classroom as a place for collective knowledge building. Emily describes herself as a mixed-race, third-generation Chinese American who is very "Americanized." She is dedicated to her church, where she goes every morning before coming to Weston, and to helping her single mother at home. She cherishes the learning environment at Weston. "I think the ideas that we learn are really exciting, [and] the small classes are great—you get to know people really well. It's a group of people that I feel like for the most part has really chosen to be here." Yet she observes that students often feel pressed "to have the perfect comment, to open the passage up to everyone. . . . You are sitting focusing on your own process and seeing how far you can jump ahead instead of really listening to the rest of the classroom and adding things on that way. . . . Everyone [is] trying to get the nod out of the teacher, or the 'yes' to the good comment."

If sometimes students' eagerness to impress their teachers and peers can interrupt the classroom discussion, at other times it is their social and cultural backgrounds that shape how students engage around the table. These can be a fruitful source of discussion, and many students talk about the importance of bringing diverse perspectives together around the table. Yet students' backgrounds may be so closely bound up with their opinions and beliefs that they find it impossible to understand opposing views.

When I arrive at Mr. Gormley's class on the contemporary Middle East, he introduces me to the group, telling the students they are "guinea pigs," and he invites them to give me "good stuff" so that my study won't "fail." The students chuckle, and one of them responds with a question: "Would *we* have failed?" Mr. Gormley quickly responds, "No, not you— you are the best students in the world. Or so we are led to believe." The students laugh with more energy this time, and another boy offers that they "have the best faculty." When the other students call him for brown-nosing, he insists that he actually believes that. Gormley begins the class by reading a *New York Times* article about democracy in Afghanistan, and after discussion about the day's news, he tells the students they are going to divide into groups of two or three for a debate.

The students are to represent the perspectives of the Palestinians, the Israelis, the Arabs, the United States, and Britain, with the sixth group representing a "neutral" view, in a debate they are to conduct as if it were taking place in November 1947. A couple of students quickly claim the U.S. and British positions, and the rest are reluctant to take either the Israeli or the Palestinian view, preferring to assume the role of the Arabs. One student asks, "What kinds of Palestinians are we talking about?" The room is surrounded by maps of the world, some of which look as old as the classroom, with national borders that no longer exist. On the board, there are statistics of the Palestinian population, and a newer map of the Middle East. Two of the students are wearing clothes that mark them as Jewish. Miriam is wearing a hooded blue sweatshirt with the word "challah" on the back and the initials of the Weston Jewish students' organization, but she has joined the group representing the Arabs. Andrew wears a Weston sports team jacket with the word "Israeli" in place of the last name across the back, but he has joined the group representing the Palestinians. A third student, Ahmed, is the last one to join a group, and there is only a spot in the group representing the Arabs. Mr. Gormley asks the students to move around, and gives them time to prepare their arguments. While most of the group moves quickly, Miriam, Andrew, and Ahmed are visibly affected by the task. Andrew moves restlessly from one chair to another. Ahmed throws his textbook on the chair next to Miriam, who puts her hood up and sits back, expressionless.

While the students representing the United States, Britain, Israel, and the neutral position get to work quickly, the two groups representing the Arabs and the Palestinians never quite convene, being interrupted by brief, indirect, caustic statements from Andrew, Miriam, and Ahmed. "Why should the Arabs be represented?" asks Andrew. "Because we got here first," replies Ahmed under his breath, barely looking up, and jiggling his legs nervously under the table, as he claims identification with the Arabs. The students representing Israel present their position as being in favor of partition, not to kick out the Palestinians but to enable them to "help themselves." Andrew responds with a feeble and cynical attempt at representing the Palestinian position. "We are not negotiating with you people," he says out loud to no one in particular. "We did not cause the Holocaust." Uncomfortable with representing Arabs, Miriam comments on the "millions of refugees" in search of a home in Israel, but Mr. Gormley interrupts her, pointing to the statistics on the board. "Not millions, thousands," he clarifies. A student in another group jumps in: "Why don't you give them Kentucky?" And while everyone laughs, another student offers, "New Jersey, New Jersey!" The group representing Britain simply says they just want to leave the conflict, and Miriam balks. "If I were an agreeing Arab," regarding whether Israel attacked Britain first, she would have to agree. Mr. Gormley, frustrated by the lack of substance, challenges the students: "Is this the best case you can make?"

As the teacher realizes that some students are unable to represent opposing views in the issue, he allows them to step out of role and redirects the discussion to the debate of whether and how land should be divided into national regions. "Are the areas defensible?" The room is filled with a silent animosity. Some students ask clarifying questions, but no one makes any arguments or defends any positions. "Seems like it should have been taken care of fifty years ago," says one frustrated student, adding that Jews "should have picked a different spot." Miriam is incensed. She explains that the land was picked "for biblical reasons," which are not the same as religious reasons, "because biblical is also ethnic and historical." But Mr. Gormley doesn't let them off the hook: "What are you going to do?" He reprimands them: "You haven't dealt with the question!" After a few more confrontational exchanges about terrorism, the bells begin to ring, indicating the end of class. Andrew and Miriam quickly grab their things and leave the room in a hurry. Several students sit motionless at the table and wait in silence, as if reflecting on what just happened. Before leaving, Ahmed turns toward me and says diplomatically, "I find it really hard to be in a group with certain people."

Of course, not every class is interrupted by angry outbursts from students unable to assume a position that affronts their particular sense of who they are. Students at Weston learn the proper way of engaging in discussions around the table quite well, and, by and large, the classes I observed—perhaps because I was observing them—were cordial, and characterized by respectful dialogue, even when the material was challenging. Differences between students were often a source of insight and enriched the discussion. At the same time, such strategies enabled students to deemphasize the role that social and cultural differences played in how students arrived at Weston and how they experienced engaging in classroom discussions. For instance, when Will Mueller talks about the group of "intellectual" students with whom he identifies, he downplays the importance of wealth and social class, claiming that there are no such distinctions.

> I can talk to a kid who lives in, in a, you know, a gigantic house, just like I can talk to a kid who's here who's poorer than I am. There's, there's no distinction here, because we're all equal on, on another level—which is, you know, our intellectual level. We're all here for a reason that's not, "The rich kids are here because they're rich and the poor kids are here because they're poor." It's, "We're all here 'cause we're smart."

> Or, you know, reasonably so. Or . . . have some, some gift that
> makes us able to enrich the school.

Such a "gift" might involve different ways of thinking: "They always say
they're looking for a diversity of thought," says Will. "They probably
want people who have high marks, but if you have all kids from New England, . . . you kind of have, have one way of thinking." Will's conflation
of "people who have high marks" with "kids from New England" is suggestive of the ways in which being smart is associated with particular social groups. Yet he also claims that there are no distinctions between rich
and poor, *because* all students are smart—which is once again to argue
against the possibility that wealth and privilege do in fact make a difference in whether and how someone is seen as smart.

This is the dream of the meritocracy: the replacement of heredity by
merit as the sole determinant of power and status. It is why Steve downplays the role of his previous schooling in how abilities "become innate,"
and why Annie describes Westonians as "rigorously" smart; it is why
Alex decides to go to Weston instead of her mother's alma mater, and
why Kevin and Jennifer want to leave behind the boredom of their public
schools. Yet it is precisely because being smart is also understood as an
inherent, innate, or inborn characteristic of the individual that students
turn to hard work as the source of their claims. In other words, to claim
that they deserve the privileges of a Weston education simply because
they are smart seems inherently elitist—a label students work against.[10]
Thus, being smart does not in itself enable a student to claim entitlement
to the privileges of a Weston education. Instead, students adduce hard
work as the source of their entitlement. But how does hard work function within the discourse of distinction?

Working Hard

At 7:57 on a Saturday morning, a steady stream of students wrapped in
heavy dark coats, hats, scarves, mittens, and a random pair of Reef flip-
flops flows down the paths that crisscross the campus from dining halls
and dorms toward the various academic buildings. The students barely
speak, as the rising sun reflects off the heaped-up snow that keeps them
on the path toward their first class of the day. I follow one wave of students that seem to walk in a huddle, perhaps to stave off the cold.

I enter the foyer of the humanities building, which is always immaculate, and find my way to Mr. Dennett's classroom, where most of the students have already settled. Mr. Dennett, a middle-aged man with graying hair and bright blue eyes, and dressed in a tweed jacket and tie, offers me a seat at the seminar table. Succinctly and half-jokingly, he describes his role, as if wanting to challenge the students to think about Existentialism before starting the class. "I don't actually teach the class, I have nothing to do with this. I just show up." The class begins with a writing task, and I lose myself observing the abundant and meticulously placed decorations that fill the room.

The seminar table is covered with icons, figures, and a collection of religious paraphernalia: two small Zen sand gardens, a couple of singing bowls, and several small statues of Ganesha, the Hindu god of success, wisdom, and luck; small wooden temples, incense boxes, praying Buddhas, and several handsome stones; a small monkey sitting on a book with a sign that reads "Godot was Here"; and three small gongs hanging by the doorway. The walls are hung with photographs of iconic buildings from around the world: Gaudí's cathedral of the Sagrada Familia, the Coliseum in Rome, the Pyramids, the Taj Mahal, and a photo of the teacher standing with the Dalai Lama. Next to the photos is a large poster titled "Living Islam," and next to it a large green hand raising its index finger: "We're Number 1! Go Green Monsters!" All of this forms an intriguing background for a fifty-minute discussion of Albert Camus' novel *The Fall*.

The teacher begins the class by reading from the Book of Matthew, and gives a brief lecture on the biblical Slaughter of the Innocents. He asks whether anyone knows the names of the Three Wise Men, but no one answers. After a few seconds of silence, I can't resist the urge and I offer, "Melchior, Gaspar, and Balthazar." The teacher looks surprised and smiles, asking me how I know their names, and I explain the importance of the Three Wise Men and the Epiphany in the Puerto Rican cultural tradition. He asks me to repeat the names, and the conversation continues. While one student reflects on Camus' references to the Bible, another draws patterns on a small Zen garden on the table. Unsure whether the student is dozing or meditating on his peer's commentary on Christianity, the teacher jokes about the difficulties of leading the first class on a Saturday. He walks to the blackboard and begins to write a sentence, "This is the story of . . . ," followed by three questions: "What?" "Whom?" "Why?" In no time, the students collectively answer the first two, but the third becomes the center of debate for the next thirty minutes. The students struggle with the difficult text, and the teacher guides the way by asking prodding questions and by writing words on the blackboard. Eventually the students take the lead and engage in the difficult task of deciding whether we are ultimately responsible for the deaths of others.

Like Matthew Briggs, I was surprised when I first learned that Weston students attend classes on Saturdays, and that their class schedules on most days run from eight in the morning until six in the evening. Saturday mornings are a busy time in the admissions office. While most prospective students and their parents are free to visit the school, Westonians are hard at work; it is a perfect time for prospective students to witness the academic life that distinguishes Weston as an exceptional community that rarely rests. On her way to class at 7:55 A.M., one student casually notes, "Every minute, . . . I know what I have to be doing. And if I don't have anything to be doing, I better be doing homework, because there is no other time to do homework. . . . Every moment is scheduled." At the end of their work week, on Saturday evenings, Westonians are ready for some distraction and rest.

During a Saturday evening in early November, after a football game, I join a group of students who have gathered to bake cookies in the common kitchen of one of the dorms—a ritual that Frank Maxwell, a third-generation Weston student, has been organizing since the previous spring. The students are relaxed and jovial as they tease one another and talk about the activities available that evening. The appliances in the kitchen look brand new, as do the gray vinyl tiles around the wooden table and two framed posters on the wall—a picture of Louis Armstrong and a Picasso reproduction. Students walk by and peer into the kitchen, drawn by the scrumptious smell of freshly baked cookies. Sandi Li sits on top of the new white counter, reading a cookie recipe book, while Frank whips a mix from a Ghirardelli Cookie Variety Pack.

While they wait for the cookies, the students entertain my questions about life at Weston, and they ask me about my work. I tell them that I'm impressed by the fact that they attend school from eight to six and on Saturdays, and add, "So, you've been doing the eight-to-six thing for three years?" Angie, a junior, exclaims, "For! Three! Years! It's long!" Her friends laugh, and she continues: "And then you are so used to, like, you have so much work, and you have so much to do, and you have so little time. You have to learn to, like, rush everywhere. When my friends come, they're like, 'Wow, you walk really fast!' I don't even realize it." I join them in their laughter, as Angie concludes, "So I just walk fast everywhere."

Sandi, still sitting on the kitchen counter and chuckling, adds, "But I like how we have so much to do, 'cause it's, like, it's supposed to be like that in high school. But I really . . ." Angie tries to interrupt her, "I know! But . . ." And Sandi cuts her off: "And we've already gone soft, since, like, it's not like we need . . ." Angie jumps and protests, screaming, *"Soft!?"* in disbelief at the idea that the school has gone soft. Frank, who is busy whipping the cookie dough, raises his eyebrows: "Yeah. Soft isn't . . ." And Angie finishes his sentence: "Soft isn't—is *not* the way I would put Weston." Sandi tries to clarify with an example: "Well, no, it's like, freshman year [*inaudible*] they have, like, Latin Department, and they had to study every day, and they were like, 'Here is what we talked about at lunch.' . . . They had so much homework!" Angie commiserates saying, "That sucks!"

Indeed, students vary in their perception of whether there is too much or too little work, but everyone agrees that it is hard. There is even what one student called "a culture of complaint" that revolves around how much work there is and who works hardest. Frank, who organized and hosted the cookie-baking party, acknowledges that while "there really is a lot of work," sometimes the complaints are a form of collegial banter that he describes as a way to relieve stress. "Someone complains about something, and you feel like you have to complain. And it almost becomes a competition to see who can complain more, who deserves more sympathy."

During meals, I often saw students trying to outdo one another by listing how much they had to do, or how late they stayed up working. While there is no doubt that students do indeed have a lot of work, Frank's comment illuminates how this competition is a way of asserting publicly their right to be at Weston. Exchanging dramatic stories about how hard they had to work is a way of reminding one another that, as Frank puts it, "if you can make it here, you can make it anywhere." Frank pauses as he thinks about what he just said, and then continues: "I'll be hard pressed to—how, how do I say this? Um, there are not many places that will make you work harder than I've worked here. There are not many places."

Having "survived Weston" is one of the ways students define what it means to be Westonian. Yet the idea of surviving Weston has a double connotation. On the one hand, it suggests "pride and excitement" about living up to the reputation; on the other, it suggests a measure of resentment for "working too hard" toward, perhaps, an unreachable goal.

"I was very angry about Weston," explains one alumna who now works at Weston, and who also believes that "kids either leave thinking they are the greatest kids in the world, or they leave feeling beat up and miserable because [they] work really hard!" But whether students feel positive, negative, or ambivalent about "surviving Weston," how they talk about hard work underscores the distinction between those "inside the bubble," who survived Weston, and what is assumed about those outside, who were excluded in the first place or did not survive once inside.[11]

"I did the best I could, but it was hard, it was really hard," comments Emily Lau, on the difficulties of living up to the image of "the best and the brightest" at Weston. Emily thinks of Weston as a place where she learns from her failures—a process that she considers not lost effort but an important learning opportunity. She reflects on the idea that not everyone can be the best:

> Weston was one of the first places where I really had to push myself really hard, and I think that in some ways that's why people complain: because you have to do things that are uncomfortable in some ways—that are hard for you. . . . One of the big things about the school is that you have to not be the best. You have to deal all the time with the fact that you aren't doing well, . . . but I think that any time you work really hard for things, you then feel very attached to it. . . . You are not number one in every area, but you feel like, "Oh, math was very hard for me and then I got better at it." . . . I own it much more . . . [because] I had to invest a lot.

Emily's connection between ownership and failure suggests that the psychic investments students make to "survive" Weston translate into the feeling that they own the privileges the school affords them. This is evident in the emotional language of the quotes I have presented throughout this chapter, and is clearly articulated in Emily's words. Emily knows that it is impossible to be the best of the best at everything, and knows what it feels like to work hard and not be the best. But for Emily, these emotions translate into further entitlement, a feeling that she "owns" her engagement and is entitled to some reward and further opportunities based on her hard work. As she explains, even if she is not the best, she does "own it much more."

This intensity of engagement is, then, a source of great pride; and despite the challenges, according to one faculty member, "you actually hear the kids talking about fulfillment, excitement, [and] enthusiasm." There are at least two ways students deal with the fact that they're not the best. First, they accept that even if they are not at the top of the smart hierarchy, being at Weston in itself makes them smart. Second, they "find a niche" within which to be smart. "You find things that you are really good at," explains Emily. "That's worth a lot to you—when you find things that you are really successful in."

Finding Your Niche

In describing what he thinks the admissions office looks for in students, Ken Ellery puts it this way: "I think sometimes they're looking for kids who, like, have that specialty—who bring, who bring in, um, something particular, something that's really unique. Like, there's—I mean there's a lot of kids here, and there's kids who've written books before they come here. . . . I would describe that as, like, you know, like a specialty, like a niche." These niches are often part of how students make sense of their admission to Weston. This is crucial to how they understand the otherwise paradoxical notion that students are alike (smart) yet different from one another (diverse). Weston students are "distinguished by excellence" because they are smart and work hard. They are also "distinguished" by the "condition or fact of being distinct or different": they bring "distinguishing" experiences to the Weston curriculum, and they assume a "niche" within which they can demonstrate excellence.

Of course, only a place like Weston can make it possible for everyone to excel in a particular niche. Elite boarding schools, with their immense pastoral campuses and ample resources, can provide enough space (physical, material, and intellectual) for everyone to find such a niche and to be elite in different ways. Still, while meritocracy provides enough impetus behind the idea of finding a niche for students to be content with not being the best, the process becomes an important strategy for them to deal with the anxiety about whether they can measure up to the Weston ideal. Having a niche is an essential part of how students construct identifications that enable them to weather the emotional toll of not being the best.

Krista Griffin's dad works in the administration of the dining services at Weston; she has been a day student for four years, and her younger sister has just been admitted.[12] Krista worries about how her sister will deal with the academic and social pressures, and I ask her what kind of advice she would give her sister.

> I'd just tell her to not compare herself to other people. Because at this school, that's what I feel like I did my first few years here, and that's hard. . . . I mean, there are some kids here who are—you're never gonna be the best at everything here, you know? And you might have your little niche here, um, but not to try to be the best at everything, you know? . . . I would want my little sister to . . . sort of find her own thing while she's here.

Students echo the sense that "anybody can find their niche at Weston." Sometimes these niches are related to academic work. "Everybody here has a subject that's easier for them," says Frank Maxwell. "Everybody has something they're good at." While all students describe academics as the main reason they wanted to come to Weston, they often find their niche in the context of other domains of work, such as sports or the arts. In fact, all students participate in some way in the other domains of work—the athletic, the artistic, and the extracurricular. How they identify as Westonians is related to how they see themselves with respect to these domains and how they construct (hierarchical) distinctions among them; finding a niche is not just about being different, but about being the best at something. What accounts for being successful varies widely from one student to another, because it is dependent on what they've identified as their own niche. Furthermore, niches are also hierarchical, and not all areas of work are valued equally or carry the same status within the Westonian hierarchies of distinction.

THE HIERARCHIES OF DISTINCTION

Before coming to Weston as a day student in the eleventh grade, Radhika Chaudari attended a regional public school where she "would always, like, rank in the top five in sports or in, like, academics or something." But she notes that at Weston, "it's, like, everyone is like that." She "never realized that there was so many talented people out there." She explains how she feels at Weston: "There are times, like, here, when I feel like second best—or, like, two hundredth best. [*she laughs*] It's like, it's overwhelming at times. . . . At my old school it was like, I was always, like, the best. And so it was kind of hard adjusting to that."

Radhika believes that all students who are admitted to Weston "must be smart in some way," but she makes a distinction between "the ones who are, like, off-the-charts smart," whom she calls "the overly achieving studious people," and Westonians who are "pretty much the same below. . . . That's why it's okay to be two hundredth best. Because you know, like, if you were back in your old high school you'd, you'd probably be up there. So that's why it's all right here." At Weston, Radhika notes, it's fine even to be at the bottom of the hierarchy: "It just means something different, because you chose to come here. You chose to be in a group of people who you knew would be better than you, who would strive to be better than you." The belief that students "choose" to attend Weston underscores the exceptional character of all Westonians, while it obscures the privilege that such choices assume. Being in the middle—or at the bottom, for that matter—does not prevent Radhika from identifying as a Westonian. Yet students spend a great deal of time talking about this academic hierarchy and trying to determine who is or is not at the top. Such hierarchies are important because they define how students enact their particular distinctions. Finding a place in the hierarchy is an essential part of becoming a Westonian.

When students talk about this academic hierarchy, they frequently offer names of specific students or categories of students as examples of people they consider smart or not so smart. By the time I started my second year of research, John Virgil, who grew up in his family's Upper East Side Manhattan home and their secluded beachfront property in New England, had become a familiar name throughout the school. Anytime a student needs an example of someone who is "smart," they either name John Virgil or Damien Ting, whom they consider a "genius" in physics and quantum mechanics. I ask John why he thinks students use him and Damien as examples of being smart.[13] "Because people are always trying to define who they are, and you're always trying to find, uh, benchmarks of what you are and what you aren't. And, uh, that's the simplest benchmark, . . . to find the extremes. I mean, you also say I'm not as stupid as a hockey player. But, you know, at, at the same time everybody knows that they're not gonna win a gold medal at the, at the, you know, IMO [International Math Olympiad]."

Although some students attempt to figure out exactly where they are in the academic hierarchy, they more often, as John argues, establish extremes against which they can claim to be "not as smart as So-and-so" yet "not as dumb as So-and-so."[14] These extremes are quite distinct in kind: whereas the "smart" extreme is associated with individual students, the "dumb" extreme is associated with whole categories of students, most often postgraduate students (PGs) and athletes.

"Dumb PGs" and the Edges of Smart

Every year, Weston—like many of its peer schools—recruits a number of students who have completed high school but who have decided to spend an additional year in school before attending college. Many of them do so in order to focus on athletic training and to improve their chances of getting into a college with a strong program in their particular sport. Many PGs are unofficially recruited by particular team coaches every year to beef up athletic teams, particularly boys' hockey, basketball, and lacrosse. These unofficial practices are controversial, and some schools have discontinued the practice. Some teachers and school officials feel that such practices contradict the express purpose of elite boarding schools: to provide an environment that is focused on academic excellence.

These "athletic" PGs (as opposed to the fewer "academic" PGs) come mostly from public high schools in surrounding cities and towns, and often from white working-class and middle-class families. For many of them, Weston is their first exposure to an elite boarding school. Despite the relatively short tenure of PGs at the school, as a category they play an important role in the Westonian social landscape.

PGs are the one category of Weston students who are not assumed to be, by definition, "smart." "That's why," says Radhika, "it's been, like, said that PGs aren't really Westonians." She elaborates: "Well, we typically think that PGs aren't really—well, I don't wanna say they're not as smart, but that they're just obviously here for one reason: for sports." Students consistently invoke the category of PGs to stand for everything that Westonians are not: public school students, students uninterested in academics, students who are unable to participate in the discussion around the classroom table.

In an Advanced Placement chemistry class, the students are scattered around the laboratory tables in the back of the classroom, wearing their protective eyewear and working in pairs to complete a titration. They slowly add drips of hydrochloride acid, waiting for the substance to change from clear to a soft rose tinge. "Too bright, too bright," says the teacher, as the test substance turns fuchsia pink in several failed attempts, until one pair of students gets the desired reaction. "Oh! Oh! That's gorgeous. Now, show that! Everyone clap! That is really, really nice!" The rest of the class claps, and quickly returns to the experiment, until another duo attains the desired reaction. "Oh, oh, oh! That is gorgeous!" the teacher exclaims happily, and one by one each pair completes the task—except for one.

The last pair move slowly as they prepare the experiment for another attempt. Mike, a PG who started at Weston this fall, seems more interested in my presence, and asks questions about my work as he rinses his instruments. "You're from Harvard, right? Maybe I'll see you there." At which the students around him laugh out loud. The teacher interrupts: "If you wanna be the best in the class, you can't joke around. . . . This is not a hockey game! . . . This is a rather-be-careful-than-screw-up experiment." The tension mounts, and the two students continue the experiment only to produce another bright-fuchsia mix. "Oh my gosh, I quit! This is ridiculous, I can't work with you!" Mike cries out. And the teacher jumps in: "Gentlemen! You're losing focus!" She asks them to make their calculations based on their failed attempts and to "pretend" that they achieved the right chemical reaction. But Mike protests, "I wanna get a round of applause!" as he closes his notebook and joins the rest of the class around the seminar table.

As soon as Mike sits down, the teacher asks him to go to the board and outline the chemical reactions involved in the experiment. "I'm going to the board, first time of the term!" Mike jokes. And in no time, he writes out the formulas, in perfect balance:

$$\sim 20 \; M^{+1} \; 2M + 2HCL \Rightarrow 2MCL + H_2$$
$$\sim 41 \; M^{+2} \; M + 2HCL \Rightarrow MCL_2 + H_2$$
$$\sim 61 \; M^{+3} \; 2M + 6HCL \Rightarrow 2MCL_3 + 3H_2$$
$$\sim 82 \; M^{+4} \; 2M + 4HCL \Rightarrow MCL_4 + 2H_2.$$

"Thank you—this is a beautiful job!" the teacher compliments Mike, who returns to his seat quietly. Together, the students determine that calcium is the unknown dissolved metal, and draw their calculators to estimate the molarity. Around the seminar table, the conversation is less organized than at the lab tables; it moves from molarities and titrations to religion, shopping, politics, and one girl's boyfriend, who waits by the door for the class to end. "Oh, that's precious!" Mike jokes. The teacher asks for the results, and as Mike is about to answer, Lionel, a three-year junior, jumps in and yells the final calculation. Mike shakes his head and stares at his foe. They exchange threats: "You wanna wrestle?" "Clear the table!" The students laugh off the exchange nervously. "We don't do that kind of chemistry around here," the teacher comments as the class ends. Perhaps worried that the PG and the three-year Westonian might continue their altercation, she asks Lionel, "Who are you walking with?"

Students are often quick to point out that some PGs are smart and capable of participating in the academic domain, stressing that the category of PG (not individual PGs) stands for just the opposite. Matthew Briggs says that it is all just a joke: "Just, you know, uh, kidding around about, 'Oh yeah, that's a dumb PG.' And most of them are, are really bright enough . . . to do well in class, but they're not—they aren't quite the same, because they come for only one year and they don't really get so much of the full experience." While individual PGs are certainly "smart enough" (maybe even "most of them"), what is crucial here is that students use the category of PG as a way to distinguish and draw boundaries around themselves as Westonians who are smart and work hard.

As an admissions tour guide, Sandi Li meets many prospective students, and she comments that she often meets prospective PGs "who I can tell have no personality." She says she doesn't want to "discriminate against PGs," yet "there are, like, PGs who are great and, like, really funny and very, uh, very modest about—they're realistic. . . . They're, like, 'I'm not smart at all—I just, you know, wanna do another year of school and try to do better and get into a better college.' You know, so I respect them."

A four-year senior, Sandi has seen many PGs come through Weston, and I ask her what she thinks about the PGs who are in her class. Her first comment is that, just as in the rest of her class, there are some PGs who are "really smart" and some who are "really dumb." "For the most part, I like them. They add interesting chemistry to senior year because they're new and they are sort of, like, hot shots on campus as soon as they set foot here." Although we are reaching the end of the interview, I can't resist asking her why. She starts to say that she doesn't "have a quick answer," and that she will think about it for our next interview. As she gets ready to go, and just before I shut off the recorder, she offers the following:

> Oh, actually, one thing that I would say about that is, they
> bring in, I don't—not that they're necessarily from a public

school, but they create sort of the public school atmosphere of, like, popularity, and of, like, posse type. I mean, we've had, we have, we always have posses [social cliques], but we know that they are, like, like us, because we've all been in this together for four years. But all of a sudden these PGs come in and, like, unless you're friends with them, you don't really know them. It's a very aloof—not even aloof, but just, like, it feels, it makes it a little more like public school atmosphere.

During our second interview, we return to her comments, and Sandi contrasts the Westonian ethos of hard work with PGs, whom she says "are like, 'Ah, we don't care about work.' You know, 'We, you know, b.s. in class and get away with our papers, and we're fine.'" Sandi claims that to make this distinction is "not to say anything bad about them either," and adds, "I really like them. Some of them are really funny, [*laughing*] highly entertaining." She adds that PGs "just bring in a much more, like, social, like, lighter sort of atmosphere—slackerish." While she doesn't "wanna put any stereotypes," she continues: "If we're talking about PG, like, most PGs, from what I've seen, they really, they're careless, you know—I mean, they're carefree. They don't, they don't really care. They're coming here to just, you know, to get Weston on their résumé, to play another year of sports, and, you know, . . . get another chance to, you know, do it the right way."

The boundary that students construct between themselves and PGs —Weston students who are not Westonians—says a great deal about how they construct "Westonian" as an elite identification. Moreover, the boundary that students draw to separate themselves from PGs implicitly reinforces class boundaries, and it clarifies some of the important ways in which public schools play a critical role in the construction of elite identifications. Westonians define themselves in opposition to what they imagine about public schools and public school students: lacking interest in learning, overly concerned with popularity, and not particularly smart, at least by Weston's very high standards. Even when students acknowledge that these stereotype are not real, they still draw a boundary between Weston and public schools in order to underscore their own distinctions. By positioning PGs as bringing in a "public school" atmosphere, a class boundary that associates smartness with higher class and athletic prowess with lower class is strengthened, and PGs are irremediably considered outsiders.

Nevertheless, some PGs do become "hot shots," as Sandi suggests. Their status derives from their position in the athletic hierarchy and from their perceived prowess in football and, particularly, ice hockey. In the discourse of distinction, the opposite of being a smart, hardworking, four-year senior is being a one-year hockey PG. At the same time, athletics are a central aspect of the image that elite boarding schools present and how they think of themselves.[15] Recruiting strong athletes is crucial to maintaining a strong image, and for some students this goes against the idea of Westonians as the smartest and most academically talented students.

Scott Jaffee, whose parents are investment bankers in the Midwest, spends a lot of time taking photos of sports events for the student newspaper. He puts it this way:

> You know that the admissions office makes a big deal about how you really need to be smart to be here. At least when I was applying, they said, you know, "We don't really accept jocks who are jocks." But—and maybe it's just that I'm sort of spoiled because there's so many intellectuals here—but there are clearly people here who are just jocks. And really, . . . I mean, frankly, they're, they're good at what they do, but they're not intellectuals, and they're not very intelligent. And there's nothing wrong with that. They're just, you know, there's just this pretense of "we want smart people who happen to be athletes."

Radhika also articulates the opposition between academics and athletics. She says that there is "definitely overlap, but if you want, like, the extremely good athletes who you consider athletes, they wouldn't be good at academics." She gives me a specific example, but quickly adds, "No one would think of him as academically smart, even though I think he is pretty smart"—thus clarifying that the distinction between academics and athletics is largely idealistic and constructed as part of the Westonian discourse of distinction.

"Niches" and the Hierarchies of Work

Part of what makes Weston an *elite* boarding school is the range of opportunities it provides its students to develop and demonstrate their particular abilities. "Anybody can find their niche at Weston" because Weston has the resources to provide ample space for those "niches" to exist in the first place. As students find their niches—whether academic, athletic, artistic, or extracurricular—these become an important part of how they distinguish among the various groups of Westonians.

Yet not all niches are created equal. Being smart is the core of the Westonian identification; and therefore, being at the top of the academic hierarchy is the apex of Westonian distinction. The academic domain, in turn, has internal hierarchies. Consider, for instance, the way Steve Hart distinguished between English and Latin. Like Steve, Michael Jonas is interested in the classics, and he likewise compares the intellectual demands of studying Latin and Greek to those of studying English. "English is quite easy," he says, adding that this is "the general consensus." He says it's easy to get A's in English.

> *Michael:*   You just—you wrote your paper, you spent time on it, um, but you turned it in, you got the book, you made some comments in class, and you were nice to the teacher, you got an A . . . in English. And also, it's a very—English [is a] very easy class to, uh, to bullshit in.
>
> *RG:*   How come?
>
> *Michael:*   You don't do the reading.
>
> *RG:*   No?
>
> *Michael:*   You just listen to what other people—you might read a paragraph, and then choose that paragraph and say some crap about it, you know, you, so—I don't know, the [Weston teaching] system has its advantages, [but it kind of has] disadvantages.[16]

The handful of Westonians who take at least three years of Latin and two years of a modern Romance language are recognized upon graduation with an official "Latin Distinction." During graduation, they are the last students to enter the ceremony, while the audience is asked to stand. They sit in a special row in front of the stage, facing their classmates, and wear specially made medals around their necks that mark their academic status.[17]

Yet success in the classics is not the only way to demonstrate excellence or hard work at Weston. When not at the top of the academic hierarchy, students can rely on the hierarchies of other domains. In athletics, the sports for which PGs are recruited are at the top of the hierarchy. These are the sports that draw the largest crowds. While "nobody wants to go watch track," as Sandi explains, everyone wants to watch what Matthew calls "marquee sports."

> It's not as if the school comes out and says, "This group is more important—they're gonna get priority." But there's more recruitment. They get postgraduates specifically for [those] sports. Sometimes the postgraduates probably wouldn't have gotten in if they didn't play this particular sport. . . . You sort of know which ones they are. . . . You know, like, in, in the fall, it's football. Um, in the winter, it's basketball and hockey. Uh, and in the spring it's probably lacrosse and to some degree crew.

Students also talk about hierarchical dynamics among and within the arts disciplines. Although these dynamics matter in how the discourse of distinction is mobilized to describe the arts domain, they are less ubiquitous than the athletic hierarchies and are ultimately less relevant to how Westonian identifications are constructed. What is crucial is that while internally hierarchical, "niches" within the arts and athletics are always perceived as secondary in terms of their status vis-à-vis academics. Thus, when not at the top of that hierarchy, students rely on the other hierarchies to claim status and distinction. Figure 1 is a graphic representation of this idea.

Students who are positioned as "smart" rely less on their identifications with athletic or artistic niches to construct their particular Westonian identifications, while students who are attributed with lower academic status rely on strong identifications with athletic or artistic domains in order to claim a niche in the Weston landscape. I will return to this figure in the next chapter, as I elaborate on how the work sphere and the social sphere overlap. It is important to note, however, that while the discourse allows for some students to be positioned as smart and athletic or as smart and artistic, there is little room for students to claim identifications as both athletic and artistic, even if a few students can claim to be excellent athletes *and* dedicated artists.[18]

The extracurricular domain of work is also an important source of identification for some Weston students, but it is not nearly as important as the academic domain (first) and the artistic and athletic domains (sec-

Academic domain

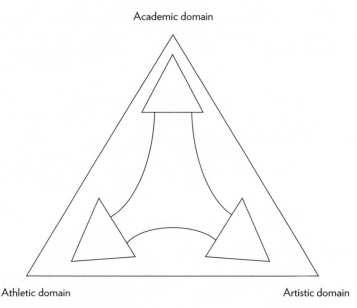

Athletic domain   Artistic domain

FIGURE 1   The hierarchies of work.

ond). This is partly due to the fact that many extracurricular activities fall within the purview of the other three domains.[19] Additionally, many students see extracurricular activities as "college suck"—something they do in order to enhance their college applications. They are often cynical about Weston's claims regarding the wide range of student clubs and organizations in its admissions materials, suggesting a parallel between how the school uses these organizations to enhance their recruitment materials and how the students use them to "beef up" their college applications.[20]

Nonetheless, extracurricular activities are important in two particular instances. First, activities that require some sort of selection process or competition, such as the school newspaper editors and the Student Council, have a high profile on campus. Students involved in these activities do incorporate them into how they distinguish themselves as Westonians, particularly students who do not identify strongly with one of the three domains described above. This is probably related, at least in part, to college admissions. If students do not believe that their academic profiles are sufficient to get them into a good college, they use extracurricular activities to improve their chances. While I was at Weston, several student leaders were known for creating leadership positions for other students who needed them for their college application, even though the positions required little or no work.

Second, extracurricular activities that involve specific aspects of how Westonians identify with other social categories are of great importance for those particular students. And the fact that they are is suggestive of how these particular identifications fit within the discourse of distinction. Two important examples of this are the school's Society of African and Hispanic American Students (SAHAS—or "Saha," as the students call it) and the Gay-Straight Alliance (GSA). The roles of these groups are directly related not to how students construct notions of "smart" or "hard work," but to how they negotiate the social landscape of the school.

THE LANDSCAPE OF DISTINCTION

The process of achieving Westonian identifications ultimately allows students to claim their distinction as students with merit who are entitled to the privileges a Westonian education affords them. This entitlement is not based either on the inheritance of privilege or on their inherent smartness, but on their effort to be the best that they can be in their particular niche. While students readily define Westonians as smart, they are at least ambivalent about claiming the label for themselves, instead claiming a personal identification as hard workers. Their commitment to hard work distinguishes Westonians as exceptional because they, unlike other students (especially public school students, they argue), are committed to academic excellence and rigor.

Ideologically, these notions are closely linked to the image of the United States as an exceptional nation in which working hard will earn anyone—with the right talents—a justified place in the meritocracy. Students not only deserve the privileges of a Weston education (because they are smart), but have earned them (because they work hard). Since not all students can be the smartest, they find other domains in which to define themselves as "the best." This echoes Michael Young's fictional meritocracy, in which "every member is a tried specialist in his own sphere"[21] and the abilities of each individual are put to their proper use in the niche in which they can provide the most social advancement. As in the well-functioning society that Emile Durkheim imagined, all individuals are educated according to their potential, and find their place in the division of labor to make their contribution.[22] As in Daniel Bell's imagined redefinition of meritocracy, everyone works to be the best in their particular niche, because everyone's needs are satisfied.[23]

This utopian vision, however, is never quite complete, and as Jerome Karabel demonstrates regarding the role of meritocracy in admission to elite universities, sustaining hierarchical relationships between groups always undermines meritocratic idealism.[24] On the one hand, becoming Westonian requires that students identify themselves as smart and hardworking individuals who deserve the privilege of a Weston education. On the other, it requires acknowledging that not everyone can "be the best" or "find a niche" in which to demonstrate excellence within hierarchically organized domains. Much of how the domains of work are understood hierarchically is manifested in how the students perceive their distribution in the physical space of the school. Indeed, the hierarchical dynamic among academics, athletics, and the arts is further clarified by how students talk about the campus.

The Weston River flows southeast toward nearby Cypress Lake, cutting the Weston campus in half. Every morning, Westonians walk to their classes across the flowing waters that feed energy to the local mill. While the river doesn't literally divide the campus in half (about three-fourths of the campus actually lies to the west), the symbolic division makes the river a physical boundary that separates two substantively different sides of the campus.

The landscape to one side of the campus is filled with trees that line the paths winding up and down the hills and around the buildings that house the academic classrooms. The other side is a vast valley that extends for more than a hundred acres, cut with straight lines of trees and paths that divide the region into athletic fields. While the theater, the music building, and the art studios are on the "hills" side, the football stadium, the athletic complex, and the baseball diamond are on the "fields." The hills/fields division spatially marks the distinctions students make between students who are smart and students who are athletic, as well as between the arts and sports. In fact, the athletic and artistic domains play an important role in the organization of the social sphere at the school.

The hills/fields distinction correlates with differences and similarities between social groups that are distinguished by other markers, such as sitting arrangements in the dining hall and in the school chapel. These arrangements are more than just separations between groups of friends. They reveal the role that privilege plays in how students assume a place within the internal hierarchies of this particular elite status group. Becoming elite is not just a process of demonstrating engagement and excellence. It implies further exclusions and the distribution of status along hierarchies that overlap in complex ways with how students make meaning from being smart and working hard.

4

RESERVED SEATING

The unmistakable voice of Bob Dylan blares from the stage and reverberates throughout the polished marble stairwell of the school chapel. Loud voices and footsteps accompany the music as the students hurry up and down the stairs. Today's assembly speaker, Ms. Martin, a veteran member of the English faculty, has asked the seniors and the freshmen to swap their usual sitting areas in the chapel. The seniors, who have waited three years to sit at the front by the pulpit area (which serves as a stage), grudgingly make their way up the stairs, while the first-year students giddily rush down from the balcony, eager to occupy the coveted spots. As they roll like rolling stones from one spot to the other, Dylan relentlessly poses the obvious question: How does it feel? I climb to the second floor with the irritated seniors, and sit in one of the back rows. My eyes scan the benches for expressions, conversations, anything that might indicate what the students are thinking about the forced shift in space. Cynicism and disbelief permeate their laughter, but it's hard to tell what they are actually thinking.

Ms. Martin draws the students' attention to the fact that while "changing seats in assembly is not a huge deal," it metaphorically points to notions of inclusion, privilege, the fragility of entitlement, and the importance of space. "How have you been unsettled?" she asks the students, as they subside into their new seats. Most of the seniors pay little attention, still incredulous that they've been asked to relinquish their treasured front-row seats to the younger students. Martin reminds them that in a few months, after they graduate, "all seniors will become newcomers, freshmen anew, lost and anonymous."

A few seniors slouch with smirks on their faces, and I wonder if they feel that Ms. Martin is proselytizing, reminding them of their own privileges. "Think of Rosa Parks's decision to sit in the front of the bus. . . . Sometimes it is important to fight for your place." She invites them to consider what it means to be granted the "status and privilege associated with the front seats." "Were you born into it? Did you work for it? Get lucky?" She wonders aloud whether things will return to the normal routine after the assembly is over, or whether the first-year students will decide they prefer the new arrangement. "What if they decide they like it down here and don't want to climb the stairs anymore?" she asks, looking up at the seniors. "Then what?" The freshmen erupt in loud applause and cheers, welcoming the idea, while the seniors hiss and boo, scornfully asserting their right to the front-row seats.

"I haven't sat up there since freshman year, and I was, like, 'This is so weird!'" recalls Sandi Li. "It made me feel, like, all small again, and I was, like, 'I don't like this,' you know?" She underscores the emotions that the sudden and unexpected shift aroused in her. "It made me feel, like, not ashamed, but just, like, more like, this—this is not where I'm supposed to be. Like, this is *so* wrong! And if those freshmen, like, try to, you know, take over our seats tomorrow, they're getting *so* kicked out!"

Sandi's comments highlight the importance of group boundaries and hierarchies, and the role that space plays in organizing and maintaining them.[1] Seating according to year might seem like a rather benign—even trivial—form of social distinction, one that highlights seniority and age differences.[2] But in the chapel, as in many other school spaces, there are also less obvious, more insidious, and just as pervasive spatial boundaries that mark distinctions and betray the deeply social dimension of the process of becoming Westonian. These spatial arrangements "naturalize" social boundaries, making the internal hierarchies of distinction appear organic, as if they should be taken for granted.

The last term of the year has begun, and students slowly make their way across the campus from their classes to another morning assembly. This time, I enter the school chapel and stand by the side wall. My attention is drawn to a series of unexpected large signs that have been posted all over the chapel, bearing words I have grown familiar with: "Fresh Posse Only," "Jocks Only," "SAHAS Senior Members Only," "A-Club Only." The signs clearly indicate that only certain students can sit in specific areas. Today's speaker, an alumna who is now an influential movie producer, seems oblivious to the signs as she speaks about the portrayal of Native American characters in Hollywood films. The students whisper about the signs, wondering who put them up, and begin to take some down. A female first-year student sitting in the first row of the balcony rips the sign reading "Fresh Posse Only" from the railing, tears and crumbles the paper, and throws it on the floor. Several black students on the first level grab a sign labeled "SAHAS" and pull it down. They write the words "Junior Posse Only" in red ink on the back and post it on the bench in front.

After the assembly has ended and the students have left for their next class, I roam around the hall, looking for the signs and reading what the students have written on them. In the back of the room, where athletes and PGs often sit, two signs remain on the wall. The word "Pimps" is written in capital letters above the words "Post-Graduates Only." And on the sign that says "Jocks Only," someone has written "Well-Hung, Cool People." Throughout the day, I hear the students talk about the signs, some of them suggesting that they were unfair and rude, and others glad that someone has pointed out the obvious—if unspoken—seating arrangements.

On my first visits to Weston, my impression of the seating arrangements in the chapel during morning meetings was that they were officially assigned; the ease with which students found a place to sit struck me as natural. Over time, I have learned from the students that there are unofficial patterns that follow an unsurprising logic: the "popular" and "attractive" students of each class (a.k.a. the "posses"); the "urban" students of color, who are typically members of SAHAS; the jocks and the PGs; the members of the squash team, along with their "groupies"; the Actors' Club (A-Club); and the Gay-Straight Alliance. These groups all have unofficially reserved seating areas that they identify with and that make finding a seat seem natural and self-evident.

When I asked students during focus groups to draw social maps of the school, many of them chose to draw diagrams of the chapel because they felt this was the clearest way to illustrate the various social groups and their relationships. The consistency with which different students drew and talked about these arrangements indicated that they tacitly shared a common understanding of the social space and of the way they decided where and with whom to sit. In all diagrams, students placed various kinds of labels to identify the various "social regions" in the chapel. Some

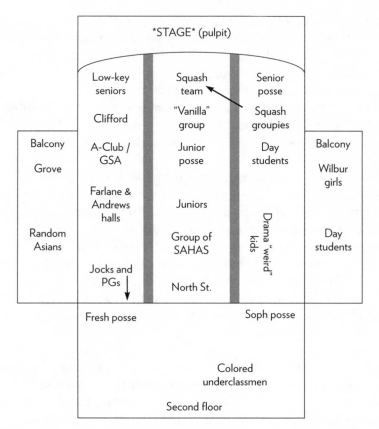

FIGURE 2 This diagram of the chapel replicates, with some alterations, one of the maps drawn by a group of students that was particularly thorough and explicit. The names of the dorms (East Street, Wilbur, Grove, Farlane, Andrews, and Clifford), as well as those of the student organizations, are pseudonyms.

of these were obvious and specific characterizations, such as where students from particular grades, particular sports teams, or specific dorms sat together. Others seemed more abstract or vague, at least on the surface—such as areas labeled "Drama weird kids," "Random Asians," or "Colored underclassmen." Still other labels pointed to a status hierarchy among various groups, such as "Senior second tier," "Third-tier guys," "Freaks," and "Confused freshmen."

The implicit ways in which students arrange and occupy the school space highlight how status groups are organized, how they interact, and how they function in the process by which students come to identify as Westonian. Of course, the fact that status correlates with a particular organization of space is not a phenomenon unique to elite boarding schools.[3] Scholars who study the culture of schools have argued that the spatial organization of different social groups not only illustrates important social dynamics, but ultimately has consequences for how different students experience school.[4] At the center of how the social space is organized is the common distinction between being "cool" and being "weird."[5] The unique ways in which this opposition is manifested in the context of an elite boarding school, however, depart significantly from the ways it is manifested in other schools. Since being a Westonian means putting a high premium on being smart and doing well academically, students who are perceived as especially talented academically are able to claim a certain kind of high status. "It's really easy to be smart and be respected," explains Patricia Sanders, a four-year senior whose grandfather is an alumnus. "Whereas in other schools, if you're smart, you're just considered a dork and no one wants to hang out with you, you know. It's, it's not okay to do work on weekends . . . at a public high school, whereas here, like, a lot of people do that. . . . Because everyone here is here because they wanna work hard. . . . And so it's—I think it changes the social scene a lot, when, when that particular aspect is there, added in there."[6]

In addition to claiming that being smart is "respected," students distinguish Weston from other schools, particularly public schools, by arguing that social distinctions and cliques are not as important at Weston. Yet the evidence—such as the seating pattern in the chapel—points to the contrary. And nowhere was the importance of social cliques more evident than in the way students talked about the two sides of the campus—the hills and the valley—and about their respective dining halls.

THE TWO SIDES OF WESTON

The two dining halls, Wyndham Hall and Alumni Hall, stand almost facing each other across the Weston River, which divides the campus. Two bridges, roughly two hundred yards from each other, span the river, connecting to the paths that lead to the two dining halls. On the hills side of the campus, to the east, Wyndham Hall is divided into three parallel dining rooms, all connected by large French doors. The dining rooms in this older building are carpeted, lit by chandeliers, and decorated with nineteenth-century oil portraits hanging over sealed-off fireplaces. Most

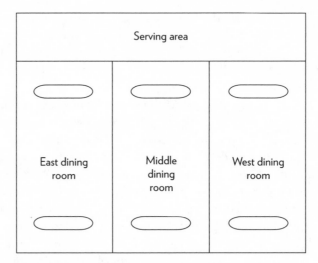

FIGURE 3   Wyndham Dining Hall. The ovals indicate various kinds of food bars.

of the tables are round, with enough chairs for eight students. During the day, the rooms are bright with the natural light that flows through the large bay windows.

On the valley side of campus, the newer Alumni Hall feels institutional and spacious in comparison to the intimate, compartmentalized space across the river. Though their redbrick façades resemble each other, Alumni Hall looks modern inside, with its angular concrete ceiling that rises high above the tables. The cavernous hall is equipped with modular food bars, which can be easily rearranged for special events and multiple purposes. Typically, the food bars—two salad bars, a sandwich bar, and a pasta bar—split the room into squares of roughly equal size. The rectangular tables are arranged in rows with enough seats for large groups to sit together. The room is always illuminated with long fluorescent lights at the sides and hanging from the high ceiling. The only natural light comes from eight narrow, equally spaced windows.

In Wyndham Hall, the dining rooms separate the process of choosing what to eat from choosing where to sit. In Alumni Hall, where the entire room can be scanned from the stack of red trays and clean plates, choosing what to eat and choosing where to sit are parallel processes. Still, in both halls, selecting where and with whom to sit is at least as important as selecting what to eat—and in some cases even more important.

To an observer, the choreography of finding a seat in the dining hall can be perplexing.[7] It takes only a few visits before I realize that groups

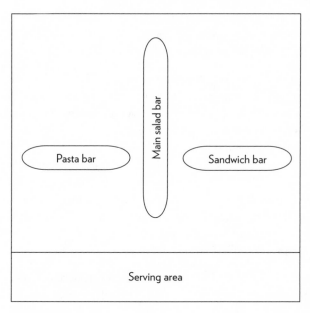

FIGURE 4   Alumni Dining Hall.

of students consistently choose the same dining hall for their meals. Yet some students—particularly in Wyndham Hall—seem to know exactly where they will eat (as suggested by the fact that they walk directly to a table and claim a chair before going through the food line). Other students—particularly in Alumni Hall—spend several minutes circling the food-serving areas and salad bars, alternating their gaze between the food and the tables before deciding what to eat.

When I ask students why they sit where they do, the most obvious (and most common) answer is that they sit with their friends or, correspondingly, that they sit "with their dorm." The latter phrase means that they sit at a specific table or cluster of smaller tables that residents of a particular dorm have claimed as "theirs." This is especially true for students who identify with Wyndham.

"It's pretty much set by dorms," explains Radhika Chaudari, a day student who claims to have figured out where every dorm has its seating area. "East Street has their own table, Salinger has their own table—like, they all have their own table. So you all sit with your own dorms, but, I guess, that's who you become accustomed to. . . . You live, spend time with them."[8]

Will Mueller, a four-year senior, says, "I know my dorm sits together regardless. There's only one or two kids who don't sit at our table with us." He describes with great specificity the tables that his fellow dorm residents claim as "theirs" and why he prefers that space.

> You go in Wyndham, you turn right. . . . The Grove tables are all along the . . . the wall, . . . the round ones. . . . I mean, there's carpet in Alumni Hall, but it's not as vibrant. In Wyndham there's carpets and smaller tables. They're not the big long ones, like a mess hall. And you know, there's chandeliers and, and it's more compartmentalized. It's—Wyndham is just a better dining hall. There's fewer people there. It's not like a cattle call and everyone is eating. I don't know. I don't know. I—you'll never convince someone on the valley that Wyndham's better, and you'll never convince someone on the hills that Alumni Hall is better. . . . But that's just what I think.

As both Radhika and Will point out, many students choose to sit with their dormmates. In both dining halls, the clearest and most consistent seating patterns are associated with "dorm tables" (in Alumni Hall, this is especially true on the "left" side of the hall). This is not surprising, as sharing meals is an important way for individuals to show solidarity and intimacy with the people who share their living space.[9] I will return to this theme of bonding in the next chapter. Here I wish to draw attention to Will's comment regarding the two sides of the campus and students' loyalties to their respective dining halls, because it suggests that social distinctions at the Weston School matter much more than students are generally willing to admit.

As we've seen, students differentiate between the hills and the valley according to distinctions between academics and athletics, which are underscored by the layout of the buildings on the campus. Wyndham, on the hills side, sits across a courtyard from the Modern Languages Department. Alumni Hall, on the valley side, is farther from the academic buildings, and its exits are oriented toward the gym and the sports arenas. Students also have strong parallel associations with the two dining halls. Wyndham and Alumni Hall anchor the social landscape of each side, and their contrasting characters manifest the distinctions between— and the identifications many students make with—the two sides of the campus.

"They are different," explains Radhika, adding that it is "a hills and valley divide. . . . You have this, like, certain, like, rivalry going. Like, they're like, 'Oh, my god, you eat at Alumni?! Why would you eat there?!'" Laurie King came to Weston on the heels of her sister, who was a senior when Laurie was a freshman. While she claims she is not as active in athletics as her sister, she has played varsity tennis and field hockey. She is close friends with other athletes, and, like them, is often dressed in sportswear bearing the Weston School logo. She lives on the valley side of the campus, and she "honestly feel[s] like the hills [side] . . . just breeds the weird ones." She claims that students from the valley have "a pretty big prejudice" against students from the hills. "It's like West Side Story. . . . We're like the Jets, and they're the Sharks. We're so much cooler." Laurie prefaces her comments by claiming that the stereotypes are "just something that we all imagine," yet she quickly turns to describing how "real" the differences are.

Like Laurie, most students express strong affiliations and loyalties to a specific dining hall and to the corresponding region of the campus on which that dining hall sits. Sandy Li, who lives in one of the large girls' dorms on the valley side, is unambiguous: "I don't really like eating in Wyndham. It scares me!" When I ask her why, she talks about the challenge of finding a place to sit in an unfamiliar hall. "They all have their, like, dorm tables. And I feel like unless I know someone there, I can't just, like, sit down with a group, or, like, sit down by myself and feel comfortable with that."[10] As a tour guide, Sandi squirms at the thought of taking prospective students to Wyndham. She justifies her choice by saying that "it's kind of out of the way," but her nose wrinkles and her expression betrays a strong distaste at the thought of even walking into the hills-side dining hall, which she describes as "much less centralized." She explains: "You walk into Alumni Hall, and you can, like, point things out. You can be, like, this is the hot-food line, this is the salad bar, that's the cereal bar, this is a bread table. So it's a lot easier, too." Sandi skirts having to describe what makes Wyndham scary by talking about how the open space in Alumni Hall makes it easier to show to prospective students. She thus avoids the contradiction of having to acknowledge that status groups do matter at Weston.

Yet students who typically eat at Wyndham likewise describe the stress of having to choose a place to sit in Alumni Hall. "Alumni just feels more crowded," explains Neil Perry, a talented theater student who usually eats in Wyndham even though his dorm is on the valley side of the campus. Neil, like Sandi, avoids talking about status groups by focusing on space, but he seems aware that his explanation is filled with contradictions. "I feel more stressful when I'm eating at Alumni 'cause it's sort of just, like, it's a smaller—even though the rooms are technically bigger, you notice that there are so many more people there. And it's just—it feels more cramped, even though the space is bigger."

"I like Wyndham a lot more," says Michael Jonas, "'cause I think it's a lot [more] unassuming."

> Alumni Hall, I feel like you're always being judged. I think it feels like you, uh, because like, that's where, like, . . . you have like all the, the athletes, and the kind of—the cool people, the drinkers, all that stuff, sitting at this table. And everyone's sitting where they're supposed to be. So when you walk in, you know, you just, you feel all these eyes kind of turned on you. And especially once you get your tray. And if you're looking for a place to sit, you feel like everyone's looking at you, seeing the way you're dressed. You know, "Who is he gonna go sit with?" . . . And people are looking at you, to see what you're gonna do. Whereas in Wyndham, you go and you get your tray, and then you go to where you're supposed to sit.

As Michael's conclusion suggests, there is a degree of prescription involved in finding a niche in Weston's social space. Preferences for one hall over another may have to do with being able to foresee a place and not feeling exposed to the scrutiny of others at the point of deciding where and with whom to eat. For instance, Sandi and Neil seem to want to avoid such scrutiny by following certain routines. Yet Michael's comment that certain students (athletes, cool kids, drinkers, etc.) eat at Alumni Hall reveals the underlying distinctions that set apart the social spaces of the two halls.

Scott Jaffee echoes Michael's observation. He describes his own identification with the hills side of campus. "There's a whole different attitude on that [valley] side of campus about social life," he explains. "I mean, I have friends who live on the valley, but, uh, it's almost like, it's almost like they're at Manchester, you know? . . . And I don't mean that in the sense that I dislike them. I'm just saying that there's a distance there." Scott's choice of metaphor is suggestive, not only because Manchester—Weston's closest rival—is nearly a hundred miles to the north, but also because students make a great deal of the differences between the two schools. Students claim that Weston is much more academically demanding and less socially conscious than Manchester, which parallels the distinctions students make between the hills side and the valley side of their campus.

Yet if those who identify with the hills describe the valley as overly social and concerned with popularity, students who identify with the valley describe Wyndham as "scary," "weird," and "freakish." Thus, students from each side choose specific status groups to characterize the social space on the opposite side and draw boundaries between different kinds of Westonians. The extremes they articulate also mark the outer boundaries of their Westonian identification by pointing to those who are hardly—if at all—Westonian. Furthermore, these extremes betray the important yet largely denied role that social class plays in the process by which students identify as Westonians.

The Valley: PGs, Sweet Posses, and "Cool Kids"

Sabrina Macy is a four-year senior. She is captain of the varsity soccer team, and was admitted early to an Ivy League university. Her parents live in an affluent eastern suburb and own a vacation house in one of New England's most exclusive oceanside cities. Since arriving at Weston, she has lived in one of the large dorms for girls that's located on the valley side, where she says most of her best friends also live. Sabrina seems keenly aware of the social groups around campus. "You just look at a dining hall—you can see *everything*." She elongates the first syllable and says it in a louder tone, to stress that she does indeed mean *everything*.

As a "valley girl," Sabrina always eats her meals in Alumni Hall. I ask whether her comments about the importance of social groups in dining halls are especially true in Alumni, and she says, "Yeah, Wyndham is different." She laughs, adding: "Well, I don't go there." Then she pauses, reflecting on the deeply felt distinctions between the two spaces. "Gosh! It's so scary, though!" As I ask her to elaborate, she acknowledges that Wyndham "is, like, a nicer dining hall. . . . I guess we're just, like—in terms of aesthetics, you'd definitely wanna go to Wyndham. And the dining hall people are a lot nicer, too." While she complains that "everyone sits with their dorms, and so you can't just, like, sit anywhere," she quickly adds: "Not that you can sit anywhere in Alumni anyway. Anyways, and also, like, the food's in different rooms, and so you have to, like, walk around, and I—it's just too complicated!" She continues to laugh, and concludes: "So I like Alumni a lot better. But, um, you can definitely sort of see that people sit in different places . . . in Alumni."

"And how does that work?" I ask.

"Um, it's partly by dorm. Um, well, this is the way I divide it." She takes a piece of paper and a pen, and begins to draw.

"The right-hand side is the cool side. And the left-hand side isn't necessarily uncool, but, um, a lot of faculty sit on the far side of the left side. And then also Salinger dorm sits there. And then a lot of weird people." We both laugh as she continues. "And then, on the closer side, there's, um—SAHAS always sits there." I recognize her descriptions, and say, "Right," to let her know I'm following her. "And then also, um, more random weird people."

"Random weird people?" I ask, and she flinches. "Yeah. Sounds so awful!" I assure her that what she's saying is helpful to me and that I'm not judging her labels. "And then on the right side, um, you have . . ." She pauses and suddenly becomes animated. "Oh! Yuppie little freshmen on the near side!" And we laugh again as she finishes her map.

> You can always tell the freshmen because there are about twenty girls sitting at *one* table and, like, sharing seats and stuff. And I admit, I did it my freshman year. But once you get past the freshman year, you get, gotta stop doing that—it's too, it's too much. And then Clifford Dorm also has their table there. And then the other side of dining hall, typically for the—for my, um, especially for my freshman and sophomore years, the sweet posse always sat there. . . . Which was, like, the cream of the crop, whatever—you know, the, the in-crowd. Um, weren't necessarily very cool people, but that's just who they were. Um, and then also the jocks and the PGs usually sit over there.

The PGs, who as a category form a boundary against which Westonians can be distinguished as smart, play an ironic role in defining the social space of the valley as the "cool" or "popular" side. In Alumni Hall, PGs anchor the space toward the back of the right-hand side, a space associated with athleticism and jocks and the standards of beauty and upper-class consumption patterns attributed to the posse. This social space is characterized by traditional gender roles and a strong and explicit heterosexuality, which is most clearly articulated in the comments that the students added to the signs that mysteriously appeared at morning assembly. Both jocks and PGs are positioned as hyper-masculine "pimps," who are not only "cool" but also "well-hung."

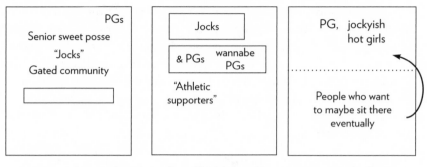

Layouts drawn by students. The labels and lines are approximately where
the students placed them.

Sandi Li's words in Chapter 3 clearly articulate the boundary that PGs
represent. Sandi suggests that PGs create a "public school atmosphere."
She blames the PGs for bringing to Weston the dynamics of "popularity"
from their public schools—dynamics that are presumably foreign to
Weston; after all, Westonians have a reputation for being concerned more
with being smart and working hard than with socializing. Yet the actual
physical space that PGs occupy at Weston has been defined before their
arrival at the school, and that the students they befriend (particularly the
girls of the posse) derive part of their status from the fact that they socialized with PGs in previous years.[11]

Consider the three layouts of the space identified with the PGs (Figure
5), which are based on three different maps the students drew during focus groups. When students drew the right-hand side of Alumni Hall during focus groups, they used more suggestive labels than Sabrina's somewhat moderate term "the cool side." In the first layout of Figure 5 (left),
the labels "Senior sweet posse," "PGs," and "Jocks" are all located behind a physical boundary (a sandwich bar) and the words "Gated community." Marking these groups as such suggests their exclusivity, at least
as felt by the students who drew the map. In the center layout of Figure
5, the same labels are accompanied by the words "wannabe PGs" and
"Athletic supporters," suggesting that these are groups with which others
at least hope to be associated. The third layout of the figure (right) labels
the females in this region "hot girls," with a dotted line (again suggesting
the boundary) dividing the room between these groups and "People who
want to maybe sit there eventually," and an arrow pointing toward the
space reserved for this particular crowd.

Whether other students do in fact want to sit with these popular

groups within their "gated community" is an open question—and often a
topic of spirited debate during focus groups, where it invariably emerged.
Students expressed a range of opinions on whether the PGs and the posse
have "higher" status or are more popular. For instance, I asked the group
that drew the center layout of the figure whether there is a hierarchy between the various social groups on campus. Will Mueller suggested that
at first glance it might seem like "the fresh posse should be running everything," but noted that this was not the case.

> *Will:*   I don't understand why they are called the fresh posse.
> Maybe 'cause they had power at some point, or—like the se-
> nior posse or something. Like the PGs. It's assumed they have
> power, but . . .
>
> *Deb:*   They really don't.
>
> *Will:*   Yeah, I think that they are just set up so that every
> other person who is not them can . . .
>
> *Andrew:*   Is aware of it.
>
> *Robert:*   Yeah, exactly, like . . .
>
> *Andrew:*   Like the posse is [*inaudible*] people being aware of
> it. Or being aware of not being a part of it.[12]

Later, I asked them again whether these students had the most status.

> *Jack:*   They have money and the ability to do whatever they
> darn well feel like.
>
> *Deb:*   A lot of them are Upper East Side [of Manhattan].
>
> *RG:*   But do they have the most status?
>
> *Deb:*   Well, not really, because people don't like them. . . .
> It's not like public school where, like, these are the popular
> people, everyone wants to be them. Because, like—sure you
> wanna be part of the posse, because they are the beautiful
> group. But you also want to be with the drama kids because
> they have a lot of talent, or the GSA because they are really
> acceptable.

While noting that the PGs and the posse are the equivalent of the popular
social groups in public schools, Deb claims that Westonians are distin-

guished as students who pay little attention to status issues. Yet she also notes that being recognized as "beautiful" may be something some students (especially girls) desire. She comments on the opposition between being among the "beautiful" and being with the "drama kids" and the "GSA." This side of the status space has a great deal to do with the characteristics of the so-called posse.

"Posse," "sweet posse," and "fresh posse" are terms of the Weston vernacular that I learned quickly. Students consistently use them to refer to the social dynamics of the school. Generally, students use "posse" to refer to any loosely affiliated group who share a notable characteristic that's relevant in the context of the school—for instance, the "day student posse," the "Korean posse," or the "leadership posse." The term most frequently used in conversations about Weston social life is "fresh posse," or, alternatively, "sweet posse" or "senior posse." To talk about *the* posse is to talk about this particular group of girls (and the boys they befriend). The use of the word "fresh" with reference to this particular group is of great significance for understanding how important this category is in the organization of the school's social life, even if many students reject it as a "public school thing." To call this group the "fresh" (short for "freshman") posse throughout the four years of school is to assign them representative value: they stand as *the* posse for that particular class.[13]

Matthew Briggs describes the fresh posse as a group of "people who consider themselves to be very, very cool, and sort of above everyone else." "You can always identify the kids who wanna be cool," says Andrew Zia. "It's this infamous fresh posse. . . . They kind of, like, stick together. [*pause*] And usually it's, like, focused around the good-looking girls." Will Mueller says, "It's kind of this exclusive, wholly white, uh, upper-crust group." He notes that "no one can ever explain" how the posse comes together.

Yet there are plenty of theories and stories. Some are improbable: "They manage to find each other. . . . They almost identify each other by the little heart-shaped Tiffany's bracelet. It's like a tracking beacon, and they're like—Whoosh!—'There you are!'" Some are unquestioning: "They said, 'You guys are—have been the decided fresh posse this year. . . . Fresh posse sits up there.' . . . Someone told us that that's where the fresh posse sat, so that's where we sat." Some are patronizing: "A core of four or five girls who are chosen, you know, who are all dating senior guys, and then become friends." And some are admiring: "[They are] confident enough to be hanging out with the senior boys. And that's, that's probably what sets them apart, is the confidence. . . . It's usually the fresh posse that's audacious enough to go speak to [the PGs]." Whatever the explanation, "there is always a fresh posse," explains Charlene Rodreau.[14] "The fresh posse will usually always consist of blond, blue-eyed, or, I mean, like, maybe there's one bru—you know, like, one or two brunettes. But for the most part, it tends to be, like, those, those girls that you would see on, um, like, Abercrombie and Fitch. . . . Those kinds of models that they usually have. . . . The all-American kind of look, or attitude, or whatnot. They all stay together."

The valley side, then, is characterized by the kind of gender norms and overt (hetero)sexuality characteristic of social groups associated with wealth and popularity in contemporary public high schools. Charlene's vivid description is telling, yet it is also ironic, because Abercrombie and Fitch is not necessarily the most popular brand among very wealthy students. In fact, the fresh posse were more likely to wear brands like Burberry, Lilly Pulitzer, Lacoste, or Polo Ralph Lauren.

Other students were able to offer specific examples of how these popular students branded themselves through expensive clothing and engaging in particular shopping practices. For instance, one student described a posse member who replaced her entire wardrobe at the beginning of each term with expensive designer clothes. The fact that Charlene—who identifies as Haitian American and grew up in the inner city—associates this crowd only with Abercrombie and Fitch suggests how little she actually knows about what it takes to "look the part." This might help to explain why PGs, many of whom actually come to Weston from public high schools in the New England region, are closely associated with this status region. The difficulty, however, is that most PGs do not come from wealthy families.[15] Instead, it is their athletic physique, their age and experience (most are over eighteen and have already finished high school), and their newness in the social space that makes them attractive to the girls in the posse—and in fact to many of the younger girls. Whatever the explanation, these athletes fit into the scheme of the valley side as the overtly masculine counterpart to the overtly feminine posse.

"When I was a freshman, I thought everyone loved the fresh posse and wanted to be them," explains Deborah Mirabelli, a day student who came to Weston because she "wanted to get a fresh start," and whose father had been a PG at another elite boarding school. I interviewed Deborah after the focus group quoted above, during which other students identified her as a former member of the fresh posse. During the focus group, Deborah seemed to delight in the fact that others knew she had been part of the posse. At the same time, she was glad everyone agreed that she was no longer part of the group:

> It was—it's weird. . . . It's like people view me that way, but then you're like—well, then they acknowledged that I'm *no* longer in the posse. So they must view me in a different way. So it's kind of—it's good and bad. It's like, "Good, oh wow, they thought I was like that. They thought I was pretty, or popular, or whatever." And then you're like, "Well, now they think of me as, like, a whole person, with likes and dislikes. And I'm not mean, like they [the girls in the posse] are."

This rejection of popularity as a way of distinguishing Westonians from other high school students is important because it suggests that the status order at elite boarding schools is far more complicated than prior studies of social groups in schools would allow. To be in the posse, in fact, is to be at one margin of a social space in which hierarchies are not linear.[16] Being pretty or athletic alone, even if it makes someone popular, does not guarantee a student high status across the social space.

The Hills: Theater Kids, the Gay-Straight Alliance, and the "Weird" Kids

Astrid Howard always catches my attention when I see her walk around campus. It isn't that I find her outfits unusual. Having worked for two years at an arts high school, I'm actually quite fond of worn-out red combat boots, fishnet stockings over black-and-orange striped tights, black jackets with anarchist buttons and patches, and orange, blue, and purple hair wrapped in bandannas. Astrid, however, is one of the few students of color at Weston who consistently dresses this way. Astrid came to Weston through one of the recruitment programs that bring inner-city students to elite boarding schools, yet I never saw her hanging out socially with the other students of color. I always saw her with a mostly white crowd that many students consistently identified as the "weird kids" or the "freaks."

After I've made many attempts to schedule an interview with Astrid, we meet close to the end of the year. We talk at length about her experiences at Weston as an openly gay Latina student who does not identify with either the "mainstream" social groups of the school or the minority students with whom she came to Weston and who are usually associated with SAHAS. During the interview, I ask Astrid to draw a map of her so-

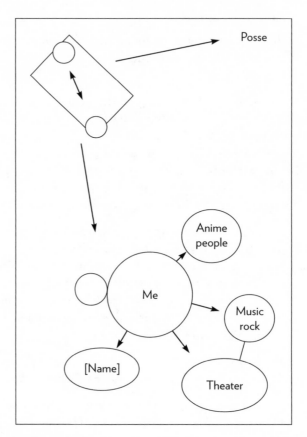

FIGURE 6   Astrid's social map.

cial space (see Figure 6). She begins by drawing a circle with the word
"Me" near the center, and the word "Posse" in the upper right-hand corner. As she draws, she explains: "Okay, so here is me, in a circle, and here
is posse. Arrgh!! I hate them." She draws a rectangle with two circles at
opposite corners, an arrow pointing down to her, and an arrow pointing
to the word "Posse." She continues drawing circles and writing words as
she explains.

Astrid plays guitar in several hard rock and alternative rock bands,
and says she is closest to the music people and the theater people on campus. But she is critical of what she sees as a stereotypical artsy crowd.

> There's, like, the annoying people that are kind of music peo-
> ple, but got into theater people, and in between, but they

wanna be, like, stoners. And, like, it's retarded! . . . It's a small people—number of people that just like to bring other people down, because they think that they're better than everybody else. Because they think that they're the actual music and theater and artsy people, but they're really not, 'cause they're just doing what everybody thinks that music and theater and whatever people should do, which is not cool.

Astrid's suggestion that these "artsy people" are also exclusive is important, because it suggests that exclusivity is rife at this end of the social space as well. Astrid describes this group as "like a posse, but anti-posse. And so anti, that they make themselves—You know when things can be so opposite that they become the same thing? That's who they are."[17] Astrid spends a lot of time with a group of students she calls "the anime obsession—like, weird people."[18] I'm struck by her use of the term "weird" to characterize her own friends. While I was not surprised to hear other students refer to her crowd as "weird" and "freakish," I didn't think this was a label they would use for themselves.

Her identification with this particular group is confirmed when she notes where they gather to eat: "We used to sit at the table, in dining hall, just, like, in the back of the far-left room in Wyndham." As mentioned above, the maps students drew of Wyndham Hall tended to be filled with names of dormitories that had claimed particular tables and eating areas. There were only two exceptions: a table in a back corner of the far-left room that was labeled "Freaks" and "Weird kids," and a long table in the middle room labeled "Theater/GSA."

The association between students who are active in theater and the arts and the Gay-Straight Alliance is likewise unsurprising, since it conforms with the stereotype of theater and "artsy" people. Sandra López, who came to Weston with Astrid, talks about the "weird" kids in relation to Astrid, with whom she still feels a connection, and she refers to the group as "Astrid and the pariahs," a term she says she made up. According to Sandra, the pariahs are "the people who, like, sort of seclude themselves. . . . They're, like, self-proclaimed weird people." She makes the connection between sexuality and being weird, as she writes down "Weird people" on a social map she is drawing.

> I think it's a trend with the *weird* people at Weston that they sort of have to be gay or lesbian too, which is really weird. Not that there's anything *wrong* with being gay and lesbian,

but it just so happens that all the *weird* people end up trying it
at some point in their career. And so then, you know, it's just
sort of like, 'Okay, I'm weird. I just have to have a girlfriend.'
. . . And it's weird, because all the gay-lesbian people are usually with the weird people.

Sandra's conception of sexuality as something that evolves through identification with a group could be seen as compelling, yet the patronizing
tone with which she dismisses the process as a "trend" illuminates how
homophobia plays out in a context of affluence.[19] Here I want to highlight how these groups are characterized as accepting of differences. For
Deb, who talked about having been part of the posse, the theater/GSA
group suggests acceptance of others—in contrast to the posse, which is
known for its exclusivity. Perhaps in her mind these students must be accepting if they are willing to be associated with the "weird" kids.[20]

The notion of acceptance, in fact, fits well with the idea that Westonians are tolerant and welcoming of diversity, and that Weston is a place
where everyone can find his or her niche. Earlier I introduced Sabrina
Macy, who said that Wyndham was "scary" and who noted that "it
sounded so awful" to call other kids "weird." When I ask her to explain
what she means by "weird," she articulates why it seems okay to be weird
at Weston.

Well, first about the weird kids. I don't know, I think that
that's what's great about Weston: is that you can be weird,
and there's a lot of other weird kids here, and so you can be—
have best friends, and they're all weird, and they're all happy
together. Which I think is nice. I mean, you know, you'll see
them sitting in dining hall, and they all [*pause*] are *so weird*.
And you just don't know what to do with them, but they're
all so happy together.

Like most other students, Sabrina has difficulty explaining what she
means by "weird," and she minces words and hesitates, only to return to
the idea that Weston welcomes everyone.

They're, they're just, they're weird. And I—I don't know.
They'll [*longer pause*] they might look weird. Like they might
have dyed hair, or whatever, which is very stereotypical. But
they also sort of—interested in different things. And I think
what's great is that at a public school they'd be eaten alive,

and at Weston, um, not only [are] they able to find friends, but I think that there is, really, um, a high level of respect on campus for everyone in general. And that, like, yes, people will sort of, like, roll their eyes, or talk about the weird people, but [*laughs*] but in the end, if they're in your class, like, um, I think in a class the, sort of, cliques tend to break down, and you can sort of form alliances with people who you wouldn't on the outside. [*laughs*]

Students talk less about this side of the social space, often just dismissing it as the "weird" side. Like Sabrina, students have difficulty pinpointing what being "weird" means, often saying little about it and almost invariably striking a condescending tone. Yet students express no ambivalence about whether being perceived as weird is desirable. No one wants to be identified with the "weird" kids—even Astrid is ambivalent about her own identification with the "weird" kids, and even those who are connected with them by association describe them as scary.

During a focus group, Neil Perry, who identifies with the Wyndham tables occupied by theater and GSA, finds himself in the company of popular boys from the valley, who ask him about the crowd of weird kids with whom they associate him. Neil responds by claiming that he, too, is scared by these kids and finds them weird. As they look over the map of Wyndham that Neil has drawn, Steve Hart points to the back corner of the far-left room and, looking at Neil, asks, "Can I sit up here?" He tries to focus Neil's attention as he taps on the map: "Over here, over here." Neil tries to clarify: "Like, with the scary granola people?"[21] He continues: "It's, like, the people who sorta dabble in the theater and music but they don't, really." But Steve interrupts him: "So wait—but they're scary to you? Or they're . . ." And Neil confirms, "They're scary to me."

Steve laughs as he sits back, and he begins to spout what he is thinking: "'Cause that means they're, like, ultra." But he breaks off, perhaps realizing he's about to suggest that he finds Neil "scary" or "weird." They go on to talk about what makes those students "weird" or "scary," mentioning their strange clothing and their interest in computer games, fantasy play, magic, and witchcraft.

But Steve's curiosity about how Neil makes sense of this group returns. He asks Neil to explain the table again. "So now, what's that table in the corner of Wyndham, in the—in, like, the far-left room?" Neil says, "That used to be the actual theater people, and then it became . . ." But

Steve interrupts again: "Now it's scary people?" "Yeah," agrees Neil. "It used—well, it used to be, the back table in that room sort of used to be a mix between . . ." Steve persists in interrupting him: "'Cause I remember you there. You used to sit there sophomore year." Neil tries to deflect Steve's pursuit: "It was theater and GSA, and that sort of fell apart."

Neil goes on to describe how the leadership of the GSA this year has been "difficult"; there's been some distancing between theater students and the GSA. He manages to avoid talking about his own relationship with the "weird" kids, though Steve appears determined to talk about it. In the process, Neil distances himself not only from the "weird" kids, but from the GSA group as well, claiming that GSA students merely "dabble" in theater and music. They're not really part of the theater scene, which he claims as his own. As he seeks to claim status in the presence of "popular" students, Neil distinguishes himself not only as different from the "weird" kids, but as better, claiming that he, unlike them, is a "real" theater student. This process is similar to the way Deborah distanced herself from the posse, by claiming to be like them (pretty), but different *and* better (a whole person who doesn't gossip).

CONTESTING AND NAVIGATING SOCIAL BOUNDARIES

The signs that mysteriously appeared in the chapel, marking and naming the seating arrangements, had been posted by the students on the Equity Committee—a group established at Weston (and other schools) to address issues of fairness across social categories such as race, class, and gender. The signs were meant to generate interest in a schoolwide forum they were organizing to discuss what they termed "the invisible lines that divide." To promote the forum, they had decided to make public the implicit seating arrangements in the chapel by putting up the signs.

A week later, at the forum, some fifty students sit on chairs arranged in concentric circles. Pizza had been brought in for the meeting, and as the room fills, Keisha, a junior from a large urban center who identifies as Caribbean American and who is the co-chair of the Equity Committee, opens the discussion. She recalls the signs that went up in the chapel and caused so much discomfort among some students. She explains that the purpose of the signs was to make lines of separation visible, and that this forum has been set up so that students can air their opinions on whether and when group separations are a good or a bad thing, as well as why the lines of separation seem invisible.

The conversation begins predictably, with brief arguments over the notion that it's "natural to hang out with people who are similar to you— who have similar interests and like similar things to do," as one student explains. Students consider the question of whether it's okay and good to spend time with the people they like and with whom they have things in common. Keisha, who is skeptical, interrupts after a few comments and challenges the group: "Is it true that what is natural is always the best?" She adds: "What is natural is not always good." Another student picks up on her challenge, agreeing that sometimes groups are not so good and wondering, "Do groups trap people within groups, as well as people outside of groups?"

One student suggests that often differences between people within a given group are greater than their commonalities, and that some individuals "can also belong to more than one group." One girl argues that some groups are actually made by academic policies, "not in a necessarily thinking way, in a way that they [the school] are conscious of—but the school itself creates those groups." She describes policies, such as theater activities occurring during sports team practices, and pre-term orientations for certain groups of students that promote the formation of cliques. Other students echo her perceptive observation. Another student explains that during sports pre-season, students "were being put into a group before they all got there." The fact that the school sponsors events for certain students—such as athletes and students of color—even before the school year begins is one of the things that the students feel promote separate groups.

It's "not necessarily just people, but the way things work here," remarks another student, commenting on the ways in which the schedule and other academic policies encourage separation between students with different interests. She says that the "choices you make, to be sports or drama, . . . [become] part of your person, create where you end up, and who you hang out with." Her words point to the complex dynamic between the structures imposed by the school, such as schedules and curricular distinctions, and students' inclinations and choices about their preferences.

Students often told me that they had to make difficult choices about which interests to pursue in different domains. I learned that when students made choices about their involvement in the domains of work, these were usually bound up with how they identified themselves socially and what kind of Westonian they wanted to be. For instance, Greta

Dunst, whom most students identified as an actress, said that her discomfort with the social dynamics and gender expectations of the athletic space had turned her away from her commitment to soccer. Ken Ellerly, on the other hand, who was convinced that being "heavy on the clarinet" was part of why he was admitted to Weston, talked about not wanting to be identified as a musician, and choosing instead to play lacrosse as a way to enhance his social status. The distinctions between sports and the arts that shape the status system in the work sphere overlap with how the social sphere is expressed and experienced, by determining directly and indirectly the companions that students choose in their nonacademic time. This is reinforced by the very programmatic structures that the school has put in place, which have a significant role in how nonacademic time is organized and experienced.

As I look around the meeting room, I notice that the group includes very few seniors, no PGs, and none of the seniors whom I've learned to associate with the posse. Marie, a junior who has been at Weston for three years, is sitting by herself about six rows from the center of the circle. She is wearing a slightly transparent white tube dress that contrasts little with her fair skin, and that accentuates her curvaceous body. Her light-blond hair is pulled back into a loose ponytail, and her blue eyes are attentive to the conversation. She sits straight on the maroon chair, legs and arms crossed, listening closely, until she decides to jump in, saying that the question of boundaries comes down to more than whom you hang out with. The heart of the question, she suggests, is: Who do you sit with, and "where do you feel more comfortable sitting?" Although she "makes new friends every term," she is "reluctant to sit at a different table." She offers a concrete example: "I would never feel comfortable sitting in the back corner of the far-left room in Wyndham, even if there were no one sitting there."

I listen to her intently, and it becomes clear that she is part of the "sweet posse" of her class. The far-left corner, the "weird people" table, is off-limits for a girl in the sweet posse, even if there is no one sitting there. That particular space is marked and distinguished; according to Marie, it's "not comfortable for anyone" who is not identified with that space. It "starts when you first get to Weston. . . . the kinds of people I met, sports teams. . . . It was the kind of people . . . from the same background, same kinds of [private] school that I felt comfortable with. . . . The right kind of people."

Adam, who has not even finished his first year at Weston as a freshman, pushes back at Marie's comments. He offers the observation that, indeed, the popular girls in his class, whom people already refer to as the "fresh posse," always sit in the same place—in the front row of the freshman area on the second level of the chapel. He describes staging a sit-in with several of his male first-year friends, to disrupt the normal flow of students sitting in the chapel. The group decided to sit down where the fresh posse typically sat. He describes the sense of discomfort that followed their disruption, the angry "looks" that the girls gave them. "We didn't do it again, because we saw all the tension," he explains. As I listen to Adam, I wonder what drove him to take the initiative to break such an obvious taboo.

During focus groups as well as informal conversations, other students confirmed the fact that the girls in the fresh posse always sat in the same place in the chapel. Two of the students who identified with the posse also confirmed this. In interviews, they described being told where to sit by older students, and being somewhat perplexed, yet also delighted, by the sudden label. "We sat in the front row of the freshman section," says Linda Merrow, "partly because, I don't know, we just felt like it, and partly because someone told us that that's where the fresh posse sat. So that's where we sat." I imagined that the girls in Adam's story—who perhaps were told that in order to be who they thought they were, and to preserve their status, they *had to* sit in those front-row seats—found themselves at a loss not just for seats, but, like the seniors at the beginning of this chapter, for a sense of identification.

Marie responds defensively to Adam's story, defending her status as a member of her class's posse: "Most of the people who are posse haters don't know half of the people on posse. They don't make the attempt to get to know the people—they go on with the stereotype." She learned during her freshman year that "all the kids hated me," and felt that she was hated because she was white and came from a private school and from an elite background. She felt that because she admittedly did not know any public school students or students of color before coming to Weston, she was isolated. She talks about meeting another student from another private school who likewise had never met any students of color or public school students, and noting that the other student also felt "hated" for being attractive and social. She talks about establishing relationships with students who "hated" her in the first year, and how now suddenly they find her to be a nice person. Marie's claim is ironic, given that most of the students that come to Weston share her class background. The idea that her class background is the source of the "hate" ignores the fact of her class privilege and the status it carries. At the same time, it illustrates the ambivalence that becoming aware of such privileges (by meeting students from other backgrounds) awakens in students like Marie. This "class guilt" may be related to the guilt that whites experience as they become aware of their complicity in the oppression of people of color.[22]

Throughout the forum, almost like a mantra, two ideas are repeated in response to the observation that students at Weston do divide into various social groups. Some students defend the tendency to group, saying things like, "This happens everywhere, in every high school." Other students retort, "What binds us together is that we are all Westonian. . . . There shouldn't be any reason for us to separate. We are all Westonians." And still others ask, "Why should Weston be any different from any other high school?" The tension between asserting a distinct identification as Westonian and justifying behavior as something that "everyone does" is at the heart of the logic of the various social arrangements. Being a Westonian means being "like other students"—that is, able to recognize social arrangements that are mapped on the school landscape. It also means challenging these arrangements and claiming a collective identification as Westonians, who are not supposed to be concerned with such distinctions. In this way, being a Westonian implies, one the one hand, finding a place in the social space, and, on the other, challenging that social arrangement as non-Westonian.

(Mis)recognizing Social Boundaries

When confronted with evidence of a community in which social distinctions matter a great deal and where space is organized in ways that reflect social boundaries, some students counter by asking, "Why should Weston be any different from any other high school?" Students assert a common identification as adolescents; they are like all other adolescents in all other schools. This is particularly true for students who identify with the "popular" crowd, or the posse.

"I think the way people choose friends here is no different than any other school, or any other big group of adolescents if they are in the same place," says Frances Sackler, who is often identified by her classmates as being part of the fresh posse. Frances is notorious around campus for wearing expensive clothes. I often see her elegantly dressed in Burberry or, more comfortably, in Lilly Pulitzer, always with a brand-name hand-bag, and minimally but carefully accessorized. Her long, straight, golden hair is always carefully brushed and her Tiffany bracelets and pearl ear-rings are always subtle but clearly noticeable. I ask Frances to describe what she means, and she says: "You are definitely gonna surround your-self with people who you are near, so your dorm friends—with people who you are, you share interests with, your teammates, your classmates. So, I mean, I think it's—friendships are formed the same ways."

By explaining clique formation as something all adolescents do, Frances ignores the important role that wealth, social networks, and cultural consumption play in the formation of student status groups, particularly the "popular" crowd with which she identifies.[23] Ironically, students who identify with the opposite side of the campus likewise fail to recognize their own class privilege; they describe themselves in opposition to the posse, which they define as being wealthy. The students on the hills side, however, are not less wealthy. After all, close to two-thirds of the stu-dents at Weston come from families that can afford the full cost of atten-dance at an elite boarding school. The students from families that cannot are distributed throughout the campus and participate in both sides of the social space. The brand names and dress styles of the students in Wyndham might be more varied, but they are no less expensive than the fashions in Alumni Hall. While the scene in the green areas of the hills lacks the skin and muscle of the valley, the threads are no less posh. Even the fashion styles of the "weird" crowd require deep pockets, as Astrid reminds me during our interview, when she mentions her desire and in-ability to keep up with her friends' wardrobes. During my second year at Weston, rumors of a high-stakes poker circuit hosted by a notoriously wealthy resident of the hills were flying about, like frisbees on a warm spring day.

Students on both sides of the social landscape seek to reject or at least downplay their economic status. The "popular" kids avoid acknowledg-ing their class status by claiming that they are building friendships just like all other adolescents (instead of like wealthy adolescents). The "weird" kids avoid acknowledging their class status by claiming that it's the posse, and not they themselves, who are wealthy, and that unlike them, the posse is concerned with fashion and conspicuous consumption (even as fashion is a crucial marker of their own particular identifica-tions).

The social space of the Weston School is organized in ways that closely

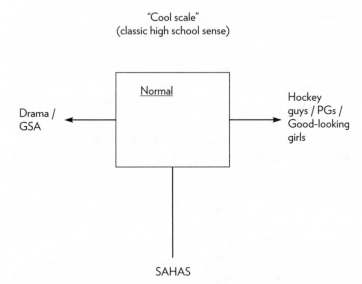

FIGURE 7   Note that the SAHAS students are placed outside the "scale" at the bot-
                tom of the diagram. This is a graphic representation of how students of
                color are positioned in the social space (see Chapter 6).

parallel the dynamics of status groups at all other schools in the United
States. The diagram in Figure 7, which was drawn by a student during
a focus group, illustrates the opposition between the two sides of the social space using what he labels the "cool scale" in a "classic high school
sense."

The social space of the valley is associated with dominant and static
gender ideals, athletic prowess, traditional definitions of beauty, and definitions of "popularity" commonly associated with nonelite school contexts. Like similar social groups in other school contexts, the students in
the valley are also identified with upper-class spending habits, as well as
an interest in future economic wealth.[24] The social space on the hills side
is associated with more fluid and thus marginal sexual and gender identifications, intellectualism, artistic interests like theater, and fringe activities like punk and "alternative" cultural repertoires. Again, these reflect
social groups in other school contexts.[25] This is important because it
challenges the assumption that a singular status logic and specific gender
ideals dominate any given elite space, particularly the upper class.[26] It
also signals the importance of understanding status systems in relation
to one another, particularly within specific economically defined spaces,

such as an elite boarding school, where different forms of "wealth," whether material or symbolic, depend on each other.[27] These patterns might confirm the idea that these status groups are concerned more with developing class-specific consumer habits than with identification.[28]

On the surface, the social space of the Weston School reflects Murray Milner's model of the "pluralistic high school," where "status inequality is relatively muted" and where tolerance for a diversity of lifestyles prevails.[29] Like Milner's Woodrow Wilson High School, the Weston School is large enough for "alternative lifestyles" to emerge and wealthy enough to support a range of areas in which students can excel—a context that promotes multiple status systems.[30] Yet at this elite boarding school, there are at least two crucial ways in which these dynamics differ.

First, being smart confers high status. The most widely recognized students at Weston are those who are perceived as the most academically talented. These students are the ones who can move most easily between the two sides of the campus—a flexibility that is related to the second critical difference between the social spaces at an elite boarding school and other school contexts.[31]

The second difference is the paradoxical claim that all students, popular and not, make about their own relation to status groups. On the one hand, students argue that such cliques are not as important at Weston as in public schools, while on the other hand they underscore the importance of such groups for their own experience—often in the same breath.[32] Students seem to resolve this paradox by shifting from a strong identification with groups on one side or the other of the school, to claiming the ability to move between groups with ease. This shift occurs particularly when students realize that the presence of social hierarchies and status groups contradicts the official school discourse regarding tolerance and inclusion—qualities that are central to how Westonians work to distinguish themselves as different from and better than other students, particularly those in public schools.

The students who are perceived as the smartest and most academically talented are also the most "recognized" and have the most flexibility in moving from one space to another.[33] Yet achieving such mobility across status groups is not solely a matter of being smart. Indeed, only a particular *kind* of smart student can move across social spaces with ease; these students are often described as the "ideal" Westonians. Rather than claiming strong identification with one group or another, a claim they readily ascribe to others, most students present themselves as being able to navigate various social spaces with ease. While this is a quality that most students try to claim, in the end, only certain students actually have the ability to traverse the range of social spaces at the school. These students must not only be able to act a certain way socially, but they must also have the right clothes and be able to talk the right way about the right things, in order to "perform" the requirements necessary to assume a place at the top of the hierarchy as "ideal" Westonians.

Moving across Boundaries: The "Vanilla Group" and the "Perfect" Westonian

Patricia Sanders claims to know something about every single member of the senior class. She is probably right. As a member of the production team of the *Westonian Notebook,* the senior-class yearbook, she has had to interact at least briefly with every single one of the students in her class. She is proud of this accomplishment, and she feels that it has given her the chance to get to know her class well. She describes her peers as "a really smart class—we really work hard." She notes her sense that her class is "better than, I think, other classes have been in the past, [where] there were definite cool people and definite uncool people." She acknowledges that this is true for her class, too, but she feels "the line is a little more blurry, and it's easier to, like, enter the mix." For Patricia, being different from *and* better than other classes means to be less like "regular high school," where "all the pretty blond cheerleader girls" are in the cool and popular group.

Patricia claims that there is no such group in her senior class, but then begins to describe her own relationship with the group she just claimed does not exist. "Like, I'm friends with some of those people who are in it, and they're not mean to me. Nor are they, like—they don't do the kinds of tricks that you expect to see." Patricia distinguishes her experience from that of her sister, who attends a "regular high school" where "there's a definite group of people who go out and party every weekend and do things together, and are really exclusive and really mean to other people. And I guess I just feel like that's not as prominent on this campus as it is on hers."

Although Patricia lives on the valley side, her boyfriend lives on the hills, and thus she claims to move between the two dining halls with ease. Yet her use of the adjectives "that" and "this" suggests that she is closer to one rather than the other: "There's a dining hall on the valley, a dining hall on the hills, so valley-ers eat in *that* dining hall and hill-ers eat in *this* dining hall. But it's pretty easy to cross over. . . . My boyfriend lives in East Street [Dorm], so we, I eat in Wyndham all the time—sometimes— and I feel accepted. I don't—I've never felt, like, 'Oh, you're a valley girl.' Like, you know, 'Go away!'" Patricia's status claims revolve around her ability to move between various social spaces with ease, and to have relationships across status groups. Other students acknowledge Patricia's social versatility and note her "friendliness." During a focus group, students label Patricia and her immediate circle of friends the "vanilla group," noting that although they sit in the dining hall near the posse, they are not part of it.

> *Deb:* They [the vanilla group] don't really overlap with posse, but they are connected to every group in some sort of way, 'cause there are drama kids in it. . . .
>
> *Will:* I like to call them the vanilla group, because they are so like, blah. Just fun and plain white-bread, vanilla kind of kids.
>
> *Deb:* Okay, so we'll call them the vanilla kids.

Will's explanation of the term "vanilla" is revealing, because it suggests that not only is this group "plain"—a necessary characteristic, perhaps, if its members are able to move between various groups—but it is also "white-bread," a term often used to racially mark a group of people as white. "Vanilla" suggests a flexible blandness that can go well with all other flavors. Later in the conversation, when I ask students to place themselves within different social groups, all of them place themselves in some way near this vanilla group. Jack Mitchell, who claims to be closer to the theater and GSA spaces, invokes a relationship to the vanilla group through a friend in his dorm. Will Mueller describes his social flexibility in terms of social networks: "I think I've done it [socialized with many groups] a lot of [this] year. Like, I talk to all the theater kids—I've done stuff in the theater. . . . I know Cam Neely [captain of the hockey team], like, Cam Neely and all his friends, and I like to hang out with vanilla kids. . . . I just try to talk to everyone that I can." Deb is more specific in her identification with this group, including herself in the "we" and claiming that she knows "all of the four-year seniors. I think it is something about the vanilla group—we all know everyone on campus. . . . I think a lot of us, because we do so much—like, I know I am really in-

volved on campus. . . . So, like, that's why I know so many people. . . .
The vanilla group is always really involved on campus." At the end of the
focus group, she turns to Will and compliments him for coming up with
a term that resonates with her. "I love the 'vanilla group' name. Will,
you're a genius!"

If the vanilla group is recognized across the social space because,
as Deb says, they are "really involved on campus," there are also a few
students who hardly need to be involved to be recognized. John Virgil,
who's one of the people often referred to as epitomizing the high end of
the smart hierarchy, is not, like Deb or Patricia, particularly "involved"
around campus. Yet every student and faculty person I met knew his
name and admired his virtues. Besides being an advanced student of classical languages, John is also an accomplished athlete on the varsity tennis
team. Students often use John as an example of the ideal Westonian. In
fact, they often tell exaggerated stories about his academic accomplishments. For instance, many believe that he has the highest academic average. John laughs with me as he jokes about people's impressions of him
and about his reputation.

> It's absurd, really—makes me sick. Because I walk into a class,
> and instead of having a C, uh, you know, and having to prove
> myself, it's, like, . . . no one will speak, you know? After I've
> spoken in class, no one will challenge me, uh, because they're
> afraid that I'm always right. And I say things that are pur-
> posefully wrong, and no one will debate me. And it's infuri-
> ating! Because no one has the guts, basically, because I have
> this, sort of, reputation. I, I know that I'm not that smart, but,
> um, apparently no one else does. I mean, even my teachers
> are, like, you know, "Oh, I have Virgil in class." I'm like, I
> mean, so what! You know, that shouldn't mean anything. But
> it's become—it's just become idiotic.

John notes that there are "so many people who are so much smarter than
I am at this school, who don't get that recognition." He offers examples
of students who he believes are smarter than he is, at least on the basis of
their grades, but whose names are not readily recognized by other students. Instead, he says, it's because he is "sort of a socially visible person"
that his reputation as the smartest "becomes a real profile" for him. John
notes his ability to move between various groups, and particularly his
association with the students in the posse. As a resident of East Street

Dorm (referred to by some students as the dorm "with the highest GPA"), John eats many of his meals in Wyndham with his fellow dormmates at a table adjacent to the corner table associated with the "weird" kids (though he says he wouldn't eat at that table). Yet he also often eats in Alumni Hall and sits with his teammates from the tennis team, many of whom are quite popular members of the posse.

John explains his ability to be with the posse by attributing it to his reputation for being smart and his academic status, saying he has "value as a smart person."

> Uh, the Alumni Hall thing, you know, sitting on that side of the sandwich table—like, most of my friends are in that group, which is, you know, a bad thing. But it's also—it's just because, um, people have accepted me because I have value as a smart person. And I know that it's, it's just like, an absurd value judgment that is the initial, like, condition for acceptance. . . . You have to be . . . really socially adept to be in that group and not have value, you know, in sports, in school. . . . All these kids wanna be friends with the best people. And so, obviously if you're outwardly weird—like, you know, the smartest people at the school aren't in that group, in general.

John's characterization of his relationship with the popular kids as a "bad thing" again suggests the ambivalence students feel about recognizing the importance of such groups in the social space. He is particularly aware of the social-class status dimensions of such dynamics, and the importance of being "socially adept" to negotiate that space. While he seems to be less articulate about what such adeptness might imply (upper-class social and cultural practices), he has a keen analysis of the role that status recognition plays in the formation of such groups. First, he notes that these popular social groups "want to be friends with the best people" in every area. In other words, to legitimize their high status at a school where being smart is a crucial status marker, being friends with the "smartest kid" is a crucial link in the hierarchy.[34] Yet not just anyone, even if the person is very smart, can fulfill that role and have the kind of access to that space John has. As he puts it, you have to be "socially adept" and you can't be "outwardly weird."

Students like John, a white upper-class male who identifies as WASPy, have a wider range of positions (or niches) available to them in the social space, and thus gain mobility across groups because they are perceived as remarkably smart, athletic, and sociable. Yet, more implicitly, they must also be perceived as "normal" or not "weird"; they must also be "plain" or "vanilla" enough to fit the social, racial, and ethnic hierarchies of the social space. In other words, to be identified as a wealthy white male who is very smart and athletic (as John is) is to have the opportunity to achieve the greatest social mobility and thus the highest social status. This has major implications for the lack of mobility of other students, especially females and students of color, for whom the discursive space at this elite boarding school is, by definition, constrained, permitting them only a narrow range of opportunities for identifying as Westonians, as we will see in Chapter 6.

The status system at an elite boarding school like Weston differs in important ways from the status systems that have been documented by scholars who study the culture of schools. To illustrate this difference, Figure 8 replicates Figure 1, but replaces the work domains with the status labels associated with each domain. At the top of the Westonian hierarchy are the "smart" students. Yet to be recognized as occupying this niche, it is not enough simply to be perceived as smart. The "perfect" Westonians are also athletic and participate in artistic activities, but do not draw their status from these pursuits. More important, as John Virgil explains, to be seen as a "perfect" Westonian requires being socially adept and able to negotiate the social landscape with ease—to know exactly where to sit, regardless of which dining hall one enters.

The "popular" group in the lower-left corner of the diagram represents mainstream ideas about what it means to be beautiful and sexy, and is associated with athleticism and economic capital. The "weird" group at the other end represents an alternative status system associated with creative activity and nonmainstream symbolic activity. It would be wrong to conclude simply that one side has more status than the other (except in their own eyes, perhaps). The students who inhabit each niche claim status within their particular social spaces in their own terms. Instead, the closer students are to the ideal of a "perfect" Westonian, the less they rely on either end of the social spectrum at the bottom of the hierarchy to make status claims. Alternatively, the farther students are from being able to claim "ideal" Westonian as an identification (PGs, "weird" kids), the more closely they identify with either one end or the other at the bottom of the status triangle. Since either extreme of this social spectrum is at the bottom of the status hierarchy, students work hard to distance themselves—at least symbolically—from both the athletic PGs and the "weird" kids.

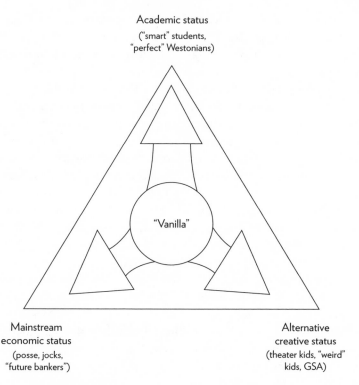

Academic status
("smart" students,
"perfect" Westonians)

"Vanilla"

Mainstream
economic status
(posse, jocks,
"future bankers")

Alternative
creative status
(theater kids, "weird"
kids, GSA)

FIGURE 8   The social hierarchies.

Few students can occupy the niche at the top of the hierarchy, and no student wants to occupy the extremes at the bottom. Instead, students claim the ability to move between social spaces, even when such mobility is rare. The vanilla group, at the center, represents a sort of "omnivorous" mobility across social spaces.[35] Acquiring the ability to negotiate this social space successfully results in the development of a social habitus that prepares students for their future lives of distinction.[36] All of these groups are, of course, ultimately elite groups, and the connections between them are critical if they are to recognize each as such. These "cultural omnivores," who can move from one space to another with ease and recognition, ensure that all Westonians are connected, reinforcing their elite status. In the status field of this elite boarding school, future bankers befriend Latin scholars, who eat with theater students; in all their differences, they share a singular elite distinction—Westonian.

In order to claim that they're "better" than other adolescents, Westonians often try to argue that at their school, social distinctions are trumped by their collective identification as Westonians and their collective experiences in the classroom. Indeed, even Astrid claims an identification as a Westonian. When I ask Astrid what it means to be a Westonian, she says that the question is hard to answer because there are so many different kinds of Westonians. I ask what kind of Westonian she is, and she pauses to reflect. "Mmmm, I don't know. I'm just me. [*laughs*] I'm, like, a [renegade] Westonian. I'm that loud girl, sort of—no, I'm, like, 'that quiet Westonian that nobody really knew until they started screaming on the stage in a rock band' sort of Westonian."

As our conversation progresses, Astrid focuses almost exclusively on her experiences in her dorm and the kinds of intimate bonds she has developed with certain friends and dormmates. Indeed, whether weird or good-looking, artistic or athletic, all students describe a sense of bonding, and all engage in rituals of intimacy that ultimately bring them together as Westonians. Knowing the difference between three-year and four-year seniors, and knowing where each belongs, is part of what endows them with a shared experience. To be a Westonian is to know how the space is divided, who belongs where, and how to make Weston a home. Even if students roll like rolling stones, they always find a niche in the social landscape of the Weston School. In the next chapter, we'll look at the rituals that "thicken" the Westonian identification, as students bond with one another to secure their status among the elite and their own future lives of distinction.

5

BONDING RITUALS

The four-year seniors are gathered in the reading room of the Student Center, a dark, warm, comfortable room that offers a quiet place to read newspapers and magazines. Some students are lying on the oriental carpets, leaning their heads on each other's torsos and shoulders, talking softly; others slouch on the gray sofas, cracking jokes and laughing loudly; a few sit on the tables, leaning against the walls, half asleep, with their feet propped on chairs or a friend's lap. Their voices form a relaxed blanket of sound, sometimes rippled by laughter, stretched by yawns, or lifted by jovial cries and friendly teasing. Trying to be unobtrusive, I pull a chair from a reading desk, sit next to a sofa in the back of the room, and pull out my fieldnotes. It's the end of the year, and by now the students seem to take my presence for granted, or at least they are no longer curious about what it is I'm writing or why I am there.

The headmaster, who has been standing in the center of the room with one of the school librarians, takes a few steps and turns her head. As if on cue, the students settle down, and the noise fades. I wonder if it's exhaustion or eagerness that causes their silence. Or perhaps, after four years, the very presence of the headmaster in the middle of the room commands their attention. Even the headmaster seems startled by the sudden silence, and she asks jokingly: "Is there something I don't know? Is it time to start? You're so quiet all of a sudden!" She looks at her watch. "I guess it's time to start."

Reading from prepared notes, the headmaster begins by commenting on how much the world has changed since these students arrived at Weston almost four years ago—back when "9-11" was no more than two consecutive odd numbers. The headmaster shares stories with the students about her boarding school education and about the many memories she "boxed" in her scrapbooks. These "boxed treasures" often revealed to her the hidden meanings of her fears and hopes. Today, the four-year seniors will be opening the boxes they filled at the end of their first semester at Weston—boxes containing letters they wrote to themselves, items they felt represented their experiences during their term, and their predictions for the years ahead. No one else is invited to the event (except for nosy ethnographers); only those who have endured life at Weston for four years can participate in the ritual, which underscores their position in the Westonian hierarchy. The headmaster concludes her remarks by noting that the memories they share form the basis of their future lives together as Westonians.

After reading a Latin text and invoking the tone of a medieval announcer, the librarian hyperbolically proclaims that these four-year seniors are the "*original* members of the Class of 2004" and that they have "demonstrated an honorable degree of school and class spirit." Two class representatives are summoned to the front to sign the proclamation and to call out the names, so that students may approach the front and receive the shoeboxes filled with the items they chose to capture their experience as first-year Westonians. As their names are called, the students come forward to open their boxes and rediscover the treasures they hid four years earlier. The excitement in the room quickly rises, and the chatter inevitably starts drowning out the names being announced. "Franklin, speak up!!" one student yells, while others try to hush the din of voices.

Once all the boxes are distributed, the noise subsides. As the students open their boxes, their memories of their lives together fill them with nostalgia. Some students embrace each other, sharing recovered items and sudden tears. I can see them reading letters, comparing photos, pulling out CDs of their first-year rock bands, old pages from the school newspaper, magazine clippings, and small hearts inscribed with names. The memories provoke laughter, yelps of surprise, gentle sobs. A few students, embarrassed by (or protective of) their younger selves, try to keep their old words secret. But even those who open their shoeboxes in private share in this moment of collective identification, when their experiences are enshrined in a group return to the beginning, a journey emphasizing that they, unlike other members of their class, are four-year seniors. At that moment, their previous four years may seem like an entire lifetime.

This moment of intimacy demonstrates what students already know: they share a particular intimacy, a collective memory that is integral to their identification as four-year seniors, a sense of closure that exists only in the memories they have gathered together and that are bound by the memory boxes. When they open the boxes, their four years at Weston are concretized as part of their identification with the school. Opening them becomes proof that they were here then and have endured; they belong together; they are here now, bonding. Even though some students sit apart, examining their boxes in private, their memories bind them to the group.

The event comes to an end and the students leave. One student arrives late, looking for his shoebox. He asks around, hunting through the boxes left on the table (perhaps they belong to students who didn't make it through the four years), but to no avail. He grabs a couple of boxes and turns to me: "Someone stole mine, so I am stealing other people's." And he walks away. A few students linger, eating the food that was set out in the back of the room. Soft drinks, cookies, and mini-churros are devoured before everyone leaves. In two days, all these students will officially become alumni of the Weston School.

Radhika Chaudari is not a four-year senior. She describes her skepticism when she read in the admissions catalogue that the friends she would make at Weston would last a lifetime. She remembers thinking: "Yeah, sure. It's just like any other school kind of thing." But after two years at Weston, she claims to know better: "Now that I've been here, and gone through it, I really think it's true. Just because you spend, like, so much time with these people, . . . you basically have that bond that will last for, like, a lifetime." Victor Martínez talks about students who may have "graduated three years ago, two years ago, whatever. And then I see 'em, somewhere random, um, during break or vacation, and I'm able to have a conversation with that person just because I knew they went to Weston." Steve Hart echoes this feeling of connection with other Westonians: "It definitely gives me true common ground with other people that went to Weston. Do you know what I mean? When I meet someone who's about my age, who went to Weston, we automatically have something to talk about. Do you know what I mean? And we have a common vocabulary." Every time he asks whether I know what he means, it feels like a subtle reminder that I am not a Westonian, and that regardless of how many times I ask the question, I will never fully understand how students experience this bond, even as I may have some ideas about what it means. It's clear that an important part of how students define what it means to be Westonians revolves around shared experience and the belief that simply going through experiences together leads to a sense of bonding.

Sandi Li explains it this way:

> The short part of it is that I think when you graduate, and you bump into anyone, like, any other Westonians on the street ever, [even] if you didn't get along with them, I think it'd just still be like a, "Hi, what's going on in your life?" sort of situation. . . . You have this common bond. Because, like, no one else who hasn't been to Weston, like, has really, like, experienced what it's like. . . . You can't really experience Weston, and experience, like, what it's been like to be here. Um, except for, like, people who graduate. So I think—I guess that's sort of what [being a Westonian] means.

These bonds that will last a lifetime are what give Westonians the clearest sense that they are different from others. This bonding is what makes all the experiences described in the previous chapters meaningful, and relevant to the process by which students identify as Westonians.

Of course, this sense of bonding through shared experience is not unique to Weston or to elite boarding schools. Constructing an identification with any group is usually the result of shared experience.[1] But seen in relation to the ways in which students come to understand themselves as being *distinguished* from other adolescents, the experience of bonding gains a unique relevance. As in all other total institutions, the hard boundaries between "inmates" and "outsiders" strengthen the sense of belonging to an exclusive group. How students experience and understand the process of bonding with other Westonians has particular characteristics and, in the end, particular consequences regarding access and entitlements to other elite settings and future elite identifications. Bonding is a crucial aspect of both engagement and excellence in the process of becoming elite, because it generates implicit boundaries around entitlement and gives students a sense of certainty about their future. The fact that students have been through this common experience, which entails the feeling of having achieved a "niche" in the meritocracy (as we saw in Chapter 3) and of having found a place on the Westonian social map (discussed in Chapter 4), ultimately connects all Westonians and gives them a sense of shared identification. This identification gives Westonians what Max Weber calls "closure" as an elite status group, making them confident that they deserve a place in the meritocracy and their access to resources.[2]

SILENTLY SHARED BONDS

Alex Crosby is a four-year senior whose parents are highly successful New York lawyers. Her dad attended an elite law school; her mom is an alumna of another elite boarding school. Alex was persuaded to enroll at Weston by the magnificent library and by the encouragement of a family friend at another boarding school who, impressed by Alex's high grades, suggested that a school focusing more on academics would be a better choice. Toward the end of our second formal interview, I ask Alex: "Would you call yourself a Westonian?"

"Yes," Alex says firmly. And I query further: "What does that mean, being a Westonian?" Alex begins, "I use it because I feel like it's—" She breaks off, and instead tells the following story:

> Over break, I went out to dinner with my dad and a few of his friends, and another girl that's a year younger than me. And I swear, everybody—like, my father knew everybody in this restaurant. . . . He's saying, "Hi, hi," and I'm sitting over somewhere, and he kind of waved me over, and he goes, um, "Hi," you know, "this is Alex. Alex, this is So-and-So." And the guy goes, "I just want you to know, you go to the best school in the country. And I'm not just saying that because I'm a graduate of the school, but I'm saying that because, blah-blah-blah-blah-blah. And, um, you know, I laughed.

Situated in a context of privilege and elite status, Alex's narrative begins by taking for granted that Weston's excellence is not just a subjective claim, but an objective claim based on "blah-blah-blah-blah-blah." Why, precisely, the alum thought Weston was "the best school in the country" does not need to be explained. It is less important in the narrative than the fact that he was also a graduate. A shared set of experiences provides a deeper sense of identification than Weston's assumed excellence. As the narrative continues, another acquaintance, who is not a Westonian, is described as talking about another alum and assuming that all Westonians are the same:

> And my dad's friend, he goes, "Oh yeah, this guy, he was a member of Jack's class," who I know, and he goes, "No, no,

no, no, no, Jack's a member of my class. I'm a four-year senior, he was a three-year." And it's, like, it was funny because
there's some—I knew what he meant. He's thirty years, forty
years older than me, and I knew exactly what he meant. And
that's why I would call myself a Westonian: because I under-
sta—because there's a bond that we all sh—kind of share silently.

Once again, the presumed excellence of Weston is, at least here, irrele-
vant to why Alex would use the label "Westonian." It's the fact that Alex
knew what this alum, thirty or forty years older, meant by the hierarchical distinction between students who spent all four years at the school
and those who only spent three. To be Westonian, in other words, is not
just to be the best, but to know such distinctions, which, as Alex articulates later in the narrative, are meaningful only to other Westonians. Alex
understands what it means to be a Westonian, "because there is a bond
that we all kind of share silently." The description of the bond as "silent"
may simply suggest its implicit character. Yet it may also indicate that the
social-class privileges that such an elite identification assumes are also
meant to be *silent*—and thus misperceived by outsiders—as part of the
core of what it means to be a Westonian.

As Alex continues her story, she notes that "some people" share the
Westonian bond "more so than others." Still, "even if you hated Weston,
. . . whether it was good or bad," all students can articulate a sense of
being Westonians and of knowing "what it was like to be here," which
silently sets them apart from those who were not. "Friends at home
wouldn't make the distinction. They wouldn't know, um, what it's like to,
you know, at midnight, be woken up, um, by the midnight run that happens sometimes—You know what, um, it's like to live in the middle of
nowhere in New England for four years, or whatever amount of years,
and, um, just the little kooky things that we have here. I mean, a skippy?
A skippy!"

Alex stresses the distinction between "friends at home" and fellow
Westonians by referring to rituals only a Westonian would know about.
Even someone who might grasp the difference between a four-year and
a three-year senior would know nothing about the "midnight run" and
other "little kooky things that we have here"—like a "skippy," the notice
that students receive from the administration when they are reported as
having missed a class. After mentioning the "skippies," Alex takes a de-

tour from the story and claims to have "never skipped a class before," noting that this somehow sets Westonians further apart from their public school peers at home. "It's an entirely different thing," Alex continues. "I go to school and I don't like snow because we don't get snow days, and I don't like getting sick because you miss a day, you're behind, you know?"

Here Alex's narrative takes a significant turn: from establishing a distinction between Westonians and those public school peers who will perhaps welcome any chance of skipping school, to establishing a connection between Westonians and "all boarding school students." "I think there's also something that all boarding school students probably can talk about, too. And we can make it more specific—but, you know, like, everything, but, like, I think, you know, the pressure to feel like we have to be the leaders of the world. Um, that's why I say that I'm a Westonian, and I'm proud to be a Westonian." Alex is describing the experience of being constantly told by assembly guest speakers that Weston students are bound to be the "leaders of the world." This is another ritual in which the Westonian identification is persistently "thickened": the repeated occasions on which students are reminded of their distinction as "the best and the brightest."[3]

Alex highlights the importance of intimacy and the role that the experience of bonding plays in making students feel that they "belong" to Weston—or rather, that the experience *belongs to them.* "It's *my* experience," Alex continues (echoing how Emily Lau talked about "owning" her work because she'd invested a lot of time and effort in it). "And it has been my home for the past four years, as much as you try to deny it. You said, freshman year, we would never call this place 'home,' and now I'll be home and like: 'Oh yeah, I go home on Monday.' My mom's like, 'You *are* home!' You know? But in my mind, it's already been changed." Why Alex thought she would never call Weston "home" in her first year might be related to the fact that she also identifies as an African American. Her story of discovering Weston, in fact, is framed by the story of her mother, who in the 1970s became one of the first black girls from the Bronx to attend an elite boarding school. The stark difference between Alex's sense of her mother's experience and her perception of her own, as an upper-middle-class young black woman who now calls her elite boarding school home, is telling. Whereas Alex says her mother rarely talked about her experiences and was apprehensive about letting her attend Weston, Alex has "already been changed." Her sense of bonding with other Westonians can be seen as continuing a process begun a generation before.[4] In the next chapter, we will look at the limits that race, class, and gender place on the experience of bonding, and why Alex suggests that "some people" identify as Westonians "more so than others." For the moment, I want to focus on her answer to my question about whether she uses the label "Westonian": "I would say I'm a Westonian because at a very basic level I know sort of how it's been. You know, I have an understanding of the people thirty years ago, forty years ago. . . . So that's why."

The gist of Alex's narrative is that being Westonian ultimately means knowing "the little kooky things" that define the experience within the borders of the school. Alex lists a number of rituals through which she identifies as Westonian. These rituals range from elaborate public performances to apparently innocuous rituals of intimacy that take place in the "backstage" of the school landscape, particularly in dormitories.[5] Such rituals, as Pierre Bourdieu defines them, "tend to consecrate or legitimate an *arbitrary boundary*" that is both created and guarded through the meanings available only to participants.[6] As such, all rituals, from the public to the intimate, are ways of enacting the discourse of distinction that both represent and enforce the process of constructing elite identifications. Alex's narrative is filled with references to rituals and practices that find their meaning in the discourse of distinction—practices ranging from midnight runs and "skippies" to rituals of introduction that create cross-generational bonds.

The Weston "Family"

Students describe Weston consistently as a "family." This is crucial, as it suggests the close bonding that cements the relationships and the networks students build at an elite boarding school.[7] For instance, although Andrew Zia is not so sure that, on the whole, there is a strong sense of community at Weston, he feels "that once you leave, then you feel, because of this common experience, that you're part of this Weston family, or something." Similarly, when talking about the friendships he has made at Weston, Terrence Wilson says he has learned "about what true friendship is, I guess. You know? Because I've wanted to call some of these people my family." Similarly, Jennifer Chung speaks of sibling-like relationships: "One thing about Weston that I definitely feel is a plus and a minus, depending on the sort of person you are—for me, has been for the most part pluses—even if you aren't friends with everyone, I feel like there are certain, like, brotherhood or, like, sisterhood, just because we're all living together. And, and there's this, like—even if you don't like someone, you still feel this connection to them, just because, I, I feel, like, here, because you are all living together, in this giant, like, family, almost."

For Jennifer, the faculty plays an important role in this feeling of family, "just because of the relationship you can develop with teachers here. That's why—that's what I meant by 'family,' 'cause you live with your teachers too. So they're like your mom and dad, in a way." She later explains:

> Everything's much more intimate here, I guess, 'cause first of all, they [the faculty] physically [live] with you, or live very near you. Secondly, they're very eager to advise you, for the most part. . . . And for the most part, they look out for your best interests, really, like, honestly. And they have fun learning with you, which makes them have a really close relationship with you, while at the same time guiding you, which I think is what a parent should be.[8]

Krista Griffin is a day student, yet she, too, says a boarding school like Weston "is just a different atmosphere. Like, going—eating with your teachers [and] being with the same people all the time." Krista describes how her biology teacher supports her academically by helping her study.

> He's just somebody who—who you can tell genuinely cares and wants you to learn and isn't just catering to the kids who it comes naturally to. And he actually told me that one day, . . . he says, "You know, it, it means a lot more to me, somebody who, you know, comes in every day and tries to learn it, more than somebody who it just comes really easily to, who just memorizes." Um, he actually offered to write my college recs. . . . He's like, "I think I see, you know, a lot in your effort, and a lot more in you than some of the teachers might," and it's like, "I think I'd like to write recs for you." I don't know— he's just a really great guy.

Krista's relationship to her biology teacher is not just academic; she describes talking with the teacher during hockey games and getting to know his son. The fact that most teachers live on campus and that many of them have families plays a paradoxical role in how Westonians think of the school as a family. On the one hand, students like Krista describe their relationships with teachers and their teachers' families in a positive light, highlighting the friendships and the intimacy that family can provide. On the other, teachers and students seem somewhat oblivious to each other's social lives. Students commented on the fact that the faculty had their own dining room tables, often filled with the noise and tumult of young children; and members of the faculty rarely ate at the same table with students.[9] Furthermore, when I initially asked teachers about the table arrangements in the dining halls, they seemed largely unaware of the dynamics happening right in front of them. They often seemed curious and even surprised when I shared the insights I had learned from the students, including comments about the teachers themselves.

Scott Jaffee takes photos of events at the school for the student newspaper. During our interview, he shares many of the photos he has taken, and we spend a lot of time talking about the significance of the photos and what he was trying to communicate about Weston through them. One set of photos shows several teachers playing with their own children in a makeshift playground near one of the dormitories. Scott comments, "You don't think of teachers as real people. They're teachers, you know?" He took the photographs because he wanted to show that teachers are "real people—they have lives, they have families, they laugh, they make fools of themselves, just like everyone else. And that's—I guess if I, if I had to have a thesis statement for these photos, that would be it."

Of course, teachers play a critical role in the learning process at an elite boarding school, and a significant part of this role consists of the relationships that students and teachers form outside the classroom. Teachers also play a range of roles in the many rituals organized around school life—from central organizing roles to peripheral enabling roles. Yet teachers were clearly marginal in the intimate experiences of bonding that students shared. This is not to discount the very deep relationships that some teachers had with specific students—relationships that might be front and center if this book were about the lives of teachers at an elite boarding school. Yet, although a few students spoke at length about their close relationships with specific teachers, this was neither a generalized experience nor—what is more important—an experience that was central to how they understood themselves as Westonians. Most of the teachers are not, after all, Westonians, and while some student-teacher relationships might well last a lifetime, it is the deep bonding between students that will be consequential for their future lives of distinction.[10]

As Alex notes, not all Westonians bond equally, and the experiences of bonding that students describe vary in quality and in the extent to which students feel part of a Weston "family." As Alex suggests, four-year seniors, those who entered Weston as freshmen, are considered the most Westonian, and they participate in institutional rituals that highlight their status, such as the memory box ritual. Jennifer says that in "talking to four-year seniors, senior friends, they definitely have, like, a very, like, brotherly or sisterly behavior towards one another."

The Hierarchy of Bonds

I ask Sabrina Macy, a four-year senior, whether she feels there are hierarchies between various kinds of Westonians. With some hesitation, she admits: "I think that there *is* sort of a hierarchy, but I think it's more . . ." She pauses to reflect. "I think that the most, uh, defined hierarchy is just in terms of seniority," she says, suggesting that the hierarchy of the grades —seniors, juniors, sophomores, freshmen—is the most obvious, and the easiest to point out.[11] "I also think that four-year seniors—" But she breaks off. "We don't think we're better than the three-years." Unable to bite my tongue, I joke: "Yeah, you do! Come on!" We both laugh and she jokes back: "But technically we are!"

Sabrina and I continue to laugh together as she seeks to make sense of the contradiction and tries to clarify, further underscoring the difference:

> Um, no, but I mean, a lot of, like, I mean, [my friend is] a three-year, and I'm really good friends with her, and I don't think that it ever [*pause*] sort of excludes certain people. But I think that [*pause*] four years at Weston is a really unique experience. . . . I think that, um, four years at Weston has people sort of bond together. So I think that there are sort of divisions that, you know, you know who's a four-year and you know who's a three-year. Um, and you know who the PGs are.

The sense that not all Westonians are the same is clear in Sabrina's response.[12] Surely all graduates are Westonians, but four-year seniors are hierarchically on top—and perhaps more Westonian than all other students. This hierarchical distinction is taken for granted, and justified by the objective reality that such students have spent four years together.

Matthew Briggs is also a four-year senior. He explains the difference:

Uh, and to some degree, there is more of a bond between four-year seniors. Because we'll remember a big assembly that we thought was hysterical, . . . and it loses something describing it to someone who came last year. Uh, so I would say that there is a closer bond between the four-year seniors, and you get in a class with a four-year senior you don't know, and you still know their name, 'cause you've seen them around for four years.

After making this claim, Matthew, like Sabrina, acknowledges the particular experiences of the three years as hard, and he enacts his own sense of equity by rejecting the hierarchy. But this appears to be mostly a way of saving face with me, who might think of such distinctions as superfluous, if for no other reason than because I'm not a Westonian myself: "I think it's got to be a lot harder on them, getting in and adjusting. But they're really very good. I've got—some of my best friends are, came as new sophomores and juniors. Because they really are equal or better to four-year seniors." But he concludes, "They just don't quite have the same bond."

Matthew, however, is a day student, and he suggests that day students may be less likely to experience this kind of bonding because "you don't make connections nearly as fast as a day student, especially as a shy day student, which, you know, like, I was. Um, like, I still am." By identifying as a "shy day student," Matthew positions himself as a particular kind of Westonian:

If you live with someone, you live with, like, forty people, you're all going to be pretty good friends, and you've got this bond that day students never really get. It's also convenient if on Sunday afternoon your friends decide: "Hey, we're all going to go down to the gym and, you know, play a game of volleyball or go skating." I've got a half an hour drive in, and I'm just not going to get [there]. . . . Sometimes it's annoying to be removed from campus by a half-hour drive and to not have the, the bond that dorm has.[13]

Matthew suggests that this Westonian bond is strengthened through social relations within friendship groups, which, as we've seen, are highly (if discreetly) organized. The inherent tension in the discourse of distinction—between claiming a collective identification as Westonian and justifying the distinctions *between* Westonians—betrays the political nature of this and all other processes of identification. Indeed, the discourse of distinction structures its own internal exclusions and shapes the hierarchies of distinction in which students must find a place. Once students find their niche in the hierarchies of distinction, they engage in rituals that confirm their right to those spaces, so that those spaces will become "home" and students are able to claim the experience as "their" experience.

In order to further articulate the different bonding experiences of boarding students and day students, Matthew offers the example of "dorm pride," a ritual I witnessed during almost every assembly I attended. Matthew describes it this way:

> If someone gets up at Weston assembly, . . . if you're from a dorm, your dorm supports you some—to varying degrees. There's, there's McMaster, there's Sa-Lin-Ger [*he accentuates each syllable*], um, but you're definitely gonna, you're gonna hear from your dorm, 'cause, you know, there's dorm pride there. Day student pride, you know, we, we know each other somewhat, um, but we don't have that same bond, because you go home with your families and, you know, your friends from your old schools.

I tell Matthew that I wondered whether I would ever hear someone yell "DAY-STU-DENTS!" during assembly, but he chuckles cynically. "If they do, it's usually, uh, it's usually jokingly."

In this instance, the notion of bonding is presented through the distinction between day and boarding students. Through this distinction, Matthew conveys the feeling that day students like him (particularly shy ones) are somehow less Westonian. Identifying as a Westonian, then, implies being able to recognize distinctions within the Westonian hierarchy of identification—such as the difference between day and boarding, or between three-, two-, and four-year seniors. To know these distinctions and to find a place in that hierarchy are central to the process of becoming a Westonian.

Matthew's explanation of the difference between boarders and day students refers to the three spheres through which students construct their identification as Westonians, and he seems to organize the differences accordingly. While Matthew talks about the differences relating to bonding and to the social sphere, he claims that the sphere of work is the one where day students are like all other Westonians:

> Dorm pride is definitely a big thing. Um, people will yell out at assembly . . . when someone from their dorm goes up, and, and there's a lot of, there's a lot of dorm bonding because [they] live together. Day student pride is almost more of a joke. Um, just as far as, we, day students, you, you do get to know a lot of day students, and you are friends with them because, you know, we all have lockers in the [same building]. But it's really, it's no different than someone in one of your classes, or someone on one of your teams. Because—and that we all go home to our own separate houses, and you don't get that, I don't know, . . . camaraderie you would have in the dorm. Because, you know, you just, you live with each other all the time, so you see people, you know, when, when they're studying, or when they're just having fun. You would have, like, a whole late-night-talk thing. Day students, you know, we do somewhat through phone and I.M., but really not quite the same.

During my time at Weston, I had the opportunity to spend many evenings with students in the dorms while they studied, had fun, or just spent time talking. Students described such friendship-building opportunities with great nostalgia, suggesting that these were indeed important moments in the process of becoming Westonian.

Dorm Bonding

On my way back to my sleeping quarters, I run into Ramón Pérez, who is saying good night to a female friend he's just escorted to her dorm—a courteous gesture that has made him late for curfew. He calls my name, and invites me to go to his dorm to watch TV. I'm happy to accept. We get to his dorm, but are stuck outside because Ramón has forgotten his keys. He yells through a window to ask another boy to let him in, just as Mr. Jesman, the faculty member on duty, comes down the stairs. Ramón leans against the door to hide, but Mr. Jesman looks out the window and sees me staring at Ramón. Ramón moves back and makes signs through the glass, saying, "I love you!" to Mr. Jesman, who opens the door. Ramón hugs him, as if playing a game with him: "I'm here, I love you, don't check me late." Mr. Jesman turns to me, and confirms that Ramón has a chronic problem with lateness. We shake hands as I come inside, and Mr. Jesman continues with check-in. I wonder if Ramón has invited me along in order to have an excuse to be late.

Ramón and I walk into the common room, where about fifteen boys are gazing at the TV. As they channel surf, they make long pauses to watch *Cops* and a Red Sox baseball game. I sit on the couch as the channels flip, until a commercial grabs their attention. A voluptuous young woman, with long blond curls and well-tanned skin, strolls on a beach wearing a short skirt, against a background of blue sky and palm trees. As the woman models the skirt and dances, one of the boys comments: "Like *that* will ever happen!" His sense of reality seems quite mature, and I wonder how much the commercial plays into the boys' fantasies, how they see Weston girls who wear similar skirts, and if they expect that a woman just like that will show up someday to please them.

I turn to look at Ramón and notice that he's sitting on a couch next to another tall boy. The boy has his arm around Ramón, who is leaning against the boy's side, almost cuddling. I'm surprised by this physical intimacy, and I notice that other boys are sitting similarly. The commercial ends and they flip to the next channel. A few more boys come in and start to get rough with one another. Ramón asks whether they want to do dorm wrestling, but the boys, who look younger, retreat. Out of nowhere, one of the boys grabs a pillow and swings it hard at another boy. They exchange pillow thwacks. One boy gets on top of the table, and another runs toward him with his right hand clenched in a fist. The sound of the punch makes me wince. The boy on the table jumps down, limping, laughing, and sore, putting an end to the fight.

At 10:25 Mr. Jesman comes down, stands next to me watching the TV, and then turns to tell me that it makes him feel old (I agree, and laugh ruefully with him). As 10:30 rolls around, the boys shut off the TV and head upstairs. Some of them go to their own rooms and others gather together in one room or another. I ask Mr. Jesman if this is bedtime. He chuckles. "Yeah—by eleven they're all in bed sleeping, to wake up at 6:30 and do homework." "Right," I deadpan, and we laugh. I say good night to the boys and leave.

As Matthew observes, students who live together in dormitories share a great deal of intimacy. Their experiences range from virulent demonstrations of manly strength, such as dorm wrestling, to brief moments of physical closeness, as when boys lean on each other while watching TV. Older boys impose their seniority on younger boys, friends spend long hours talking well after the official bedtime, homework is often shared, and students engage in all sorts of illicit activities—smoking, drug dealing, gambling, sneaking out to have sex on classroom tables.[14] As an adult observer, I had no access to these activities. Yet the stories students told were filled with references to such events, and I have no reason to doubt that they were happening. I cannot determine how widespread such activities are, but I can confidently claim that they play an important role (perhaps only as myths) in the narratives through which students talk about what it means to be Westonians.[15] It is at such times that the experience of bonding simmers into the thick brew of Westonian identification. Yet these moments of bonding are not experienced equally by all students.

Jennifer Chung, who earlier described feeling that Weston was like a family, offers a different perspective when I ask her directly about her friends in the dorm. Jennifer came to Weston as an eleventh grader. While students who come in as freshmen and sophomores are typically placed in large dormitories, students like Jennifer are usually placed in smaller "houses" that accommodate ten to twenty students. The rationale for this choice was never clearly explained to me, but it was obvious that students who come to Weston later in their high school years experience this housing arrangement as a form of hierarchical segregation from the "real" or "original" Westonians—to use the language of the memory boxes ritual.

Jennifer is a diminutive girl who looks much younger than the rest of the juniors and seniors with whom she lives. I ask her whether she has friends in her house, and in contrast to her earlier comments about family, her answer is hesitant.

> Sort of. Um, not really I guess. . . . I guess when I interact [with] them, I don't feel like I'm being honest, and that makes me feel uncomfortable. So I don't really wanna, like, hang out with them as much as—I mean, I *do* hang out with them, 'cause, you know, I live with them, and they're really nice people. It's just that, I guess I really like—I don't know, not, like,

in a romantic way, but, like, really passionate relationships. And I feel like I can't, I can't develop it with them."

I ask Jennifer what she means by not being honest with her house-mates, and she answers with a rich and extended narrative about her childhood, her Korean immigrant parents, and how she came to identify as a bisexual female. Jennifer explains that she doesn't "advertise" her sexuality, but that, when people ask, she says she is "bi." She describes her sexual identification as part of why she feels separated from the other girls in her dorm: "'Cause they're, like, what people would label, I guess, like, 'girly girls.' That kind of, like, freaks me out. Because sometimes I realize that's what I really wanted to be, just so I could, like, fit into, like, the female image." Her answer begins to suggest how the discourse of distinction is gendered in particular ways, and points to the fact that heterosexuality remains the norm (we'll look at this topic more closely in the next chapter). Indeed, as she suggests below, having "status" as a female depends on enacting a particular kind of femininity that "fits" within the discourse of distinction.

Jennifer returns to her childhood narrative and speaks about the ex-pectations of her conservative mother and open-minded father, her admi-ration for her male friends, and the way these "colored [her] experience of living with only girls, in a house full of girls." She then tells a story about getting involved with a male friend and about feeling that she had to "pretend" she was "one of those girls who's always wanted a boy-friend, and, like, feel cool now that they have a boyfriend," while she was "really not that person at all."

> When I'm, like, talking with, like, other people in my dorm—
> 'cause they're really into, like, sharing their personal lives and
> stuff, just 'cause I feel, like, it's almost like a status thing. I re-
> member, like, in the beginning of the year, this girl was, like, "I
> bet I've kissed more boys than you" to some other girl in my
> dorm. And, like, I was like, "That's so weird!" Like, I don't
> even find that, like, even the least bit interesting. . . . One time,
> like, one girl asked me, "Do you have a boyfriend that you are
> seeing?" And I was like, "Yeah," 'cause I didn't wanna, like,
> be, like, "No," 'cause that's kinda silly, to lie about that. But
> then, like, I don't really feel like talking [about it]. . . . I guess

they sort of, like, talk about that kind of stuff a lot. And that's one of the reasons why I just feel a little bit out of it.

I ask Jennifer to explain what she means by "girly girls," a term she claims to have picked up from her aunt, who is worried that her eight-year-old daughter, like Jennifer, is too much of a tomboy and not girly enough. She explains why she feels disconnected from the other girls in her house.

> I guess they're all into, like, the sort of, like, typical girl things, I guess. Like shopping and, like, dressing up and stuff like that. And, like, we had, like, a freaking, like, prom dress fashion show one time, and I was like, "Geez, this is so weird!" I mean, it's kind of cute and, like, nice. And then sometimes I chastise myself because I'm like, "Jennifer, just, like, loosen up and, like, just go with it." You know, like, "Maybe, maybe you'll wanna, like, have this experience and, you know, thirty years down the road you won't be able to necessarily, like, just, like, hang out with the girls," or whatever. I mean, I could, but I mean, like, not like these, and so I guess I'm sort of like, chastising myself at the same time. [*pause*] I don't know. "Girly girls" is a bad expression.

Despite feeling excluded from the ritual, Jennifer feels that she needs to loosen up and participate. While there are many layers of subjective meaning in her narrative, the point I wish to stress is that being part of the ritual feels, to Jennifer, like a necessary aspect of the dorm bonding experience. Even as her sexuality and her particular gender identification fall outside what is acceptable in the context of the dorms, where girls are expected to compete for boys and practice looking good, she chides herself for not participating.

Rituals, in fact, play a central role in how members of a group come to feel that they are part of the group and in how they construct a sense of belonging.[16] Rituals carry—often explicitly, though most of the time implicitly—the underlying symbolic structure, or discourse, that gives meaning to the experiences of participants.[17] The Weston School is a place filled with rituals of all kinds. Some of these rituals are subtle, inconspicuous practices that are often taken for granted and that might even go unnoticed.[18] Others are spectacular—not in their magnitude, but in their character. Some of these rituals are public and open to the whole school community, while others are highly selective and private. Regardless of their character, the various rituals in which the students at Weston engage, whether institutionally sponsored or beyond the purview of the institutional gaze, are a form of what Clifford Geertz famously calls "deep play."[19] As such, rituals are highly symbolic and give the observer a glimpse into the underlying logic that organizes the experience of a given group in a given space, at a given time.[20] The discourse of distinction and its inherent contradictions are displayed in the details of every ritual.

RITUALS OF DISTINCTION

The various Weston rituals I had opportunity to observe (and occasionally participate in) can be generally classified as either *institutional* or *organic*. Institutional rituals are organized, overseen, and controlled by the school authority, particularly by the faculty, even when students are in charge of organizing the details and carrying out the actual ceremonies. Most of these rituals have a long history at the school, and they involve not only the students and the faculty, but often administrative staff. Students' families are often spectators, if not participants (for instance, on alumni weekends).[21]

Rituals that I am calling organic take place generally beyond the gaze of adult authority. This is not to say that adults are unaware of them; at times, adults may even be complicit. But students are the primary organizers, the main participants, and for the most part the only audience. Many of these rituals likewise have a long history at the school, but they are not officially sanctioned by the institution. Some organic rituals are sponsored and supported by the institution (pep rallies, student rock band concerts, and so on). Some institutional rituals are carried out entirely by students in ways that are rather organic; examples are the senior-class yearbook and the organization of the prom. Yet by and large, these two kinds of rituals have distinct characters and play fundamentally different roles in the process of identification.

Both institutional and organic rituals vary in how elaborate they are. While all rituals involve a degree of formality and regularity (otherwise they would not be thought of as rituals), some rituals are loose and somewhat unpredictable in form, while others are carefully planned and unfold with great regularity.[22] The latter is most typical of institutional rituals, whereas the former tends to be the norm in organic rituals. Events such as awards ceremonies and formal dinners recur every year, and their logistics have been formalized in writing so that anyone can follow the script. Organic rituals often involve illicit activities, which means that they must be organized (so that the students don't get caught) yet flexible, and they often occur spontaneously.

One additional characteristic of rituals that is essential to the process of identification is the nature of their intended audience: the choice of who gets to witness and participate in the ritual. Organic rituals are almost entirely for, by, and about the students and their experience. Some institutional rituals are meant to be private, like the process of dealing with the disciplinary committee, which is the same for all students but which students go through on their own. Others are highly public, like graduation. Some organic rituals are also public, like the kinds of cheering that accompany athletic games, but the audience for such public rituals is composed of the students themselves, whether playing or cheering. Yet organic rituals are mostly restricted to an audience of students, often a subset of all students—those in specific groups or categories, such as a particular dorm, a particular grade, or specific social networks. These sorts of rituals are often about confirming the inherent distinctions in the hierarchies of the Westonian identification. The ritual of opening memory boxes is a case in point.

Other rituals are about vulnerability, about risk taking, about building loyalty, and about the internalization of roles.[23] During my time at Weston, I observed many rituals, and in each instance, I had the sense that a particular dimension of the Westonian identification was being "thickened."[24] Institutionally sponsored and openly public rituals like pep rallies and morning assemblies are mostly about students' strengthening their collective identification as Westonians. At the morning assemblies, the headmaster stands in front of the student body and calls them to attention with a loud "Good morning, Weston!" Or she asks the students to give a "Westonian welcome" or a "Westonian applause" to a special guest or speaker. Often these special guests make reference to the idea that Westonians are "the best of the best," or that they are expected to make great contributions to society or assume leadership roles. In a place where the pressure to be "the best of the best" is keen, stress and tension build exponentially. Like any bubble, the "Weston bubble" is susceptible to the building up of internal pressure. This pressure finds escape through what one student described as "pipes"—organic rituals that can be thought of as pressure release valves, such as the "midnight run."

During my visits to Weston, I often spent the night at one of the faculty houses near the athletic fields, which allowed me the comfort and the space to write and reflect on my visits to the school. After transcribing fieldnotes and writing journal entries, I often read the week's *Westonian,* with the clanking of the heating pipes and the buzz of my bedside lamp providing the soundtrack. One night, just as I was falling asleep over the school newspaper, a torrent of voices screaming what sounded like "Freedom!" flooded through the window. I sprang up, disoriented. The "midnight run" returned several times, and only after a couple of iterations did I have the presence of mind to look out the window. As I watched, a group of what seemed like a hundred students came running by, half dressed and screaming, "We're free!" I realized that the accumulated pressure had found its end-of-semester release valve. The next day, students explained that at midnight on the last night of each term, students gather in an undetermined spot and run through campus in their pajamas, yelling to release the tension of their final exams. They commented that the neighbors, who apparently find it as startling as I did, have complained numerous times. Yet despite the efforts of the school to stop this organic ritual, it continues to startle the uninitiated, distinguishing town from gown.

During a visit I made to another dorm during final exams, a dorm faculty member invited me to join all the boys in a game of dodge ball, which he hoped would release some of the "unhealthy" tension the students were carrying. Other official and unofficial rituals seem to serve similar purposes, as do shuttles to the mall or the nearby city, out-of-town permissions, Saturday dances, and Café Casinos.[25] Other "pipes" are not so easily monitored. One of the largest and most important is Homecoming Weekend, when Weston competes against its rival, Manchester Academy. Every year, hundreds of alumni and parents of current students descend on the campus of one school or the other (the scene of the competition alternates), ready to attend tailgate parties and to witness the games. Feuds are recalled, chants are performed, and the bonds between Westonians of many generations are strengthened.[26]

More hidden and organic rituals take place in the dorms and other private spaces of the school. Examples are the prom fashion show that Jennifer mentioned, the "porno night" initiation rituals for new students, and the "wall of shame" on which students post their rejection letters from colleges and universities. In an effort to alleviate the weight of rejection, the students not only share the "shame" publicly, but symbolically denigrate the image of the rejecting school by embellishing the letter with new sentences and phrases, such as "community college" in place of "university."[27] Indeed, these rituals play a crucial social role in consecrating and legitimizing otherwise implicit or subtle boundaries.[28]

The discourse of distinction is in full symbolic display in the most elaborate rituals: from the very public graduation exercises, which are usually held outside in full display, to the very hidden rituals that students organize in the privacy of their dorm rooms and basements; from the rituals that engage the entire school to those that are specific to particular groups. Each group that fills the social space of the Weston School has its own rituals of bonding, and each ritual has symbolic layers that make it intimate and perhaps even secret. My access to these rituals was somewhat limited. The more organic and student-centered a ritual was, the less access any adult had. While I did witness some highly symbolic late-night rituals among the boys, I learned about rituals in the girls' dorms only through stories. Because of the gender and sexual dynamics that govern the ethics of fieldwork, I could not witness girls' dorm rituals that may have been equivalent to rituals I observed among the boys.[29] Whether I directly witnessed these rituals or learned about them from the stories students told, what is crucial is that each of these rituals underscores a sense of shared experience, and, at a deeper level, a sense of shared intimacy.[30]

Whether filled with spectacular bravado or innocuous simplicity, every ritual carries elements of what it means to be a Westonian and plays a role in how students become elite. Each of these rituals—the bells that mark the Weston daily schedule, the sudden release of the midnight run, the pomp and circumstance of graduation, the excitement of senior night —thickens the Westonian identification and the corresponding bonds that may last a lifetime.

"HAVE YOU MADE ANY CRONIES?"

If the lives of social distinction that I described in the previous chapter are about structuring exclusions among groups, including how groups appropriate and negotiate space, the sphere of bonding and intimacy that I describe in this chapter is about the bonds that thicken through relationships within and between those groups. All of these distinctions are constructed in relation to a collective Westonian identification that distinguishes these students as a class apart from others. These processes of collective identification that students describe as bonding are not unique to elite boarding schools. The forging of family-like bonds and the kinds of loyalties that these experiences produce can also be found in other contexts, including total institutions with less benign manifest goals. Yet in the context of an elite boarding school, the intensity of these shared experiences is crucial for creating and cultivating "the illusion of earned status," and for achieving closure around the entitlements that such status implies.[31] The significance of the rituals described in this chapter lies in how they underscore the boundaries that distinguish the graduates of an elite boarding school as an elite status group.

Linda Merrow plans to attend a prestigious undergraduate business program after commencement. Her mother is an office clerk in a nearby town, and her dad is a salesman; they're proud of her accomplishments. This term, Linda will be attending Weston's internship program in Washington, D.C., where she'll spend a couple of months working for a high-profile U.S. senator with connections to the school. I ask her what it means for her to be a Westonian. She thinks for a moment, and says: "One of the things that [*pause*] is a big deal about being a Westonian is that any—I could be [*pause*] standing in any airport in the world with a Weston sweatshirt on, and someone's gonna come up to me and say, 'You go to Weston? Oh, I had,' you know, 'a step-brother that went to Weston.' Or, 'I had—' You know, somebody knows somebody who went here."

I ask Linda if this has happened to her before, and she offers that it happens "all the time," making the crucial link to one of the ultimate class consequences of such identifications: "And what goes along with that is just connections. And anywhere you go, you're gonna be able to find somebody who will help you just because you went here. And that may not be right, but maybe there's something about having gone here that does warrant some kind of a trust. I mean . . ." She pauses to consider the implications of what she is saying. After a moment's contemplation, she adds: "I don't know. I mean, I know wherever I—wherever I'm gonna end up, I would [*pause*] feel totally confident, hiring nearly any of my four-year friends. Because I, I mean, I've, I've known them, and I know that they've gone through a lot of what I've gone through, and that, that they've learned a lot of the same work ethic."

Matthew Briggs offers a similar view, but with some added apprehensions and caveats:

> Part of me would feel guilty about, you know, sort of, the whole cronyism thing, which I really do not like. . . . For my own personal, moral, ethical reasons, I would not hire some-

one for being from Weston. But if I saw a résumé that said Weston, they would get an interview, I would say. Like, like, I would, I would read that as, that, that packet or whatever, very carefully. And just put some weight into—not like, "You're from Weston," you know, "you're gonna use the good-old-boy network here." But "You went to Weston, so that means you had to get in, you had to survive the place, and you're—there are certain base qualifications that you probably have."

Matthew's words clearly illustrate how the experience of bonding relates to the experiences of students in the sphere of work and the ideology of meritocracy. In order to justify any preference he might give in the future to a fellow Westonian, Matthew invokes the discourse of distinction as it is articulated through the notion that Westonians are smart, work hard, and have demonstrated the excellence expected of every Westonian, especially those who have graduated.

Julie Lasky is the fourth of four siblings to attend Weston. She identifies as half Jewish and is proud of her father's rise from poverty to high status as both a lawyer and a doctor. Unlike Matthew, she is much less concerned with the "moral" implications of cronyism, which she finds perfectly acceptable. Yet in order to provide a justification, she makes a connection to the broad social map of the Weston landscape. As to whether she would call herself a Westonian, Julie laughs: "Sure! Yeah! You know, you've got your cronies." She laughs again, as she utters the word, "Westonians!" Curious, I ask her what she means by "having your cronies." She describes a cartoon in the *New Yorker* in which a father and son sit in their posh living room, both wearing suits and ties. The father sits back smoking a cigar, and the son leans forward in his tie and blue blazer attentively. The caption reads, "How's school? Have you made some cronies?"[32]

Julie and I laugh as she describes the cartoon, and I tell her that other students have talked about this. She responds:

I believe it—I think it exists. I don't know if I, I—I don't think it's a bad thing, you know? I think people take themselves so seriously, but if you just—you have to have fun with it, because there's, there is, like, all the stuffy, sort of, old-school way of, of being. . . . But it dissipates with, with the diversity, I think. And that's a good thing, probably. Because it can be, it can be very sexist, and very classist, and all that stuff. And so long as it isn't that, and you allow—you know, when I'm around with four-years, I always, I always get this whole four-year, like, you know, we're four-years, like, you know, it's great. And I'm talking about people from every walk of life, you know—certainly not just white wealthy Americans.

For Julie, the apparent diversity of a school like Weston offers a rationale for mobilizing what sociologists call "social capital," and for securing the social resources that Westonians have "earned."[33] Julie's words might suggest that all social groups are equally bound by the same Westonian identification. The relationships that they have built at Weston, even as they are distinguished in the social space, lead to the same access to future social networks. But as we will see, not all Westonians are positioned in the same way. Indeed, distinction is a kind of "scarce resource" that some groups protect even as all students identify as Westonians. Social processes related to race, class, and gender as categories of identification weigh heavily on the distribution of distinction at Weston, and shape how students come to identify as racialized, classed, and gendered Westonians preparing to lead lives of distinction.

6

UNEQUAL DISTINCTIONS

Lee Fiora is the daughter of a mattress salesman. In her midwestern sub-urban milieu, a boarding school is seen as a mystical walled enclave, either "a place for screwups" or a place for the very rich. At the age of ten, on a road trip to Florida, Lee discovers the picture-perfect landscape of affluent suburbia and learns from her father that "people like us don't live in these houses. These people keep their money in Swiss bank accounts. They eat caviar for dinner. They send their sons to boarding schools." Too young to appreciate her father's civics lesson, Lee wonders if "they send their daughters to boarding school." Lee learns more about elite boarding schools "from TV shows and *Seventeen* magazine." To her parents' bewilderment, she applies to the prestigious Ault School and gets accepted.[1]

After four years of elite boarding school education, and despite her best efforts to fit in, Lee remains an outsider. Having "spent a lot of time here feeling left out," she learns to accept her "membership in a subculture I felt I belonged to only when I was away from it." Lee admits to the reader that at the time of her graduation, the "highlight" of her elite boarding school experience was a boy—a popular boy who sneaks into her bed at night and whom she fellates under a classroom table. Lee's elite boarding school experience is distinctly marked not only by her inability to participate in the culture of affluence, but also by her becoming a wealthy boy's sex toy, a role she embraces with ambivalent bliss.[2]

Lee's naïveté about elite status leads her to share her experiences with a *New York Times* reporter, who takes advantage of her openness to expose the persistent exclusivity of elite spaces like the Ault School.

Shunned by everyone except her closest friend, Lee is accused of pissing "in your own pool," as one student puts it, and lives the last few days of her elite boarding school years in the shadow of her own strangeness. In the end, at graduation, the only one who can commiserate with Lee is, ironically, a black male student. More popular than Lee, yet precariously managing his own status, Darden Pittard shares his secret with Lee: "Black people who live in a white world learn to be careful. . . . You learn not to make waves. . . . Because once you do, that's it. You're a trouble-maker, and they never think of you any other way." Having sealed her fate as an outsider, Lee moves on to the rest of her life.[3]

Lee Fiora is a fictional student, the main character in Curtis Sitten-feld's loosely autobiographical novel *Prep*. Lee's predicament is not new; in many of the fictional accounts of life at elite boarding schools, the main theme is exclusion. From *Rushmore*'s Max Fischer and John Ir-ving's Owen Meany to Jonathan Ogner in *Class* and Odin James in *O*, novels and films set in boarding schools are filled with characters who can't seem to find their niche in the ample space of their elite schools. In the popular film *School Ties*, a working-class Pennsylvania teenager named David Greene is recruited at the end of his high school career to enhance the winning chances of the football team at "St. Matt's," a fic-tional (if all too lifelike) elite boarding school.[4] Despite his classmates' curiosity about his roots and their skepticism about how he got to St. Matt's, David manages to establish his reputation as a friendly and hard-working student. After he leads the school to a football victory over its rival, "St. Luke," his teammates discover that he is Jewish, which they take not only as an affront to their WASP sensibilities, but as a betrayal. David is shunned and ridiculed by his peers; he is also falsely accused of cheating by a wealthy legacy student who brags about his fifth-generation rights to Harvard. When the accuser's guilt is revealed, David is "ab-solved" for breaking the honor code, and the headmaster sighs with relief and hopes "to forget this ever happened." David retorts, "No sir, you are never going to forget it happened, because I am going to stay here. And every day you see me, you'll remember that it happened." Arguably, an important part of the narrative energy behind any story set at an elite boarding school is supplied by the tensions inherent in a character's ex-clusion from, or failure to fit within the constraints of, the culture of af-fluence.[5]

Beyond the many fictional accounts, actual instances of exclusion are rife. Lorene Cary's autobiography *Black Ice*, Johanna Vega's story in the

PBS documentary *American Dreams at Groton,* the journalistic account of Eddie Perry's story in *Best Intentions*—such accounts of outsider status tell us a great deal not only about individual experiences, but about the institutional conditions that promote exclusion.[6] At the same time, these narratives also show how much elite boarding schools have changed in the past one hundred years. Yet their main role in society has not changed: they ensure that students embrace their elite status and justify their privilege as they are socialized into future positions within the power elites. This much has been abundantly argued and illustrated by scholars who have written about elites generally, and about elite boarding schools in particular.[7]

Since the civil rights movement of the 1960s, coeducation and cultural diversity have done little to raise questions about what is perhaps the most fundamental characteristic of an elite boarding school: exclusion. The very fact that there is a complex gatekeeping procedure defines elite schools as exclusive. Exclusion is not, however, simply about who does or doesn't get in. Rather, processes of exclusion permeate the landscape of elite boarding schools in unique ways that contribute to the consolidation of systems of oppression—specifically sexism, racism, and classism. This point has been neglected by the literature on elite schooling, in which such dynamics are typically ignored, or subsumed within larger arguments about the role of elite boarding schools in preparing students for power.[8] While elite status defines the experiences of all students at the Weston School, not all students are equally elite. Each of the previous chapters suggests how race, class, and gender shape the three spheres of experience I discuss. In this chapter, I pull these strands together to emphasize that elite boarding schools remain institutions for the consolidation of an upper class that is fundamentally Anglo-Saxon and patriarchal.

It is important to explain at the outset that I try to avoid a static and essentialist view of race, class, and gender in which those who identify with particular categories are assumed to have particular experiences because of *who they are.* For instance, how girls talk about their experience at Weston is not determined by their biology or by their essential nature as girls. Rather, how girls identify as Westonians is shaped largely by the gender assumptions that underlie the very definition of what it means to be a (male) Westonian. The dynamics of race, class, and gender—as socially constructed categories—restrict the ways in which different students identify as Westonians and how they make meaning of their experience. In other words, access to the range of meanings available in any given space is determined not by who the students *essentially are*—their identity—but rather by how they understand themselves and how they are perceived by others: their identification.[9] The dynamics of race, class, and gender ensure that *all* students will construct Westonian identifications differently. Yet the social and political consequences—including the costs and rewards of identifying as a Westonian—are not equally distributed. By taking this approach, I hope to stress rather than skirt the question of how real people experience *actual* and *lived* processes of identification within categories of race, class, and gender that have a direct impact on their particular subjectivities. My aim is to show that the social constructs of race, class, and gender are not simply free-floating categories with relatively immaterial effects on how people identify and are identified by others, but that these processes of identification have real political consequences.[10]

Furthermore, race, class, and gender do not operate as discrete categories but are deeply intertwined.[11] Many social scientists dealing with questions of race, class, and gender have underscored the complex ways in which these categories intersect, while also noting the difficulty of talking about them all at once. One way to deal with this challenge is to foreground the dynamics of one category while keeping the others, at least analytically, in the background. For instance, in Chapter 4, where I discussed the story of Marie, the student who identifies as a member of the fresh posse, I focused on her class status to make sense of how she identifies with a particular status group. Yet her experience is also premised on her particular experience of gender and sexuality. She identifies as an attractive female who is perceived by others to embody the characteristics of the popular girls in her peer group, most of whom identify as white. Similarly, when I discussed the experiences of Alex Crosby, I focused first on her class status as the daughter of upper-middle-class parents and then shifted attention to her identification as black, both of which intersect in complicated ways with how she experiences being female.

This process of shifting categories of race, class, and gender analytically between foreground and background allows us to see how the dynamics of each operate distinctly yet always in relation to the others. Ultimately, my aim is to make clear that these constructs interact in complex ways to shape the experiences of *all* students, always in specific circumstances and in places that determine how categories come to bear on situations yielding unequal distinctions.

RACE: BEING "IN" BUT NOT "OF" WESTON

Like most of its peer schools, Weston proclaims a commitment to diversity as one of its central goals.[12] This goal is articulated in most of its admissions materials, and students are quick to talk about diversity when asked about admissions criteria. Diversity, however, proved to be one of the most complex aspects of the Westonian discourse of distinction. These complexities reflect in powerful ways the national anxieties about affirmative action and about the role of race and ethnicity in college admissions.[13] In this section, I describe some of the ways in which the discourse of distinction is *racialized*—that is, how the idea of being a Westonian is itself implicitly marked racially in ways that inevitably exclude. For Westonians who identify as nonwhite this process of identification might be characterized, in Lorene Cary's words, as being *in* but not *of* this elite boarding school world.[14]

Being "Diverse" versus Being "Smart"

Laura Miller is a day student who describes herself as a "white student from [a neighboring town]"—an identification that, given the lack of racial diversity among day students, seems almost redundant.[15] When I ask her what she thought when she was admitted to Weston, Laura leans over the dining hall table where we're having breakfast, and ponders: "I figured for a while that in order to get into Weston you had to be either very smart, very wealthy, or very diverse. . . . 'Diverse' meaning, like, you're from North Dakota, or you've sailed around the world. . . . You know, people from Alaska, people whose parents are ambassadors."

"There's always something that makes us special," Laura comments, and we laugh together as I suggest that, according to her definition, she must have been smart. Her response to my compliment is puzzling: "I must have been smart, cause I'm white, and I'm from [this New England state], so I must have been smart." She implies that, absent other characteristics and experiences, students enter Weston on the basis of their intellect alone, and that students who bring some sort of "diversity" (that is, who aren't white or from a New England state) are perhaps held to different (perhaps lower) standards. To be "undiverse," as some students put it, is, by elimination, to be smart.

Laura defines "being diverse" as a quality possessed by individuals, as opposed to a characteristic of a group. This way, she avoids speaking directly about race and ethnicity. This avoidance is typical of the comments on diversity, which students—even students of color—prefer to define in terms other than those of race and ethnicity. Terrence, who identifies as black, hesitates as he explains that the admissions office is looking for "a diverse group of people who, um, you know, who hold diff—" He breaks off, thinks for a moment about what he is about to say, and resumes his thought: "who are able to express their opinions and who are able to add something to their community." With this euphemism (which repeats almost verbatim the official school discourse), Terrence echoes the notion that the school is looking for a "diversity of thought," and likewise avoids race and ethnicity as important aspects of diversity. His hesitation and his shift from "difference" to the ability to express ideas also suggests that talking about diversity in terms of the ability to articulate different points of view is easier to reconcile with the idea of being smart than justifying diversity for other reasons, such as supporting justice or equality.[16]

Ken Ellerly is from the western United States. He believes diversity is part of what makes Weston a good school, and I ask him why.[17] He, too, answers with hesitation, describing how he brings diversity to the campus and likewise defining diversity as an individual rather than a group trait: "Um, perhaps maybe it's, part of it is bec—, from the fact—well, okay, I mean, I, I bring diversity to the school in a way. I mean, though I'm, you know, I'm Caucasian, I come from a different area—I come from [a western state]. . . . This is an East Coast boarding school." Though noting that he's Caucasian, which would mark diversity as a racial matter, Ken believes he brings diversity because he comes from a western state rather than the East Coast, suggesting that diversity might be an issue of geography. He continues: "I wanted to meet other kids, maybe like me, who were from [my home state] and from other countries, who have made the decision to go—not just go away to boarding school, but really go, like, a distance to school. And I think that, I mean, diversity just adds to the whole educational experience." Ironically, Ken begins explaining his rationale for diversity by stating that he wanted to meet students like himself, as opposed to meeting those different from him. Such students, who have chosen to go "a distance to school," are also perhaps like him in that they can afford to travel this distance. I ask him to explain further, and he insists that "people bring different, um, being from different backgrounds, and they bring, like, they bring different things to the table, you know, and a different perspective."

His construction of diversity, which is racialized at the beginning, becomes less related to race as I continue to ask him why it is important. He moves to equating diversity with geographic distance, and identifies himself as someone who didn't just want to "go away to boarding school" but wanted to go "a distance," without noting the economic resources necessary to do so. In this way, Ken turns the political dimension of diversity into a kind of commodity possessed by students with privilege, such as "children of ambassadors" or "people who have sailed around the world," as Laura puts it. By talking about "geographic diversity," "diversity of experience," and "diversity of thought," students avoid the tensions that may arise if diversity is viewed as a strategy for social justice perhaps at odds with the discourse of distinction, and with the meritocratic ideology that so strongly influences it. Thus, particularly for students who identify as white, diversity is about enhancing their educational experience with students from different backgrounds and not about social justice or equity.[18]

Annie Kasper identifies as white, and she echoes the notion that students must be smart and have a "certain level of education" to be admitted. She says that the admissions office looks, first, for "engagement and enthusiasm" and a level of "competency in terms of academic work. I mean, if you don't have a certain level of education you obviously—it's going to be hard to float in this type of environment." Unlike Ken and Laura, Annie talks about diversity as the characteristic of a group. Yet she echoes Laura by suggesting that diversity as an admissions criterion is secondary to "engagement and enthusiasm, . . . and competency in terms of academic work." This understanding of being "smart," as distinct (both different and better) from being "diverse," has direct consequences for how nonwhite students identify as Westonians.

Expressing some hesitation about sounding "elitist," Sandra López describes Weston as "the best of the boarding schools." She describes herself as the only "Dominican girl from Harlem" at Weston, and she is proud of what she sees as a great accomplishment. Her long brown curls are pulled back tight into a ponytail, and her dark brown eyes squint behind her glasses. She describes the recruitment program that brought her to Weston as "the best of the programs of its kind. . . . The way they start off with, like, over a thousand kids, or thousands of kids, or something like that, and narrow it down to sixty per contingent." Having established that she is different from other students by virtue of her academic inclinations and that some external source has identified her as smarter than those "thousands of kids," she concludes: "So I like to think, you know, I was probably, you know, best of the kids in the city. You know?"

Sandra describes the role that diversity and smartness play in the admissions process:

> I guess they look for, like, a lot of different things. . . . I mean, . . . it's a really diverse school. So I'd say, like, they look for not only, like—they look for [pause] diversity in experiences and maybe [pause] ethnicity, um, you know, and not only, not, well, [pause] I'd say that a lot of the kids that come to Weston are really smart at their other schools. So, like, they're the smartest in their class, or something like that. And what they do is just bring all the smartest kids, all over the country, and, like, the world even, to just one place, you know. And then you're not so smart anymore, once you come here.

Sandra's claim to smartness is qualified by the context from which she comes to Weston—a context in which she's considered smart because she goes away to school, which points to how "smart" references class status and upward mobility. While Sandra describes herself as being "the best" from Harlem, once at Weston she feels "not so smart anymore." Her self-construction as Westonian identifies her not as "smart" (even though she might believe she is smart), but as "diverse." This narrative turn places students who do not identify as white (and therefore smart) in a quandary regarding why they were admitted and how they construct Westonian identifications.[19]

One way students of color make sense of their admission to Weston is by assuming that they are brought in to "enrich" the curriculum. Radhika Chaudari feels certain that her ethnicity played a role in her admission. Although she grew up in the United States, she was born in South Asia, and she feels it is her responsibility to bring this background into the school. Coming to Weston, she says, made her aware for the first time that she was different:

> I never realized that I was South Asian, or that I was different. And then, when I came here, it seemed like I was, and that's what I brought to the school, in a way—my culture. And then I realized that I didn't really know much about my culture

to actually bring it and, like, add my experiences. So when I came here, we had [a South Asian Society]. And I never, like, had that anywhere else. And so I was thinking: What will they do? What will they talk about?

While she says she doesn't feel pressured, she notes: "I just felt like I should be that South Asian because that's why they accepted me. [*laughter*] Because, like, I feel like diversity really had a role in it. Like, my culture had a role in why I was admitted here. And so that's why I felt like I should know more about it, in a way." Both Radhika and Sandra believe that they were admitted because they bring diversity (even if they're also smart). Being positioned as *the* curriculum of diversity shapes how they identify as Westonians. For Radhika, it means that she's supposed to be more South Asian than she was before. At the same time, for both Sandra and Radhika it means realizing that at Weston they're no longer the smartest. In this way, students of color are in the predicament of wondering whether they've been admitted to Weston because they are identified as students of color, rather than because of their academic achievements or merits. Thus, the discourse of distinction affirms white students' status as smart, while it makes students of color insecure about their own academic status.

The fact that achievement is racialized is also evident in how the various niches students participate in are organized into hierarchies. Niches at the top of the hierarchy happen to be areas in which students of color seldom participate. For instance, during the time I was at Weston, I never saw a student I identified as nonwhite taking advanced courses in Latin or Greek.[20] This meant that students of color would not be seen at the front of the graduation ceremony to receive the Latin Distinction.

I am not arguing that students of color see being smart as "acting white."[21] On the contrary, students of color were as eager and enthusiastic about their academic work as any other student I met. They described their families' commitment to high academic achievement and said they worked as hard at their academic work as other students did.[22] The difference related to whether they felt they belonged in a certain space or chose to participate in certain activities. Indeed, it is the way the discourse of distinction restricts what nonwhite students are able to claim that sets them up for an inferior place in the academic hierarchy of distinction. This is not because they are less smart or less academic, or because their "culture" rejects academic success,[23] but because the range of

academic roles and ways of articulating their smartness are limited by
the discourse of distinction. As a cultural explanation, this analysis departs drastically from the claim that students of color don't take on academic challenges because of their "culture."[24] Instead, it is the "culture"
of an essentially racist institution that positions students of color in a
discursive space they can hardly occupy.[25]

In addition to becoming the curriculum of diversity for their white
peers, students of color experience pressure to conform to the dominant
culture. Attending an elite boarding school gives them an opportunity to
learn the "culture of power" that will prepare them for future success.[26]
Roland Carter, a four-year senior, argues that for students of color like
him, adapting to Weston involves a measure of assimilation. For him, this
assimilation has both positive and negative dimensions.[27] He recognizes
the degree to which Weston values and teaches "tolerance," and praises
the efforts of the school to "bring people from every corner of the world,
you know, from different backgrounds." The exposure to living "with
people who are not like you" provokes what Roland sees as a positive
shift in interactions among all students, including students of color, and a
valuing of difference.

Yet Roland doesn't think that the process of adaptation is the same for
white students, for whom it's "not really losing too much to come here
and to learn from one of us. But for us to . . . come here, where there are
very, very few of us, it's a lot to really dive into this culture." He reflects
on the conversation about the topic at a meeting in which students of color
discussed whether "by coming here as a minority . . . you are losing any
of [your culture], or exactly how you keep it and teach other students"—
a question which suggests, once again, that students like him are somehow responsible for the curriculum of diversity. He concludes that he has
lost "some of the way that at home I would interact with my counterparts": "[I] don't want to make Weston out to be very sophisticated, but
I think that there is a lot of language that I would use at home just between friends that I don't feel is, ah, sophisticated enough to use here.
Sometimes you change yourself to really be a Westonian, whatever that
—what it might mean."

Roland describes the injurious nature of the experience of being selected for the privileges of a Weston education. Ironically, his commentary suggests that while students of color contribute to the diversity that
constitutes Weston's explicit curriculum, there is an implicit message that
they must somehow separate themselves from what makes them "di-

verse," or different from the white norm that defines Weston. This norm implicitly defines the characteristics that make an individual "diverse" and governs how those individuals experience "being diverse." It also determines how diversity is supposed to be enacted and how diverse others are expected to be—not only academically, but also socially and in the sphere of intimacy.

Diversity and Tolerance

In the discourse of distinction, Weston is framed as a school where diversity is valued and difference is embraced, even if the value of diversity is not consistently articulated. The notion of tolerance, which students and faculty often use to describe the school's commitment to diversity, is central to how diversity is understood, in part because to tolerate—rather than embrace—difference makes it less threatening to the status quo that the discourse preserves. For diversity to be a tolerable part of the curriculum, it also needs to be enacted in particular ways. This is an important dimension of how diversity is negotiated at Weston. What counts as a tolerable and educative kind of diversity? When and how might diversity become intolerable? How are different kinds of diversity valued, negotiated, and enacted?

As discussed in Chapter 4, students look for opportunities to be, as one student put it, "surrounded by people who are like you." Students search for affinity groups, both formal, as in student clubs, and informal, as with tablemates in the dining hall. Yet these patterns fly in the face of the official institutional discourse, which seeks to distinguish Weston as a place where differences are actively embraced. This may be one reason that—as a student observed in a letter to the campus newspaper, *The Westonian*—students of color appear to have "tacitly reserved their own table throughout the years." This letter sparked a contentious debate in which students argued over the experience of cultural difference, racism, and the role of student organizations dedicated to particular racial or cultural backgrounds. The initial letter suggested that students also grouped according to their grade level, but it was the lack of "a union between the races" that the writer focused on as intolerable. "Diversity truly means the coexistence of different kinds of groups of people," this student maintained, embracing the notion of tolerance as a form of distinction but accusing students of color of "making it virtually impossible to comfortably be one community."

Yet close observations of the seating patterns in the dining hall suggested a more complicated story. While students of color often did sit together at a specific table, it was much more common to see white students sitting together.[28] But only when students of color joined for a meal was the accusation of self-segregation leveled. When students sat together for other reasons (to be with their teammates, with their dormmates, and so on) this did not draw attention or make it "virtually impossible to comfortably be one community." Nor was the fact that most tables were entirely filled with white students perceived as a threat to the "union between the races."

For instance, although Frances Sackler was ready to justify the apparent exclusivity of her posse friends as adolescent behavior (see Chapter 4), she expressed anger at the apparent exclusivity of students of color. She felt they acted against the ideal of diversity and compromised her own experience of difference. One possible explanation for this double standard is that the discourse of distinction positions students of color as being *in* Weston, for the purpose of becoming the curriculum of diversity, but never as being *of* Weston.

Just as some ideas and values are tolerated while others are not, actual practices—from dance styles to modes of speech—are more or less tolerated, depending on which groups of students engage in them. These practices constitute the repertoire and particular articulation of behaviors, forms of engagement, and ways of acting in the world that identify certain groups and distinguish them from others. Such practices are often negotiated with humor and ease—for example, debating whether gangster rap constitutes a type of artistic expression worthy of inclusion as legitimate music. Others burst into controversy and debate, like the heated exchange in *The Westonian* over whether student "cultural" groups are a form of segregation or a source of support for minority students. Still others become the subject of measured debate, as in the following interaction.

At a meeting of the Student Activities Committee, a racially mixed group of students and faculty members sit around a square table and discuss general concerns about sexually explicit movements during school dances. Although the concerns about these events include whether they are, as one student puts it, "the same scene over and over," and whether students have the time to be more creative with their dance parties, the conversation always returns to the sexual atmosphere. Some students describe the style of dancing as "sandwich dancing," "leg humping," and "rubbing their behinds." I recognize features of the popular reggae and rap styles that dominate the contemporary dance scene, typically associated with hip-hop and black popular culture. This impression is confirmed when a student of color says, "Weston is trying to make our life separate from the outside world by asking us to dance differently here than we do when we go home." He identifies the dancing as the "culture that is out there, clubs, MTV." Naïvely, I assume that the concern refers to the dance practices of students of color, but my initial impression is quickly corrected at the autumn semiformal dance.

Inside Alumni Hall, temporary curtains and flower arrangements have transformed the space, and the tables and chairs have made way for a wide-open dance floor. Top-40 songs and the latest R&B blare from the speakers, and the professional DJ adjusts the club-style lighting to fit the tunes. One large mass of teenage bodies moves around the dance floor, as the mostly pink flushed faces sweat their way through eager yet precarious physical contact. Young girls bend forward, hands on their knees, and awkwardly rub their buttocks against the enthusiastic khakis of their male classmates, who seem distracted and can barely keep to the beat. Some students are clearly more experienced than others. Two of the very few brown-skinned students at the dance (both female) make the least physical contact but demonstrate the most agile moves, prompting praise from the rest of the self-conscious crowd.

"Seven years ago there was none of this," remarks one faculty member. "It crossed the line a couple of years ago." Although her assessment could suggest that the style of dancing crossed from tolerable sexual "exploration" to intolerable "harassment," as some members of the Student Activities Committee described it, the dance practice has apparently "crossed" other lines. In an informal conversation, students of color explain that the parties organized by the Society of African and Hispanic American Students—often spontaneous, and hardly supervised at all—have become quite popular among some groups of white students, who are curious about the popular, and sexualized, dance styles associated with black culture. Though this particular style of dancing seems to have entered the school as part of the repertoire of cultural practices of some black students, it "crossed the line," moving beyond the boundaries of the informal SAHAS meetings and the bodies of black and Latino students, to the dance floor of the school semiformal, where it is enthusiastically adopted by the white majority in evening gowns.

Students of color have long been dancing like this within the bounded space of their SAHAS meeting room, drawing on the club scene, street parties, and hip-hop venues outside Weston. But for white students, the style is a novelty. They may see it not only as a form of "cultural expression," but also as an outlet for sexual exploration. The sexual nature of the dance is underscored and becomes the focus of concern when it becomes a more widespread aspect of the school culture. It crosses the border from a black "tolerable" (or perhaps invisible) *cultural* activity, to a schoolwide "intolerable" *sexual* activity, which needs to be policed and even curbed by the faculty responsible for protecting the integrity of the —mostly white—students' bodies.

There is another way students of color are positioned outside the Westonian discourse of distinction in the social sphere. The "cool scale," which a student drew during a focus group and which we saw in Chapter 4 (Figure 7), clearly illustrates this separation. The diagram places SAHAS students outside the horizontal scale entirely, suggesting that they do not participate in the social space that is formed by the opposition between the posse, the PGs, and the jocks at one end, and the Drama/GSA group on the other. Students of color are not *of* this scale, but they have ties to it; they are *in* the scale, linked with the "normal" center, perhaps as an ad hoc group.

Students in general, and students of color in particular, readily identified this distance. They talked about the fact that students who identified as black and Latino were outside the social space. In fact, any student of color who could lay claim to a niche within the otherwise white social space ran the risk of being labeled a "wannabe" or an "incog-negro." As Terrence puts it, black and Latino students "who try to fit into a certain category [within the social space]—wannabes—like, don't really associate themselves, with, you know, with, like, racial groups. Especially, like, SAHAS and things like that." This doesn't mean that students who identify as black or Latino avoid claiming further identifications as athletes or as "artsies." But they do so at the risk of not being identified as "real" students of color.

Objectified Intimacy: On Being a "Pet" at Weston

Even in the spaces of intimacy and bonding, students of color experience diversity as they themselves become (often involuntarily) the curriculum of diversity. Sunday evenings bring a mix of tempers and moods to the dorms, as the one day of rest at Weston comes to an end and students realize, "Oh, shoot, there goes the weekend." Students prepare for their classes, put finishing touches on a paper due the next day, or vacuum their rooms. Every dorm room is personalized, reflecting the adolescent culture of the living space as well as the range of styles, backgrounds, commitments, and beliefs with which students identify. Some students have lofts built into their rooms; others have colorful draperies, posters of half-naked pop stars, political slogans, or reminders of the September 11 attacks.[29] The hallways feel sterile by comparison. A sign by the custodian's office reads, "Your mother doesn't work here—clean up after yourself!" indicating a complex (and gendered) relationship between students and the working-class staff that provide them with services.

A group of girls are sitting in one of the rooms, near the door. A few of them read, while others talk about attending an antiwar rally in Boston. The mood is calm and friendly. Monica, the only brown-skinned student I've seen in the dorm so far, bursts into the room and captures everyone's attention. She looks comfortable in her white cotton pajama pants and blue T-shirt, and she talks excitedly as she reports her day's activities with a religious group. Then two other students enter the room and direct their attention to Monica's hair.

The duo, one with long red curls and the other with straight blond hair, take special interest in Monica's black hair, which is carefully pulled back. The two newcomers ask if they can style her hair. Self-consciously, Monica replies that she pulled it back because she thinks it looks terrible, but the curious duo persist. They touch Monica's hair and ask the other girls whether they also think that Monica's hair is "beautiful." Monica's head bobs from side to side to avoid their hands, while the duo interrogate her about how and why she "straightened" her hair. Monica insists that she's done nothing to it. Their determination to see Monica's hair loose seems to verge on obsession and is clearly, at the very least, intrusive. I wonder what the others in the room are thinking. None of them—including the dorm faculty member who is escorting me—seem concerned or ready to intervene. They continue reading, conversing about their homework, and sharing "boyfriend" advice.

Monica's head continues to swerve, avoiding the four pale hands, and she continues to protest that she does not want to let her hair loose. She's concerned that her hair will "stick out" and "will not look good." The girls disregard her protests, and one of them reaches for her headband. Monica tries to wrestle her way out, but the headband comes off as she escapes, and her hair fans out in every direction. She looks down, and her hands struggle to bring her hair back together, as one of the assailants exclaims, "Look how beautiful it looks straight!"

Monica screams, "I'm being pet! I'm being pet!"

The students back off, and Monica finally gives in, letting go of her hair and shaking her head. As she predicted, her hair sticks out, but the other girls insist that it looks "beautiful straight." Monica pulls it back again. Her voice is cynical and filled with frustration, "I feel like I'm in an '80s movie!"[30]

Monica's hair becomes part of the curriculum of diversity that white students assume they should explore. Touching her hair is tonight's lesson, yet Monica resists becoming the object of their learning. She cannot experience this moment as bonding or intimacy because she is positioned as the exotic other, an object being used to provide a lesson about diversity. Perhaps the two white students are just being playful or are curious to learn something from touching her hair.

Monica's predicament echoes the words of Victor Martínez, a four-year senior from New York City who identifies as Hispanic. Victor is dedicated to his leadership role in SAHAS and the Salsa Club. He comments on the assumptions he thinks white students make about him as a minority:

> Um, that, you know, I was fast because I was a minority. Um, that I could dance because I was a minority. . . . Uh, my hair was special because I was a minority. Because I always had a, you know, a straight hair line or something, you know, that—they found that really weird. And up till now they always ask me, you know, "How do you keep your hairline so straight?" [*laughter*] Um, I find that really funny all the time. And, you know, they like touching my hair because it's different than theirs. You know, it's sometimes I feel like, if I'm, like, some sort of lab monkey.

Rather than being part of an environment in which *all* benefit from diversity, students of color *are* the diversity. Like lab monkeys (as Victor puts it), students of color are subjected to the scrutiny of the white norm that positions them as objects to learn from. They enrich the curriculum of the school simply by being there, giving white students opportunities to learn about people different from them—and about their hair.

CLASS: THE "HIDDEN INJURIES" OF THE MERITOCRACY

In the meritocracy, higher-class status is based on an individual's "innate" or "inborn" abilities, to use the words of Steve Hart (Chapter 3). According to Michael Young, the upper class in a meritocracy consists of individuals deemed intellectually superior by virtue of their demonstrated talents or their genetics.[31] Thus, to be a Westonian, an identification related to being smart and working hard, means to belong to an elite class, if not an upper class. In the United States, belonging to an elite class is no neutral matter, because the country was founded on anti-elitist principles. Alexis de Tocqueville wrote that the "emigrants" who founded this country had "no notion of superiority one over the other. . . . The soil of America was opposed to a territorial aristocracy."[32] Throughout the nation's history, U.S. citizens have been ambivalent about intellectualism and about the role of the educated elites in the formation of the class system.[33] This ambivalence shaped the emergence of the academies, as we saw in Chapter 1, and it continues to play a role in how students at an elite boarding school, where being intelligent is socially valued, experience their own identification as smart.

The sense that to be smart implies belonging to an elite status group means that students try to avoid being perceived as elitist. Sandi Li describes herself as a Midwesterner, and although she says she is Asian American, she adds in her self-description that she tends "not to associate myself with that very often." She comments on how she saw herself before she came to Weston: "I think I was really snobby because I thought I was smart"—a remark that suggests a connection between being smart and having (class) status. At Weston she rejects the label: "Everyone at home thinks that I'm like, really, really smart. And I'm like, 'I don't get very good grades at Weston.'"[34] Getting mediocre grades at Weston is paradoxically both a claim to smartness (I'm a Westonian) and a rejection of smartness (I don't get good grades). Indeed, at home, Sandi will always be considered smart, regardless of her grades, simply because she attends an elite boarding school. To be smart, then, is classed in the sense that it implies a higher status, particularly when it entitles students to certain privileges, like attending an elite boarding school. As Sandra López puts it, her family and neighbors explain her absence from home by saying, "She's smart—she goes away to school."[35]

This privilege that the meritocracy affords students who are smart and hardworking comes at the risk of experiencing separation from home, both physically and emotionally.[36] Yet this rupture doesn't affect every student equally. For students like Frances Sackler, Steve Hart, Ken Ellerly, and Frank Maxwell, whose attendance at an elite boarding school was almost assumed from birth, movement between home and school is seamless and requires few personal adjustments. For students like Roland Carter, Sandra López, Sandi Li, and Matthew Briggs, separation from home often requires a great deal of psychic energy. "Sometimes you change yourself to really be a Westonian," said Roland Carter when he was making a distinction between the "sophisticated" language of Weston and the way he speaks with friends at home.[37] "As much as you try to deny it," Alex Crosby has observed, coming to identify Weston as "home" means accepting a necessary distance.[38] These "injuries" of upward mobility through intellectual merit are not too far from or unrelated to those experienced by upwardly mobile blue-collar workers.[39] Like being upwardly mobile, being smart and becoming an elite boarding school student often means the loss of an identification with home.[40]

To claim an identification as smart, then, is to class oneself, to be a "snob," to be better than others, by virtue of what students understand as an inherent characteristic and not the result of hard work. Yet as we saw in Chapter 3, to claim an identification as a hard worker is to suggest that one has earned the right to be a snob and that one is entitled to upward mobility through contest rather than sponsorship.[41] Still, such identifications can also be mixed with great ambivalence about the claims of distinction, even when students come from elite backgrounds.

Elite Ambivalence: To Bond, or Not To Bond

Michael Jonas is one of those students who, as Alex suggests, do not like to identify as a Westonian. Michael is a two-year senior from a southern city. Although his dad is a well-known lawyer and philanthropist in his hometown, his family doesn't quite have enough income to cover the Weston tuition, and thus he receives a partial scholarship. I ask him whether he would ever call himself a Westonian. "That's an interesting question," he says, "because in some ways I really hate that, like,"—he pauses to say the word slowly, extending the "oh" and infusing his tone with a degree of contempt—"Wes-*tohh*-nian."

Michael continues, "There's just something like, really—maybe it's just the sound of the words. Maybe it's just the image that comes to my head of a—the people. Oh, probably the speakers, the speakers who use it, like, Wes-*tohh*-nians." Again he utters the word in a mocking tone, deepening his voice and extending the syllables. "It just like, gives you that, that, that feeling, that icky feeling." I look at him puzzled, waiting for more, and he recalls an earlier part of our conversation, when he described the popular kids that eat in Alumni Hall and hang out on the valley side of campus. "Well, like, the same feeling that I got when I saw the Wall Streeters, future Wall Streeters of America, out playing hacky-sack, and all the trophy wives sitting, tanning their, their bare arms. That's the way I feel when I hear the word 'Westonian.'"

For Michael, there is a direct connection between what it means to be Westonian and the image of wealth, beauty, and power that is stereotypical of prep schools and which he associates with the valley side. I ask him whether that's the image he associates with the term, and he offers a slightly more nuanced interpretation:

> Yeah, in a way. I mean, I don't, it's not, I think it's much less so than it used to be—the classical boarding school concept, where everyone's rich. But it still, it exists. Um, and especially you see, like, these people, like, some of the people who came from [my southern state], from my old hometown, they're kind of full of it. They're like, "Oh, I go to Weston." I'm like, "Shut up!" They wear little Weston tee–I wear Weston T-shirts just 'cause they're cool T-shirts. People probably think I'm flaunting it, but I get really uncomfortable when people ask me where I go to high school.

The discomfort of claiming a Westonian identification at home and his annoyance at others who bluntly claim it suggest the emotional toll that becoming a Westonian has taken on Michael. He acknowledges that he, too, wears Weston T-shirts, but claims this is only "'cause they're cool T-shirts." He acknowledges, though, that he does identify with the term "Westonian" and is likely to use it, pointing to his knowledge of Greek and ancient Greek culture as a justification.[42] "But now I'm just like, 'Well, I'll just be honest and tell them' [that he goes to Weston], because being honest isn't being prideful. So, but, um, it's like the Greeks. The Greeks were honest. If, if, if the guy was the best boxer, then he would say, 'I'm the best boxer.'" Ultimately, Michael is willing to claim the distinction of being a Westonian because—according to the Greeks—it doesn't mean he is prideful; it's simply the "honest" truth. In the end, he admits, "I don't know. I guess I'll probably . . ." He pauses for several seconds and begins to say the word quietly to himself, as if trying it out. "I am a Westonian," he whispers. And tries it again, a bit louder: "I was a Westonian." And again: "I was a student at Weston." He finally concludes, "I'll use the—I'll use the word. . . . I'll use it. I mean, I'll say, I would say 'Weston'—no, I'll probably [say that I] went to Weston," suggesting that this is "probably the least Westonian."

Michael returns to the image of self-satisfied graduates and mimics what he imagines a future alum might sound like: "'Westonian'—that's kind of a term you use among the boys. 'Remember Westonian days?' [*jokingly*] You know? But that's—it kind of implies intimacy, kind of an understanding, like a tacit [*sigh*] 'It was great to be a Westonian, wasn't it?' And then a smug smile. I don't know." Michael's ambivalence about being one of "the boys" (which suggests how distinction is gendered), and his comment that it "implies intimacy," point to the theme of bonding—the "smug smile" implying the tacit bond of all Westonians.

Steve Hart likewise says he is not sure that he would call himself a Westonian. Yet his explanation for his ambivalence is distinct from Michael's and denotes a different experience of class. Whereas Michael is working against the injury that claiming a Westonian identification can inflict, Steve is more concerned with being recognized as deserving and highlights his status as one based on contest rather than sponsorship. Indeed, Steve doesn't ever want to feel sponsored by his own elite status, but wants always to prove that he deserves what he has, even if winning that contest depends on his class status. Steve remarks, in a mocking tone, that he "would never say, 'I'm a Westonian.'" I laugh with him, and challenge him to explain what he means. "Like, when I'm an alum, I'm gonna come back [to Weston], you know, to my tenth reunion. I'm gonna come back to my twenty-fifth reunion. Uh, I don't think I'm gonna come back here every year, um, but I'm definitely gonna try and stay in touch with all the people who I met here. It definitely gives me true common ground with other people that went to Weston. . . . And that's great, to meet people who are like you, and that's cool."

Steve describes the implied intimacy that Michael referred to and that is part of bonding. He's proud of this experience and wants to honor it by staying in touch with his fellow Westonians. Yet he describes negative emotions as well. "I guess I'm ashamed of having gone to Weston, in some way, because it means that I'm privileged, or whatever. Um, and I sort of wish that I could say I did it all by myself. Uh, I sort of feel like I haven't accomplished anything." Steve is worried that his class privilege will automatically grant him the (undeserved) respect of others.

> I don't wanna be able to walk up to people and say, like, "I went to Weston," to a person, and have them be like, "Okay," you know, "We respect you." I don't want that to be the case. Like, I would like it, when I walk into a room, and people are like, "Oh, here's the new kid—he's dumb," and then you just

take them. Because that's, like, that's what's important, is like, winning people's respect in that way. And that's much more worth anything than having a name that gives people a false respect.

On the surface, it seems that Steve is simply stating that he doesn't want the Weston reputation to follow him, and that he hopes to be treated like any other "dumb kid" wherever he goes. Yet his desire to conceal his status as a Westonian points to his need to "disguise [his] eliteness."[43] Steve wants to ignore the fact that his own class privilege has enabled him to obtain the kind of elite education that will prepare him to walk into a classroom at any Ivy League university and impress his peers. To acknowledge such privilege might imply that he is not deserving of his niche in the meritocracy. In fact, Steve is wary of the negative consequences his identification as Westonian might have when he begins his first year of college at his father's Ivy League alma mater, where he believes he will be "hated" for having gone to Weston: "I mean, I don't think it's gonna be, like—I imagine that there are gonna be people at [the Ivy League school], like, who are just gonna wanna beat the shit out of me because I went to Weston, do you know what I mean? Like, I can totally see that. Uh, as weird as that may sound, I don't know, but I—I want to win their respect."

By comparison, Steve feels no such ambivalence when describing his home environment, where he is surrounded by other elite boarding school students and by Weston alumni in his immediate circle of family and friends. While most students say they feel distanced from home, students from families that have historically attended elite boarding schools and whose entire education has been a carefully laid-out path toward Weston don't describe a stark tension between home and school.[44] Frances Sackler, for instance, describes spending vacations at her family's summer home surrounded by students from other elite boarding schools. She explains that her circle of friends at home is not much different from the one at school, since "a lot of my best friends outside of school are my summer friends, who I just don't get to see during school. . . . Most of my summer friends also go to boarding school."

Confronting Class in the Social Space

The New England spring arrives in full force by the last days of April. Flip-flops, khaki shorts, and miniskirts are everywhere on the student body, supplanting heavy winter clothes, and skin becomes ubiquitous. Bare-chested adolescent boys sprint after frisbees flying over the grass in front of the library and Weston Hall. Girls in bikinis lie on beach towels next to radios turned up full blast. Eighties rock 'n' roll has made a comeback, and I find myself mumbling lyrics I remember from my own high school days. I watch the scene, giddily waiting for an invitation to run after the smooth-flying frisbee.

Though playing with frisbees in the open spaces adjacent to the dining halls is an everyday ritual once spring arrives, not all frisbee spaces are created equal. Behind Wyndham Hall, students stand in a circle fully clothed and toss the disk lightly to each other over the heads of others who are reading or chatting. Next to Alumni Hall, the disk flies in a fury, and muscular torsos gleam with sweat as the boys leap into the air. On the edges of the lawn, girls in bikinis sun themselves and listen to music. Michael Jonas calls the crowd on the valley side the "future Wall Streeters of America and their trophy wives," once again marking the space not only with a specific sexuality, but also with economic wealth.[45]

Other scholars who have studied social groups in high school contexts argue that the organization of the social space corresponds to class relations.[46] Their analyses suggest a straightforward correlation between wealth, status, and place. At Weston, this view proves too simplistic. While it is true that the popular kids on the valley side are associated with economic wealth and the "weird" kids on the hills side are associated with cultural production, wealth characterizes both sides of the campus. While hanging out on the lawns of the hills, I heard conversations about cigar collections, secret poker games involving large sums of money, and the expensive fashion tastes of the "freaks" and theater kids. Yet the students themselves make distinctions about wealth, saying that it's crucial to determining which side of the campus a student identifies with, and that being on the valley means confronting wealth and upper-class conspicuous consumption head-on.

Krista Griffin, the day student whose father works in the administration of the dining services, describes developing friendships with the valley girls in the fresh posse. "I remember, like, clothes were a big deal. Like, uh, all the, um, you know, like, a lot of the boarder girls who, like, that I was friends with from New York would go shopping at, like, you know, they'd have, like, Versace clothes, and they'd have like new th—, you know, boutique, like, awesome clothes." She describes going shopping with two of her new friends and being stunned at the way they made purchases.

Like, my, my non-Weston friends, um, like, we'd go shopping, and we'd look at the price tags before we bought something, or before deciding whether we would buy something. And I remember going to [the city], or something, with a couple of my friends from Weston. We went with one of their moms. And it was, like, I noticed that they didn't even look at the price tag. Like, they just piled things in their carriage and bought them—like, no problem! It was really, I mean, I don't think that's, like, a Weston thing, but I think a lot of very privileged kids come here, and they don't even realize the privileges they have. Especially, like, monetary privileges, you know?

Krista notes the particular class affiliation of the girls in the posse whom she befriends, and she observes the girls' patterns of consumption.[47] Her story points to the way the experience of femininity intersects with class and material resources.[48] For girls, inhabiting the social space of the valley also means that they have to downplay their academic interests and identifications as smart, or risk being dismissed as too smart and thus not feminine enough to become the trophy wives of the "future Wall Streeters" who inhabit this space. In this sense, when such girls are perceived as smart, they give up a crucial dimension of their class status.

GENDER: BEING PRETTY, BEING SMART

The experience of becoming the curriculum, or being asked to represent the "point of view on things" of an entire group, is not new or unusual at Weston. When the first group of female students arrived at Weston in the early 1970s, many experienced what one alumna describes as "usually unintentional persecutions": "The young woman at the seminar table would feel both gratitude that her presence had been acknowledged and anger or embarrassment that attention had been drawn to her solely because of her sex."[49] Gender dynamics appear to have changed since the 1970s, yet sexism, and relationships with boys, are still powerful determinants of how girls come to identify as Westonians. One way to explore these dynamics is to consider how girls and boys talk about their intimate relationships with each other.[50] Here we'll take a different and perhaps less obvious angle. We'll look at the gender assumptions that permeate the way students talk about being Westonian, and will explore how gender dynamics are manifested in other spheres of their experience.

For instance, there is a hidden gender dimension to the way students understand and navigate the space of the school. This becomes evident when the hierarchies of work (discussed in Chapter 3) and the social hierarchies (Chapter 4) are considered in relation to each other. Whenever students used specific dorms to characterize one side of the campus or the other, they always used boys' dorms as referents. When talking about the hills as being studious and smart, they referred to East Street Dorm; when they talked about the valley as being athletic and "jockyish," they referred to Salinger or Wendell. On the other hand, students used girls' dorms on the valley side as examples of popularity and attractiveness, while they described girls' dorms on the hills side as being "weird" or "unattractive." This suggests that being smart and being athletic are gendered as primarily male qualities, which positions girls almost by definition as less smart and less athletic than boys.[51]

The discourse of distinction not only implicitly sets up boys as different, but allows them a wider range of opportunities for enacting distinction. For instance, while boys are able to be smart as well as popular and athletic, girls explicitly say they have to make choices between being popular and being smart. To be a "popular" or a "hot" girl is to avoid being too smart. If a girl is smart, then she must sacrifice other markers of feminine status. Indeed, girls often said that in order to find a niche at Weston, they had to choose between being pretty and being smart.

Being Smart and (Too) Aggressive

Julie Lasky is a four-year senior who has a lot to say about the social life at Weston. She describes herself as "an independent thinker who thrives on diversity, an opinionated yet contemplative member of the community. Explorative, compassionate, outspoken." During the interview, we talk about her outspokenness and her active participation in classroom discussions. She says that students, especially guys, often feel uncomfortable when girls have a strong voice in class. I ask her to elaborate.

> Well, I think—I think you can be either an attractive female here, or an intellectual and an aggressive female here. And I know of one girl who is both, but she really wasn't that intellectual. She was just very forthright, and she was a real ex-

ception to very many rules. But she's also, like, bipolar, and [*pause*], like, she was, she was like an Amazon. She was like, really tall, and good at tennis, and, uh, but she was cool, she was a good friend of mine, we're still in touch, and she goes to [college] now, and she's awesome, she's a cool girl. . . . She was one of a very, very select group of people, women, who I think were able to speak out, be themselves.

Julie also offers several examples of female teachers—"a very select group of women"—whom she admires because they are outspoken, say what they think without apologies, and command respect when they speak on the assembly stage. She says female students tend to avoid being aggressive in the classroom, "because that's reserved for men." Yet Julie insists on being outspoken in class, and she feels that she is "being pressured to be one or the other."

I've had specific relationships [with boys] crumble as a consequence of the fact that they, in the end, couldn't deal with the fact that, that I was gonna be aggressive about my opinions, that I was going to get better grades than them in classes, and that, you know, that I was gonna be a female who was, who was maybe attractive to them. And, and the, the point of the matter is that I'm probably more aggressive than I am attractive. And that—that's when I felt the division. And, uh, and that's when it, you know—parts of your social life suffer.

Julie establishes that because she has chosen to be assertive and outspoken in class, her social life has suffered, and that she feels excluded from certain groups on campus because she is "more aggressive than I am attractive." She says "there's a line being drawn" between her female friends, who fit a particular "archetype" of beauty, and herself, an "aggressive" girl: "And maybe I'm among a very select group, and, and it could be just all in my head, but, um, you know, I, I've been basically told by people, um, you know, that, that it's [*pause*], that for whatever reason, it's, it's an unattractive quality."

Ken Ellerly is a handsome guy, and a key informant on the posses from a guy's perspective. He confirms Julie's sense that being smart and aggressive is seen as unattractive by wealthy, athletic, handsome boys like him. Ken talks about the girls from his West Coast hometown with some nostalgia, saying they are easygoing and laid back. Here, Ken has taken to dating girls from the local public high school. He says that in comparison, Weston girls are "bitchier and less nice." He says he is not sure why, but he is "absolutely certain that they are bitchier, harder girls to get along with." Although he keeps repeating that he doesn't know why that is, he offers some telling explanations.

> I don't necessarily know why that is. But maybe it's—a lot of it has to [do] with, I think, like, the fact that this is such a competitive place, and it's such, like, a strong school. . . . A lot of it has to do with the fact that we're, like, competitive guys, right? Who, who might, like, be borderline cocky-slash-arrogant. In a place like Weston, aren't the—I mean, it's almost rewarded. I mean, that, that works. That, like, formula can work at a place like Weston.

Ken acknowledges that there are girls who are assertive in class discussions, but, like Julie, he agrees that "in girls, that's not rewarded." He notes that this contradicts the discourse of Weston as an egalitarian place: "Here is definitely a place where, like, you know, males and females can [be] considered equal, and that's really important. . . . This school has—holds that in high regard. Like, it's something that it wants —you know, like, [girls and boys] are equal. But I still think that it's like the old school. Like, certain qualities are rewarded more in boys than in girls."

Ken offers a particular example of a female student whom he describes as "unbelievably overbearing in class," and he notes that she was "ripped on" by other students for this. But his compassion is short-lived, and he begins to describe her as a seminar hijacker—someone who tries to control classroom discussion or who is too aggressive during debates.

> She's brutal. . . . She's *the* seminar hijacker. *Of* the hijackers. . . . I mean, that quality wasn't rewarded. If I were like that in a class, if, I mean, if I were like that in class, that wouldn't be rewarded either, 'cause she takes it to an extreme, like, but I can see how a guy who's more aggressive in class, might be re—Like, well, well, they use that, that, that adjective "aggressive," but then in a positive way. But if a girl's—if a girl does it, they might describe it as, like, "intimidating."

As I listen to Ken, I wonder whether he realizes that in his earlier description of Weston girls as "bitches" he was also devaluing girls who were not afraid to speak their mind. So I ask directly whether he believes this, and he replies: "I think it's a little—I mean, that's a little bit of the class here. But I mean generally the girls here are more aggressive. Whereas maybe, like, where I'm from, [my hometown], those girls fit in a more traditional female role. Like, less outspoken maybe. More like cute, funny—that kind of thing."

Being Pretty and Playing Dumb

It's the first day of June, and my time at Weston is coming to an end. Today I attended several rituals, including an awards ceremony in which it seemed as if nearly every graduating senior received some institutional recognition. In the afternoon I observed a rehearsal for the graduation ceremony; not only will the ceremony be scripted, but there was also a script for the rehearsal itself.

This evening I've joined a group of girls who have gathered in the apartment of their faculty advisor to celebrate the birthdays of the month. We joke while munching on the rich chocolate cake, and we play word games (Westonians are fond of word games, which enable them to show off and improve their "vocab"). I'm so exhausted that all I can do is scribble a list of single words in my fieldnotes.

More students join in, and Stephanie sits next to me. She asks if she can see what I'm writing. I look through the pages to see if there's something I can share, hoping she'll get distracted and forget about the request. She does, but others begin to ask about my work. Though I usually have standard responses to the questions they're asking, tonight I feel evasive, and explain that I don't yet know what I'll write about or what the main thesis of my research will be. "Would you send your kids to Weston?" Patricia finally asks, frustrating all my attempts at evasion.

I've posed the same question to many students during interviews, and often they've asked me as well. I was always ready to answer, "I don't know yet, but I'm thinking about it." This time, as I envision my daughter, almost four years old, attending Weston in the future, I can't muster a simple, straightforward, uncommitted answer. "I don't think I would send my daughter as a boarding student," I say. In that room full of female boarding students, my murmured declaration falls like a thump, and suddenly the room is quieter. All eyes and ears are on me. "Why?" asks Chloe. "Because you love her?" The weight of her question makes my sense of vulnerability feel minuscule. How can I possibly suggest that her parents, or the parents of any of the girls in the room, don't love their children? I am obliged to come clean.

I decide to risk opening Pandora's box and share my thoughts with the group. After two years of observing, interviewing, and thinking about Weston, I've come to the conclusion that I wouldn't want my daughter to deal with the pressures of being a girl in such an enclosed environment. The girls respond to my honesty by taking up—and challenging—the idea that Weston is sexist. They discuss it with great fervor, talking about everything from bras and feminism to trophy wives and the social cost of being smart. Most of their initial responses to my views on the treatment of girls at Weston are incredulous. They focus on my suggestion that sexism is pervasive and accepted at Weston, and begin to argue against it.

Patricia begins by claiming that Weston isn't sexist; boys simply have more "potential" to be smart than girls. When she thinks of students she considers "very smart," they're always boys—Damien Ting and John Virgil, for example. This is proof, Patricia says, that boys are inherently smarter. Some of the other girls are quick to counter Patricia's claims, while others agree with her. Melanie thinks the reason more boys are known to be smarter is that they are more outspoken and aggressive in class and are thus more noticeable. Several students offer examples of girls who they think are very smart but who go unacknowledged or unrecognized by others as smart. After some back and forth, Patricia seems persuaded that guys are more outspoken, more outgoing, and "more visible" than girls.

Some of the students begin to describe girls as more emotional (or "emo," as Linda puts it). They suggest that girls are more open to being emotional and expressive than guys, and that since the school values more "intellectual," unemotional contributions to debate, boys are seen as smarter. "Why are all geniuses like Einstein male?" asks Patricia, and the conversation turns to biology. Even though they see the way boys are positioned as smarter, and recognized as such, they lean toward explaining the inequity as a matter of nature rather than sexism.

Chloe protests this conclusion, and expresses dismay at being "dismissed by the boys" in class simply because she's a girl.[52] Chloe says that boys often dismiss female authors like Virginia Wolf as "just some feminist" and describe books like *To the Lighthouse* as a "feminist angry woman rampage." They smirk whenever the topic of feminism comes up in class, and are dismissive and contemptuous whenever the issue of sexism comes up. The other girls say they've had the same experience. Linda admits that she dreads it every time feminism comes up in class, because she doesn't want to have to put up with the boys and their comments. They agree that to be identified as a feminist is to risk not only being wholly dismissed in the classroom, but being stigmatized socially as well.[53]

I ask the students whether there are differences between the ways girls and boys are expected to look attractive. All of them agree that girls are expected to "look good" and get "made up" to go to class, while it is fine for boys to go in sweats and shirts. I ask them why they feel such pressure to "look good" for class, and they explain the importance of getting attention from the boys, whom they believe are the ultimate judges of who is considered "hot" and determine the "pool of pretty girls." Olga explains that boys are often intimidated by girls who participate in class, and that therefore girls will often "play dumb" in order to make sure the guys don't feel insecure. Some of the other students agree, adding that they often "play dumb" in order to get closer to guys they like, because they believe guys are not attracted to girls who come across as articulate or outspoken. As I listen to them talk about whether they do or do not want to be thought of as smart, I wonder what the girls want, and why they would downplay their own intelligence to have a relationship. Are they looking for acceptance? Legitimacy? Status? Future financial stability? What do they think they're seeking, and how do they think they'll obtain it by "getting with the boys"?[54]

Patricia says that girls are naturally attracted to smart boys, while boys are naturally attracted to pretty girls. She describes talking with her female friends about the fact that they're at Weston in order to become "trophy wives," and how they see all the hard work of being at Weston as a way to enter a circle of future successful men and "marry a rich husband." Julie adds that girls come to Weston so that they can "prepare to be chosen" by the boys of the Westonian elite. I ask them whether this is the reason so many girls like to lie out in the sun in their bikinis and wear miniskirts once the weather warms up. Alex, the only black female in the room, explains that only girls with the "right bodies" wear bikinis, and asks whether there's an item of clothing that's considered "scandalous" for the boys to wear. No one can come up with an example—or an explanation for the fact that they can't come up with one. Julie jumps in again, suggesting that Weston girls are preparing themselves to be pursued by the "right guy."

Yielding to the urge to share my thoughts about gender with these students opened up an intense debate about sexism at Weston that, in the end, I was lucky to witness. The two-hour conversation profoundly enhanced my understanding of the powerful way gender shapes the process through which these girls come to identify themselves as Westonians. That conversation, of course, reflected the individual experiences of the girls in the room. Yet it echoed many of the experiences other girls shared with me during interviews. It confirmed what I saw in classrooms and dining halls, where the social and academic spheres intersect, and where everyday interactions shape the way girls experience becoming Westonians.

Femininity and Bonding Rituals

When talking about life in the dorms and asking the girls for stories about their memorable experiences, the most common ritual I learned about was "porno night." Older girls lure younger girls into a room, where they're locked in for several hours while a series of pornographic videos play on a TV screen. This and other rituals underscore for girls that there are particular ways of being a girl that are premised on their relationships with boys. The annual prom dress fashion show, for instance, heralds the overwhelming display of traditional gender roles and values that constitutes the senior prom.[55]

Another ritual, the "V-Tree," likewise points to the important role traditional heterosexuality plays in the way girls construct identifications as Westonians. During a focus group, Sandi Li offers to describe the ritual, first reminding everyone present that the conversation is confidential. The name of Sandi's dormitory, Gould, is carved on the threshold of the building as "GOVLD." The "V" in the center of the word is the sign that the girls use to claim an identification with the space, by placing their fingers over their heart and making a "V" with their middle and ring fingers.[56] Every year, the names of entering first-year girls are added on individual leaves to the cardboard V-Tree in the basement of the building, and as the girls lose their virginity, the leaves "fall" from the tree.

There is an important contrast between rituals like the V-Tree and the prom fashion show, and the rituals that boys engage in within the gender-segregated dorm space. Boys' rituals involved enactments of masculine bravado, such as hot-dog-eating competitions and midnight dodge ball, or of homosocial intimacy, such as Halloween drag parties and photo shoots of students sitting in Santa Claus's lap.[57] While these boys' rituals are ultimately about self-exposure, bonding, and building loyalties within the group—a process that goes back to the very founding of these schools as all-boys schools[58]—girls' rituals are about constructing a female sexuality that is defined by their role vis-à-vis the boys. The girls construct identifications as female Westonians that *depend* on their relationships with Weston boys, who are, presumably, the true Westonians. Boys (white boys in particular) construct Westonian identifications that depend only on their relationships with one another, and that acknowledge the girls only as decorations. In fact, when boys described rituals that referenced girls, the rituals involved the boys' sexual exploits or the ranking of girls based on their looks. For instance, in one dorm the boys would rank each girl on the basis of the number of beers they would have to drink before they would be willing to have sex with her—zero being the top ranking.[59]

Noting how ubiquitous miniskirts are at Weston in the spring, Annie Kasper expresses her frustration:

> Um, [*long pause*] I think a lot of girls—I think it's just in [*longer pause*] general society—I think that's what girls are told to look like and told that that's attractive, and it's a way that they're gonna *get* somewhere. . . . It's about sex, it's about, um, appealing to guys, and, um. One, that's not the point of this school, um, and it's also just not tasteful, I guess. And it's also *degrading!* I think there are definitely girls at this school who think of themselves as sex objects, um, and it's, it's really hard to look at, um. And I think they play down how smart they are, um, like, those particular people, because they don't want to be intimidating, um, to guys.

For Annie, the problem isn't that girls who "think of themselves as sex objects" are not smart, but rather that they "play down" how smart they are.

Krista Griffin remembers how important it was for her and the other girls in the posse to look good:

> What girls would do is they would get all dressed up and go to the [snack bar] and just sit there and, like, look pretty. . . . It was really weird. And, you know, you would, like, call boys, or you'd, like, hang out, like, at the football games, 'cause all the boys are at the football games. And, um, I remember, like,

when I would hang out with my friends [at the local public high school], we'd do what we always used to do. We'd have, like, you know, sleepover parties and go out for pizza, like, just us. And it was never—it was never, like, this huge, uh, focus on appearance. That was—that I noticed when I came here.

Krista also speaks of girls' difficulties in the academic sphere, saying that it's "harder for girls here than it is for boys." She feels that the older teachers, most of them men, "still think boys are smarter, . . . and still think boys are more successful." She believes that these teachers will often encourage the boys to apply to Ivy League schools, and she seems to mock them as she changes her tone to imitate how she thinks they sound: "I went to Princeton, my father went to Princeton, you seem like a nice young man to go to Princeton." Frustrated by her perception of male teachers, she concludes, "And people don't really say that to the girls."

Gendered Niches

In the domain of work, boys overwhelmingly dominate the niches at the top of the hierarchy. This is most clearly seen in sports. The athletic activities that receive the most attention are always the male sports teams. In the case of football, which is perhaps the most well-attended sport, there simply is no girls' team. Only one sport, field hockey, is solely for girls, and the spectators at such games are usually few and far between, mostly limited to the players' families and close friends. While there are girls' teams in ice hockey and basketball, attendance at girls' games is markedly lower than at boys' games. Furthermore, there are stark differences between the facilities available for boys and girls, particularly in ice hockey. According to the students, the second year I was at Weston was the first time the girls' hockey team was allowed to play in the main ice rink—and only if the boys were not playing.[60]

Other hierarchies are also gendered—for example, the fact that most of the students who excel in Latin and Greek are not only white, but also boys. Girls who excel in this area are considered unattractive by the boys and are most often associated with the "weird" crowd on the hills side of campus. Extracurricular activities are also gendered, and leadership roles are almost exclusively reserved for boys. The president of the Student Council, perhaps the most prestigious of leadership positions, has historically been a male student, while girls are often selected as secretaries. Even when the representation of girls and boys in a given organization is mixed, some students describe the organization with gendered language. Consider the way Sandi Li, for instance, describes her perception of the editorial board of the student newspaper: "I don't know what the atmosphere with the *Westonian* is now, but in the past it was, like, a boys' club, sort of. And, like, you see the people at the top, and they are all so, like, self-confident and, like, dignified, like, they go into the meetings with, like, their dress coat and, like, tie, and sit at the head of the table, and they're like, 'We are so cool.' . . . I like that a lot, though, and I think I tried to emulate that a li—, a little too much."

Alex Crosby is largely quiet during the conversation about girls in the classroom. She finally jumps in to say that things aren't all that different in the theater, a space she claims as her niche. Alex has assumed important leadership roles in the theater and in various stage productions, but she feels that Neil Perry, who also works in the theater but assumes far less responsibility, is recognized around campus as the "king of theater." During our interview, Alex suggested that in the theater she has a double burden of proving her worth as a leader: she's not only a girl, but also black.

Greta Dunst likewise experiences the theater space as sexist: "I've always been given the roles, like, the sex girl patrol member." I ask her to elaborate, and she describes the limited choice of roles she's been given in student productions. She says that student-produced plays always have to do with sex (usually heterosexual sex). Kristen and Alex have tried to challenge the Actors' Club students, who produce theater shows, to do different things, but have had little success.

> A-Club review shows have to—something to do with sex, or else people don't care. And mostly that means, like, girls not wearing very much clothes, and, like, making some funny— you know, like, acting all voluptuous and stuff. And it's just— it's really tiring. And I know Alex and I are just, like, "Can we not have an A-Club show that involves—that, like, that *can't* be the only thing that's funny on this campus." Like, that's what brings people to see a lot of the shows!

Thus, the discourse of distinction positions boys and girls hierarchically, allowing females less space for finding their niche (or their roles in the social and academic theater), constricting their ability to find their niche by forcing them to make either/or choices. Some girls circumvent this hierarchy, of course, and it may be that in the end it's the girls who choose to "be smart" and ignore the pressures to "be pretty" who end up achieving success in their particular academic niche. Girls who make such choices appear to do it fully conscious of the fact that either they're excluded from the popularity game because they don't "look" the part, or they're relinquishing the comforts of becoming decorations for the true (white male) Westonians.[61]

By shaping the space in which Westonians must find a niche, the discourse of distinction limits the range of possibilities that students have and unequally distributes their opportunities to distinguish themselves. This point can be extended to the entire education system. It indicates how a study of elite schooling can help us understand processes of identification in other schools, even those at the opposite end of the educational spectrum.

ON THE UNEQUAL DISTRIBUTION OF DISTINCTION

Scott Jaffee describes himself as a "rich, white, good-looking, Anglo-Saxon, male," and says he's "really glad" that he is not black: "Because black people have to live with this whole history of, you know, being, being afraid of being lynched, you know, being afraid of having their church burnt down, you know, being [in] slavery. . . . Even if, you know, the kids at this school never experience that first-hand, they still experience the racism, and sort of, of the legacy of that."

While Scott has at least some insight into what it might mean to be black, he is far less clear about what it means to identify as white. He describes being white as having "anti-meaning."

> I've never felt separate from anything. That's why, I mean, it has anti-meaning. You haven't had any struggle, I mean, I mean frankly, I, . . . I'm a rich, white, good-looking, uh, you know, Anglo-Saxon, white, you know, male, and that's sort of the majority of everything, you know. So it's sort of, it's like, it's almost like, I have, I, I'm less deserving because I'm so— because I've never had any struggle. That's—and that's sort of what I mean by anti-meaning, if that makes sense.

The ambivalence and contradictions in Scott's words defy a simple interpretation. One way to make sense of his explanation is to ask: What is it that Scott feels he is "less deserving" of? I would propose that the answer is privilege—not just the privilege of attending a school like Weston, but the privilege of being rich, white, male, and of course good-looking. These privileges are, as we've seen, interconnected. The reason being a rich white male at Weston has "anti-meaning" is that, in fact, they mean the same thing: being a Westonian means, by default, to be rich, white, and male, and anything else would imply some sort of "struggle." His suggestion that lacking such a struggle makes him "less deserving" implies that he's ambivalent about his privilege and perhaps beginning to understand how it is defined in relation to the struggles of others—nonwhite, nonmale, nonrich, and, I would add, non-Westonian.[62]

Westonians, like other students at elite boarding schools, have the distinct privilege of receiving an education that is abundantly resourced, while the majority of students in the United States attend underfunded and overburdened schools. This is no accident, but an integral part of a system that is designed to reproduce inequalities and class distinctions. These inequalities are mirrored in elite boarding schools like Weston. Because exclusion is a premise of distinction, the internal hierarchies at such schools are likewise no accident. The very discourse of distinction in which elite identifications are rooted is in turn rooted in broader processes of social exclusion, and the discourse itself is therefore unequally distributed. This *unequal distribution of distinction* underscores and perhaps strengthens the status hierarchies in the broader society, pointing to at least one way in which elite boarding schools are implicated in the perpetuation of social inequality. They reinscribe the social dynamics of class, race, and gender oppression in the production of elite status groups.

Yet despite this unequal distribution of distinction, all students leave Weston with the sense that they are Westonian, even as this means something different to each of them. Indeed, as I hope I have shown, the fact that different Westonians occupy distinct positions in the Westonian space is central to the way an elite boarding school produces students who identify as members of an elite status group, as well as to the way all of them manage to avoid recognizing the privileges associated with their status as an elite. To be a Westonian is not only to be distinct from all other students, but to find a distinct place in the Westonian landscape of distinction. It is also merely the beginning of what presumably will be a life of many more distinctions. At the threshold of their Westonian lives, students prepare to pass collectively through elaborate rituals that attenuate their differences and underscore their identification as an elite group of students. While they may or may not be "preparing for power," they are most certainly preparing to enter other spaces of elite distinction and are forming strong and often clear visions of what those futures will look like.[63]

7

ENVISIONING AN ELITE FUTURE

The blue skies that usually follow every nor'easter make New England winters bearable. Regardless of how much snow falls or how windy it gets, the calm brightness that comes afterward promises hours of sledding and skiing, snowballs and snow sculptures. While most schools close after large storms, at Weston there's no such thing as a "snow day." This doesn't mean, of course, that students don't know how to take advantage of a clear day after a heavy dose of the "white stuff." Dining-room trays make excellent sleds, and the snowbanks along the school paths make perfect snow forts.

The day after a particularly massive snowstorm, I'm on my way to Wyndham Hall when I encounter a group of six students, two on one side of the walkway and four on the other. They toss enormous snowballs at each other, directly over the path I intend to cross—so I dodge, barely eluding one cold missile. I bend down to scoop up some snow, and with my best Puerto Rican snowball technique, I toss it and watch it crumble in midair. I walk on, sheepishly, as they laugh and continue playing.

I arrive at Wyndham, where I meet Emily Lau, a four-year day student who has been a key informant during my first year of exploratory research.[1] It's early December, and like many of her fellow seniors, Emily is anxiously awaiting the early-decision responses to her college applications. We talk about schools, and when she mentions Harvard as one of her choices, she asks whether I think Harvard is anything like Weston. Ducking the question, I turn it around and ask her what *she* thinks. She says Harvard "was the school I could find that was most like Weston."

She worries, however, that Harvard is also "all of the parts of Weston that I don't like." She comments on her visit to the campus. "When I went to Harvard I looked around and I said, 'Oh!' [*she slaps her hand on the dining-hall table*] 'I recognize the landscaping that we're trying to copy!' So some people think that Weston is trying to be like Harvard!" I laugh, and together we list other ways in which the schools are similar: the yard, the seminar tables, the football rivalries, the uniformed staff, the décor, the abundance, and the wealth. From her perspective as a senior, she notes, "I don't know—I mean, I don't know if we love Harvard, or we hate Harvard, or we want to be Harvard, or we don't want to be Harvard, but we think about Harvard a lot." She adds, "Not everyone can go to Harvard," echoing the notion that "Weston is not for everybody"—an idea that is at the center of how students understand their own admission to Weston.

Emily and I continue our conversation long enough for me to run out of audiotapes. We pause, and I walk across campus to my quarters for more tapes. On my way back to Wyndham, at the very spot I dodged the snowballs, I encounter six young children, positioned almost exactly like the earlier group of Weston boys, tossing snowballs at each other. This time I'm not so lucky, and as I walk by, thinking about Harvard's relationship to Weston, about social reproduction and elite boarding schools, one of the snowballs lands splat on my red wool coat.

When I get to Wyndham, I share the story about the snowballs with Emily, which leads to a conversation about the literal and symbolic boundaries of the "Westonian bubble." Emily offers an example of the way Westonians draw symbolic boundaries to distinguish themselves from other people: they use the idea of "working at McDonald's" to represent the opposite of being a Westonian. The image of failure that "working at McDonald's" evokes "is very dear to people's hearts," says Emily. "It comes up in all kinds of different contexts." For instance: "You're complaining about math and you say, 'Ah, who cares? . . . I'm not gonna do my math work—I'm just gonna fail.' Like, 'I don't care—I don't care about math, therefore I'm not gonna do it.' And somebody else says, . . . 'Do you not wanna go to college? What, are you just gonna work at McDonald's?'"

According to Emily, Weston students do not envision themselves as service workers earning a minimum wage, "because that is symbolic of failure."[2] Yet when I ask if people who do that kind of work are seen as failures, she adds a layer of nuance: "If you really sat anyone down and you said, 'Do you really think people at McDonald's have failed?' they'd say, 'No, no, no!' You know, 'People! Lifestyles! The common man! Yay! We support everybody!'"

Weston students have two distinct views of a career as a low-wage service worker: it has one value for them, and another value for individuals outside the bubble border. They may envision an ideal world of fairness and equity, where the "common man" is valued, but they do not see themselves as "common." Doing what the "common man" does, in fact, would be deemed failure for proper Westonians. As Emily explains: "When [students] are standing at the checkout line, they talk about school. So it's like, you are carrying your own bubble with you, and you don't—I mean, you interact with the cashier, [but] they spend their whole lives thinking, 'I was the best of the best, which means *you* are still the cashier.'"

These distinctions between the envisioned futures of Weston graduates and the lives of "others" are further complicated by the students' relations with the people whose daily efforts and hard work form the invisible backbone of excellence at the Weston School: those who clean the seminar tables and change the light bulbs that illuminate every classroom discussion. Every day, dozens of staff members—who outnumber the faculty nearly two to one—cross the bubble border to their jobs. They wear green uniforms emblazoned with the Weston logo—another feature that distinguishes them from the casually dressed "real" Westonians.[3] The symbolic distance separating the staff from the students and faculty erupts into view only when the flow of the school operation is interrupted by unusual events, such as student pranks.[4] Otherwise, the complex dimensions of the relationships between those who work for Weston, and those for whom Weston works, remain hidden.

Students realize that their experiences at Weston depend on the labor of those who keep the "underworkings" in motion, and some students reconcile this division of labor by forming personal relationships that they assume will override status distinctions. For Robert Joyce, in fact, it is the lack of formality in his relations with the staff that allows him to befriend them in more familiar terms. "Sometimes we don't talk, really talk about anything—just, like, 'How was your day?'" says Robert, describing his friendship with one dining-room staff worker. "[She] might tell me about, like, you know, her grandchildren or something." Roland Carter says, "The staff can be real, can speak to you in a manner that you feel is not measured or metered in any, in any way." He describes a running theme among the students: "There's this joke that, you know, we should really get to know the staff because they're the only real people on campus."[5]

While Roland notes that over the years he has become more aware of the support staff, his "joke" underscores the boundary between the staff and true Westonians.[6] Indeed, Westonians would never see the work that staff members do as a worthy future for themselves. As the students learn to lead lives of distinction, their effort to celebrate the "common man" without actually becoming "common" entails the perpetuation of privilege and the dependence of the upper class on the lower, not the development of any solidarity between them. It is also further evidence that "the power of social class is hidden in notions of and feelings about individual worth, dignity, and respectability."[7] The relationships that students (and perhaps some faculty as well) develop with the staff are likely to continue beyond their lives at Weston—not with the same people, but with other, equally invisible, uniformed workers. Students will encounter many custodians and secretaries, but so long as being a Westonian means being "the best of the best," everyone else will "still be the cashier."

REVISITING THE FIVE E'S OF ELITE SCHOOLING

This chapter is not about what Westonians reject, but about what they envision as a worthy future. The way they talk about their future involves, first, the expectation of attending an elite college or university (preferably an Ivy League school), and second, the desire to enter high-status professions or at least to assume leadership roles in whatever careers they choose, high status or not. Of course, anyone can contemplate the idea of attending Harvard or imagine a career as a lawyer or a politician, but not everyone feels entitled (or has direct access) to such futures. How Westonians *envision* their future is embedded in other aspects of the process of becoming elite: *exclusion, engagement, excellence,* and *entitlement,* the five e's which I have discussed throughout this book. The model presented here deepens our understanding of the relationship between elite schooling and the production of elite status by illustrating how Westonians internalize privilege. It draws on the insight that social class works from the outside in, through public discourses and ideologies; and from the inside out, through the articulation of internalized elite identifications.[8]

Exclusion: "Weston Is Not for Everybody"

Perhaps the most critical step in the creation of elite status is the rationalization of a method of exclusion that determines who gets a place inside the Weston bubble and who does not. In the case of Weston, as with all elite colleges, universities, and other institutions, this happens through the admissions process. This process involves distinctions that separate Westonians from all other students—who are barred from entering this particular elite space—and at the same time connect them with all other Westonians (that is, all other members of this elite group of students). The words of a first-year student are revealing: "You need to see yourself on the same level as everyone else."

Students begin to identify as Westonians through implicit messages that, rather than suggesting the complexity of the admissions selection process, reduce it to a matter of each student's intrinsic characteristics, or, to put it in students' own terms, to what makes each of them "special." This shift suggests to students that they, more than others, deserve to be part of this elite group—a belief that is further justified as they reassure themselves that while "Weston is not for everybody," it is for them, because they are smart and work hard. Some students may be aware that there are external factors which led to their admission, but since they don't know what role these factors may have played in their particular case, they have only what they know or think about themselves as a reference. There must be something about *who* they are (that they are "smart," or that they are "diverse") which makes them eligible to be a Westonian.

Of course, different students, particularly students who do not already belong to elite groups, experience the process of exclusion differently. For instance, while students of color do construct identifications as Westonians, the discourse of distinction limits the kinds of claims they can make and the positions they can assume. Indeed, the experience of becoming the curriculum is akin to a kind of "double consciousness" that may keep students of color from completely assuming an elite identification.[9] As we saw in Chapter 6, this is not a problem of the "culture" of students of color.[10] Rather, it is the result of a discursive space in which students of color have little room to maneuver. If there is a "cultural problem," it is the (racist) cultural dynamics of the elite space they enter that limits their possible identifications and positions.

When diversity becomes part of *what* someone is ("this student is diverse") as opposed to a description of the *relationship* among people ("this is a diverse group of students"), individuals become identified solely by their presumed race (actually, by their external "racial" identifiers).[11] Similar processes may occur for white working-class students, particularly since the discourse of distinction deepens the psychic injury of crossing class boundaries.[12] In his classic study of British youth, Paul Willis argues that it is through *identification* with their working-class positions that "working-class kids get working-class jobs." I would suggest that it is through a direct *rejection of* that same working-class identification (and all—or most—of the identifiers that go with it) that students are able to construct a new Westonian identification as they join the elite.[13]

Thus, despite the assertion that elite boarding schools seek to be inclusive, it is through exclusion that the process of producing an elite status group begins. The arbitrary boundary between those who are included and those who are excluded is the first step through which future Westonians begin to think of themselves as smart and hardworking students who are worthy of the education that the Weston School provides. Once inside, further exclusions shape the processes through which students find a niche and the hierarchical positions they assume as Westonians. Being admitted to an elite boarding school, however, does not guarantee admission to an elite college or university. To continue the path toward an elite future, students must demonstrate that they belong inside.

Engagement: "Finding Your Niche"

When students are accepted at Weston, the presumption is that they come with a passion for learning, inside and outside the classroom. Students often come with previously developed interests in music, theater, sports, or specific academic areas, and the school provides them with ample opportunities to refine their skills and talents. The school also expects students to take risks and explore new interests and challenges by taking advantage of the many opportunities the school offers. Through all of these activities, students develop their identification with particular niches that are hierarchically organized within the space of distinction, but which are also constrained by an overriding, implicit, Westonian elite identification. Their particular niches also become central to the process of applying to college, which requires them to stand out among other equally elite applicants.[14]

I ask Radhika, a day student, how she thinks her experience compares to that of boarding students, and whether she experiences the school as self-contained. "Yeah. Except I feel like I live here," she laughs.

> I spend more time here than I do at home. I get here, like, at seven in the morning, and I don't leave until, like, nine, ten at night every day. . . . Weston doesn't really force you into it anymore—it's basically your own involvement. And so, when you're a day student, you have to make yourself involved, if you wanna fit into the cog at Weston, into the Weston machine, I guess. It's just that it's—since you're not forced into staying in this environment, you don't have to be here. You can just use it for the school, you can use it for the classes, and then you can leave, like, at six. But if you want to be a Westonian and do everything else in it, then you have to do more than just classes.

Radhika confirms that day students are not considered as Westonian as boarding students, because they are not "forced" into the totality of the institution. At the same time, she performs her own identification as Westonian by presenting herself, like all Westonians, as a willing and eager participant in her schooling process.[15] Once students enter the Weston bubble, they encounter the challenges and opportunities they are entitled to by virtue of being admitted to Weston and which only a context of abundant resources and ample space can provide. The academic space at Weston is taken for granted, because it seems extensive and endless, with enough room for everyone to find a niche. Through these opportunities and challenges, students "thicken" their Westonian identifications, but not without dealing with further exclusions based on other identifications and social categories. In this sense, whether and how students engage the opportunities that are provided at a school like Weston is also about the practice of exclusion. This negotiation is essential to how the curriculum of distinction hierarchically organizes the whole range of elite identifications students construct, even as the Westonian identification binds students together as a status group. Indeed, part of becoming Westonian involves finding a place in a hierarchy in which not everyone is equally elite.[16]

When students internalize a sense of bonding with all other Westonians, which is underscored by their sense that they belong inside the space of distinction, they can focus on what distinguishes them from other Westonians by constructing new identifications and negotiating various *diversities*. By focusing explicitly on difference and by accommodating a range of diverse identifications, the discourse of distinction masks the fact that students are developing a common elite identification as Westonians, even as their particular identifications are hierarchically organized. Furthermore, by framing diversity as an individual asset that *all* students bring, they manage to avoid dealing with social dynamics of exclusion that are based on categories of race, gender, and class. In other words, by underscoring their *individual* distinctions, students learn to misrecognize the privileges of their *collective* distinctions and avoid dealing with the social consequences of their status.[17]

Ultimately, this Westonian identification is cemented by what some students—even teachers—describe as the overwhelming experience of "surviving Weston," which becomes the ultimate form of shared distinction. This distinction is premised on the abundance of resources, the commitment to a particular style of learning and teaching and to specific kinds of diversity, and the embrace of an ethos of excellence and hard work, all of which are essential to the distinguishing of Westonians. In order to justify these privileges, students must turn the internalized mystery of being included as Westonians into an externalized proof that they are, indeed, special, different from all other *excluded* students.

Excellence: "Be the Best That You Can Be"

Once students are allowed inside, Weston demands in return that they work hard to be "the best of the best." Students do not necessarily (and are not likely to) work to be the "best of the best" at every challenge they encounter. In reality, most of them won't be *the* best at any particular thing (there aren't as many opportunities as there are students for each of them to be the best at something!). Instead, as Emily explains, "You find things that you are really good at. . . . That's worth a lot to you—when you find things that you are really successful in." On the one hand, the process of finding a niche is about locating a position within a hierarchical space; on the other, it is about finding a space in which to "survive Weston" and demonstrate excellence, which are crucial for internalizing a sense of entitlement to elite status.[18]

The abundance of material resources and opportunities that Weston offers its students is an implicit necessity for this part of the process. Students are more likely to find something that they are successful at—even if they are not the best—if there is a wide range of experiences from which to choose. While a few well-funded comprehensive public schools may be able to provide such extensive opportunities, most cannot possibly offer educational opportunities that cost more than $50,000 per student. The privilege of entering Weston, then, entitles students to these opportunities, but demands in return that students work hard to excel and to be "really successful" in at least some aspect of the education that the school offers. But this is no easy task. The discourse of distinction sends a clear and overwhelming message, as a former headmaster demanded of all Westonians: "Make a reasonable effort to learn, or go where the demand is less urgent."

I asked Jennifer Cooper, who spoke about wanting to come to Weston to escape the boredom of her public school, whether she thought the school should ease the pressure to work hard and be the best. She thought about it for a few seconds, looked down, and replied: "I think it might kind of take away the motivation of students [who] sort of feel like this is the academic, the end-all-be-all, and if you can get through Weston, you can sort of get through anything. . . . And maybe that's why a lot of people come here, 'cause they feel like this is sort of the epitome of [the] academic race, and if that race weren't here, I don't think it would necessarily attract the kind of students that it does."

This "academic race," then, is an important part of what being a Westonian means for Jennifer. Without this sense of working to be the best, Jennifer would find it difficult to fathom a Westonian identification. The idea of a community that never rests is present from the moment students begin to construct their identification as Westonians. Demonstrating that they are indeed the best of the best entitles students to claim future privilege, and to envision themselves inside future elite bubbles.

This image is necessary because it becomes the external representation of entitlement while internally emphasizing an elite identification. In other words, though students often must imagine why they are entitled to enter Weston, their hard work, and the fact that they have embraced and conquered at least some of the challenges they have faced, are clear indications that they are indeed entitled to a Westonian elite identification.

Patricia Sanders confirms this when I ask her whether she thinks there are fair statements that can be made about all Westonians. "Yes, I do. I do. I do believe that every Westonian is," she pauses and takes her time to consider her answer, "very intelligent and deserves everything that they, um, they worked really hard to go to—just to stay here for four years. So yeah, I do believe that. Um, that you deserve recognition for being— working hard, and [getting by]. Yeah, I do."

Entitlement: "If You Can Get through Weston . . ."

Whether they envision themselves as legislators or lawyers, authors or librarians, surgeons or ministers, Weston graduates can hardly imagine anything more difficult than surviving Weston, which entitles them to a place among the "distinguished alumni" of the school. Their Weston diplomas carry with them a long-standing reputation for rigor, high standards, and enduring excellence.

As Weston alumni, students are entitled to social connections that are likely to shape their elite futures. In Chapter 5, Linda Merrow talked about the experience of being in airports around the world wearing Weston clothes and having strangers approach her to ask whether she is an alum. Wherever she goes, it seems like "somebody knows somebody who went here, . . . and anywhere you go, you're gonna be able to find somebody who will help you just because you went here." Linda feels entitled to the opportunities that such connections make available, because she feels that surviving Weston "does warrant some kind of a trust." She says that in the future she would feel confident hiring her peers because she knows firsthand the experience and the "work ethic" they share as Westonians.

In her last term at Weston, Linda will be joining a group of Westonians who will be doing internships with members of congress in Washington, D.C., a program similar to others provided by elite colleges. Radhika Chaudari is also going to Washington, and she looks forward to meeting other Westonians during her internship, which she describes as an opportunity to "get access." "We were talking about that last night at [our] Washington internship dinner. . . . They said access is the most important thing in this country—and so, when you have such access, you can do anything you want. And so, to have other people wanting to help you just because you went to this school—it's kind of cool."

The summer before her senior year, Radhika had already begun to benefit from this "access," getting a job as a paid intern at a law firm in New York City, "just because I told them I was from Weston," she explains. "They expected me to be a certain way because of the school. And so that's why I got such opportunities." "Thus," as Cookson and Persell put it, "the web of affiliation . . . continues to grow, becoming more interwoven, entangled, and in the end, the basis of status group and class solidarity."[19]

Securing the entitlements of a Weston education begins before graduation, and is tempered by other aspects of the curriculum that mitigate the possible elitism implied in the idea that Westonians "can get through anything." The Weston School is built, in part, on the Puritan moral ethic of its founders, and the belief that the purpose of a privileged education is to be useful to mankind.[20] Whether citizenship and civic responsibility as ethical ideals are actually outcomes of the education Weston provides is open to debate, and would be of interest for future research. But what is more important is that the presence of this ethos as an ideal provides some justification for the very existence of an institution like Weston, where presumably "the best of the best" are prepared to fulfill some civic duty, perhaps to oversee those who are excluded from the Weston bubble. If the impressive wealth of elite boarding schools presents a stark parallel (perhaps a contradiction) to the economic challenges of the public school system, the elite identifications of these students can be understood in relation to processes of identification in nonelite schools. As students of an elite school, Westonians learn to rule because other (nonelite) students learn to labor.

Envisioning

The process of producing an elite status group may reach its apex at the point where students can envision themselves as a future elite, as the decision makers of society, caretakers of those who were excluded from the Weston bubble. It is also at this point that they take over the role of excluders from those who once determined that they were worthy of a Weston education. At the school level, the process ends in the college counseling office, where future identifications are envisioned and students are connected to the social networks that will ensure their position among the Westonian elite. As students graduate, they cross the threshold of their exclusive Weston bubble and take on new challenges through which they can demonstrate their presumed excellence and justify their entitlements to future lives of distinction.

"Getting into a Good School"

Almost as soon as students enter the Weston bubble, they begin the process of exiting. When they visit the school, prospective families are often intrigued by Weston's impressive college matriculation record; overall, the largest number of Weston graduates have attended Harvard, Yale, and other Ivy League schools.[21] Just as students begin by imagining themselves as certain kinds of students in order to enter Weston, they have plenty of room—and support—for seeing themselves as students at the most elite colleges and universities.

Given Weston's impressive record of placing students in prestigious colleges, the expectations of students and their parents are often the biggest restraint on a process that is supposed to allow students maximum freedom to make wise choices. According to some faculty, many parents have unrealistic expectations about what ought to be the outcome of an expensive Weston education and about what students have earned through their hard work. These expectations are particularly misguided in the contemporary terrain of college admissions, where a Weston diploma is no longer a "magic wand."[22]

Applying to college returns students to the same processes of identification involved in their arrival at Weston, in which their individuality becomes the fulcrum of the process, overshadowing the underlying machinery that delivers them to the "right" college. Today's college application process is far more complicated than in the days when a Weston officer literally "placed" candidates with a simple phone call. These days, "college counseling," like admissions, is presumed to be much more about "finding a match."[23] Students make decisions about colleges, prepare for standardized tests, collect letters of recommendation, write essays, and prepare their applications through a carefully crafted and elaborate process that provides close and thorough support. The resulting applications offer portraits of the individual students for the colleges they have selected, some of which may best fit their particular personalities, interests, and goals, and the repertoire of identifications they have each constructed at Weston.

Today, Westonians end up enrolling in close to a hundred different colleges. Yet the school still sends many students to Ivy League schools, where they will find buildings with familiar names. Some students are not sure that these schools are all that they're cracked up to be. "I don't know if I'll apply to Harvard. I mean, it seems so clichéd to me," said Andrew Zia as he began the process of generating a college list. Eventually, Andrew was admitted to three of the most selective universities in the country, including Harvard. He claims that he made the final decision through a luck-of-the-draw game with two of his closest dorm friends. "Randomly," they determined that one of them would be attending Harvard, another Princeton, and the third Yale.

Students are well aware that competition for getting into the most elite colleges and universities is stiff, and some are dubious about whether going to Weston actually improves their chances of getting into an Ivy League school. "There's sort of a, a saying among the students," says Scott Jaffee, "Weston helps you, it increases your chances of getting into a good school, but decreases your chances of going—getting into a great school." Many students echoed this common statement, particularly if they were excluded from admission to their first college choice; they wondered whether their chances would have been better if they'd stayed at their local public school. While statistically some students may in fact have lessened their chances of attending such institutions by choosing to attend Weston, they still envision themselves as a future elite, perhaps largely because of the opportunities and the demands of their Westonian experience.

"It definitely has been endurance," says Michael Jonas about attending Weston. "I mean, just studying day in and day out." Michael was disappointed when he didn't get into Harvard. "I was just like, 'Fuck! . . . Here I worked all this time for this, but to no avail.' But then that's when you start realizing, well, actually, it *was* to some avail, because I actually learned some things that are useful." In the long run, Michael's membership in the Weston Alumni Club may provide him with more than just "things that are useful," and his Westonian identification will render the college attendance distinctions moot.[24]

Still, the realization that Weston is no guarantee of admittance into an elite college is often hard to accept. Wilbert Overend, a third-generation Westonian, says Weston has lived up to almost all of the expectations he's had since he first visited the campus as a little kid with his grandfather. "Probably the only expectation that it didn't meet was guaranteeing me a, a little space in an Ivy League school," he says regretfully. Wilbert was deferred from early admission to an Ivy League school and was eventually denied admission. When he describes the small West Coast college where he was admitted, he doesn't even pretend that I might recognize the name, and instead compares it to small liberal arts colleges in New England, like Bates, Bowdoin, and Colby. "It's definitely, like, a very small disappointment factor that I think, 'Yeah, stuff like that happens for a reason,' I guess." Wilbert is debating his options as he considers deferring his admission. "You can think, 'I'll be able to do just as much in life if I excel at [this college] as if I dragged by my toes at, you know, at a place like [Ivy League University], so I'm not too concerned." As he prepares to leave Weston, Wilbert is disappointed about his college prospects, but not dismayed. "I regret so few things about my experience here, which is another thing that, like—if you look back on it, and you don't regret a lot, that's, that makes me pretty happy." For Wilbert, Weston "is an astonishing place."

"For the Rest of Your Life"

At the end of a crisp day in early May, Andrea Moon and I sit at an empty seminar table and converse about her spending four years at Weston, receiving early admission to an Ivy League university, and leaving the "Weston bubble." She is excited about the "new start—but at the same time, . . . it's just a continuing step from Weston." She believes the university she's heading to will continue to demand the best from her, but that the lessons she learned at Weston will ease her transition. "Weston is not necessarily an institution that just teaches you facts, but it teaches you how to get them, like, for the rest of your life, and I think that is something that will continue. Like, the learning process and the little tricks, and whatever that I've gained here."

Andrea is an elegant and courteous Asian American who speaks with ease about everything from rowing to the Supreme Court. She is academically self-assured, and her demeanor radiates self-confidence and maturity. Beyond being able to engage in serious inquiry and discovery, Andrea can envision her success at a prestigious Ivy League institution because of the lessons she learned around the seminar table. While she is still "clueless" about what she wants to do "in terms of career," Weston has enabled her to envision herself assuming roles in government or politics.

Andrea talks about taking a popular course on American constitutional law, explaining that the goal of the class is to "have more or less a

balanced court in our classroom, which makes these debates very interesting. . . . It's almost like the real-life court." Andrea envisions herself
"between O'Connor and Rehnquist—so a little bit off, like the sway vote
towards the conservative." By the time she graduates, Andrea will have
studied the Constitution, prepared arguments in cases about civil rights,
the First Amendment, abortion, and the separation of church and state,
and argued in front of nine students, each assuming the role of a Supreme
Court justice.

There are students who imagine themselves as leaders in less exalted
though just as illustrious endeavors. One student remarks that the seminar classroom "makes it easy for people to imagine themselves as the
teacher." While this may be the case, students who talked about considering careers in teaching, for example, also talked about the lack of support for such choices from parents and colleagues. Kevin Bausch also
feels that "most people can do anything if they just . . . put effort into it,"
and he feels "like if I chose to do [anything], like, I have a strong enough
background to sort of move forward." Kevin has considered teaching as
a career, "but then my family quickly is like, 'No—you won't make any
money.' For me, it's just gonna come down to whatever I feel like I'm
gonna be happy doing. Because otherwise, I don't know, I can't do something that I'm not—that I'm going to hate. Like, I just won't do it for
money."

Amy Stein already envisions her role as a school principal and de-
clares, "I wanna start a school when I'm older." Weston has honored Amy
for her academic excellence, but she seems more committed to public service, and highlights her work with public officials and local government
through the Westonian Society of Social Services. Amy values the opportunities she's had to engage in organizing events with the town, and says
she's "learned a lot about how to deal with bureaucracy." Having grown
up in a large city on the West Coast and attended urban schools with
mostly black, Latino, and Asian populations before coming to Weston,
Amy recognizes the privilege of being identified as white in the broader
social context. She claims to be deeply concerned with class disparities
and social inequality, and envisions a school like Weston that is tuition-
free and that serves less affluent and less privileged students. Realizing
that the biggest challenge for her enterprise will be fundraising, she jokes
about securing a pledge from a Weston colleague who "plans on making
tons of money."

Whether as school founders or school funders, many Weston students envision themselves in positions of power—from Supreme Court justices to school directors. Other students talk about wanting to be head librarians or leaders of environmental organizations, about attending Harvard or working for the Peace Corps, and, of course, about running for president. When I asked students how Weston had prepared them for their future careers, students talked about the exposure they'd received to ideas and experiences through their courses and their extracurricular opportunities; the skills and the social and relational dispositions they'd developed around the seminar table; and the network of alumni and colleagues they would be able to draw on in the future. The first point is presumed in the definition of an elite boarding school as "scholastically elite," and is illustrated in the classroom descriptions throughout this book. The interactions in those classrooms, as well as the way students have described the demands that the school makes on them, illustrate the second point. The last is related to the way students justify cronyism, and to their sense that they're entitled to future connections.

Weston students feel entitled to assume leadership roles and envision their future successes, even as they sit around the seminar table. The table is "similar to many boardroom meetings," explains Roland Carter. "Each person at that table has something different that they have to add, in order for the overall project to be complete." Roland adds that if one member "doesn't come ready," then "the entire project can't go forth, or the entire company can't grow as a whole." Sharply dressed in a pressed white shirt and a bright-red necktie, this young black student seems ready to enter any boardroom and be part of a team. He underscores the importance of being able to envision himself as instrumental to the process and entitled to participate: "When a student feels that they are needed at the table, [when] the student feels that their questions as well as their comments, as well as just listening, that *all* aspects of their being there is important—then they really start to understand more what goes on. They are not as hesitant in conversations." As students internalize the sense that they're entitled to be at the seminar table, they begin to identify with the idea of being a Westonian and with the particularities of what they believe this means.

"We all think differently here," says Roland, but "there's a particular way in which you want to analytically look at the text, and we want to sort of make these broad conclusions." Roland is not sure whether he wants to become a minister or go into law, but he knows he wants to serve the public in some way in the future. Like many other Westonians,

Roland is also taking the elective course on American constitutional law that Andrea Moon described earlier, in which students assume roles either as attorneys arguing cases before the Supreme Court or as justices listening to the cases. Roland invites me to go to class with him after the interview, and I eagerly join him, excited to finally witness the students developing legal arguments and discussing the merits of Supreme Court decisions.

We make our way from the library to Weston Hall. Instead of going up the front marble steps, we use the side entrance, which is closest to the History Department and Mr. Lieberson's classroom. It's a rainy Saturday morning, and the squeaking of wet shoes on the marble floor echoes from every polished surface. The classrooms in this older part of the building are large, with high ceilings and bay windows. Like the old library, the room is lined with tall, overflowing bookshelves. Yet the room feels pristine and clean. The wood gleams, and the maps stored above the blackboard are neatly rolled. The center of the room is taken up by the seminar table, looking ceremonial and surrounded by thirteen chairs, on a crimson Persian rug. A large image of a Native American chieftain presides from the wall.

By the time Roland and I arrive, most of the students have already found their seats. I can't help noticing the seating pattern. Four boys—Will Mueller and three others I recognize as PGs on the varsity hockey team—are sitting together on the far side of the table. Opposite them are five girls sitting next to each other near the door. Roland looks around at the available seats and settles right next to Will. The teacher sits near his desk, the boys to his left and the girls to his right, as if arbitrating between the two sides.

Mr. Lieberson begins by reminding the students that next Saturday they will be running a mock court dealing with *Plessy v. Ferguson*—the 1896 case that upheld legally enforced racial segregation, so long as blacks had "separate but equal" facilities—and he starts assigning the students their roles. One of the girls, who has been assigned to defend segregation, complains that she does not want to be put in the position of presenting a racist argument. But the teacher stands his ground: "In your future legal careers, you may have to argue cases that you don't agree with." Will asks Mr. Lieberson if he can be Chief Justice, and the teacher snickers back at him, asserting his authority to assign the roles. Once all the roles are assigned, Mr. Lieberson directs the students to pay close attention to the case and to build their arguments carefully. He reminds them that the judges will be ruthless with questions and challenges, and that they may interrupt the attorneys' arguments at any time. Students must be ready to respond and to predict the kinds of arguments and questions that could come their way.

Today the class is discussing the 1873 Slaughter-House Cases. Before starting, Mr. Lieberson points out my presence, and without asking me to introduce myself, he asks whether someone will volunteer to explain the case to me. No one speaks up. He asks humorously, "Who's in charge?" Will and two of the boys raise their hands, as the girls mumble in apparent dismay, rolling their eyes and sighing. Before any of the boys begins, one of the girls, Aurora, jumps in to explain. Unfamiliar with the case, I become even more lost as Aurora freely uses terms from various constitutional amendments and legal concepts that I've never heard of. Utterly confused, I nod my head as if I am completely familiar with what she is saying. I thank her, and the class continues.[25]

The students discuss state citizenship versus federal citizenship, and the teacher encourages them to develop their own judicial philosophy and to think about the contrast between substantive and procedural due process. Throughout the conversation, only Will and the five girls participate actively in the conversation. The three PG hockey players sit quietly. It is Aurora, who knows the details of the case and is able to articulate the ideas, who overwhelmingly dominates the conversation. Will attempts to interject ideas and challenge her, but she challenges him back immediately, apologizing when she doesn't understand what Will is trying to say. The teacher rarely interrupts, except to clarify, to introduce a concept, or to note when a student, usually Aurora, has offered an important point.

Later, I ask Will what he thinks about the teacher's remark that in their "future careers as lawyers" they'll have to be able to argue for the "other side." He laughs, jokes about the challenge of "arguing the racist side" in the mock trial of *Plessy v. Ferguson,* and notes: "I think that the school really does, you know, kind of like—it prepares you to be someone who is very assertive. If not a lawyer, someone who is, is in a company and is just, you know, like a board member, I would say. Because one of the things about the seminar classroom that is unique is, you *do not* back down." He stresses the phrase "do not" as if his reputation depended on it, and he explains: "You can see something from another person's perspective. You can say, 'I, I understand it,' but you never kind of . . . " He pauses for a moment, and jokes, "Unless you're wrong." We laugh together at his comment, and I joke back, saying that I thought he was going to say that he would never back down, even if he was wrong. He jokes back, "Yeah! Even if you are, you still defend it. Like I, you, you wanna be as, like, as—you wanna concede sometimes to someone else, but not totally. You wanna still have a bearing at the table that doesn't make you look like you've been beaten up."

If the fear of being "beaten up" drives students to persist, it's the fact that they feel entitled to be right that justifies what Linda Merrow describes as "some kind of egotism. Even if it's not necessarily apparent, I think we all learn that at some point." Though she says that not all Westonians are outwardly egotistic, "even the kids that don't show it— that don't act, like they, they think they're [*pause*] better than the other kids—I think it's still there. I think they still . . ." She pauses again, trying to make sense of her own claims but unable to answer her own question. "I don't know how to describe *why* that's there."

This book offers an explanation of precisely why Westonians come to believe that they are, as Linda puts it, "better than other kids." Becoming elite involves the forging of "a certain type of elite consciousness."[26] The way students claim and enact their identification as Westonians shows how the self is necessarily remade in the process of becoming elite, and how students come to convince themselves that they deserve their privilege.[27] Being "the best of the best" involves authenticating the boundaries established through *exclusion,* by demonstrating *engagement* and emphasizing *excellence.* The outcome is a sense of *entitlement* to privilege and the ability to *envision* an elite future.

"PERFECT WESTONIANS"

During one of the many lunchtime conversations I had with students at Weston, Annie Kasper, Frank Maxwell, and Radhika Chaudari are discussing the idea that Weston is like a well-oiled machine. I ask Radhika during our interview to elaborate on what this means, and I point out that she has used the machine metaphor several times in the interview. She explains succinctly: "Anyone can come in, but you all come out a certain way." Intrigued, I ask her to say more.

> Like, everyone comes in with varied interests, and, like, you're good at this and you're good at that. And I guess on some basis you're all, like, on, at this standard. But then you come

in, and you go through this mill, and it doesn't become important anymore. You may have been, like, the world-class pia-
nist at your last school, but it doesn't matter here, because
there's probably another one just like it. And so, when you
come out of here, you don't have that special something that,
like, distinguishes you from the rest. Yet you know that you're
special, just because of everything that you do. And so you
don't identify yourself, I guess—you don't identify yourself by
that one thing anymore.

Radhika's suggestion that Westonians lose their distinctions as they
acquire their elite identifications might contradict the idea that there are
many different kinds of Westonians and that some students are more
Westonian than others. Yet her words underscore the fact that even if
some students lose a sense of distinction from other Westonians, they
know that they're special. What she means by "special" is grounded in
the same idea of what makes Westonians exceptional and how their engagement becomes part of their elite identification. She echoes the words
of many of her fellow students as they envision their elite futures: "Um,
you think, like, you can handle anything that comes your way now, just
because you've tried so many different things, and you've experienced
so many different things that you probably wouldn't have at your old
school. And so when you're—they think that you, they've prepared you
for the world, kind of thing. And so I guess you feel like you can handle
any situation that comes at you."

For Radhika, distinction is no longer (just) about being different. It's
about having the ability to tackle and succeed at any endeavor she
chooses. What binds Westonians together is not just knowing where they
each fit into the Westonian hierarchy, but the fact that this is an *elite* hierarchy. Having demonstrated that they're willing to work hard and be the
best they can be, Westonians are entitled to claim future distinctions and
to enter future elite spaces. Even if some students are less Westonian, they
are, nonetheless, *all* Westonians. "You come out like one of these, like,
perfect people," says Radhika. "Perfect Westonians."

One month before graduation, during one of the final focus groups,
Steve Hart, Ken Ellerly, Michael Jonas, and Neil Perry discuss what this
means. When Steve suggests that being a Westonian simply means that
someone went to Weston, Michael is incredulous: "Ooh! I don't know
how I, I think there *is* some sort of vague conception of what a Westo-

nian is. And I don't know how to put it. I mean, it's, it's like . . ." He chuckles as he searches for the words and everyone listens intently. "It's like saying what an American is. I mean, I guess you can try to point out a few characteristics maybe—a feeling of superiority. But I mean, there's always gonna be iconoclasts."

Steve agrees. "I guess there's, uh—you're right that there's, like, an idealized picture of what a Westonian is. But, like, nobody fits that. There's no such person." I'm intrigued by Steve's statement, particularly because he and Michael are two of the people most other students associate with the ideal of a Westonian. Michael confirms this: "Well people, people used to say that, I mean people like you and I were kind of considered— I was considered until my, like, [disciplinary committee], they're like, 'Yeah, you work hard, you, you go to a lot of clubs, uh, you're respectful, you're a nice kid.' Like that was the, like, ideal of a Westonian." Steve teases Michael about the fact that he was caught with marijuana in his dorm a few weeks earlier, and everyone laughs as Michael jokes: "Yeah, I smoke ganja, right, so I lost my ideal Westonian status." As the laughter breaks, Michael jumps back in: "But I mean, that's what it is. Being an ideal Westonian is being, like, well rounded, nice to everyone, but, you know, having the little good time on the side, working hard. Um, I think that's the ideal. And, like, what a Westonian entails? Someone who's motivated, ambitious, who goes here—I don't know."

"I almost consider myself the ideal Westonian," says Scott Jaffee. His declaration takes me by surprise, in part because, unlike Steve and Michael, no one has ever mentioned Scott as an example of the ideal Westonian. When describing the ideal Westonian, students often offered descriptions that in some way or another paralleled how they described themselves; but they never claimed that they themselves were the ideal Westonian. Scott Jaffee, however, is far more direct, and I ask him to describe what makes him the ideal Westonian.

> I have good grades, you know, I do well in class. I'm smart, but I don't care about academics. Um, I don't do varsity sports, but I'm in the gym [twice a week]. I am not a theater junkie, I don't live in the theater like some kids do, but I've directed plays, I've acted in plays. Uh, I am not a, uh, music junkie, I don't live in the music building and sleep on the, on the, on the, uh, sofas in there, like some people do. But, you know, I'm still in there a lot, I still, you know, play two instru-

ments. I'm in, in sev—, two bands, and several, two, two jazz bands and a, and a rock band, and, um—or I should say I make guest appearances on rock bands. Um, and so in that sense, I mean, and, also, I, I, I wouldn't, I'm also not a popular person, um. I, uh, I have friends, I am well liked. I wouldn't say I'm well known on campus. . . . Probably most people don't know I am, who I am, or anything about me. But people who do know about me like me. I don't really think I have any enemies, as far as I know. Um, I stay away from people I dislike, so maybe that helps.

We laugh together, though I'm not quite sure why we are laughing, and he concludes: "The point is, I'm not skewed in any one direction. I'm not a total socialite. I'm not a total, you know, academic nerd. I'm not a total, like, you know, drama junkie or, you know, I'm not a jock. . . . I still enjoy dabbling in lots of different things and I, I have a lot of—I hang out in a lot of different social groups. Um, and so that—in that sense, I almost consider myself the ideal Westonian."

Whether Scott is or is not the ideal Westonian is beside the point. What is crucial is that his description of himself is almost a perfect summary of what all the other students say about what it means to be a Westonian. It means to be intellectually curious and have good grades without being an academic nerd, to be an athlete without being a jock (or, worse, a PG), to be artistic without being a junkie, to be known socially without being a socialite. Keeping the "perfect balance" of sports, academics, the arts, and extracurricular activities while maintaining a solid academic record and a steady group of friends: this is what makes the ideal Westonian. "If you're achieving the best status in every one of these, that would be the perfect Westonian," says Radhika. "Although that is virtually impossible."

DEPARTURE RITUALS

At the end of their Weston careers, students leave the Westonian bubble without much fanfare, but with plenty of ritual. The senior prom, for instance, is dull in comparison to the spectacular and highly dramatic displays of consumption that characterize senior proms elsewhere.[28] Yet it is a community event, as parents come from far and near and gather with the faculty outside Weston Hall to take photographs of their sons and daughters, who are dressed in tuxedos and designer dresses and preparing to board the buses that will take them to the dance. There is an assembly dedicated to the seniors during which the yearbook is presented, and at least three major award ceremonies, including an invitation-only ceremony for the top-ranking students in the graduating class. There are rock concerts, sit-down dinners, farewell parties in the dorms, and many organic and unofficial rituals that take place in dormitory basements, away from the gaze of teachers and ethnographers.

After two years at Weston, during which I developed close relationships with many students, I wanted to have my own departure ritual. Departures are important for ethnographers, because they mark a shift—if not the end—of relationships that have become significant.[29] At the end of the spring semester, as students completed their final exams and began graduation plans, I organized an ice cream sundae party for the thirty-six seniors who had generously given their time and energy to my research. I invited them to bring anyone they wanted, and I invited others with whom I had interacted during my time at Weston. The party was held in a room in the Student Center where I had attended many meetings and informal events. The day before the ice cream party, students had received their senior class yearbooks, and many of them brought them to get signatures. I was surprised when students began asking me to sign their yearbooks, and I started asking them to sign the copy I had purchased. The messages they wrote in the front cover and back pages of my yearbook were a reminder of the relationships we'd built in the course of the ethnographic fieldwork. The following three messages were typical:

> Hey!
> What can I say. . . . You have become part of the senior class of '04! I had a fabulous time working w/ you—your questions helped me reflect on my own background and experience while @ Weston. I learned a lot about myself, and I was able to start discussions with my friends which helped define my time here. So: thank you. I think your project was great for our grade. I hope it turns out well. My email as of now is [address] Good luck in the future!
> [heart]
> Sabrina
>
> Rubén—
> I really enjoyed working with you this year. It made me happy to see a real-life Puerto Rican role model. I really re-

spect what you do. All my best for the rest of your project. Hope to keep in touch.

[*heart*] Sandra

[*email*]

Rubén—

Talking with you was scary because I found that when my thoughts about social things were voiced they sounded . . . awful. The discovery of what those thoughts were was exciting, though, and I thank you for that. Good luck w/ all of your work, and I hope we're interesting enough for a year of work on us.

Sincerely,

Steve, '04

[*email*]

While all yearbook inscriptions follow a particular form and are meant, by definition, to contain some sort of personal connection (real or not) and even flattery, I like to think that what the students chose to write (and the fact that they asked me, a non-Westonian, to sign their yearbooks) reflected at least to some extent the relationships I developed with the students—relationships of mutual respect, trust, and even admiration. As I read through their messages, I noted that most of them spelled my name correctly, with an accent over the *e*. Indeed, all the students knew my name was pronounced "Ru-*ben*" (something some faculty members always stumbled over). This took me back to the very first day of my research, when I sat paralyzed in the middle of my room, wondering how I should introduce myself.

The graduation ceremony is held outside—a symbolic display of the importance that the pastoral landscape has for elite boarding schools. For the past couple of days, the headmaster and the class president have been closely monitoring the weather forecast. Unfortunately, today rain is expected, and the staff members arrive especially early to prepare two spaces for graduation—one outside, in front of Weston Hall, the other in the gymnasium. The morning is gray and chilly, but word spreads quickly that the ceremony will proceed outdoors. By sunrise, many of the white plastic chairs arranged in front of the stage have been reserved with long strings of masking tape and improvised paper labels.

The students begin to gather in their lineup areas. From my vantage point, under a tree by a white picket fence, they're distinguished only by their undistinguishing plainness. I recognize their faces, but they are all dressed alike: boys in blue blazers, khakis, and neckties; girls in white dresses—except for two girls who have defied the threat of removal from the ceremony by wearing sleek pearl-colored pants. The one Native American student in the entire school wears a colorful feather necklace and a red scarf around her waist. The students receiving the Latin Distinction wear their silver medals around their necks and stand closest to the stage, where a select group of adults, including the headmaster, the deans, and members of the board of trustees, all dressed in casual suits, are finding their seats.

The graduation ceremony is unassuming and restrained. The only signs of opulence are the luxury cars that line the road and fill the parking lot, and the designer clothes worn by family members sitting in the neat rows of plastic chairs. A large crowd of current and former students stand around the periphery, leaning against the picket fence or mingling with the faculty, who stand to the side, in the shade of the surrounding trees. Many members of the custodial and maintenance staff stand at the outer edge, uniformed in their green polo shirts, khaki pants, black shoes, and Weston baseball caps. They look proud of the students, and of the lush grass they've carefully tended for two months in preparation for the ceremony.

Roland Carter gets up to read the invocation, asks everyone to rise and hold hands, and thanks the audience for their support through the "years of struggle, pain, and victory." He welcomes everyone to "join in the tradition of Weston to fully realize the Weston community," and half jokingly invites everyone to "make yourself as comfortable as you can," to endure what promises to be a long and repetitive graduation ceremony. Though the speeches are few, the list of awards is long, sprinkled copiously with the names of elite universities and famous alumni. By the end, almost all of the students have visited the stage at least twice, to receive some sort of award and the final validation of their Westonian-hood: their diploma.

After all the awards have been given, diplomas delivered, hands shaken, and hugs received, the headmaster delivers her farewell speech. She reminds students of the importance of putting "ourselves into community with others who have different lives," and helping "those in the margins of society," implying, perhaps, that Westonians are at the center. "You have worked hard, contributed to life, and opened doors of opportunity," she tells them, inviting them to develop a sense of "sophisticated selfishness." At noon on the dot, she wishes them "Godspeed." The bells of the Weston tower begin to toll, and the students erupt in excitement. They laugh and cry, sway and jump, gather in groups to take photographs, smoke cigars, cling to each other, pace, dance, and celebrate their eagerly anticipated graduation. As the new alumni express their elation, the guests proceed across the bridges that connect the hills side to the valley side. They take plain yellow lunchboxes from the carefully arranged tables, and gather under trees or on blankets in the middle of the field to unwrap their lunch.

I left Weston along with the Class of 2004. I did not receive a diploma; the alumni office did not collect my permanent address; I did not walk with students at graduation; I did not smoke cigars with the students after the ceremony. My family and I stood at the sidelines with the parents and friends, we ate from the lunchboxes that the uniformed staff handed out, and we sat on the cautiously manicured lawns, saying goodbye to students, meeting parents, shaking hands, and exchanging hugs. Between smiles, tears, and candid reflections, I once again tried to envision my four-year-old daughter as a student at Weston. I wondered if Mercedes Irene would wear pants or colorful necklaces at graduation. What sort of Westonian would she become? As I contemplated the scene around me, I wondered whether she would toss frisbees or lie on the grass. Was she smart enough to be successful here? Would she work hard and feel entitled to the privileges of a Westonian education? Would she become a trophy wife? How would she negotiate the perilous social geography inside the Weston bubble? Would she find a niche among the best of the best, and believe that everyone else is just a cashier?

RESEARCHING IDENTIFICATION AT AN ELITE BOARDING SCHOOL

Throughout this book, I have tried to make myself, as the "instrument of research," explicit.[1] As much as possible, I have done this by exposing myself as a participating subject, trying to find my own niche in the Weston landscape. Whether I fib when introducing myself to others, hesitate in classroom conversations, or dodge the question when asked to share my fieldnotes, the imperfections of the ethnographic process always reveal much about the self as well as about the research context. These moments of "vulnerability," when I, as ethnographer, expose myself to the intimate process of establishing relations in the field, are as much about the process of doing ethnography as they are about coming to understand how identifications are constructed and boundaries are negotiated in a context of privilege.[2] Because so much of the ethnographic endeavor is about how I present myself and negotiate interactions with participants, my own participation reveals a great deal about the very processes I am interested in understanding. Ethnography is not just the methodology; it becomes part of the process under study, as it shares its underlying logic. In the process of observing how others present themselves to me, I present myself to them, and the interaction is shaped by the specific context of our encounter. In fact, to a large extent, this context sets the terms under which we engage and through which our interaction evolves. While we are "actors" in these encounters, interactions cannot evolve unless we are able to recognize and follow the "rules of engagement" that have been set prior to our encounter,[3] and even prior to our entry into this particular space—a space of privilege and high status that is rarely a site for this kind of research.[4]

The dynamics of power—which have been the object of constant reflection among ethnographers and educational researchers, particularly those informed by critical, postcolonial, and feminist traditions—manifest themselves in unique ways when the research context can be defined as elite.[5] This is particularly true regarding the dynamics of insider/outsider status. Many scholars assume that researchers have either insider or outsider status as they enter the research process.[6] Furthermore, this status is assumed to be evident prima facie, as though the researcher and/or the community had stable and readily evident identifiers that defined their relationship. Yet as Michele Foster argues, the process is far more complicated than this, and the ways in which presentation is negotiated and identifications are constructed through the research process in a context of affluence and privilege clearly challenge such static notions of the insider/outsider dichotomy.[7]

Indeed, one of the central challenges of this work stemmed from the fact that I—a light-skinned Puerto Rican male with well-educated, middle-class parents—was in some sense looking "up" at the educational experiences of students at an elite boarding school in the United States. Yet this formulation is simplistic. The power relations that shaped my work were far more complex than metaphors of verticality allow.[8] If anything, I might say that I was researching up, down, sideways, and all around. As a researcher in training I was identified with the academy, which by and large has a hierarchical position over schools as the object of research. Even in a context of privilege, the role of researcher and academic scholar bears a great deal of status; at Weston, it shaped how people perceived me and affected the degree of authority they granted me. Although mediated by my status as a graduate student, my identification with a university in a secondary school context allowed me a certain kind of status. This was particularly so with students, with whom I also related as an adult (married, with children, and so on), with the authority that such status grants. I negotiated this adult status with great care, reassuring students about my ethical responsibilities to protect their privacy and anonymity, as well as looking after their well-being.[9]

My status as a student, however, also allowed me a certain insider status, particularly as a Harvard student—an identification many Weston students have at some point or another envisioned for themselves. After all, I, too, was a student at an elite educational institution, a "Harvardian," if there is such a thing, and as much as graduate students at Harvard can claim such an identification, which is an open question.[10] I was often asked whether I was an undergraduate at Harvard as well, and of course, my status quickly diminished when I explained I had a degree in music from a conservatory. I rarely explained that admission to my own high school, although public, was also subject to an entrance exam and that it is considered an "elite" public school. Most times I downplayed the status of my own high school education, in part because I didn't want students to assume a common experience that might keep them from articulating things they took for granted. Indeed, while my own education would be considered "elite" or at least privileged in the Puerto Rican context, it hardly compares to the privileges of a Weston education.[11] At the same time, there were also instances when I worked to present my own high school as in some ways similar to Weston, in order to establish some basis for a common identification with students as smart or as academically inclined.

There were many ways, though, in which I was inescapably an outsider, and a "lower" outsider at that, looking "up" to study the lives of a group of students who had, in many ways, higher status than I did. For one, I am and was always perceived to be a non-Westonian, clearly incapable of ever knowing what it really means to be a Westonian. I was also, despite my fair skin, always identified as nonwhite. My name is irrevocably nonwhite, my accent, which thickens over extended conversations and with physical exhaustion (inevitable in long periods of fieldwork), is clearly not a U.S. accent. Despite all the claims of my own high school to elite status within Puerto Rico, I can hardly claim anywhere near the status of any elite boarding school in the United States.

The various ways in which I was both an insider and an outsider within the context of the school determined what I was able to know and what experiences were outside my purview.[12] This was most obvious regarding my own gender identifications: whereas I was able to hang out in boys' dorms on my own and at all hours of the night, I could not do the same in girls' dorms. Additionally, students of color admitted to feeling like they could talk about issues that concerned them and which they would not have shared with me had they identified me as white. On the other hand, though they did not articulate it, white students may have felt that they had to talk about issues of race and ethnicity in particular ways because I was their audience. As Joan Hoffman puts it, "who I was or was perceived to be influenced the information to which I would be given access. The management of my identification thus became an important aspect of my research strategy."[13]

Entering the research context always involves a complicated process of negotiation that does not end when the Committee on the Use of Human Subjects and the Internal Review Board approve the research protocols. Indeed, it only begins this way. Negotiating access to spaces with high status, such as elite boarding schools, might seem particularly difficult.[14] Joan Hoffman argues that this is one reason there is a "relative scarcity of literature on society's higher social strata."[15] In beginning their study of elite boarding schools, Cookson and Persell describe being grateful and even "perplexed" by the "graciousness" with which they were received by the schools they sought to study. They speculate that perhaps the heads of the schools thought their "study would highlight the positive aspects of boarding school life," suggesting that they lacked a general understanding of social science research and were more concerned with journalists and being exposed through scandals.[16]

I also did not experience any of the difficulties described by Ian Weinberg when I secured access to the Weston School.[17] This was largely due to the fact that the school's Curriculum Review Committee initially invited me as a consultant, as I've described in the introduction.[18] The work of my initial research at Weston directly informed the development of research questions for the second research project. The data I collected during the second year, however, was much more focused and specific to the research questions I developed.

RESEARCH METHODS

To observe how different students construct and enact Westonian identifications under different circumstances, I focused my second year of fieldwork on four different kinds of interactions: those that took place in official school activities, in informal school contexts, in one-on-one interviews, and among focus group participants. I employed four complementary methods of data collection: participant observation, a student questionnaire, in-depth narrative interviews, and focus groups. This combination of methods proved extremely generative, and the various data I collected suggested particular insights and informed one another in the analysis in rich and interesting ways. Still, throughout the process, I had to make several crucial decisions to limit the scope of my research in ways that would make the research manageable while still "good enough."[19]

One of these early decisions was to limit the focus of the second year of research to a subset of students in the senior class, which allowed my analysis to center on social categories, rather than developmental differences. Seniors, especially those who attended the Weston School for two or more years, had more experience negotiating boundaries through a wider range of contexts and had a more developed sense of what it meant to be Westonians. Seniors also had more flexible schedules, particularly during the spring term, when I conducted in-depth interviews; and they had completed their college admissions process, which put them in a unique position to reflect on their experiences and on what it meant to be graduates of an elite boarding school.[20]

Participant Observation

Participant observation is an essential tool for understanding culture.[21] Given this study's focus on symbolic boundaries, observing the interactions of students in a range of contexts is an important starting point. For the portrait I prepared at the request of the school, I spent two months visiting the school on a regular basis, often for several days at a time, attending classes, assemblies, eating with students and faculty in the dining hall, hanging out in dorm lobbies and, when appropriate, student rooms, attending faculty meetings, sports games, pep rallies, student group and advisee meetings, and talking with anyone willing to speak with me—with or without the tape recorder. During the second year, I continued the "deep hanging out" I had begun in the first year.[22] This time, I identified particularly salient contexts in which students enacted their Westonian identifications and observed how social distinctions and other symbolic boundaries emerged and shaped interaction in specific contexts. For instance, I ceased visiting faculty meetings, and spent less time eating with faculty. While their experiences as teachers at such a rarefied institution are indeed worthy of exploration, I made a deliberate decision to focus strictly on students during the second phase of the research.

For nine months, from October 2003 to June 2004, I visited the school on a weekly basis for periods ranging from several hours to several days.[23] During these times, I continued to observe classes, student meetings, extracurricular activities, and informal gatherings. Through this "hanging out," I initially sought to establish a rapport with students and to identify key informants.[24] As the research progressed, I focused my observations on specific interactions and sought to observe situations in which Westonian identifications were being enacted, either explicitly (during alumni visits, admissions open houses, sports events, official school rituals) or implicitly (during "unofficial" rituals in the dorms, meetings of student organizations, classes). In these instances, I paid close attention to the ways race, class, and gender shaped how students interacted with each other and how they negotiated the school space. These social categories became increasingly relevant and significant to my evolving understanding of the ways students experienced the school and negotiated various identifications, including their own identification as Westonians.

Student Questionnaire

Over the winter break and during the month of January, I administered an online questionnaire to all seniors in which I asked them to provide "thumbnail sketches" describing themselves in their own words,[25] as well as general questions about themselves and their activities at the school (see below). The questionnaire was voluntary, and students could choose to respond anonymously or to provide their contact information if they were willing to participate in the interview and focus groups. The questionnaire gathered preliminary data about students, which I then used to refine the interview protocols.

Selecting students from the survey responses was a fascinating process, and I learned a great deal about the importance of certain categories and criteria. For instance, answers to the question, "How would you describe your ethnic or racial background?" yielded answers that ranged from the straightforward ("white") to the comical ("Northern European mix—i.e., very very white"), the complex ("I consider myself a cultured/semi-worldly American"), the angry ("I am white, but I really hate not only that question but also being forced to say I am white"), and the confused ("I wouldn't, until you defined the terms precisely"; "What eth[n]ic or racial background?").

The thumbnail sketches were also a fascinating window into how identifications are constructed, and made it that much more difficult to select students, as each sketch suggested something interesting about each student. It was fascinating to see how students chose to represent themselves in this small space. Consider the following examples:

> I want to learn, tons of history, a basic understanding of the sciences, to read all the works of the major philosophers especially Kant and Plato, to play the piano, to speak French and

German and maybe Japanese, Italian, Spanish, Russian, Hebrew, Mandarin, Arabic, and to read Latin and Greek, to take enough math to uncover the mystery that I'm just starting (in real analysis) to experience, to write books and poems, and to marry, have children, and teach and live a simple, fulfilling life.

This is my third year here, and my feelings toward Weston are still ambivalent. I love the [seminar classes], but I believe the academically competitive atmosphere cultivated by the institution is counter-productive to the stated goals of cooperative learning and discovery through process. I'm a bit of an individual and dislike schedules. I've also been diagnosed with mild ADD, but I don't use medication. I went to public schools until I came here. I live in the South, in an upper-middle class [home].

I am a four-year senior on a full financial aid package. I came to Weston through [a minority recruitment] program, whose mission is to get inner-city kids interested in boarding schools. My parents are Colombian immigrants without a college education. I spend most of my free time here working on the student newspaper, *The Westonian.*

Four year day student. White. Catholic. Male. Interested in Drama, Music, Sciences. Socially liberal, economically conservative (political views). Closely connected to my family. Straight edge (no drugs, alcohol). I must also add that I am somewhat divided. I sometimes feel that I exist between Weston and home, as I lead a different life at home. I have a different circle of friends, all of whom are very unWestonian —which I like. A dose of reality, you know?

Each of the dozens of personal descriptions students offered invited more questions and pointed to intriguing dimensions of the experience.

I used the student questionnaire to select participants based on the criteria outlined in the next section. First, I categorized the students who had volunteered or whom I had recruited through direct contact. I did so primarily on the basis of how they identified along categories of gender or race, and the social cliques with which they most identified. I also categorized them based on whether they had been at the school for two, three, or all four years, whether they were boarding or day students, and whether they received financial aid. Based on this initial group of students, I looked through the questionnaires for various combinations of categories. Often, there were more than a few volunteers who fit certain category combinations. In those instances, I shared the questionnaire responses with a group of colleagues, and we selected volunteers based on how much or how little they fit particular stereotypes. We also read the thumbnail sketches carefully, looking for unusual responses and responses that either challenged or confirmed our assumptions about who they were, on the basis of the rest of their survey responses.

Although by and large it was easy to recruit students with a wide range of backgrounds, recruiting students who identified as Asian American proved challenging. Several of them completed the questionnaire, but most did not volunteer their contact information or agree to be interviewed. It was never quite clear to me why this was the case, and I did not develop a better understanding of this as the research evolved.[26] In the end, I was able to recruit two males and two females who identified as Asian Americans and who were not immigrants—that is, who were primarily raised in the United States. One female student who identified as South Asian–American also agreed to participate.

Participant Selection Criteria

The cohort of thirty-six students I interviewed represented a wide range of experiences and backgrounds, reflecting what Miles and Huberman call "maximum variation."[27] Through direct contact during observations and through the student questionnaire, I selected students with diverse backgrounds and experiences through "purposeful sampling"[28] strategies driven by theoretical, context-specific, and practical criteria.[29]

Ethnographic studies do not typically predetermine the criteria for selecting key informants and participants.[30] The assumption is that by being a participant-observer and becoming familiar with the setting, the researcher can identify key informants and build relationships that lead to participation.[31] Yet in studying an array of student experiences, the researcher encounters an inherent tension between choosing students according to predetermined (etic) social categories (such as race, class, and gender) drawn from previous research, and choosing students according to what emerges from the context as salient differences (emic) determined through immersion in the context. This study focused on how different students construct different versions of their Westonian identifications, as well as on how race, class, and gender shape student experiences. In this way, the study departs from others that focus specifically on the experiences of girls, boys, or black students in elite schools.[32] In order to get as much variation as possible, I selected participants according to the following criteria.

Theoretical Criteria. Previous research indicates that race, gender, and class are central forces in how students construct identities.[33] Therefore, I sought to include students who identified themselves with various categories within these criteria. The questionnaire asked students directly how they would describe their racial/ethnic background. As proxies for assessing a student's social-class background, the survey also asked about parents' jobs and whether the student received financial assistance, which is determined based on need. The research focused exclusively on U.S. domestic students, even though the school has a large population of international students, particularly from Asian countries. From an analytic standpoint, I made this decision because I did not feel that I could adequately address how the background of international students shaped their experiences at the school. I assumed that international students experience race, class, and gender in ways that are directly shaped by their home cultures, about which I knew very little.[34] I did include students who were born in the United States to immigrant parents and who had spent most of their childhood in the United States.

Context-Specific Criteria. During the first year of research at Weston, I found that students' academic interests and extracurricular activities (including sports, arts, and other extracurricular activities) were crucial to the way they talked about their experiences and described the school. For example, I learned that being part of the classics program, which involved advanced levels of Latin, was an important marker of academic status among students. The grade in which a student entered Weston was also a marker of difference, with "four-year seniors" getting special attention in school events. I paid close attention to ensure that participants had a range of extracurricular and academic interests. The number of students starting during different grades loosely paralleled the proportions of the senior class (see table on page 230).

Practical Criteria. Participation in this study was entirely voluntary. Some participants self-selected as volunteers and approached me independently to express their interest, once they learned about my study.[35] On the other hand, those I recruited directly based on their responses to

Profile of the Weston School Class of 2004[a]

Category	Percentage of total
Total enrollment	100.0
Gender	
Females	43.7
Males	56.3
Starting year	
9th (4-year seniors)	51.0
10th (3-year seniors)	23.5
11th (2-year seniors)	12.8
12th (1-year seniors)	0.9
Postgraduates (1 year)	11.9
School residence	
Boarding students	83.5
Day students	16.5
Home residence	
U.S.	93.0
International	07.0
Racial/ethnic affiliation of U.S. students (self-described)	
Asian/Asian American	10.1
Black/African American	5.8
Latina/o/Hispanic	4.6
Middle Eastern	0.6
Native American	0.3
White/Euro American	67.3
Multiracial	1.5
Undeclared	2.8
International students	
Asian	4.5
European	2.4
Financial aid distribution (largely determined on basis of student need)	
Students with no aid	69.4
Students with aid	
Less than 50%	3.1
50–99%	19.6
100%	4.6
Faculty/staff children[b]	3.3

[a] All data provided by the Headmaster's Office of the Weston School. Actual number omitted to protect anonymity.

[b] 100% tuition remission.

the questionnaire, or through a recommendation from other participants or from teachers, sometimes were unable or chose not to participate. In very few instances, parents of students who had not turned eighteen preferred that they not participate. In one case, a participant was expelled from the school for possession of a controlled substance before I was able to interview him. These and other unforeseen practical issues certainly played an important role in determining which students participated and the kinds of interactions I had with students.

Profile of Participants

A total of thirty-seven students agreed to participate in the in-depth interviews and focus group phase of the research. All participants were U.S. citizens and had spent most of their lives in the United States. The student who was expelled is not counted in the numbers that follow. Of the thirty-six remaining students, nineteen students identified as female and seventeen as male. Paralleling the senior class as a whole (see the table), five students (14 percent) were day students and thirty-one (86 percent) were boarders. Four-year seniors were somewhat overrepresented, with twenty-six students (72 percent); there were six three-year seniors and three two-year seniors. One postgraduate was interviewed but did not participate in the focus groups, and no one-year seniors participated. For comparison purposes, the table on page 230 provides a profile of the 2004 senior class as a whole.

Students varied as to how they chose to identify in terms of race or ethnicity. Some described themselves in the questionnaires and others in the interviews. Twenty students claimed an identification as white, Caucasian, Anglo, or some related variation, including identification with specific European immigrant groups. Three students claimed a Latina/o identification, two Puerto Rican, and one Dominican; one student identified as mixed, with one Hispanic parent and one white American parent. Five students identified as black or African American; one student identified as Haitian American, and another identified as biracial, with one black parent and one white. Four students identified in some way as Asian American: one as Taiwanese American, one as Chinese American, one as Korean American, and one as biracial, with one parent Asian and the other white. One student identified as South Asian.

Students on financial aid were also overrepresented in the sample. Seventeen students indicated that they received financial aid from the school, ranging from full to partial scholarships. Eight of these students identified as students of color, while nine identified as white (one was the child of a staff member). The other nineteen students either did not specify (seven) or indicated that they did not receive financial aid (twelve). Only six of these students did not identify as white.

The thirty-six students also varied as to their involvement across the curriculum. At least four students were active and had leadership positions in artistic activities, and at least four were involved in varsity sports, including two team captains. Students also varied in terms of the social spaces with which they associated or identified; about half considered themselves valley-siders and half hills-siders.

In my initial meetings with participants, I provided them with a project description, discussed the details of the study, and addressed their questions. I explained to each of them that while I would use pseudonyms to protect their confidentiality, it was possible that their friends might recognize some of the details of their shared and individual experiences at Weston. Participants signed consent forms and obtained permission from their parents to participate in the research (with the exception of students who were eighteen or older).

Narrative Interviews

The third stage of the research involved in-depth narrative interviews. With each participant, I conducted two sixty-minute open-ended narrative interviews following a protocol (see page 246). In a few instances, I conducted only one interview, either because I recruited the student later in the term, or because the student spent the last term at a program off-campus. Narrative interviews are opportunities for the collection of stories about participants' experiences.[36] These narratives provide examples of the ways in which participants see themselves and how they make sense of their experiences.[37] Furthermore, through these stories participants construct and enact particular versions of various identifications in the context of a relationship with an interviewer.[38]

Focus Groups

As the interviews were completed toward the end of the spring term, I organized the participants into three groups that ranged from five to ten students. I ran two focus group sessions with each group.[39] Focus groups provided opportunities for data collection beyond the constraints of interviews and unique opportunities to observe interactions, combining observation with self-reported data.[40] The focus groups were another specific context in which participants enacted identities through their narratives and interactions, not only with me, but also with their peers. Since I was facilitating the activities, it was difficult to record fieldnotes during the focus groups. I recorded each focus group on audio as well as videotape. Video was a way to add descriptive validity to the analysis because it captured details that I missed. In this way, videotape is not only a form of "visual 'note taking,'" but a tool for reflexivity.[41] As Lomax and Casey argue, "the involvement of the researcher in the interaction can be analyzed and understood from the video text."[42] Following Sarah Pink, I took "note of the collaboration and strategies of self-representation that were part of [the video] making," as a way to take into account how students responded to the video recording.[43]

Drawing on observation data, questionnaire responses, and interviews, I developed two focus group activities. In the first meeting, I gave students an admissions brochure with the heading "We are Westonians . . ." I asked students to read the text of the brochure and to look carefully at the details of the design. I asked them to identify details of the brochure that reflected their experience at the school as well as details that sounded unfamiliar or in any way misleading. I also asked them to share experiences that either confirmed or contradicted what they read or saw in the brochure and whether they agreed with what others were saying.

In the second focus group, I paired the students and I gave them large pieces of paper and a box of markers. I asked students to work with their partners to draw a map representing the social life of the school. I told them that the map could be as abstract or as literal as they wanted, and that they could choose any way of organizing the maps. After twenty minutes, each pair had to explain their map to the others, and the others could comment on, challenge, and ask questions about the graphic representations. At the end of both focus groups, I gave students paper and pencils so they could record any thoughts, questions, or suggestions about the activity, about what they'd heard students say, or about things they wished they had said or had felt uncomfortable saying in the large group. Following each focus group, I wrote memos about my impressions of the activities.

Focus groups yielded surprisingly rich data. As is common with focus groups, students interacted in ways that reflected their thoughts and fears about themselves in relation to the group.[44] As one student commented in her written reflection: "I think the responses given by each individual person reflect their own insecurities, or confidences—what their own opinions on their [social] deficits are. There may be some accuracy to the statements made, but [what they drew] is defined by the desires and ideals of the individual behind the definition. Very illuminating."

These dynamics generated data about student interactions that could not possibly have emerged in interviews, or even during participation in formal or informal school activities.[45] The artifice of the focus groups as a structured, semipublic form of data gathering created a very particular kind of context in which students interacted in ways that were similar to the kind of engagement that occurs at the seminar table—interactions that are central to the school's classroom culture.

Students as Social Analysts

One of the richest and most satisfying ways of generating data was through engaging the "sociological imagination" of the students themselves. Toward the end of my fieldwork, and especially as I started to conduct the focus groups, I engaged the students in a kind of "member check" or "respondent validation" (as Sara Delamont calls it) as a means of "checking with participants to see if they recognize the validity of the analysis being developed."[46] As I developed ideas and recognized themes in what I was hearing and observing, I started to ask the students if they could clarify, expand, or correct any of these emerging impressions of their experience.[47]

Generally, I did this in three ways: through informal conversations, through specific interview questions or tasks (as described above in the interview section), and through the focus groups. As my time at Weston progressed and I spent less time observing and more time "hanging out," I was able to present the students informally with ideas about what I was seeing (often prompted by them), and ask them to tell me what I was missing or how they thought my observation was incomplete or even wrong. I asked them to direct me to places and people who might add more information or offer an alternative view. Some students engaged in this process eagerly, often quite determined to "prove me wrong" or show how my perspective was skewed or misdirected. Through this process, students became social analysts of their own experience, and often offered insightful elaborations that proved to be quite fruitful.

Toward the end of the second set of interviews, I deliberately asked students to consider what I was observing. Often these questions emerged at the request of the students themselves. At the end of every interview, I asked students if there was anything that they wanted to ask me. Sometimes they asked me personal questions, about my family, my background, what it was like to be in graduate school, or whether I would send my children to Weston—a question I usually asked them as well. But most commonly, they wanted to know what I was seeing. I took these opportunities to share with them some of my observations and to ask them specific questions about things that puzzled me. As much as possible, I always tried to present my questions and observations in ways that positioned the students as the experts (which they were!), and which downplayed my researcher role. I reminded students that they, more than anyone else, knew what it was like to be a student, and that I, in my short time there, could not possibly know what they were experiencing. I asked them to show me how I was wrong, or what I was missing, and how they would modify my analysis to capture their own experience.

During the second set of focus groups, I also worked to create a space in which students engaged in the same kind of social analysis. I wanted to take advantage of their academic interests and inclinations and their passion for debating around the table to generate data that would complement my own analysis. These dialogues were not out of the ordinary at this school, where students are used to engaging evidence and presenting counterarguments. In fact, students often were ready to prove me wrong, offering counter-examples and pointing out what I was missing or how my perspective was blinding me. Students appeared to relish this process, and often came back to me when they saw me around campus or in the dining hall to offer new insights and observations. Like the student quoted above, often what they wrote in the final reflections suggested their deep awareness of important dynamics that would often go unmentioned during the group conversation. For example, one student who identified as white and upper-middle-class said: "I think that we did not dive into the more sensitive/intense issues of race and socioeconomic background. . . . I don't have anything specific to say, but would emphasize the importance of these distinctions. Also, come senior spring, I am noticing a lot more universal mingling—our class is bonding."

My understanding of the process of becoming elite at this American boarding school was shaped in fundamental ways by the critiques that the students themselves offered and the ways in which they directed my attention throughout the process.

DATA ANALYSIS AND VALIDITY

One challenge that ethnographic work poses is the difficulty of making sense of data that is by definition "messy," complex, and multidimensional.[48] Making sense of and "creating coherent, focused analyses from a mass of fieldnote data, which by now number several hundred pages," can be an arduous and overwhelming task, and this challenge is compounded when multiple types of data are added to the mix.[49] Throughout the two years of my research, I recorded more than a hundred hours of interviews and focus groups, and collected nearly a thousand pages of fieldnotes. During the focus groups, students produced twenty-three maps; I collected boxes of school documents; and 106 students responded to the online questionnaire.

In ethnography, there is also little separation between the processes of collecting and analyzing data. In fact, "substance cannot be considered independently of method; *what* the ethnographer finds out is inherently connected with *how* she finds it out."[50] Fieldnotes are filled with analytic memos and other reflective commentaries that help the researcher keep track of an evolving analytic process. There is no "program" that spits out a report from which conclusions are drawn. Observation, analysis, ideas, hypotheses, and questions are embedded in an iterative process that is constantly informing and regenerating itself. Throughout the research, I used "open coding," noting the themes that emerged in my fieldnotes and memos on a daily basis.

The "jungle of data" (as I used to refer to it) that such processes yield can be overwhelming, and often I felt paralyzed by what seemed like mountains of transcripts, fieldnotes, and memos.[51] In order to make sense of these data, I developed what I call "analytic maps," with which I parsed the data and defined "paths" for traversing it in a somewhat systematic fashion. I began this process by organizing the interviews, all of which were transcribed either by myself or by an independent transcriber. Once transcribed, I listened to each interview and focus group with the transcript, correcting mistakes, and trying to clarify those pesky "inaudibles," noting pauses and shifts in tone that might add nuance to the words. Transcripts, of course, are always incomplete representations of what is said in an interview.[52] In listening to them repeatedly, I wanted to capture more than just the words, by returning to the space of the conversation and reviewing whatever thoughts I had recorded in the subsequent memo.

After revising each transcript, I used the digital software Atlas-ti to code the interviews.[53] I used several coding strategies, including open and focused coding, automatic coding, and searching for specific strings of words and ideas. I created analytic network maps to try to understand how codes were related to each other and how "thick" or "embedded" various codes were with one another. After doing open coding of several interviews, I developed focused coding strategies in order to begin developing theoretical connections, as well as to streamline what could otherwise become an unwieldy list of codes.[54]

This semi-closed coding (or semi-open coding, as I called it) involved coding the data with a set of questions involving the content of the narratives. Rather than coding line by line, I read and coded "chunks" of narrative data. First, I determined whether this particular "chunk" was a narrative, using the definitions and strategies for narrative analysis drawn from the works of William Labov, Elliot Mishler, and Catherine Riessman.[55] I coded each narrative according to the topic(s) from the interview it addressed or illustrated. I then asked who the "characters" or participants, either obvious or implied, were in each narrative, and how they were positioned (what roles they played) in the narrative. I was especially interested in narratives about the self, about friends, about particular constituents (such as faculty and family) and specific status groups among students. Another dimension of the narratives that became increasingly important as I developed my analysis was their context, or the particular places in which the narratives took place, as well as whether and how these places were presented as characters in the narrative. I also coded narratives with the dimension(s) of the official curriculum that students referenced (academic, athletic, artistic, extracurricular, or residential).[56]

As I began to make sense of the interview data, it became increasingly clear that students organized their experiences at the school in three general "spheres of experience," as described in Chapter 1. I therefore began to organize the data according to which spheres of experience were referenced, and I also noted whether and how these spheres were separated or overlapped in how students understood them. Throughout data collection, and particularly as I began the initial coding phase, I developed a list of themes and concepts that were of theoretical significance, such as codes related to dynamics of race, class, and gender. I noted the various ways in which students explicitly referenced these issues, as well as whether and how these dynamics were implicit in what they were saying. In addition, given my interest in processes of identification and boundary work, I coded the data for instances when either of these processes was evident.

To analyze my fieldnotes, I began by constructing scenes based on my observations, in which I highlighted whether and how race, class, and gender were playing a particular role in what I was observing.[57] I adapted Strauss's basic coding paradigm for grounded theory, focusing on the interactions through which identifications were constructed and the strategies students used to enact those identifications, and focusing, as well, on the conditions under which identifications were constructed and enacted.[58] These conditions included the salient characteristics of the contexts in which students participated and the kinds of interactions that students had with different people.

The various coding strategies I used for organizing the different kinds of data proved extremely fruitful as I explored whether and how different pieces of data came together and illuminated one another in the overlaps between various codes and groups and subgroups of codes.[59] This is perhaps one of the advantages that digital qualitative data analysis allows the researcher, as it enables the almost unlimited (while time efficient) exploration of relationships between codes and data.[60] This kind of "axial coding," in which categories of data are related "to subcategories along the lines of their properties and dimensions," illuminates how codes and other analytic categories "crosscut and link."[61] This process can generate increasingly complex and more complete explanations of how individuals make meaning of particular experiences.

Methodologies are not just statements about methods, but arguments about the philosophical positions I take regarding the nature of knowledge (ontology) and how we come to know (epistemology).[62] Being explicit about who I am and how I experienced being at the Weston School, as I've done throughout this book, is not just about navel gazing. Indeed, given the relational focus of this work, reflexivity—the role that the researcher's own identifications and subjectivities play in the process—is one of the largest validity concerns.[63] Just as in my interaction with Mr.

Gardiner described in Chapter 2, throughout my time at Weston I negotiated social and cultural boundaries and engaged in the production of
particular identifications for myself.

Throughout the research process, I remained keenly aware of how I
was perceived and how my reactions toward others shaped what I observed. I used several tools to monitor and scrutinize my role in the research: reflexive memos and journaling, interactional analysis of narrative interviews and video data, peer collaboration and feedback, and
member checks. Reflexive memos and journaling are ethnographic tools
that allow researchers to be aware of their emotions and to observe themselves as they become part of the setting and the culture under study.[64]
These memos were essential in my effort to understand how I interacted
with others in the Weston setting, and what this revealed about myself as
well as the school.

Two additional strategies involved sharing parts of the data with others who might offer unique insights and suggest alternative explanations.
One involved review by peers in an interpretive community.[65] Interpretive communities provide opportunities to strengthen coding strategies
and analytic tools by enabling the ethnographer to get feedback from
skilled researchers who are not intimately connected to the data. I shared
my coding schemes and asked fellow study group members to develop
their own as points of comparison. They often offered alternative interpretations and pointed to discrepant data. A final strategy involved my
soliciting the assistance of research participants, asking them to review
transcripts of interviews and to clarify or expand on any issues raised.[66]
As I described above, I also shared some of my initial analysis with participants and asked for their impressions, clarifications, and suggestions.
Both of these strategies were important tools for developing interpretive
validity and for guarding against researcher bias.[67]

RELATIONSHIPS IN THE FIELD

If entering a research site is a complex process of negotiation, exiting can
be at least as difficult, often complicated by the fact that personal relationships have been developed and emotions are at stake.[68] The researcher is responsible for being as careful and ethical in negotiating exits as in managing entrances. In Chapter 7, I describe the sundae party I
organized for the participants in my study, and highlight the experience

of being asked by the students to sign their yearbooks. The fact that they asked me to sign and the content of the messages they left for me are an indication of the positive relationships we developed during my time at Weston.

Their messages also raised questions about reactivity—the ways in which the research process influences the participants. Almost all of the messages contained some reference to how the students' participation in the study had somehow shaped their perception of the school and how they saw the school differently. All research with human subjects, even experimental designs, has unavoidable (and most often direct) consequences for those who participate.[69] Only researchers who engage in action research acknowledge this fact from the start, and begin their inquiry with this assumption.[70] Ethnographers do worry about the "effect" that their research will have on participants, but mostly frame this as a problem of representation.[71]

Processes of identification do not end when the data are collected and the analysis comes to a (temporary) rest. Throughout this book, I have constructed a narrative about myself as a researcher that (implicitly and explicitly) seeks to persuade the reader that I have done a "good enough" job and that the narrative I offer is reliable and valid as social science research.[72] Like identification, analysis is never complete. Even as I revise the pages of this book, I see new themes and new ideas that will remain unarticulated here. This is both the virtue and the quandary of ethnography. The process of coming to know the subject is never quite complete; the representations imprinted here are no longer "true," and thus the text is always "essentially contestable." Even as I write these words, I remain in a constant process of coming to know, or at least imagining that I know, something worth telling. As Clifford Geertz explains: "Cultural analysis is intrinsically incomplete. And, worse than that, the more deeply it goes the less complete it is. It is a strange science whose most telling assertions are its most tremulously based, in which to get somewhere with the matter at hand is to intensify the suspicion, both your own and that of others, that you are not quite getting it right. But that, along with plaguing subtle people with obtuse questions, is what being an ethnographer is like."[73]

In this book I have constructed a representation of the students and of the school that is contingent and partial. The analysis contained in these pages is by no means complete, and there is far more to the experiences of students at a school like Weston than I can convey here. The thirty-six participants whom I "plagued with obtuse questions" generously shared with me far more than my analysis can possibly capture, and to them I extend my deep gratitude for allowing me into their lives.

ONLINE SURVEY (UNFORMATTED)

Weston Student Profile Questionnaire

This poll's results will not be available to respondents online.
* An asterisk indicates that an answer to the question is required.

Thank you for taking the time to complete this questionnaire. Your responses will help me to better understand students' experiences at [Weston] and what it means to be a [Westonian]. Please answer the questions briefly. The questionnaire should not take more than 25 minutes to complete. All of the information you provide below will remain confidential. At the end of the questionnaire, you will be asked whether you would like to participate in the latter stages of this research. If you think that you would like to participate, please enter your email address in the space provided so that I may contact you. Your answers to the questionnaire will remain confidential, even if you provide your email address. You will also have an opportunity to make your answers to the questionnaire anonymous if you so wish.

In order to authenticate your responses to this poll, please enter your campus phone extension in the space below. Your responses will not be identified with your extension.

* Extension Authentication
Enter your four-digit campus extension.

Thank you. Next, click the "Submit for Error Checking" button below to continue the questionnaire. On the next page, review your answers and click the "Next" Button at the bottom of the page to continue.

Personal sketch

QUESTION I

Please provide a few sentences to describe yourself in the space provided here. *Text Limit: 500 characters (approximately 10 lines)*

QUESTION 2

Which of the following are your strongest subjects or areas of study?
(Choose all that apply.)

Anthropology
Art
Biology
Chemistry
Classical languages
Computer science
Dance
Drama
Economics
English
Health and human development
History
Mathematics
Modern languages
Music
Physical education
Physics
Psychology
Religion/philosophy
Other (please specify below):

QUESTION 3

Which of the following subjects or areas of study do you find most challenging? (Choose all that apply.)

Anthropology
Art
Biology
Chemistry
Classical languages
Computer science
Dance
Drama
Economics
English
Health and human development
History
Mathematics
Modern languages

Music
Physical education
Physics
Psychology
Religion/philosophy
Other (please specify below):

Extracurricular activities

QUESTION 4

Do you participate in any of the following extracurricular activities? If so, please click under "Yes" and specify which ones in the box to the right. You do not need to describe them, but please provide the full name of each group.

A. Clubs or student organizations
B. Performance ensembles (including informal groups)
C. Drama or other theater activities
D. Other activities (including club sports)

QUESTION 5

Are you (or do you plan to be) on any of the following Varsity teams? (Choose all that apply.)

Baseball
Basketball
Crew
Cross-country
Cycling
Field hockey
Football
Golf
Hockey
Lacrosse
Soccer
Softball
Squash
Swimming
Tennis
Track
Volleyball
Water polo
Wrestling
Other sports (please specify):

QUESTION 6

Which of the extracurricular activities listed above do you enjoy the most? Why? *Text Limit: 250 characters (approximately 5 lines)*

Plans after graduation

QUESTION 7

How many colleges are you applying to? (If more than 20, please choose "20.")

QUESTION 8

What is your first choice, and why? *Text Limit: 250 characters (approximately 5 lines)*

QUESTION 9

If you are not planning to go to college next year, what are your plans following graduation, and why? *Text Limit: 250 characters (approximately 5 lines)*

Background questions

QUESTION 10

What do your parents / does your parent do for a living? (You may include step-parents.) *Text Limit: 200 characters (approximately 4 lines)*

QUESTION 11

Has anyone else in your family attended (or currently attend) Weston? If so, when? And how are you related? *Text Limit: 100 characters (approximately 2 lines)*

QUESTION 12

Do you receive financial assistance from the school in order to attend Weston?

Yes
No
Prefer not to answer

QUESTION 13

In what grade did you enter Weston?

9
10
11
12
PG

QUESTION 14

Are you a day or boarding student?

A. Boarding
B. Day
C. Term abroad

QUESTION 15

What is your gender?

QUESTION 16

How would you describe your ethnic or racial background? *Text Limit: 100 characters (approximately 2 lines)*

Click the "Submit for Error Checking" button below to confirm your responses to the questions above. On the next page, you may review your responses. Click the "Next" button at the bottom of the page to answer the last question. You must answer this last question in order to complete the questionnaire.

Below, you are given two choices regarding future participation in this research project. You must choose one of these options in order to complete the questionnaire. None of these options obligates you to participate in any of the future phases of this research. Regardless of what selection you choose, your answers to this questionnaire will remain confidential (your name will never be used). If you would like to keep your responses to this questionnaire anonymous, please click "No" below. Your answers will not be identified in any way.

* Would you be willing to be contacted regarding participation on this study?

A. No, I do not wish to be contacted.
B. Yes, you can contact me. (Please enter your email address and/or campus extension in the space below.)

Thanks for completing the questionnaire. Your answers will be very helpful in guiding my research. All of your responses are protected and saved in a secure server and are strictly confidential. If you indicated interest in participating further in this research, I will contact you shortly. Thanks again!

STUDENT INTERVIEW PROTOCOL

Part 1

INTRODUCTION

Hello. Thanks for agreeing to participate in my study. I appreciate your time. The whole interview will take about two hours, which we will divide into two sixty-minute sessions, but we can end the conversation at any point in the interview. Before we start I want to make sure that you agree to have the interview tape-recorded. This will help me to return to our conversation later and make sure that I capture your stories completely. It will also allow me to listen to you closely. You can ask me to stop the recording at any point. Our conversation is confidential; and if I quote you in my work, I will not use your name or any details that may identify who you are. Is this okay with you?

1. I'd like to begin by asking you to tell me about your decision to apply to Weston.

Narrative Prompts

- How did you find out about this school?

- What were some of the reasons you chose to attend Weston?

- When did you come to the school for the first time, and what was your first impression of Weston?

2. Can you share with me one of your first experiences at Weston that has stayed with you?

3. Tell me about what it is like to come to Weston in terms of your friends at home and family.

Narrative Prompts

- Where is your hometown?

- What is it like when you go home?

- What do your friends at home think about Weston?

- What does your family think about Weston?

*******First interview will stop here*******

Part 2

Before we continue with the second interview, I'd like to know if you had any thoughts after our last conversation that you would like to share with me. During this interview, I would like to return to your impressions of Weston and also focus on your plans for the future.

1. I'd like to learn more about your experience here and your impressions of the school.

Narrative Prompts

- In the questionnaire, you described your academic strengths as _____. Can you tell me more about that? And how has Weston supported your interest in this?

- In the questionnaire, you also said that you found _____ most challenging. Do you recall an instance that illustrates how challenging this is for you?

- What has been most important to you about Weston? Can you give me an example?

- Do you believe that your background and your experiences prior to coming to Weston have shaped your experience here? If so, what aspects of who you are have been most important in your Weston experience? How does being _____ influence your experience at Weston? If not, why not?

- What have been the most challenging aspects of being a student at Weston? Can you give me an example?

- Would you say that Weston would be a good place for any student? Why or why not? Do you know any friends at home that you think would be good Westonians? Can you describe them for me?

2. I'd like to learn about your future goals, and how you feel Weston has prepared you to pursue those goals.

Narrative Prompts

- Have you thought about any career pursuits? If so, what are they, and how has Weston helped you develop those interests?

- What kinds of jobs do you see yourself doing in the future?

- If you had children, would you send them to Weston? Why, or why not?

3. Is there anything else that you would like to share with me about your experience at Weston?

4. Do you have any questions for me that I may be able to answer?

Thanks again for spending this time with me and for sharing your experiences. I am very grateful for your participation. I will transcribe the tape of our interview and will send you the transcription, so that you can review it and let me know if there are things you'd like to correct or clarify.

NOTES

INTRODUCTION

1. R. W. Connell et al., *Making the Difference: Schools, Families, and Social Division* (Boston: Allen and Unwin, 1982); Laura Nader, "Up the Anthropologist: Perspectives Gained from Studying Up," in Dell Hymes, ed., *Reinventing Anthropology* (New York: Pantheon, 1972).

2. Ross Gregory Douthat, *Privilege: Harvard and the Education of the Ruling Class* (New York: Hyperion, 2005), 12 (italics in original).

3. The names of all people and places in this book have been changed. In addition, some of the physical details of the descriptions have been altered in ways that do not undermine the analysis. Physical descriptions and other personal details thus may at times be incomplete or intentionally misleading. In deciding which details to keep and which to alter, I consulted with officials from the school, who helped to identify details that might make the school recognizable and offered alternatives.

4. Sara Lawrence-Lightfoot, *The Good High School* (New York: Basic Books, 1983); Sara Lawrence-Lightfoot and Jessica Hoffmann Davis, *The Art and Science of Portraiture* (San Francisco: Jossey-Bass, 1997). The aim of portraiture is to develop rich descriptions based on data collected through qualitative research methods, such as participant observations and interviews. Portraiture focuses on "goodness" through an "intentionally generous and eclectic process that begins by searching for what is good and healthy and assumes that the expression of goodness will always be laced with imperfections" (Lawrence-Lightfoot and Davis, *The Art and Science of Portraiture,* 9). Portraits are descriptive accounts of particular institutions or people in which the analysis of the data is embedded in the richness and aesthetic dimensions of the descriptions.

5. Michael Apple, *Ideology and Curriculum* (London: Routledge, 1979); Elliot Eisner, *The Educational Imagination* (New York: Macmillan, 1979); Theodore R. Sizer, *Horace's Compromise: The Dilemma of the American High School* (Boston: Houghton Mifflin, 1984); Philip W. Jackson, *Life in Classrooms* (New York: Holt, Rinehart and Winston, 1968).

6. Gerald Grant, *The World We Created at Hamilton High* (Cambridge, Mass.: Harvard University Press, 1988), 4.

7. The school was originally named University High School, and to this day is commonly known by its English initials, UHS. The official name of the school, however, is the Escuela Secundaria de la Universidad de Puerto Rico.

8. E. Digby Baltzell, *Philadelphia Gentlemen: The Making of a National Upper Class* (Chicago: Quadrangle Paperbacks, 1958); idem, *The Protestant Establishment: Aristocracy and Caste in America* (New York: Vintage, 1964); Peter W. Cookson and Caroline Hodges Persell, *Preparing for Power: Amer-*

ica's Elite Boarding Schools (New York: Basic Books, 1985); Steve B. Levine, "The Rise of American Boarding Schools and the Development of a National Upper Class," *Social Problems,* 28, no. 1 (1980); C. Wright Mills, *The Power Elite* (London: Oxford University Press, 1956); Alan Peshkin, *Permissible Advantage? The Moral Consequences of Elite Schooling* (Mahwah, N.J.: Lawrence Erlbaum, 2001); John Wakeford, *The Cloistered Elite: A Sociological Analysis of the English Public Boarding School* (London: Macmillan, 1969); Ian Weinberg, *The English Public Schools: The Sociology of Elite Education* (New York: Atherton, 1967).

9. As stipulated in the initial letter of agreement between the school and myself, I obtained permission from the school to use the data I collected on its behalf during the first year. Brief sections of this book originally formed part of my report to the school. I then revised them for the purposes of this book, with the school's approval.

10. See Harry Wolcott, *Ethnography: A Way of Seeing* (Lanham, Md.: Altamira, 2008).

11. This phrase was originally coined by James Clifford in *Routes: Travel and Translation in the Late Twentieth Century* (Cambridge, Mass.: Harvard University Press, 1997). The concept was developed later by Clifford Geertz in *Available Light: Anthropological Reflections on Philosophical Topics* (Princeton, N.J.: Princeton University Press, 2000).

12. The idea that social structures reproduce through complex social processes is as old as Auguste Comte and sociology itself. The role of schooling in social reproduction has been at the heart of education sociology, and was eloquently and famously articulated in Samuel Bowles and Herbert Gintis, *Schooling in Capitalist America: Educational Reform and the Contradictions of Economic Life* (New York: Basic Books, 1976). See also Basil Bernstein, *Class, Codes, and Control* (London: Routledge and Kegan Paul, 1971); Pierre Bourdieu and Jean-Claude Passeron, *Reproduction in Education, Society, and Culture* (London: Sage, 1990).

13. Legacy practices abruptly entered public discourse when a reporter at the "Unity: Journalists of Color" convention challenged George W. Bush, himself the beneficiary of legacy admissions, to justify the practice in light of his opposition to other forms of affirmative action and his claim that admissions should be solely based on merit. Bush and other politicians have called for an end to legacy admissions, but so far there is no movement in that direction. See Amy Goldstein, "Bush Hits 'Legacy' College Admissions: President Addresses Minority Journalists," *Washington Post,* August 7, 2004. See also Jerome Karabel, *The Chosen: The Hidden History of Admission and Exclusion at Harvard, Yale, and Princeton* (Boston: Houghton Mifflin, 2005).

14. The range of per-pupil spending is quite broad from state to state. In 2005, while Utah spent $5,216 per pupil, New Jersey ($14,117), New York ($13,703), the District of Columbia ($13,348), and Connecticut ($12,263) were well above the national average. See National Center for Education Statistics (NCES), U.S. Department of Education, "National Public Education Financial Survey, 2004–2005" (Washington, D.C.: NCES, 2008). The $46,000 figure is a conservative estimate based on the reported average for all boarding school members of the National Association of Independent Schools (NAIS). "NAIS Facts at a Glance, 2007–2008" (Washington, D.C.: NAIS, 2008), available at www.nais.org/resources/statistical.cfm?Item Number=146713 (accessed February 10, 2009). Not all of the boarding schools included fit the category of elite boarding schools. It is safe to assume that elite boarding schools spend more than the average, given their resources. Based on informal estimates, schools like Weston spend closer to $80,000 per student.

15. According to the NAIS, tuition covers only about half the cost of educating each student, with another third coming from investment income and the remainder from other sources such as gifts and external grants. National Association of Independent Schools, "2006 NAIS Non-Tuition Survey" (Washington, D.C.: NAIS, 2006), available at www.nais.org/resources/seriesdoc.cfm?ItemNumber=148270 (accessed December 15, 2008). In 2008, the combined endowment of twenty-eight schools that fit the criteria for elite boarding schools totaled a staggering $6.3 billion, with an average of $225 million per school. See Rubén A. Gaztambide-Fernández, "What Is an Elite Boarding School?" *Review of Educational Research,* 79, no. 3 (2009).

16. See Paul William Kingston, *The Classless Society* (Stanford, Calif.: Stanford University Press, 2000); Jan Pakulski and Malcolm Waters, *The Death of Class* (Thousand Oaks, Calif.: Sage, 1996); Jan Pakulski and Malcolm Waters, "The Reshaping and Dissolution of Social Class in Advanced Society," *Theory and Society*, 25 (1996). For a critique of these arguments, see Erik Olin Wright, *Classes* (London: Verso, 1985).

17. See, for instance, Jonathan Kozol, *Savage Inequalities: Children in America's Schools* (New York: Harper Perennial, 1992); Jonathan Kozol, *The Shame of the Nation: The Restoration of Apartheid Schooling in America* (New York: Crown, 2005).

18. In outlining the differences between reproduction, social reproduction, cultural reproduction, and cultural production, Paul Willis argues that the term "reproduction" refers strictly to the biologically grounded process of replacing parents with their children. Paul Willis, "Cultural Production Is Different from Cultural Reproduction Is Different from Social Reproduction Is Different from Reproduction," *Interchange*, 12, nos. 2–3 (1981).

19. See Robert Granfield, *Making Elite Lawyers: Visions of Law at Harvard and Beyond* (New York: Routledge, 1992); Peter Kuriloff and Michael Reichert, "Boys of Class, Boys of Color: Negotiating the Academic and Social Geography of an Elite Independent School," *Journal of Social Issues*, 59, no. 4 (2003); Richard Sennett and Jonathan Cobb, *The Hidden Injuries of Class* (New York: Norton, 1972); Valerie Walkerdine, "Workers in the New Economy: Transformation as Border Crossing," *Ethos*, 34, no. 1 (2006).

20. Max Weber, "The Distribution of Power within the Political Community: Class, Status, Party," in Max Weber, *Economy and Society: An Outline of Interpretive Sociology* (Berkeley, Calif.: University of California Press, 1978), ch. 9, sect. 6.

21. Fredrik Barth, "Introduction," in Fredrik Barth, ed., *Ethnic Groups and Boundaries* (Boston: Little, Brown, 1969); Michèle Lamont, *Money, Morals, and Manners: The Culture of the French and American Upper-Middle Class* (Chicago: University of Chicago Press, 1992); Michèle Lamont, *The Dignity of Working Men: Morality and the Boundaries of Race, Class, and Immigration* (Cambridge, Mass.: Harvard University Press, 2000); Charles Tilly, *Identities, Boundaries, and Social Ties* (Boulder, Colo.: Paradigm, 2005).

22. According to Michèle Lamont and Virág Molnár, boundaries are "conceptual distinctions made by social actors to categorize objects, people, practices, and even time and space." Lamont and Molnár, "The Study of Boundaries in the Social Sciences," *Annual Review of Sociology*, 28 (2002): 168. See also Michèle Lamont, "Symbolic Boundaries," in Neil J. Smelser and Paul B. Baltes, eds., *International Encyclopedia of the Social and Behavioral Sciences* (New York: Elsevier Science, 2001).

23. The dominant view of identity comes from developmental psychologist Erik Erikson. For Erikson, identity is the result of a developmental process that is particularly intense during adolescence. The process of developing an "identity" involves a series of "crises," occurring at all stages of life, through which an individual deepens a sense of himself or herself as a social being by internalizing various labels and characteristics. Erikson was careful to provide a dynamic enough view of identity to be able to capture the deeply social nature of what he ultimately defined as an internal, psychic "process 'located' *in the core of the individual* and yet also *in the core of his communal culture,* a process which establishes, in fact, the identity of those two identities" (22). Yet Erikson was particularly concerned with specifying the mental processes involved in defining individual identity, even as he asserted that this was an inherently social process, and his definition of identity reflects this focus on identity as a cognitive rather than a social process. Erik Erikson, *Identity: Youth and Crisis* (New York: Norton, 1968).

24. Rogers Brubaker and Frederick Cooper, "Beyond 'Identity,'" *Theory and Society*, 29, no. 1 (2000); Philip Gleason, "Identifying Identity: A Semantic History," *Journal of American History*, 69, no. 4 (1983); Stuart Hall, "Introduction: Who Needs 'Identity'?" in Stuart Hall and Paul du Gay, eds., *Questions of Cultural Identity* (London: Sage, 1996); Richard Jenkins, *Social Identity* (London: Routledge, 1996). This approach to understanding identification has a long trajectory within feminist intellectual traditions, particularly the work of multicultural radical and Third World feminists. See Chandra

Talpade Mohanty, *Feminism without Borders: Decolonizing Theory, Practicing Solidarity* (Durham, N.C.: Duke University Press, 2003).

25. These strategies might involve: public behaviors and linguistic patterns (see Shirley Brice Heath, *Ways with Words: Language, Life, and Work in Communities and Classrooms* [Cambridge: Cambridge University Press, 1983]); clothing and music preferences (see Dick Hebdige, *Subculture: The Meaning of Style* [London: Methuen, 1979]; and ways of consuming and producing culture (see Paul Willis, *Common Culture: Symbolic Work at Play in the Everyday Cultures of the Young* [Boulder, Colo.: Westview, 1990]).

26. "Identity repertoire" theories have evolved since the early work of interpretivist sociology and the work of George H. Mead, *Mind, Self, and Society* (Chicago: University of Chicago Press, 1934). One of the important strands that grew from this work, and that has had significant influence on how the notion of identity has evolved, is the dramaturgical definition of identity as performance. See Erving Goffman, *The Presentation of Self in Everyday Life* (Garden City, N.Y.: Doubleday Anchor, 1959). In his classic text, Goffman is concerned with understanding how individuals mobilize their symbolic resources to particular ends, depending on the task at hand. Goffman argues that we can understand broader social processes and institutions by considering the roles that individuals assume and perform in those settings. He argues that social institutions "may be studied profitably from the point of view of impression management. Within the walls of a social establishment we find a team of performers who cooperate to present to an audience a given definition of the situation" (238). More than "the general notion that we make a presentation of ourselves to others," which Goffman notes is not particularly novel, his point "is that the very structure of the self can be seen in terms of how we arrange for such performances" (252). For Goffman, all presentations of the self (or identities) must be actualized in real time—they must be performed—in order for them to acquire significance.

27. See, for instance, Richard Ashmore, Kay Deaux, and Tracy McLaughlin-Volpe, "An Organizing Framework for Collective Identity: Articulation and Significance of Multidimensionality," *Psychological Bulletin,* 130, no. 1 (2004); Brubaker and Cooper, "Beyond 'Identity'"; Hall, "Who Needs 'Identity'?"; Stuart Hall, ed., *Representation: Cultural Representations and Signifying Practice* (London: Sage, 1997); Dorothy C. Holland and Jean Lave, eds., *History in Person: Enduring Struggles, Contentious Practice, Intimate Identities* (Santa Fe, N.M.: School of American Research Press, 2001); Jenkins, *Social Identity;* Bradley Levinson, Douglas Foley, and Dorothy Holland, eds., *The Cultural Production of the Educated Person: Critical Ethnographies of Schooling and Local Practice* (Albany, N.Y.: SUNY Press, 1996).

28. See, for instance, Lois Weis, ed., *Class, Race, and Gender in American Education* (Albany, N.Y.: SUNY Press, 1988); Lois Weis and Michelle Fine, eds., *Beyond Silenced Voices: Class, Race, and Gender in United States Schools* (Albany, N.Y.: SUNY Press, 1993); Lois Weis and Michelle Fine, eds., *Construction Sites: Excavating Race, Class, and Gender among Urban Youth* (New York: Teachers College Press, 2000).

29. On resistance, see Michelle Fine, *Framing Dropouts: Notes on the Politics of an Urban Public High School* (Albany, N.Y.: SUNY Press, 1991); Signithia Fordham, *Blacked Out: Dilemmas of Race, Identity, and Success at Capital High* (Chicago: University of Chicago Press, 1996). On reproduction, see Dorothy C. Holland and Margaret A. Eisenhart, *Educated in Romance: Women, Achievement, and College Culture* (Chicago: University of Chicago Press, 1990); Jay MacLeod, *Ain't No Makin' It: Leveled Aspirations in a Low-Income Neighborhood* (Boulder, Colo.: Westview Press, 1995). On redefinition, see L. Janelle Dance, *Tough Fronts: The Impact of Street Culture on Schooling* (London: Routledge, 2002); Wendy Luttrell, *Pregnant Bodies, Fertile Minds: Gender, Race, and the Schooling of Pregnant Teens* (New York: Routledge, 2003).

30. For instance, while Willis clearly demonstrates how the "lads" draw boundaries between themselves and the "ear'oles," we know nothing about how the "ear'oles" experience their schooling and the ways in which they also engage in processes of identification. See Paul Willis, *Learning to Labour*

(Farnborough, U.K.: Saxon House, 1977). Wendy Luttrell offers an insightful account of the paradoxical complexities in how the women in her study related to the notion of the "teacher's pet" as a kind of "good student" identification. Wendy Luttrell, *Schoolsmart and Motherwise: Working-Class Women's Identity and Schooling* (New York: Routledge, 1997).

31. Dorothy Holland and Kevin Leander define "positioning" as the process through which a powerful body, such as an elite boarding school, calls upon an individual to assume a specific social position that the institution has created for him or her in the social space. Dorothy C. Holland and Kevin Leander, "Ethnographic Studies of Positioning and Subjectivity: An Introduction," *Ethos*, 32, no. 2 (2004).

32. Catherine Riessman, "Narrative Analysis," in Michael S. Lewis-Beck, Alan Bryman, and Tim Futing Liao, eds., *The Sage Encyclopedia of Social Science Research Methods* (Thousand Oaks, Calif.: Sage, 2004). The early work in linguistics by William Labov has been especially influential in this tradition of narrative analysis. See, for instance, William Labov, *Language in the Inner City: Studies in the Black English Vernacular* (Philadelphia: University of Pennsylvania Press, 1972); William Labov, "Speech Actions and Reactions in Personal Narrative," in Deborah Tannen, ed., *Analyzing Discourse: Text and Talk* (Washington, D.C.: Georgetown University Press, 1981). See also W. J. T. Mitchell, ed., *On Narrative* (Chicago: University of Chicago Press, 1981).

33. Jerome Bruner, *Acts of Meaning* (Cambridge, Mass.: Harvard University Press, 1990), 111. This is what Bruner calls "narrative discourse." See also Jerome Bruner, *Actual Minds, Possible Worlds* (Cambridge, Mass.: Harvard University Press, 1986).

34. J. A. Simpson and E. S. C. Weiner eds., *OED Online* (Oxford: Oxford University Press, 1989), s.v. "distinction," available at dictionary.oed.com/cgi/entry/50067355? (accessed March 17, 2009).

35. *OED Online*, s.v. "distinction." In the sociological literature, the term "distinction" was made famous by Pierre Bourdieu, *Distinction: A Social Critique of the Judgment of Taste*, trans. Richard Nice (Cambridge, Mass.: Harvard University Press, 1984). Bourdieu brought the analysis of the relationship between class status and cultural consumption to new heights by arguing that taste—that most elusive dimension of cultural engagement—was a way for status groups to demarcate boundaries that distinguished those with high cultural capital from those without. Bourdieu also mobilized the term "distinction" for its dual meaning by suggesting that taste is not only a marker of difference but, more importantly, a marker of social rank. He was interested in explaining taste as a marker of status and social-class boundaries, and the ways these are maintained through cultural practices.

36. According to Michel Foucault, discursive formations have three characteristics: (1) they delimit what is "sayable" and who is authorized to make truth claims; (2) they limit the range of meanings that are possible for individuals; and (3) they impose specific roles on the agents of discourse and set the conditions for speaking, and restrict who can obtain that formation. Thus, he writes: "Any system of education is a political way of maintaining or modifying the appropriation of discourse, along with the power and knowledge to carry." Michel Foucault, "The Order of Discourse," in Robert Young, ed., *Untying the Text: A Post-Structuralist Reader* (London: Routledge and Kegan Paul, 1971; rpt. 1981), 66. For Foucault, discourses reflect the relations of power which underlie their formation and which, in turn, are maintained through that discourse. This means that discourses can never be neutral—and the discourse of distinction is no exception.

37. James Paul Gee, *An Introduction to Discourse Analysis: Theory and Method* (New York: Routledge, 1999), 7.

38. This is what James Gee calls "big D" Discourse. This distinction is useful in Gee's presentation of D/discourse analysis. I will be talking only about discourse in its encompassing definition, and will use the "little d" spelling. I will use "language," instead of "discourse," to describe how words are used in particular instances.

39. Critical discourse analysis "argues that language in use is always part and parcel of, and partially constitutive of, specific social practices, and that social practices always have implications for in-

herently political things like status, solidarity, distribution of social goods, and power." James Paul Gee, "Discourse Analysis: What Makes It Critical?" in Rebecca Rogers, ed., *An Introduction to Critical Discourse Analysis in Education* (Mahwah, N.J.: Lawrence Erlbaum, 2004), 33. In other words, discourse is the product of social, political, and ideological processes, as well as the means through which they evolve. As such, analyzing discourse can yield insights about the processes that underlie its production. For an excellent review of the literature, including definitions, approaches, and debates in critical discourse analysis, see Rebecca Rogers et al., "Critical Discourse Analysis in Education: A Review of the Literature," *Review of Educational Research,* 75, no. 3 (2005).

40.   "Culture," too, is a term that has suffered a great deal of conceptual diffusion. For discussions of the conceptual development of "culture," see Clifford Geertz, *The Interpretation of Cultures* (New York: Basic Books, 1973); Adam Kuper, *Culture: The Anthropologists' Account* (Cambridge, Mass.: Harvard University Press, 1999); Raymond Williams, *Culture and Society, 1780/1950* (New York: Columbia University Press, 1958). If, as anthropologist Fredrik Barth argues, culture is "nothing but a way to describe human behavior," then discourse is one of those things people do that we can describe as part of cultural analysis. Barth, "Introduction," *Ethnic Groups and Boundaries,* 9. Alternatively, if we take culture to be the "webs of significance" human beings have spun and upon which they are suspended, discourse is one way in which these webs are organized and gain coherence, and in which they manifest and make themselves knowable. Geertz, *Interpretation of Cultures.*

41.   Holland and Lave, "History in Person: An Introduction," 4.

42.   This antiquated view of culture dates back to the early work of anthropologists like Margaret Mead, who saw "cultures" as objective and predetermined entities that could be "collected" through observation; see the discussion in James Clifford, *The Predicament of Culture: Twentieth-Century Ethnography, Literature, and Art* (Cambridge, Mass.: Harvard University Press, 1988). While this view of culture has been thoroughly dismantled by cultural theorists, it persists as the most pervasive view of culture. For recent articulations of this view of culture as a way to explain academic inequality, see Orlando Patterson, "A Poverty of the Mind," *New York Times,* March 26, 2006; Ruby Payne, "Nine Powerful Practices," *Educational Leadership,* 65, no. 7 (2008); Ruby Payne and Kim Ellis, *A Framework for Understanding Poverty* (Highlands, Tex.: Aha! Process, 1996); Abigail Thernstrom and Stephan Thernstrom, *No Excuses: Closing the Racial Gap in Learning* (New York: Simon and Schuster, 2004). Bill Cosby has become the most famous celebrity to foment this view of culture as a way to explain academic failure. For a sustained critique of this discourse, see Michael Eric Dyson, *Is Bill Cosby Right? Or Has the Black Middle Class Lost Its Mind?* (New York: Basic Civitas, 2005).

43.   This departs somewhat from Geertz's original view of culture as webs of meaning (Geertz, *Interpretation of Cultures*). It suggests that meanings are also politically and economically organized for the achievement of particular hierarchical arrangements that are sustained symbolically by those very webs.

44.   Stanton Wortham, "Curriculum as a Source for the Development of Social Identity," *Sociology of Education,* 76, no. 3 (2003); idem, "From Good Student to Outcast: The Emergence of a Classroom Identity," *Ethos,* 32, no. 2 (2004).

45.   Willis, *Learning to Labour,* 194. See also R. W. Connell, *Schools and Social Justice* (Philadelphia: Temple University Press, 1993); Holland and Lave, *History in Person;* Holland and Leander, "Positioning and Subjectivity"; Paul Willis, "Foot Soldiers of Modernity: The Dialectics of Cultural Consumption and the 21st-Century School," *Harvard Educational Review,* 73, no. 3 (2003).

46.   See Barbara Ehrenreich, *Nickel and Dimed: On (Not) Getting by in America* (New York: Metropolitan Books, 2001); Douglas Massey, *Categorically Unequal: The American Stratification System* (New York: Russell Sage Foundation Publications, 2007).

47.   Erving Goffman, *Asylums: Essays on the Social Situation of Mental Patients and Other Inmates* (New York: Anchor, 1961).

48.   Wortham, "Curriculum and Social Identity"; idem, "Good Student to Outcast."

49. See Kevin Kumashiro, *Troubling Education: Queer Activism and Antioppressive Pedagogy* (New York: Routledge, 2002).

I. TOTALLY ELITE

1. J. D. Salinger, *The Catcher in the Rye* (New York: Bantam, 1945), 131.

2. Curtis Sittenfeld, *Prep* (New York: Random, 2005), 15.

3. John Irving, *A Prayer for Owen Meany* (New York: Ballantine, 1989); John Knowles, *A Separate Peace* (New York: Macmillan, 1960).

4. *Dead Poets Society,* dir. Peter Weir, screenplay by Tom Schulman (Touchstone Pictures, 1989); *School Ties,* dir. Robert Mandel, screenplay by Dick Wolf (Paramount Pictures, 1992).

5. *O,* dir. Tim Blake Nelson, screenplay by Brad Kaaya (Lions Gate Films, 2001).

6. The catalogue of fictional literature and feature films that use boarding schools as the narrative context is too extensive to quote in its entirety. In addition to the few cited here, some recent examples include the Harry Potter series by J. K. Rowling, published by Scholastic, and Taylor Antrim, *The Headmaster Ritual* (New York: Houghton Mifflin, 2007). There is also a growing catalogue of young-adult fiction that takes place in private schools, such as the book series *Private,* by Kate Brian and Julian Peploe, published by Simon Pulse, and the *Upper Class* series by Hobson Brown, Taylor Materne, and Caroline Says, published by HarperTeen. Lists of novels and films that take place in boarding schools are available through Web resources like Wikipedia. See Wikipedia, s.v. "boarding school," en.wikipedia.org/w/index.php?title=Boarding_school&oldid=249520222 (accessed November 3, 2008).

7. Richard Barbieri, "Different Forms of Independent Education," in Pearl R. Kane, ed., *Independent Schools, Independent Thinkers* (San Francisco: Jossey-Bass, 1992), 27.

8. In a sustained attempt to distinguish among various kinds of "nonpublic" or "private" schools (the terms are used interchangeably), Otto Kraushaar develops a distinction between "denominational" and "independent" schools. Catholic "parochial" schools are the most typical, but there are also Protestant, Jewish, Muslim, and other religiously affiliated schools. See Otto F. Kraushaar, *American Nonpublic Schools: Patterns of Diversity* (Baltimore: Johns Hopkins University Press, 1972). Kraushaar notes that some independent schools are associated with particular denominations, usually Episcopalian, the denomination most often associated with the Protestant establishment described in E. Digby Baltzell, *Philadelphia Gentlemen: The Making of a National Upper Class* (New York: Free Press, 1958); and idem, *The Protestant Establishment: Aristocracy and Caste in America* (New York: Vintage, 1964). Barbieri also notes that the distinction between "denominational" and "independent" is somewhat complicated by the fact that many "independent schools are religiously affiliated, . . . with Episcopal and Quaker schools clearly falling well within the accepted independent school definition" (Barbieri, "Different Forms of Independent Education," 28).

9. See, for example, Leonard Baird, *The Elite Schools: A Profile of Prestigious Independent Schools* (Lexington, Mass.: Lexington Books, 1977); Kane, *Independent Schools, Independent Thinkers;* James McLachlan, *American Boarding Schools* (New York: Scribner, 1970); Arthur G. Powell, *Lessons from Privilege: The American Prep School Tradition* (Cambridge, Mass.: Harvard University Press, 1996); Theodore R. Sizer, ed., *The Age of the Academies* (New York: Bureau of Publications, Teachers College, Columbia University, 1964).

10. I discuss the first and second groups in more depth in this chapter. For examples of the third group, see J. E. Chubb and T. M. Moe, *Politics, Markets, and American Schools* (Washington, D.C.: Brookings Institution, 1990); E. Vance Randall, *Private Schools and Public Power: A Case for Pluralism* (New York: Teachers College Press, 1994). Educational historian Diane Ravitch, for instance, in her personal and impassioned defense of private schools as de facto protectors of diversity in the school system, treats all private schools, from elite boarding to urban Catholic schools, as if they were the same, or at least as if they served the same role in the broader educational system. See Diane Ravitch, "Differ-

ent Drummers: The Role of Nonpublic Schools in America Today," *Teachers College Record,* 92, no. 3 (1991).

11. Max Weber, "The Definitions of Sociology and of Social Action," in Max Weber, *Economy and Society: An Outline of Interpretive Sociology* (Berkeley, Calif.: University of California Press, 1978).

12. Specific details or examples in this chapter are not necessarily drawn from the Weston School and should not be interpreted as identifiers of the school.

13. I define boarding (or residential) schools as those in which 80 to 90 percent of the student body lives in dormitory-style residential halls for the majority of the time during the academic year. Nonpublic schools are either "day" or "boarding" schools. At most boarding schools, a relatively small number of students live at home and attend as "day students." Likewise, some day schools have small residential programs. Yet with few exceptions, schools identify as one or the other.

14. Erving Goffman, *Asylums: Essays on the Social Situation of Mental Patients and Other Inmates* (New York: Anchor, 1961).

15. Philip W. Jackson, *Life in Classrooms* (New York: Holt, Rinehart, and Winston, 1968). The notion of the "hidden curriculum" is based on Max Weber's distinction between "manifest" and "latent" functions. Manifest functions are those that are clearly articulated as the primary goals of the institution; latent functions are those that, while not articulated or self-evident, are crucial for the perpetuation of society. See also Michael Apple, *Ideology and Curriculum* (London: Routledge, 1979); Elliot Eisner, *The Educational Imagination* (New York: Macmillan, 1979); and Henry A. Giroux, *Theory and Resistance in Education: Towards a Pedagogy for the Opposition* (Westport, Conn.: Bergin and Garvey, 2001).

16. Goffman, *Asylums.* See, for instance, Peter W. Cookson and Caroline Hodges Persell, *Preparing for Power: America's Elite Boarding Schools* (New York: Basic Books, 1985); Thomas James, "Totality in Private and Public Schooling," *American Journal of Education,* 97, no. 1 (1988); John Wakeford, *The Cloistered Elite: A Sociological Analysis of the English Public Boarding School* (New York: Praeger, 1969). More recent authors take the categorization for granted and offer no further discussion; see Sarah A. Chase, *Perfectly Prep: Gender Extremes at a New England Prep School* (New York: Oxford University Press, 2008).

17. Goffman outlines five types of "total institutions": (1) those that protect vulnerable inmates from danger due to some incapacity (homes for the blind, assisted-living residences, etc.); (2) those that care for inmates who pose a threat to public health (mental hospitals, leprosaria, etc.); (3) those containing inmates who pose a threat to society (prisons, concentration camps, etc.); (4) those that allow inmates to pursue a particular task or endeavor (army barracks, ships, servants' quarters, boarding schools, etc.); and (5) those that provide a retreat from the world for their inmates, who may be in search of religious enlightenment (convents, abbeys, etc.).

18. Goffman, *Asylums,* 5–6.

19. Ibid., 6.

20. Goffman's own research focused on mental hospitals, and he draws the most compelling and detailed examples from his own work. His discussion also focuses largely on those institutions "serving" the needs of individuals who are incapable of taking care of themselves and who may pose an involuntary threat to society (e.g., mental patients), and those overseeing the lives of dangerous individuals (e.g., prisons). It is not surprising, therefore, that the framework of total institutions has been most influential in the analyses of these settings, and only loosely used in the analysis of boarding schools and similar institutions that might otherwise fit Goffman's categories. See George A. Hillery, "Villages, Cities, and Total Institutions," *American Sociological Review,* 28, no. 5 (1963); Madeline Karmel, "Total Institution and Self-Mortification," *Journal of Health and Social Behavior,* 10, no. 2 (1969); C. A. McEwen, "Continuities in the Study of Total and Nontotal Institutions," *Annual Review of Sociology,* 6 (1980).

21. George Orwell, "Such, Such Were the Joys," *Partisan Review* (1952).

22. Goffman, *Asylums,* 62.

23. Ibid., 72.

24. Sara Lawrence-Lightfoot, *The Good High School* (New York: Basic Books, 1983), 340.

25. The concept of presentation "management" is also Goffman's. See Erving Goffman, *The Presentation of Self in Everyday Life* (Garden City, N.Y.: Doubleday Anchor, 1959).

26. Goffman, *Asylums*, 5–6, italics added.

27. This difference is crucial to the relationship between the inmates (students) and the staff. While Goffman argues that inmates in total institutions are highly unlikely to ever become the staff, and even less likely to ever rise above the staff, in total institutions like boarding schools the crossing between inmates and staff is not only likely, but common. Even more distinct is the fact that those who ultimately have governance over the institution, and therefore over the staff, are mostly former inmates. Goffman also argues that staff members are placed in a hierarchical position in terms of their association with the institution, and that both staff and inmates come to associate the institutional name and facilities with the staff first and the inmates second. The situation is quite different at an elite boarding school, where only the students (and former students) can claim the label "Westonian."

28. Goffman does address the fact that there are aspects of inmates' lives which take place "backstage"—behind interactions with and outside the gaze of the institutional authority. Building on Goffman, Anthony Giddens suggests that these spaces of intimacy are ultimately more important in the construction of social bonds than the solitude of an activity like sleep. For Giddens, "at least one connotation of 'privacy' is the regional isolation of an individual—or of individuals, for privacy does not seem inevitably to imply solitude—from the ordinary demands of the monitoring of action and gesture." Anthony T. Giddens, *The Constitution of Society: Outline of the Theory of Structuration* (Berkeley, Calif.: University of California Press, 1984), 129. This distinction in the "monitoring" of behavior is the crucial difference between the social sphere and the sphere of intimacy: whereas the former involves monitoring by (and thus performing for) relative strangers in a public space, the latter involves monitoring by intimate others and the self. As Giddens explains, "Back regions which allow the individual complete solitude from the presence of others may be less important than those which allow the expression of 'regressive behaviors' in situations of co-presence" (129). By "regressive behaviors" Giddens means acts which are not socially acceptable when performed in public, but which may imply a sense of intimacy when enacted in the presence of intimates. Giddens cites Goffman to provide examples, such as "profanity, open sexual remarks, elaborate griping, . . . inconsiderateness for the other in minor but potentially symbolic acts, minor physical self-involvements such as humming, whistling, chewing, nibbling, belching, and flatulence." According to Giddens, these intimate experiences with others lead to bonding and "reinforce the basic trust in the presence of intimacy originally built up in relation to the parental figures" (128). As such, they yield a sense of belonging with others.

29. The term "group closure," as Weber uses it, means the process through which status groups "close" access to the resources they control, both symbolic and material, by delineating group boundaries. See Max Weber, "The Economic Relationships of Organized Groups," in Max Weber, *Economy and Society: An Outline of Interpretive Sociology* (Berkeley, Calif.: University of California Press, 1978). Credentialism, for instance, is a closure strategy; see Randall Collins, "Functional and Conflict Theories of Educational Stratification," *American Sociological Review,* 36, no. 6 (1971).

30. For a discussion of the problem of definition, see Rubén Gaztambide-Fernández, "What Is an Elite Boarding School?" *Review of Educational Research,* 79, no. 3. (2009).

31. Caroline Hodges Persell and Peter W. Cookson, "Chartering and Bartering: Elite Education and Social Reproduction," *Social Problems,* 33, no. 2 (1985). Cookson and Persell carefully distinguish between the larger group of "leading" boarding schools and the "truly socially elite" schools. They show quite persuasively, and without lumping together all kinds of boarding schools, that elite boarding schools are able to place their students at a decidedly advantageous position vis-à-vis the students' non-elite peers, particularly in the ability to enter elite colleges. Social networks and informal relationships among admissions officials at both kinds of institutions play a crucial role in the successful placement of students in particular schools. Mitchell Stevens demonstrates this process in rich detail in his book based

on ethnographic research with the admissions office of an elite liberal arts college. See Mitchell Stevens, *Creating a Class: College Admissions and the Education of Elites* (Cambridge, Mass.: Harvard University Press, 2007).

32. Using the *Social Register* as a way to determine a school's eliteness is problematic, if for no other reason than that the same social groups would be in charge of making such distinctions. Furthermore, while in the early 1980s the *Social Register* may have been a more or less accurate representation of elite status, in the past twenty years its authority has declined and it is no longer a reliable index of eliteness. When Tom Jones, who was in charge of the *Social Register,* retired from Forbes, Inc., the news triggered speculation that the days of the register were coming to an end. See Frank DiGiacomo, "The Forbes Family Is Scaling Back *Social Register,*" *New York Observer,* June 17, 2002; Shelley Emling, "*Social Register* Less Influential in Egalitarian Times; Directory's 'Days Not Numbered,' Forbes Insists," *Atlanta Journal Constitution,* June 21, 2002; Rittenhouse Review, "'Oh Dear, Bunny!' What Will Become of the *Social Register?*" rittenhouse.blogspot.com/2002/06/oh-dear-bunny-what-will-become-of.html (accessed November 4, 2008).

33. The term "correspond" is an allusion to Bowles and Gintis' "correspondence principle," which suggests that the organization of the school system parallels the organization of social classes in a way that reproduces that order. Samuel Bowles and Herbert Gintis, *Schooling in Capitalist America: Educational Reform and the Contradictions of Economic Life* (New York: Basic Books, 1976).

34. There certainly are private day schools that could be classified as elite, according to the criteria I present here. I would speculate, however, that the experiences of students in elite day schools are much more similar to those of students in elite public schools than to those of students in elite boarding schools. Kraushaar makes a similar observation when he notes that there are "resemblances in style and atmosphere [between] smaller high schools in affluent suburbs [and] elite private day schools" (Kraushaar, *American Nonpublic,* 12). Jay Mathews' work on elite public schools is informative. He makes the case that about 10 percent of the schools in the public school system could be considered elite, according to his criteria. See Jay Mathews, *Class Struggle: What's Wrong (and Right) with America's Best Public High Schools* (New York: Random House, 1998), 5–7. See also Peter Demerath and Jill Lynch, "Identities for Neoliberal Times: Constructing Enterprising Selves in an American Suburb," in Nadine Dolby and Fazal Rizvi, eds., *Youth Moves: Identities and Education in Global Perspective* (New York: Routledge, 2008); and Adam Howard, *Learning Privilege: Lessons of Power and Identity in Affluent Schooling* (New York: Routledge, 2007).

35. Pearl R. Kane, "Independent Schools in American Education," *Teachers College Record,* 92 (1991). "Independent" is a term that *some* nonpublic schools claim as an alternative to the term "private," which carries a more politically charged and, according to Kraushaar, even "pejorative connotation" (Kraushaar, *American Nonpublic,* 54). It is worth noting that the term "independent" resonates deeply with advocates of nonsectarian private schools, and that it draws on visions of American exceptionalism and libertarian ideology. While "private" may betray the dimension of exclusivity of all nonpublic schools (in that they all get to choose who can enter), "independent" resonates with notions of individualism, meritocracy, and exceptionalism that are ultimately the ideological frames that shape the discursive formation I will describe in the chapters to come. Kane argues that independent schools are "as diverse in character as any comparable number of U.S. citizens" ("Independent Schools," 396). Scholars who have studied independent schools argue that part of the difficulty in defining them lies in their diversity. Indeed, advocates of independent schools go to great lengths to make this argument about diversity in order to reject the "aura of exclusivity and elitism" that is at times associated with private education" (Kane, "Independent Schools," 396). See also Mary E. Henry, *School Cultures: Universes of Meaning in Private Schools* (Norwood, N.J.: Ablex, 1993); Paul William Kingston and Lionel S. Lewis, "Studying Elite Schools in America," in Paul William Kingston and Lionel S. Lewis, eds., *The High-Status Track: Studies of Elite Schools and Stratification* (Albany, N.Y.: SUNY Press, 1990); Alan Peshkin, *Permissible Advantage? The Moral Consequences of Elite Schooling* (Mahwah, N.J.: Lawrence Erlbaum, 2001); Powell, *Lessons from Privilege.* In 2008, the National Association of Independent

Schools (NAIS) counted 1,083 member schools, including 145 boarding schools. See National Association of Independent Schools, "NAIS Facts at a Glance, 2007–2008," www.nais.org/resources/statistical. cfm?ItemNumber=146713 (accessed December 15, 2008). According to NAIS estimates, there are 369 schools, including nine boarding schools, that fit the criteria of "independent" but that are not members of NAIS. The Association of Boarding Schools (TABS) lists 289 member schools, of which 243 are U.S. secondary schools. But these include parochial as well as public schools that do not fit the "independent" category. See Association of Boarding Schools, "School Finder General Search," www.schools.com/directory/adv_search/gen_search (accessed December 15, 2008).

36. For an explanation of what it means to have a government charter and a broad historical overview of the academies that set the precedent for charter schools, see the essays in Nancy Beadie and Kim Tolley, eds., *Chartered Schools: Two Hundred Years of Independent Academies in the United States, 1727–1925* (New York: Routledge, 2002). In their closing chapter, Beadie and Tolley offer an excellent account of the legacy of the academies for today's charter schools. Some early academies were more accountable to the public than others. See, for instance, the case of New York State and the role of the Board of Regents in overseeing early academies; Theodore R. Sizer, "The Academies: An Interpretation," in Sizer, ed., *The Age of the Academies* (New York: Bureau of Publications, Teachers College, Columbia University, 1964).

37. Elite boarding schools vary in the size of their endowments, from about $50 million to $1 billion, with an average of $118 million. See Gaztambide-Fernández, "What Is an Elite Boarding School?" See also Geraldine Fabrikant, "At Elite Prep Schools, College-Size Endowments," *New York Times,* January 26, 2008.

38. Eric Konigsberg, "Never Having to Say, 'Too Expensive,'" *New York Times,* December 30, 2007.

39. McLachlan, *American Boarding Schools;* Sizer, "The Academies." This was not the case for all academies, as many were also founded with the express purpose of educating freed slaves, children in farming areas, and girls. For more examples of alternatives, see Beadie and Tolley, *Chartered Schools.*

40. Sizer, "The Academies."

41. Elite boarding schools like the Weston School receive upward of 1,000–2,000 applications, of which fewer than 500 are usually admitted and 100–300 eventually enroll. By comparison, in 2008 the average for NAIS boarding schools was 1,630 inquiries, 426 applications, 189 admissions, and 110 enrollments (this is called the "admissions funnel"). National Association of Independent Schools, "NAIS Facts at a Glance, 2007–2008."

42. Gaztambide-Fernández, "What Is an Elite Boarding School?"

43. Today, some elite boarding schools have well over a hundred buildings. Their campuses are comparable in size to those of liberal arts colleges. Gaztambide-Fernández, "What Is an Elite Boarding School?"

44. Both Lorene Cary's autobiography and Curtis Sittenfeld's novel offer interesting commentary on the role of admissions in setting the character of the student body. Lorene Cary, *Black Ice* (New York: Knopf, 1991); Sittenfeld, *Prep.*

45. For an intimate and insightful description of how progressive curriculum and pedagogy are implemented and explored in the context of one elite (although not boarding) school, see Susan Semel, *The Dalton School: The Transformation of a Progressive School* (New York: Peter Lang, 1992).

46. Very few public schools have the ability to select their students. Those that do are typically magnet schools, which are dedicated to specific programs and able to select students based on the criteria specific to the programs. Examples are high schools devoted to the arts, programs for "gifted" students, and schools for athletes. See Mary Haywood Metz, *Different by Design: The Context and Character of Three Magnet Schools* (New York: Teachers College Press, 2003); Claire Smrekar and Ellen Goldring, *School Choice in Urban America: Magnet Schools and the Pursuit of Equity* (New York: Teachers College Press, 1999).

47. Cookson and Persell, *Preparing for Power,* 96. Cookson and Persell do a thorough job of de-

scribing this dimension of the schools' curriculum, and they comment: "Today the Socratic method lies at the heart of the boarding school teaching craft. The dialogue of a seminar implies a certain amount of intimacy and sharing among teachers and students that in turn suggests small classes" (97).

48. Cookson and Persell's assumption that there is "intimacy" around these seminar tables is simplistic and doesn't begin to suggest the complexities of interacting in a seminar, a process that is filled with power dynamics and that is central to the way in which identification evolves.

49. The term "cocurricular," which some schools use instead of "extracurricular," underscores the important role such activities play in education and, more important, in students' preparation for college admission. See Stevens, *Creating a Class.*

50. On public high schools devoted to the arts, see Jessica Davis, ed., *Passion and Industry: Schools That Focus on the Arts* (Natick, Mass.: National Arts and Learning Foundation, 2001); Brent Wilson, "Arts Magnets and the Transformation of Schools and Schooling," *Education and Urban Society,* 33, no. 4 (2001).

51. Cookson and Persell, *Preparing for Power,* 80.

52. Like those documented in Mathews, *Class Struggle.* These activities are necessary for college admissions, and elite public schools are often quite successful at providing them (see Stevens, *Creating a Class*). It is interesting to note the ways in which elite boarding schools take on the role of parents by providing the sort of "concerted cultivation" that Annette Lareau identifies as typical of upper-middle-class parenting styles. See Annette Lareau, *Unequal Childhoods: Class, Race, and Family Life* (Berkeley, Calif.: University of California Press, 2003). Given the large amounts of money and time some parents spend on extracurricular activities, it would be interesting to compare how the cost of attending an elite boarding school is viewed by parents who are anxious about upward mobility.

53. For a critique of the role of progressive educational approaches in the education of the elite, see Mary Eberstadt, "The Schools They Deserve: Howard Gardner and the Remaking of Elite Education," *Policy Review,* 97 (October–November 1999). See also Beth Rubin, "Unpacking Detracking: When Progressive Pedagogy Meets Students' Social Worlds," *American Educational Research Journal,* 40, no. 2 (2003).

54. The discussion in this section draws primarily on the historical work of Ted Sizer, James McLachlan, and Steven Levine, all of whom provide historical accounts of how elite boarding schools emerged and evolved in the United States. Sizer ("The Academies") offers a history of the academies (the institutional precursor of independent schools), which developed rapidly in the eighteenth century only to decline even more quickly after 1850. McLachlan's book *American Boarding Schools* is a detailed account of how these schools developed and expanded, offering substantial detail on the social dynamics and the people involved in the spread of American boarding schools. Levine's "Rise of American Boarding Schools," a briefer social history that focuses specifically on elite boarding schools, seeks to challenge McLachlan's argument about the purpose and social forces behind the rise of boarding schools.

55. My discussion here draws primarily from Sizer, *The Age of the Academies.* The term "academy" derives from Plato's home in Athens and the garden where he taught his disciples.

56. Beadie and Tolley, *Chartered Schools;* Sizer, *The Age of the Academies.*

57. Sizer, "The Academies," 45. Sizer offers no explanation of just why these schools were more widely known or better positioned to make such a change. While he decries the fact that historians have dismissed the academies as elitist and have assumed that these elite schools represent all academies, he also offers no analysis of why these schools became the symbol of all academies, despite their lack of similarity. If, as he claims, "the best-known academies were often the least representative" (46), why, then, were they the "best-known" and why did they survive while most others died? I argue that it was their historically elite status and accumulated cultural and social capital that accounted for their longevity, their rise to fame, and their prominence as the symbol of all academies.

58. Levine, "Rise of American Boarding Schools"; McLachlan, *American Boarding Schools.*

59. Yasushi Watanabe describes the Brahmins as "one of the oldest and most distinguished aristo-

cratic groups in the United States"; Watanabe, *The American Family: Across the Class Divide* (London: Pluto Press, 2005), 2. He locates the origin of the term "Brahmin" in the 1857 novel *Autocrat of the Breakfast Table,* by Oliver Wendell Holmes (himself from a Brahmin family), who uses the word to refer to old families that traced their lineage to the original founders of Boston and who claimed cultural sophistication (203). The Brahmins were central to the early institutionalization of culture in Boston through the establishment of the Museum of Fine Arts, the Boston Symphony Orchestra, and educational institutions like MIT. Paul DiMaggio, "Cultural Entrepreneurship in Nineteenth-Century Boston: The Creation of an Organizational Base for High Culture in America," *Media, Culture and Society,* 4, no. 1 (1982).

60. Levine, "Rise of American Boarding Schools"; McLachlan, *American Boarding Schools.*

61. Royal "charity" schools were originally established as far back as 1179 (the Westminster School) for the purpose of educating the children of local peasants in communities surrounding monasteries. Over the centuries, nine charity schools were opened throughout Britain, building connections to universities and gaining great prestige. Following reports of abuse and poor conditions, the nine schools became regulated under the Public Schools Act of Parliament in 1868. Far from the modern conception of "public" as state funded, these schools were originally called "public" because members of the public (i.e., nonclergy) could attend. "Public" also because education happened, as it were, "in public," these private boarding schools became one of the most important preservers of the British aristocracy, which they continue to serve today. See Wakeford, *The Cloistered Elite.*

62. See McLachlan, *American Boarding Schools,* which demonstrates that some of the founders of U.S. schools had close connections with, and a deep understanding of, boarding schools in Britain.

63. As Sizer and McLachlan show quite clearly, those schools that had direct contacts with elite universities were most adept at revising their curricula to meet the universities' demands. While other academies struggled to provide instruction in as many subjects as possible, elite boarding schools tended to limit their offerings to what the elite universities required of them. This influence continues to shape the goals and curricula of these schools, including the recruitment and preparation of athletes, students of color, and other groups. See Jerome Karabel, *The Chosen: The Hidden History of Admission and Exclusion at Harvard, Yale, and Princeton* (Boston: Houghton Mifflin, 2005).

64. McLachlan, *American Boarding Schools,* 11, italics in original.

65. Ibid., 12.

66. Levine, "Rise of American Boarding Schools." On credentialism, see Collins, "Functional and Conflict Theories of Educational Stratification"; and Weber, "Economic Relationships."

67. Attitudes toward private education were also changing at this time. It is worth noting that most of the institutions founded prior to 1850 call themselves "academies," whereas those founded after that date call themselves "schools." This suggests some awareness of the shifting public attitudes toward the academies, a shift that Sizer notes. (The pseudonym "Weston School" should not be interpreted as suggesting a founding date.)

68. Most often this leader was a male educator. Groton School's Endicott Peabody is perhaps the most well-known. See the documentary *American Dream at Groton,* dir. David Grubin (PBS Video, 1991); and McLachlan, *American Boarding Schools.* But almost every elite boarding school has some sort of "founding father" that is regarded by the institution as its patriarch.

69. According to a recent newsletter from the president of the NAIS, "only the top 4 percent of families in terms of income ($200,000+) can readily afford an independent school education for their kids." Patrick F. Bassett, "Bassett Blog: Affordability and 'the Family Ford,'" May 1, 2006, www.nais.org/about/article.cfm?ItemNumber=148304&sn.ItemNumber=4181&tn.ItemNumber=147271 (accessed December 15, 2008).

70. For a candid look at the experiences of children from extreme wealth, see the HBO documentary *Born Rich,* dir. Jamie Johnson (Shout Factory Theater, 2002).

71. The purpose of this diversity, however, remains an open question and is often a point of con-

tention. The debates within elite boarding schools in many ways reflect the controversies over diversity in higher education and over affirmative action. They range from politically oriented arguments about justice and social change to arguments about the importance of diversity for learning and for the enhancement of the curriculum students receive. The latter arguments tend to be depoliticized and often unclear about what "diversity" means. Moses and Chang argue that the tension between a diversity rationale that is oriented toward social justice and one that is oriented toward educational benefits ends up undermining the value of diversity for democracy. Their analysis of how courts have wavered in the justification of diversity is insightful. Michele S. Moses and Mitchell J. Chang, "Toward a Deeper Understanding of the Diversity Rationale," *Educational Researcher,* 35, no. 1 (2006).

72.   Stevens, *Creating a Class,* offers perhaps the best description of the complex, lifelong process that leads a student toward admission to an elite college—which is strikingly similar to the process leading to matriculation at an elite boarding school.

73.   Much like the elite colleges and universities that their students seek to attend, elite boarding schools adjust their public image by playing number games that downplay their actual demographic character. In constructing how they present an image to their intended public, elite boarding schools work against the "spoiled identity" of elitist institutions by claiming that their student bodies are more inclusive than they actually are. Goffman argues that "a performer tends to conceal or underplay those activities, facts, and motives which are incompatible with an idealized version of himself and his products" (*Presentation of Self,* 48). Institutions like elite boarding schools likewise perform idealized versions of the identifications they wish to present.

74.   Gaztambide-Fernández, "What Is an Elite Boarding School?" The SSAT is administered by the Educational Testing Service and is designed much like the SAT.

75.   Cary, *Black Ice,* 127.

76.   Sara Lawrence-Lightfoot describes in rich detail the "aesthetics and comforts of abundance" that mark the atmosphere of elite boarding schools (*The Good High School,* 221). Cookson and Persell likewise pay special attention to the role that architecture and spatial aesthetics play in shaping the "tone" of elite boarding schools. Such aesthetic features, they maintain, carry a "subliminal message" that complements "the actual educational resources and classroom facilities the schools provide" (*Preparing for Power,* 47).

77.   Only two southern schools are listed in Baltzell's sixteen elite schools.

78.   Sizer, "The Academies," 40.

79.   Baird, *The Elite Schools,* 7–8. While there are certainly many elite schools that are not boarding, including elite public schools, private elite schools in urban areas are without exception day schools, and their students reside at home. I would speculate that the experiences of these students are much more comparable to those of students in elite public schools—with one crucial difference: whereas elite public schools tend to be in suburban areas, elite private schools tend to be in or near large cities.

80.   In his sociohistorical analysis of why boarding schools flourished at the turn of the twentieth century, Levine points out that day schools were decreasing in popularity as boarding schools were expanding. He speculates that perhaps "parents preferred that their sons be educated in a pristine rural environment rather than in the city. In a rural environment their children would be far removed from the contaminating aspects of city life, including the dangerous habits and ideas of working-class children whom they were likely to meet on their way to and from school" ("Rise of American Boarding Schools," 72). Levine supports his argument by noting that Noble and Greenough, the only day school that survived the spread of the boarding schools, chose to move to a rural setting and started a small boarding program.

81.   Cookson and Persell, *Preparing for Power,* 47.

82.   James Duncan and David Lambert, "Landscapes of Home," in James Duncan, Nuala Johnson, and Richard Schein, eds., *A Companion to Cultural Geography* (Malden, Mass.: Blackwell, 2004), 391.

83.   Peshkin, *Permissible Advantage;* Powell, *Lessons from Privilege.* On changes in higher edu-

cation, see John D. Skrentny, *The Minority Rights Revolution* (Cambridge, Mass.: Harvard University Press, 2002); Stevens, *Creating a Class.*

2. GETTING IN

1. The processes of identification involved in such impression management are indisputably complex, as participants struggle to define the situation and to determine their legitimacy and the terms by which they will engage each other. Erving Goffman, *Encounters: Two Studies in the Sociology of Interaction* (New York: Bobbs-Merrill, 1961); Erving Goffman, *The Presentation of Self in Everyday Life* (Garden City, N.Y.: Doubleday Anchor, 1959). The kind of exchange that occurred between Mr. Gardiner and me might be interpreted as what Goffman (in *The Presentation of Self*) calls "role idealization," the process by which we choose how to idealize particular identities in particular situations, so as to present ourselves in more admirable or, in this case, legitimate terms.

2. My own arrival, as described in the introduction, depended on the connections that my elite graduate education provided and on my ability to make the right impression by using language and other cultural symbols properly in order to gain acceptance and legitimacy. In this sense, the process of admission to an elite boarding school is very much like the process of admission to a college or university, elite or otherwise. While the literature on college admissions is abundant, scarcely anything has been written about admissions to elite boarding schools, other than accounts within the context of other arguments or in autobiographies. On admissions to higher education, see Louise Archer et al., eds., *Higher Education and Social Class: Issues of Inclusion and Exclusion* (London: Routledge, 2003); William Bowen and Derek Bok, *The Shape of the River: Long-Term Consequences of Considering Race in College and University Admissions* (Princeton, N.J.: Princeton University Press, 1998); Jerome Karabel, *The Chosen: The Hidden History of Admission and Exclusion at Harvard, Yale, and Princeton* (Boston: Houghton Mifflin, 2005); Mitchell Stevens, *Creating a Class: College Admissions and the Education of Elites* (Cambridge, Mass.: Harvard University Press, 2007).

3. For a detailed account and incisive analysis of the life of an admissions officer at an elite liberal arts college, see Stevens, *Creating a Class.* Stevens' descriptions resonate with and closely mirror (though on a smaller scale) my own experience as an admissions officer at another boarding school and my observations and conversations with the admissions staff at Weston.

4. Pierre Bourdieu, "The Forms of Capital," in John Richardson, ed., *Handbook of Theory and Research for the Sociology of Education* (New York: Greenwood, 1986); Alejandro Portes, "Social Capital: Its Origins and Application in Modern Sociology," *Annual Review of Sociology,* 24 (1998); Robert Putnam, *Bowling Alone: The Collapse and Revival of American Community* (New York: Simon and Schuster, 2000).

5. A thorough description and discussion of these programs is beyond the scope of this book, but there are sources that deal with these programs in more detail. See, for instance, Judith Griffin, "Catching the Dream for Gifted Children of Color," *Gifted Child Quarterly,* 36, no. 3 (1992); Gary Simon and Prep for Prep, eds., *Be the Dream: Prep for Prep Graduates Share Their Stories* (Chapel Hill, N.C.: Algonquin Books, 2003); Ron Suskind, *A Hope in the Unseen: An American Odyssey from the Inner City to the Ivy League* (New York: Broadway, 1999). See also G. William Domhoff, *Who Rules America? Power and Politics,* 4th ed. (Boston: McGraw-Hill, 2002); Richard L. Zweigenhaft and G. William Domhoff, *Diversity in the Power Elite: Have Women and Minorities Reached the Top?* (New Haven, Conn.: Yale University Press, 1998).

6. This is consistent with the general consensus among social and cultural psychologists, who argue that individuals in the United States tend to highlight the self as the cause of their success and to engage in self-enhancement when talking about their experiences. See, for instance, Marilynn Brewer and Ya-Ru Chen, "Where (Who) Are Collectives in Collectivism? Toward Conceptual Clarification of Individualism and Collectivism," *Psychological Review,* 114, no. 1 (2007); S. Kitayama et al., "Individ-

ual and Collective Processes in the Construction of the Self: Self-Enhancement in the United States and Self-Criticism in Japan," *Journal of Personality and Social Psychology,* 72, no. 6 (1997).

7. The process of admissions involves a complicated "funnel" that begins with the inquiry. Inquiries yield applications that yield admissions. Yet the fact that a student has been admitted does not necessarily mean that he or she will enroll. The final number of students that actually enroll is called the "yield."

8. This is an example of what Stanton Wortham calls the "thickening of identity." This thickening is part of the relational processes by which particular identifications become further internalized. Stanton Wortham, "Curriculum as a Source for the Development of Social Identity," *Sociology of Education* 76, no. 3 (2002); idem, "From Good Student to Outcast: The Emergence of a Classroom Identity," *Ethos,* 32, no. 2 (2004). Wortham explores processes of "positioning" in the classroom, borrowing the term "thickening" from Holland and Lave. See Dorothy C. Holland and Jean Lave, "History in Person: An Introduction," in Dorothy C. Holland and Jean Lave, eds., *History in Person* (Santa Fe, N.M.: School of American Research Press, 2001).

9. Commensuration is the process by which people establish metrics that allow them to compare otherwise incommensurable ideas or even relationships. As Wendy Espeland and Mitchell Stevens argue, such processes often illustrate complex and implicit boundary constructions and are suggestive of how individuals make meaning of their experience. See Wendy Nelson Espeland and Mitchell Stevens, "Commensuration as a Social Process," *Annual Review of Sociology,* 24 (1998).

10. While students described Weston as being unique in its emphasis on participation, this kind of pedagogy is widespread in elite boarding schools, and most other accounts of teaching and learning in elite boarding schools today reflect the kind of seminar-style dialogue that students engage in at Weston. See Sarah A. Chase, *Perfectly Prep: Gender Extremes at a New England Prep School* (New York: Oxford, 2008); Leslie Margolin, "A Pedagogy of Privilege," *Journal for the Education of the Gifted,* 19, no. 2 (1996); Arthur G. Powell, *Lessons from Privilege: The American Prep School Tradition* (Cambridge, Mass.: Harvard University Press, 1996). This is also evident in fictional accounts. See Taylor Antrim, *The Headmaster Ritual* (New York: Houghton Mifflin, 2007); Curtis Sittenfeld, *Prep* (New York: Random House, 2005).

3. BEING SMART, WORKING HARD

1. For a detailed and incisive discussion of the internal contradictions of meritocracy as an ideology, see Jerome Karabel, *The Chosen: The Hidden History of Admission and Exclusion at Harvard, Yale, and Princeton* (Boston: Houghton Mifflin, 2005). Karabel does a masterful job of elucidating how these contradictions have unfolded throughout the history of admissions policies at Harvard, Princeton, and Yale. See also the essays in Kenneth Arrow, Samuel Bowles, and Steven Durlauf, eds., *Meritocracy and Economic Inequality* (Princeton, N.J.: Princeton University Press, 2000).

According to Amartya Sen, "the concept of 'merit' is deeply contingent on our views of a good society" (Sen, "Merit and Justice," in Arrow et al., *Meritocracy and Economic Inequality,* 5). As such, there are bound to be contradictions, as different notions of "the good" come into conflict. For Sen, one basic tension arises between, on the one hand, rewarding people for the "good they do, and more particularly the good that can be brought about by rewarding them," and, on the other, rewarding people for the quality of what they do, regardless of the outcome or the "goodness of the consequences generated" (8). John Roemer outlines a tension that is more germane to the Weston context, contrasting a view of merit that highlights "ability" with one that highlights "effort" (Roemer, "Equality of Opportunity," in Arrow et al., *Meritocracy and Economic Inequality*). The tensions discussed by Sen and Roemer point to how competing conceptions of meritocracy relate to notions of egalitarianism and competition, individual justice and fairness. As Karabel notes, whether meritocracy is in fact a good idea is also highly contested, and dependent on the interests that various groups are trying to protect, particularly as they are related to access to elite education. Yet Karabel goes further: "The ideal of meritocracy . . . is inherently unattainable" (*The Chosen,* 550).

2. This misrecognition of class privilege has been documented and researched by other scholars in different contexts. Ellen A. Brantlinger, *Dividing Classes: How the Middle Class Negotiates and Rationalizes School Advantage* (New York: Routledge Falmer, 2003); Sarah A. Chase, *Perfectly Prep: Gender Extremes at a New England Prep School* (New York: Oxford University Press, 2008); Adam Howard, *Learning Privilege: Lessons of Power and Identity in Affluent Schooling* (New York: Routledge, 2007); Jenny Stuber, "Talk of Class: The Discursive Repertoires of White Working- and Upper-Middle-Class College Students," *Journal of Contemporary Ethnography,* 35 (2006).

3. Italics in transcript material indicate words that were uttered with emphasis.

4. The connection between being smart and working hard is related to an inherent tension in the ideology of meritocracy: whether merit should be rewarded as an intrinsic characteristic of a person, or as a result of the way that person uses his or her merit "toward a greater goal" (see Sen, "Merit and Justice"). The combination of intelligence—as measured by IQ tests—and effort is explicit in Michael Young's definition of "meritocracy." See Michael Young, *The Rise of the Meritocracy, 1870–2033* (London: Thames and Hudson, 1958). Young's farce, written as a dissertation by a fictional student of sociology in the year 2033, outlines the rise and fall of a meritocracy in Britain. The writer extols the virtues of rule "by the cleverest people; not an aristocracy of birth, not a plutocracy of wealth but a true meritocracy of talent" (18–19). Yet in this fictional future, the excesses of the meritocratic elite have led to the uprising of the "lesser" underclasses, led by a group of feminists whose battle cry, "Everyone can be beautiful," is an ironic retort to the claim that not everyone can be smart.

5. This boundary suggests how the ideology of meritocracy, as articulated at a school like Weston, is linked to exceptionalism through the idea that the elite status of a school like Weston is bound up with its "exceptional" character (and that of its students). This is related to the broader notion of "American exceptionalism." Seymour Martin Lipset, *American Exceptionalism: A Double-Edged Sword* (New York: Norton, 1996). Schools like Weston are seen as a manifestation of the exceptional character of a society in which competition and merit seamlessly produce the best possible outcome. Such a perception draws on the image of the United States as a true meritocracy, where hard work rather than inheritance yields upward mobility. Alexis de Tocqueville, *Democracy in America,* trans. Richard Heffner, abridged ed. (New York: Signet Classics, 2001); Nicholas Lemann, *The Big Test: The Secret History of the American Meritocracy* (New York: Farrar, Straus and Giroux, 1999); Stephen McNamee, *The Meritocracy Myth* (Lanham, Md.: Rowman and Littlefield, 2004). Jerome Karabel, however, demonstrates in *The Chosen* that the ideal of meritocracy fails as a model for admissions to elite universities.

6. This number is translated from Weston's unique grade point system into a 4.0 scale. In Weston's system, the equivalent of 3.29 is considered relatively good.

7. This misrecognition of privilege parallels observations on middle-class parenting that are discussed in Annette Lareau, *Home Advantage: Social Class and Parental Intervention in Elementary Education,* 2nd ed. (Lanham, Md.: Rowman and Littlefield, 2000); idem, *Unequal Childhoods: Class, Race, and Family Life* (Berkeley, Calif.: University of California Press, 2003). It also echoes Ellen Brantlinger's and Julie Bettie's descriptions of how successful white students fail to recognize class and race as sources of privilege that greatly determine their academic success. Julie Bettie, *Women without Class: Girls, Race, and Identity* (Berkeley, Calif.: University of California Press, 2003); Ellen A. Brantlinger, *The Politics of Social Class in Secondary School: Views from Affluent and Impoverished Youth* (New York: Teachers College Press, 1993); idem, *Dividing Classes.* See also Stuber, "Talk of Class."

8. Wendy Luttrell, "Working-Class Women's Ways of Knowing: Effects of Gender, Race, and Class," *Sociology of Education,* 66, no. 1 (1989). Will echoes anxieties similar to those documented in Richard Sennett and Jonathan Cobb, *The Hidden Injuries of Class* (New York: Norton, 1972). For an analysis of how social-class mobility is experienced emotionally as a site of pain, see Valerie Walkerdine, "Workers in the New Economy: Transformation as Border Crossing," *Ethos,* 34, no. 1 (2006).

9. The subtleties are significant and are related to what Bourdieu terms "habitus"—socially acquired propensities that are manifested in attitudes, preferences, and opinions, and embodied through movements, dress, and posture. Pierre Bourdieu, *Outline of a Theory of Practice,* trans. Richard Nice (New York: Oxford, 1977). This is important because, as I will argue in Chapter 6, race, class, and gender—in particular—play an important role in whether and how students can succeed at being perceived as smart without coming across as arrogant.

10. William Henry maintains that the word "elitist" "has come to rival if not outstrip 'racist' as the foremost catchall pejorative of our times." William A. Henry III, *In Defense of Elitism* (New York: Doubleday, 1994), 2. He bemoans the anti-elitist attitude that pervades politics in the United States, advocating a necessary elitism in the pursuit of social and cultural progress.

11. The experiences of students who choose to leave or are expelled from Weston are beyond the scope of this book. There were several such students during my time at the school—and although I did not have time to pursue their stories, or to investigate the particulars of their situations, it would have been interesting to explore how such students understand what it means to be a Westonian and whether and how they would claim the label.

12. At most elite boarding schools, the children of staff and faculty can attend the school tuition free. But they must go through the admissions process and meet the criteria for admission. The experiences of these "fac-brats" and "staff-kids," as they are known, would be of great interest, as they seem to have a rather particular experience as Westonians. See, for instance, the novels of John Irving, himself a faculty brat. Irving's fiction (e.g., *A Prayer for Owen Meany*) makes many references to boys growing up at a boarding school.

13. Interestingly, students seldom used the term "genius," except to describe Damien. For an interesting history of how the word is used to position individuals, see Ray McDermott, "Materials for a Confrontation with Genius as a Personal Identity," *Ethos,* 32, no. 2 (2004).

14. Wendy Nelson Espeland and Mitchell Stevens, "Commensuration as a Social Process," *Annual Review of Sociology,* 24 (1998).

15. The notion of the scholar-athlete has its roots in elite schools, particularly Ivy League universities. See James Axtell, *The Pleasures of Academe: A Celebration and Defense of Higher Education* (Lincoln: University of Nebraska Press, 1998); Douglass Shand-Tucci, *The Crimson Letter: Harvard, Homosexuality, and the Shaping of American Culture* (New York: St. Martin's, 2003). Mitchell Stevens, *Creating a Class: College Admissions and the Education of Elites* (Cambridge, Mass.: Harvard University Press, 2007), devotes a whole chapter to sports. Stevens' discussion illustrates the complex relationship between academic and athletic expectations and how these are negotiated in the admissions process.

16. I did not get the sense from observing classes that the level of discourse was different in different languages, although I did observe that the methods and perhaps the aims of studying different languages differed. Classes in Greek and Latin are conducted in English, while courses in modern languages are conducted in the target language. This difference suggests that, as cultural capital, classical languages play a different role from modern ones. While modern languages have practical utility and can bridge barriers between cultures, classical languages are symbolic status markers that actually underscore social-class distinctions. "I find that [Latin] has gotten into my English writing," explains one student, which suggests that learning Greek and Latin may ultimately be more about *refining* English and earning cultural capital than about learning another language.

17. The practice of distinguishing students who study advanced Latin harks back to the early nineteenth century. Academies were struggling to find a balance between the classical education they took pride in offering and the more vocationally oriented education their constituents were demanding. They began differentiating the two through practices like the Latin Distinction. To this day, some schools offer two diplomas, one in English and one in classics—a practice that began in the early nineteenth century. See James McLachlan, *American Boarding Schools* (New York: Scribner, 1970); Theodore R.

Sizer, "The Academies: An Interpretation," in Sizer, ed., *The Age of the Academies* (New York: Bureau of Publications, Teachers College, Columbia University, 1964).

18. During my second year at Weston, the captain of the lacrosse team was also an accomplished violinist who gave a solo concert prior to graduation. He was at Weston for only two years. Before that, he had attended schools in Canada, where the opposition between the arts and sports among the elites does not seem as clearly delineated.

19. For instance, extracurricular club sports are part of the athletic domain, theater clubs are part of the artistic domain, and academic clubs (such as math) are part of the academic domain. Although these are officially "extracurricular," students talked about these activities in relation to their experiences in those academic domains, and not as extracurricular per se.

20. Mitchell Stevens *(Creating a Class)* shows the important role that extracurricular activities play in admission to elite colleges. In his analysis, he assumes (as do the admissions officers) that these extracurricular activities occupy a large portion of students' time and effort. I found that students talked strategically about these experiences, often revealing that they required little effort, and that at times they could do just enough to give the impression in a college application that they were involved in extracurricular activities even if they weren't. For instance, they would start a club that never met or that met only to socialize. This is part of what they described as learning how to "bullshit," or how to give the appearance of hard work despite making little effort. For an interesting and engaging philosophical treatment of the idea of bullshit, see Harry G. Frankfurt, *On Bullshit* (Princeton, N.J.: Princeton University Press, 2005).

21. Young, *The Rise of the Meritocracy,* 83.

22. Emile Durkheim, *The Division of Labor in Society,* trans. George Simpson (New York: Free Press, 1933).

23. Daniel Bell, *The Coming of Post-Industrial Society: A Venture in Social Forecasting,* special anniversary ed. (New York: Basic Books, 1999).

24. Karabel, *The Chosen.*

4. RESERVED SEATING

1. James Duncan, Nuala Johnson, and Richard Schein, eds., *A Companion to Cultural Geography* (Malden, Mass.: Blackwell, 2004); Don Mitchell, *Cultural Geography: A Critical Introduction* (Malden, Mass.: Blackwell, 2000).

2. As Sarah Chase points out, age distinctions form an important hierarchical system. In the school she studied, students openly argued for seniority privileges as an acceptable form of inequality. Sarah A. Chase, *Perfectly Prep: Gender Extremes at a New England Prep School* (New York: Oxford University Press, 2008). The same was true at Weston. Milner notes that even in schools where social group hierarchies are minimal, the dominance of students in higher grades over those in lower grades is stark. Murray Milner, *Freaks, Geeks, and Cool Kids: American Teenagers, Schools, and the Culture of Consumption* (New York: Routledge, 2004).

3. The fact that student status correlates with a particular organization of school space was noted long ago, in Hollingshead's brief observations on the way social class is related to students' movements from, to, and inside their school space—observations he makes within his larger study of the social context of schools. August B. Hollingshead, *Elmtown's Youth: The Impact of Social Classes on Adolescents* (New York: Wiley, 1949). More recent detailed analyses of spatial arrangements can be found in Julie Bettie, *Women without Class: Girls, Race, and Identity* (Berkeley, Calif.: University of California Press, 2003); Penelope Eckert, *Jocks and Burnouts: Social Categories and Identity in the High School* (New York: Teachers College Press, 1989); Milner, *Freaks, Geeks, and Cool Kids;* Laurie Olsen, *Made in America: Immigrant Students in Our Public Schools* (New York: New Press, 1997); Barrie Thorne, *Gender Play: Girls and Boys in School* (New Brunswick, N.J.: Rutgers University Press, 1993).

4. Rist, for instance, shows how one teacher places students based on her perception of their

class status and how this process ultimately shapes the way she relates to them. Ray Rist, "Student Social Class and Teacher Expectations: The Self-Fulfilling Prophecy in Ghetto Education," *Harvard Educational Review,* 40, no. 3 (1970). Thorne, *Gender Play,* attends closely to how boys and girls move in the space of the schoolyard and other spaces they inhabit, as she analyzes how gender roles are learned in the early grades. Olsen, *Made in America,* illustrates how groups of immigrant and nonimmigrant students are segregated through space and the school policies that promote such segregation. She shows that the way students perceive spatial arrangements illustrates how they think about themselves and others and how they find their place in the racial hierarchy of the United States. Milner, *Freaks, Geeks, and Cool Kids,* compares the different ways in which status is organized between whites and blacks at one school by looking at spatial arrangements and movement across specific spaces. Bettie, *Women without Class,* observes the way different groups of girls maintain control over certain spaces in order to strengthen social group boundaries.

5. This distinction is similar to the one described in Eckert, *Jocks and Burnouts;* and in Milner, *Freaks, Geeks, and Cool Kids.*

6. I rarely heard students use the term "geek" while I was at Weston. In fact, they never used it to refer to themselves or to smart students at the school. They used it only to draw a boundary between Weston and public schools—by arguing, for example, that at their old school they were considered "geeks," or that "So-and-So, who is smart," would be considered a geek at another school but not at Weston.

7. I often found myself gravitating toward the tables where adults sat, particularly at the beginning of my time at Weston, before I got used to sharing the social space with students who were half my age. Sitting with adults was easy; I was much closer in age to most of the adults on campus, and many of them were, like myself, in the process of starting families of their own. As a teacher myself (who had spent two years teaching and living at another boarding school), I shared their passion for and commitment to education. I often spoke with them about education, from the kinds offered at Weston to our educational efforts with our own children. A number of teachers had degrees from Harvard as well, and in many ways we were colleagues, even as my role as researcher was distinct from theirs as teachers or administrators. But perhaps most important, particularly during my second year at the school, was the fact that teachers knew I wasn't "studying" them.

8. Radhika's conclusion is consistent with the idea that identification is constructed through experience in shared space and time. See Anthony T. Giddens, *The Constitution of Society: Outline of the Theory of Structuration* (Berkeley, Calif.: University of California Press, 1984); Richard Jenkins, *Social Identity* (London: Routledge, 1996).

9. The "feed," as Goffman points out, is an important part of building bonds with inmates. See Erving Goffman, *Asylums: Essays on the Social Situation of Mental Patients and Other Inmates* (Chicago: Anchor, 1961). Cookson and Persell point out the importance of eating as a group: Peter W. Cookson and Caroline Hodges Persell, *Preparing for Power: America's Elite Boarding Schools* (New York: Basic Books, 1985). Milner, *Freaks, Geeks, and Cool Kids,* likewise notes how important shared meals are to the functioning of status groups within a public high school.

10. A participant in Milner's study *Freaks, Geeks, and Cool Kids* comments that sitting alone was worse than failing a test. I didn't find this extreme fear of social isolation prevalent at Weston, but the student's comment suggests that sitting alone may at least be undesirable, especially in the presence of strangers.

11. In this sense, they are clearly "positioned" well in advance of their arrival. The PGs enter a space in which they have almost no room for mobility; see Dorothy C. Holland and Kevin Leander, "Ethnographic Studies of Positioning and Subjectivity: An Introduction," *Ethos,* 32, no. 2 (2004). To date, there are no studies of the particular experiences of PGs. Sarah Chase (in *Perfectly Prep*) does devote some discussion to students who would be similar in background and in the way they are positioned at the pseudonymous Bolton Academy, but her analysis is focused much more on the wealthier students.

12. The students' words very much reflect Murray Milner's theory of status relations. See Milner, *Freaks, Geeks, and Cool Kids*; idem, *Status and Sacredness: A General Theory of Status Relations and an Analysis of Indian Culture* (New York: Oxford University Press, 1994).

13. According to students, each class has its respective posse, and sometimes they differentiate among the "fresh," "soph," junior, and senior posses. Most often, however, they retain the term "fresh posse" to designate the students who were and continue to be identified as good-looking and popular since their freshman year and throughout the four years at Weston.

14. I explored this question with several students, including two girls who identified with the posse. While their stories may or may not be an account of what actually happened, their narratives confirmed the details I discuss here regarding not so much which students constitute the posse and how they come together, but rather how the notion of the posse fits in the social landscape.

15. In fact, many PGs come from blue-collar suburban and rural areas in New England, where they are considered athletic stars. Some are sent to Weston by college recruiters, who want them to improve their academic record so that they can be admitted to selective institutions. Most of the PGs I talked with knew little about schools like Weston before they arrived, and often said they felt overwhelmed, not just with the academic demands but also with the social demands. The PGs I spoke with resented being considered less smart and were well aware of the stereotypes placed on them by other students—labels they firmly dismissed.

16. Milner's analysis, in *Freaks, Geeks, and Cool Kids,* with his notion of the pluralistic high school, is probably the most nuanced treatment of status relations. Yet his assumption that hierarchy implies a linear order leads him to suggest that pluralistic high schools are nonhierarchical. I would disagree, suggesting that nonlinear hierarchy is a more accurate way of interpreting status relations, at least within an elite boarding school in which status is somewhat contested. The problem is that "popularity" is not the same as having "high status." Rather, the two are intertwined, forming a complex and multidimensional hierarchy.

17. Astrid echoes Penelope Eckert's analysis (in *Jocks and Burnouts*) of the way social groups define themselves in opposition to one another. Eckert argues that in the middle-class context of her study, this identification by opposition has stark social and economic consequences for both groups. In an elite boarding school, these consequences are mitigated by the fact that students who have access to wealth inhabit both sides.

18. Anime is a Japanese style of cartoon animation that has become quite popular throughout the world in recent years. It is similar to "manga" cartoons, and often involves computer and other animation techniques.

19. Chase (in *Perfectly Prep*) says that homosexuality was a completely taboo subject at the elite boarding school where she did her study, and she notes that gay, lesbian, bisexual, and transgender (GLBT) students were pushed almost entirely to the periphery of the school's social space. I did not find an extreme aversion to GLBT issues at Weston. In fact, in comparison to what Chase describes, the Weston School is a very open and welcoming place for GLBT students. Yet, as I will discuss later, sexuality is a crucial aspect of how students construct elite identifications, and this point is quite clear in Chase's analysis.

20. Alternatively, following Eckert's analysis *(Jocks and Burnouts),* as Deb distances herself from the posse—who, she believes, are not accepting—she identifies the opposite group as accepting.

21. The term "granola" is suggestive. It is often used to refer to groups of people who consume health foods, such as granola, and who are committed to the environment and progressive left politics. "Granola" also suggests a particular kind of dress style that is associated with progressive, perhaps even radical politics, characteristic of neo-hippies and other earth-oriented groups. The term is typically used disparagingly as a sort of put-down, similar to "tree hugger."

22. See Ruth Frankenberg, *White Women, Race Matters: The Social Construction of Whiteness* (Minneapolis: University of Minnesota Press, 1993); Peggy McIntosh, "Understanding Correspondences between White Privilege and Male Privilege through Women's Studies Work," in *National Women's*

Studies Association Annual Meeting (Atlanta, Ga.: Spelman College, 1987); Tim Wise, *White Like Me: Reflections on Race from a Privileged Son* (Brooklyn, N.Y.: Soft Skull Press, 2005). I will discuss these "hidden injuries" in the next chapter.

23. Frances' description echoes the words of students in Milner's study of cliques *(Freaks, Geeks, and Cool Kids)*. Milner, however, accepts these explanations at face value and fails to develop an analysis of how such claims obscure more subtle dynamics. Indeed, he quite explicitly states that his analysis does not consider broader relations of power in shaping the status system of the high school. In doing so, he arrives at the wrong interpretation of what appears on the surface to be a pluralistic status system, in which there appear to be no consequential hierarchies.

24. Like the "jocks" in Eckert, *Jocks and Burnouts*, the "cool kids" in Milner, *Freaks, Geeks, and Cool Kids*, and the "preps" in Bettie, *Women without Class*.

25. Like the "burnouts" in Eckert, *Jocks and Burnouts*, the "freaks" in Milner, *Freaks, Geeks, and Cool Kids*, and the "skaters" in Bettie, *Women without Class*.

26. See, for instance, Chase, *Perfectly Prep*. Perhaps because of its smaller size, the social space at Chase's Bolton School is far narrower and apparently less "tolerant" of alternative lifestyles, following Milner's logic *(Freaks, Geeks, and Cool Kids)*. The fact that gender ideals are somewhat contested within this elite space should not, however, be confused with a lack of sexism or of homophobia. Milner and Chase draw opposite conclusions about the extent of gender equality and sexual tolerance, and whether feminism has affected how girls deal with status. I suspect they both miss the mark, Chase by overemphasizing sexual behavior and Milner by underemphasizing desire. The truth probably lies somewhere in the middle, and fictional accounts of life at elite boarding schools seem to capture it most accurately. For instance, Curtis Sittenfeld, *Prep* (New York: Random House, 2005), is much more nuanced than either Chase or Milner in her account of gender and sexuality in high school experience.

27. This is related to what Bourdieu calls "homologies" between fields. Pierre Bourdieu, *Language and Symbolic Power*, trans. Gino Raymond and Matthew Adamson (Cambridge, Mass.: Harvard University Press, 1993); Pierre Bourdieu, *The Field of Cultural Production: Essays on Art and Literature* (New York: Columbia University Press, 1993).

28. See Milner, *Freaks, Geeks, and Cool Kids*.

29. Ibid., 130.

30. Milner's analysis (ibid.) is insightful and provides a complex understanding of status relations within American high schools. Yet Milner confuses the apparent harmony of the social space at Woodrow Wilson High School with the notion of pluralism. Milner defines pluralism in opposition to notions of assimilation, hierarchy, and intolerance. On the basis of his observations inside the school lunchrooms, Milner argues that within most large public high schools, a tolerance for different lifestyles and an abundance of resources mute hierarchical arrangements and competition for scarce resources, including status itself. But Milner deliberately stays at the surface and fails to explore the underlying hierarchies that organize and, I would argue, sustain the peace between status groups. Indeed, as some of the data presented in this chapter suggest, when the normalcy of status relations is interrupted (when, say, sitting arrangements are shifted), even the most tolerant and pluralistic spaces turn chaotic and those with the most status usually prevail. I would suggest that the very idea of tolerance, in fact, implies the sort of hierarchical order that Milner rejects as definitional for status relations within high schools.

31. In Milner's study (ibid.), academic achievement seems to play a minimal role in status relations. In addition, mobility and visibility operate very differently in the way social relations are manifested.

32. The students in Milner's research simply accepted status groups and refrained from arguing that they were nonexistent or unimportant. Status groups, whether hierarchical or not, are simply a part of life at American high schools, Milner suggests (ibid.).

33. I use the term "recognized," as opposed to "popular," to avoid confusion about a particular kind of status. By "recognized" I mean students whom everyone (including nonseniors and faculty) could identify by name and who were often used as "symbols" of particular status groups. I reserve the term "popular" to mark a particular kind of "recognition" similar to what Milner calls "cool kids" (ibid.).

34. This illustrates Bourdieu's point (in *Language and Symbolic Power*) about the role of homologies in sustaining status relations. High status in any autonomous part of the status field requires a relationship with the high-status circles of all other parts of the field.

35. The concept of cultural omnivores was first developed by cultural sociologist Richard Peterson to suggest that rather than drawing boundaries according to distinct forms of cultural consumption, middle- and upper-class people shifted to more wide-ranging forms of cultural consumption. Richard Peterson and Roger Kern, "Changing Highbrow Taste: From Snob to Omnivore," *American Sociological Review,* 61 (1996). Bethany Bryson shows that such practices become a new form of cultural capital that distinguishes omnivores (usually middle- and upper-middle-class consumers) from univores (usually working- and lower-class consumers). Bethany Bryson, "Anything but Heavy Metal: Symbolic Exclusion and Musical Dislikes," *American Sociological Review,* 61 (1996). I use the term "cultural omnivores" to suggest that espousing wide-ranging tastes not only distinguishes these students as elite, but also allows them to traverse the status field and strengthen status relations between various elites.

36. Shamus Khan, "The Production of Privilege" (diss., University of Wisconsin, 2008).

5. BONDING RITUALS

1. See the discussion of processes of identification in the Introduction (citations in notes 23 and 24).

2. On status groups and closure, see Max Weber, "The Distribution of Power within the Political Community: Class, Status, Party," in Max Weber, *Economy and Society: An Outline of Interpretive Sociology,* vol. 1 (Berkeley, Calif.: University of California Press, 1978).

3. These rituals have a lot in common with the processes described by Stanton Wortham, except that Wortham is describing the process of shifting positions from "good to outcast," whereas here Westonians are positioned as the "future leaders of the world." See Stanton Wortham, "Curriculum as a Source for the Development of Social Identity," *Sociology of Education,* 76, no. 3 (2002); idem, "From Good Student to Outcast: The Emergence of a Classroom Identity," *Ethos,* 32, no. 2 (2004).

4. Domhoff and Zweigenhaft argue that minorities never fully accomplish entry into the elite; this remains an open question, particularly in light of Barack Obama's election. Richard L. Zweigenhaft and G. William Domhoff, *Blacks in the White Establishment? A Study of Race and Class in America* (New Haven, Conn.: Yale University Press, 1991). Yet the difference between Alex's understanding of her mother's experience and her perception of her own suggests at least a shift in how she and her mother make meaning of the experience and identify as part of an elite class.

5. On the concept of the "backstage," see Anthony T. Giddens, *The Constitution of Society: Outline of the Theory of Structuration* (Berkeley, Calif.: University of California Press, 1984); Erving Goffman, *The Presentation of Self in Everyday Life* (Garden City, N.Y.: Doubleday Anchor, 1959).

6. Pierre Bourdieu, *Language and Symbolic Power,* trans. Gino Raymond and Matthew Adamson (Cambridge, Mass.: Harvard University Press, 1991), 118, italics in original.

7. The idea that one of the most important outcomes of an elite education is the array of relationships and social networks students build with one another has been central to earlier analyses of elite boarding schools. See the discussion in Chapter 1.

8. Students had a lot to say about their relationships with teachers. I have chosen not to explore that dimension of their experience of Weston as family, because I feel it is only loosely related to the sense of bonding they experience with other students. There are no systematic studies of the experiences of teachers at elite boarding schools, which would be a rich way to explore these institutions.

9. The most obvious exceptions to this were formal dinners, when the seating was to a large extent assigned, and where faculty members were expected to sit with students. This was one of those institutional rituals that, by changing the routine and mixing faculty with students, actually highlighted the usual practice of keeping them separate.

10. "Research on peer relations frequently suggests the important role peers play in shaping youth identification processes, a role that can sometimes eclipse those played by parents and teachers seeking

to guide adolescent decision-making. Adolescents' growing need for autonomy and differentiation, coupled with their decreased emotional dependence on the family, can cause a shift in allegiances and identifications away from adults and toward peer groups. Belonging, in this sense, can become more a matter of peer group membership than family connection" (Eric Toshalis, personal communication, December 9, 2008). See also Luba Falk Feinberg et al., "Belonging to and Exclusion from the Peer Group in Schools: Influences on Adolescents' Moral Choices," *Journal of Moral Education,* 37, no. 2 (2008); Michael J. Nakkula and Eric Toshalis, *Understanding Youth: Adolescent Development for Educators* (Cambridge, Mass.: Harvard Education Press, 2006).

11.   Likewise, it's the easiest and most obvious to point out in most other high schools. See Murray Milner, *Freaks, Geeks, and Cool Kids: American Teenagers, Schools, and the Culture of Consumption* (New York: Routledge, 2004).

12.   The irony in this exchange is important: students may *claim* there is no hierarchy, but this doesn't necessarily mean there *is* no hierarchy. Particularly in a place like Weston, where the notion of equity is a dominant part of the discourse, acknowledging internal hierarchies becomes problematic. To be able to understand these often hidden dynamics requires extensive engagement with participants. I suspect the reason Milner concludes that hierarchies played a minimal role in his study *(Freaks, Geeks, and Cool Kids)* is that he and his research team simply did not spend enough time in any given school to understand the subtle yet critical ways in which hierarchies are manifested, particularly when resources and space are abundant.

13.   The experiences of day students like Matthew challenge the notion that an elite boarding school is a complete "total institution" (see Chapter 1). It is important to note, however, that despite this lack of "totality," and even if day students have a lesser "bond," they, too, call themselves Westonians. Their place in the Westonian hierarchy underscores the bond that boarding students have by virtue of the boundary drawn between the two groups. Chase also discusses the important distinctions between day and boarding students. At the school she studied, most day students were less wealthy than the boarding students, which accentuated the difference. Sarah A. Chase, *Perfectly Prep: Gender Extremes at a New England Prep School* (New York: Oxford University Press, 2008), 197–202. This is not the case at Weston, where some of the day students are among the wealthiest students at the school.

14.   Cookson and Persell *(Preparing for Power)* speculate about the extent of these "intimate" activities and make insightful suggestions about how important the activities may be. But their research did not document such behavior.

15.   Chase, *Perfectly Prep,* offers a more detailed analysis of how students talk about these activities. Her discussion illustrates the importance of such intimacy, and it confirms much of what Cookson and Persell say in *Preparing for Power.* See also Abigail Jones and Marissa Miley, *Restless Virgins: Love, Sex, and Survival at a New England Prep School* (New York: Harper, 2008).

16.   Bourdieu, *Language and Symbolic Power;* Giddens, *Constitution of Society;* Goffman, *Asylums.*

17.   Clifford Geertz, *The Interpretation of Cultures* (New York: Basic Books, 1973); Cynthia Lightfoot, *The Culture of Adolescent Risk-Taking* (New York: Guilford, 1997); Peter McLaren, *Schooling as a Ritual Performance* (New York: Routledge, 1986); Victor Turner, *The Ritual Process: Structure and Anti-Structure* (Chicago: Aldine: 1969).

18.   Drawing on Turner, *The Ritual Process,* others have framed schooling as a particular kind of ritual. See, for instance, McLaren, *Schooling as a Ritual Performance;* James Seale-Collazo, "Charisma and Its Discontents: Religious Education and Cultural Change in a Puerto Rican Protestant High School" (diss., Harvard University, 2006).

19.   Geertz, *Interpretation of Cultures.* See also Lightfoot, *Adolescent Risk-Taking,* for an excellent discussion of play as symbolic activity, from a psychological perspective.

20.   McLaren, *Schooling as a Ritual Performance.* McLaren's is perhaps one of the most thorough and compelling analyses of the rituals of schooling. He offers a detailed and complex framework for analyzing ritual. For my purposes here, I have drawn a simpler framework based on my own observations of rituals at the Weston School.

21. These rituals are most like the ones described by Goffman *(Asylums)* as being an essential part of how a total institution reorients the psychic lives of its inmates toward internalizing an identification with the institution. These are also closest to Bourdieu's definition of a "rite of institution" *(Language and Symbolic Power)*.

22. Turner's and Bourdieu's definitions of ritual are quite different in scope. For Bourdieu, rituals are more specific and bound in time; Turner's definition is more vague and can accommodate a wider range of situations that might be deemed ritualized. See McLaren, *Schooling as a Ritual Performance,* for a more detailed discussion of what constitutes a ritual and the range implicit in the definitions.

23. Lightfoot, *Adolescent Risk-Taking,* offers an insightful analysis of the role of risk-taking in processes of group identification and bonding.

24. Wortham, "Curriculum as a Source"; idem, "Good Student to Outcast."

25. There are also less ritualized release valves. For instance, sports activities not only allow students to engage in learning through their bodies; they also provide school-sponsored opportunities to release built-up pressure. On several occasions, physical education faculty and staff commented that the training room was a place where students vented their frustrations. "I see my job as stress release," explained one trainer. Other faculty members noted that students often had wild conversations in the back of the bus on their way to games: "I've had to remind them that I am there," said one coach. While these examples are not especially ritualistic, their role as a spontaneous form of communication that promotes bonding and intimacy is similar to that of ritualized play.

26. The film *School Ties,* directed by Dick Wolf (Paramount Pictures, 1992), provides a wonderful illustration of these interschool rituals.

27. Nancy Gibbs and Nathan Thornburgh, "Who Needs Harvard?" *Time,* August 13, 2006; Peter Schworn, "Wall of Rejection Letters Is Teens' Group Therapy," *Boston Globe,* April 8, 2008. Gibbs describes the wall of shame as "a great way for [students] to realize they're not alone in having their Ivy dreams dashed."

28. These rituals are in many ways similar to the kind of "rites of institution" that, Bourdieu argues, signal to each participant "what his identity is, but in a way that both expresses it to him and imposes it on him by expressing it in front of everyone . . . and thus informing him in an authoritative manner of what he is and what he must be" *(Language and Symbolic Power,* 121). This way of understanding rituals parallels quite closely the notion of "positioning" that Holland and Leander articulate. Dorothy C. Holland and Kevin Leander, "Ethnographic Studies of Positioning and Subjectivity: An Introduction," *Ethos,* 32, no. 2 (2004).

29. I have chosen not to share details of rituals I witnessed that might be interpreted as scandalous or that might mislead readers to interpret this book as an exposé of "rich kids acting badly." While such details would illustrate my argument about the symbolic content of these rituals, they would not necessarily make the argument stronger.

30. Bourdieu, *Language and Symbolic Power,* maintains that these rituals confer an air of objectivity and reality on otherwise arbitrary boundaries—the sort that protect the status of Westonians as an elite group of students.

31. Cookson and Persell, *Preparing for Power,* 164.

32. Cartoon by William Hamilton, *New Yorker,* May 3, 2004, 78.

33. See note 4 in Chapter 2.

6. UNEQUAL DISTINCTIONS

1. Curtis Sittenfeld, *Prep* (New York: Random, 2005), 363.

2. Ibid., 362, 324.

3. Ibid., 369, 387.

4. *School Ties,* dir. Robert Mandel, screenplay by Dick Wolf (Paramount Pictures, 1992). The movie was shot at three different schools, all of which fit the profile of an elite boarding school. See imdb.com/title/tt0105327/.

5. Even when the main characters are adults, their outsider status provides the tension needed to carry the story forward. John Keating, in the film *Dead Poets Society* (dir. Peter Weir; Touchstone Pictures, 1989), is the classic example of a teacher who can't seem to understand the true purpose of an elite boarding school. More recently, Taylor Antrim, *The Headmaster Ritual* (New York: Houghton Mifflin, 2007), portrays a headmaster bent on radicalizing the school's brightest students. In both stories, the main characters have turned against their own eliteness and seek to reject the status quo—a form of protest that costs them their jobs.

6. Two books edited by Louis Crosier contain essays by insiders, mostly former students, reflecting on a range of experiences within boarding school contexts. When the first book was published, Crosier was criticized for focusing on the negative aspects of the boarding school experience. The second collection sought to address this concern by focusing primarily on the positive. See Louis M. Crosier, ed., *Casualties of Privilege: Essays on Prep Schools' Hidden Culture* (Washington, D.C.: Avocus, 1991); idem, ed., *Healthy Choices, Healthy Schools: The Residential Curriculum* (Washington, D.C.: Avocus, 1992).

7. See the Introduction and Chapter 1.

8. Peter W. Cookson and Caroline Hodges Persell, *Preparing for Power: America's Elite Boarding Schools* (New York: Basic Books, 1985).

9. For a discussion of the difference between an essentialist view of identity and a process view of identification, see the Introduction (with citations in notes 23–27).

10. For a similar approach toward processes of identification and cultural production, see Dorothy C. Holland and Jean Lave, eds., *History in Person* (Santa Fe, N.M.: School of American Research Press, 2001). Comparable arguments are made in Stuart Hall and Paul du Gay, eds., *Questions of Cultural Identity* (London: Sage, 1996); Richard Jenkins, *Social Identity* (London: Routledge, 1996); Lois Weis and Michelle Fine, eds., *Beyond Silenced Voices: Class, Race, and Gender in United States Schools* (Albany, N.Y.: SUNY Press, 1993); idem, eds., *Construction Sites: Excavating Race, Class, and Gender among Urban Youth* (New York: Teachers College Press, 2000).

11. This idea is what social and cultural theorists refer to as "intersectionality." They argue that race, class, gender, sexuality, and other social categories can be understood only in relation to one another, and that to do otherwise is to miss crucial pieces of how these categories shape experience. This view has been developed primarily by scholars of feminist, critical race, and postcolonial theory. See Patricia Hill Collins, *Black Feminist Thought: Knowledge, Consciousness, and the Politics of Empowerment* (New York: Routledge, 2000); Kimberle Crenshaw, "Mapping the Margins: Intersectionality, Identity Politics, and Violence against Women of Color," *Stanford Law Review,* 43 (1991); Chandra Talpade Mohanty, *Feminism without Borders: Decolonizing Theory, Practicing Solidarity* (Durham, N.C.: Duke University Press, 2003). For examples of scholars that take an intersectional approach to their research, see Julie Bettie, *Women without Class: Girls, Race, and Identity* (Berkeley, Calif.: University of California Press, 2003); Ann Arnett Ferguson, *Bad Boys: Public Schools in the Making of Black Masculinity* (Ann Arbor: University of Michigan Press, 2000); Wendy Luttrell, *Pregnant Bodies, Fertile Minds: Gender, Race, and the Schooling of Pregnant Teens* (New York: Routledge, 2003); Laurie Olsen, *Made in America: Immigrant Students in Our Public Schools* (New York: New Press, 1997); Lois Weis, ed., *Class, Race, and Gender in American Education* (Albany, N.Y.: SUNY Press, 1988); Lois Weis and Michelle Fine, eds., *Beyond Silenced Voices: Class, Race, and Gender in United States Schools*; idem, *Construction Sites*.

12. See Pearl R. Kane, ed., *Independent Schools, Independent Thinkers* (San Francisco: Jossey-Bass, 1992). A quick look at recent issues of *Independent School,* the magazine of NAIS, makes this quite clear. Former editor Catherine O'Neill Grace, in her recent review of articles, identifies multiculturalism and gender equity as two of the recurrent themes of the 1990s: Catherine O'Neill Grace, "Before the World Change: Independent School in the 1990s," *Independent School,* 65, no. 3 (Spring 2006). As in higher education, social class has become a central aspect of the diversity debates in secondary education. See, for instance, Caroline Blackwell, "An Uneasy Fit: Socioeconomic Diversity and Independent Schools," *Independent School,* 65, no. 2 (Winter 2006); and other articles featured in the same issue.

13. These anxieties are well documented in the literature on affirmative action. See William Bowen and Derek Bok, *The Shape of the River: Long-Term Consequences of Considering Race in College and University Admissions* (Princeton, N.J.: Princeton University Press, 2000); Patricia Gurin et al., "Diversity and Higher Education: Theory and Impact in Educational Outcomes," *Harvard Educational Review*, 72, no. 3 (2002); John D. Skrentny, *The Ironies of Affirmative Action: Politics, Culture, and Justice in America* (Chicago: University of Chicago Press, 1996). The contemporary challenges of affirmative action are explored in Michel S. Moses and Patricia Marin, "Moving Beyond *Gratz* and *Grutter:* The Next Generation of Research," *Educational Researcher*, 35, no. 1 (2006); see all of the articles in this theme issue. See Chapter 1, note 79. For a compelling history of affirmative action at elite universities, see Jerome Karabel, *The Chosen: The Hidden History of Admission and Exclusion at Harvard, Yale, and Princeton* (Boston: Houghton Mifflin, 2005). Mitchell Stevens, *Creating a Class: College Admissions and the Education of Elites* (Cambridge, Mass.: Harvard University Press, 2007), provides an insightful account of the role of "diversity" in the admissions process at elite liberal arts colleges.

14. Lorene Cary, *Black Ice* (New York: Knopf, 1991), 59.

15. The day student population at Weston is starkly homogeneous along racial/ethnic lines. The large majority of day students identify as "white" or "Caucasian," a fact that reflects the demographics of the New England region, in which most day students reside.

16. See Chapter 1, note 71.

17. In his very insightful chapter on diversity in college admissions, Stevens *(Creating a Class)* points out that the idea of diversity has become one of the defining elements that make elite liberal arts colleges competitive. The populations that traditionally supply these colleges now seek diversity as an important part of their education. This, I would suggest, raises critical questions about the purpose of diversity and the benefits that different groups derive from it.

18. This is the same strategy that the University of Michigan took in defending its affirmative action policies. University officials argued that diversity was necessary for the enhancement of the educational experience of all students (Gurin et al., "Diversity and Higher Education").

19. This echoes the experiences of students of color and students from working-class backgrounds who are described in Robert Granfield, *Making Elite Lawyers: Visions of Law at Harvard and Beyond* (New York: Routledge, 1992). See also Theresa Perry, Claude Steele, and Asa Hilliard, *Young, Gifted, and Black: Promoting High Achievement among African-American Students* (Boston: Beacon, 2003); Skrentny, *Ironies of Affirmative Action.*

20. Advanced courses in math and science were somewhat more diverse, often because more international students from Asia or students who identified as Asian American took these classes. The few participants who identified as Asian American worked hard to distance themselves from the idea that Asians were somehow naturally smart and mathematically inclined. For a critique of the "model minority" stereotype that informs their responses, see Stacey J. Lee, *Unraveling the "Model Minority" Stereotype: Listening to Asian American Youth* (New York: Teachers College Press, 1996); Vivian S. Louie, *Compelled to Excel: Immigration, Education, and Opportunity among Chinese Americans* (Stanford, Calif.: Stanford University Press, 2004). A recent report noted that stereotypes about Asian Americans contradict and are often confused with the experiences of international students who come to the United States from Asia; see Tamar Lewin, "Report Takes Aim at 'Model Minority' Stereotype of Asian-American Students," *New York Times,* June 10, 2008.

21. Signithia Fordham, *Blacked Out: Dilemmas of Race, Identity, and Success at Capital High* (Chicago: University of Chicago Press, 1996); idem and John Ogbu, "Black Students' School Success: Coping with the Burden of 'Acting White,'" *Urban Review*, 18, no. 3 (1986); John Ogbu, *Black American Students in an Affluent Suburb: A Study of Academic Disengagement* (Mahwah, N.J.: Lawrence Erlbaum, 2003). The "acting white" hypothesis has been the subject of great debate among education scholars. See, for instance, Erin McNamara Horvat and Carla O'Connor, eds., *Beyond Acting White: Reframing the Debate on Black Student Achievement* (Lanham, Md.: Rowman and Littlefield, 2006).

22. For similar observations, see Dorinda Carter, "'In a Sea of White People': An Analysis of the Experiences and Behaviors of High-Achieving Black Students in a Predominantly White High School"

(diss., Harvard University, 2005); Prudence Carter, *Keepin' It Real: School Success beyond Black and White* (Oxford: Oxford University Press, 2005).

23. This is the kind of reductive argument developed in Orlando Patterson, "A Poverty of the Mind," *New York Times,* March 26, 2006.

24. This is typically labeled as the "culture of poverty" thesis, which proposes that students of color and poor students fail because their "culture" doesn't value academic achievement or because their "cultural practices" undermine academic efforts. The thesis was developed initially in Oscar Lewis, *La Vida: A Puerto Rican Family in the Culture of Poverty—San Juan and New York* (New York: Random House, 1966); Oscar Lewis, *The Children of Sánchez: Autobiography of a Mexican Family* (New York: Vintage, 1963). Early (and staunch) criticisms of the culture-of-poverty thesis were developed in Eleanor Burke Leacock, *The Culture of Poverty: A Critique* (New York: Simon and Schuster, 1971); Charles A. Valentine, *Culture and Poverty: Critique and Counter-Proposals* (Chicago: University of Chicago Press, 1968). Despite ample evidence to the contrary, however, the thesis continues to thrive as an explanation of academic failure. For a recent example, see Ruby Payne, "Nine Powerful Practices," *Educational Leadership,* 65, no. 7 (2008); Ruby Payne and Kim Ellis, *A Framework for Understanding Poverty* (Highlands, Tex.: Aha! Process, 1995).

25. For a similar cultural argument, see Carter, *Keepin' It Real;* Mica Pollock, *Colormute* (Princeton, N.J.: Princeton University Press, 2004).

26. Lisa Delpit, *Other People's Children: Cultural Conflict in the Classroom* (New York: New Press, 1995).

27. Milner's use of the term "assimilation" directly undermines the applicability of his concept of the pluralistic high school, as it is one of the dynamics against which he defines pluralism. Murray Milner, *Freaks, Geeks, and Cool Kids: American Teenagers, Schools, and the Culture of Consumption* (New York: Routledge, 2004).

28. Sandra S. Smith and Mignon R. Moore, "Interracial Diversity and Relations among African-Americans: Closeness among Black Students at a Predominantly White University," *American Journal of Sociology,* 106, no. 1 (2000); Beverly Daniel Tatum, *Assimilation Blues: Black Families in a White Community* (Westport, Conn.: Greenwood, 1987); idem, *Can We Talk about Race? And Other Conversations in an Era of School Resegregation* (Boston: Beacon, 2008); idem, *"Why Are All the Black Kids Sitting Together in the Cafeteria?" And Other Conversations about Race* (New York: Basic Books, 1997).

29. Chase offers a detailed account and an interesting analysis of the ways students decorate their dorm rooms and how these reflect gender ideals. See Sarah A. Chase, *Perfectly Prep: Gender Extremes at a New England Prep School* (New York: Oxford, 2008).

30. Monica's reference to 1980s movies could be interpreted in multiple ways. For instance, it might allude to the hairstyles of white middle-class female characters in movies aimed at teenagers of that decade. She may also be referring to the many black female characters in 1980s movies who were portrayed as poor black women in need of rescue. Generally, adolescent females in 1980s "teenybopper" movies were portrayed as needing to be rescued and as easy victims of male curiosity. See, for example, *Sixteen Candles* (1984), *The Breakfast Club* (1985), *Girls Just Want to Have Fun* (1985), *Heathers* (1989), and *Say Anything* (1989). In any case, Monica appears determined to reject a somewhat classed stereotype that would be inappropriate for a distinguished Westonian.

31. Michael Young, *The Rise of the Meritocracy, 1870–2033* (London: Thames and Hudson, 1958).

32. Alexis de Tocqueville, *Democracy in America,* trans. Henry Reeve (London: Longmans, Green, 1875), 26. Tocqueville described the settlers of New England, where elite boarding schools developed and flourished, as belonging "to the more independent classes of their native country." He observed that they "possessed, in proportion to their number, a greater mass of intelligence than is to be found in any European nation . . . [and] brought with them the best elements of order and morality" (28).

33. Richard Hofstadter, *Anti-Intellectualism in American Life* (New York: Vintage, 1970).

34. In Sandi's case, she is working against two sources for being identified as smart: the fact that

she is Westonian and the fact that she is Asian American—a category associated with academic achievement by virtue of the model-minority stereotype (see Lee, *Unraveling the "Model Minority"*; Louie, *Compelled to Excel*). The model-minority stereotype is alive and well at Weston, and Asian American students, some of whom, like Sandi, work hard to avoid identifying with international students from Asia, have the double burden of rejecting the identification as smart. Sandi's description of her family and her parents' investments in her education is consistent with descriptions given by the middle- and upper-middle-class participants in Vivian Louie's work. Yet in contrast to Louie's suburban students at Columbia, Sandi does not claim any kind of ethnic advantage. On the contrary, she actively seeks to distance herself from anything that might identify her with Asian students from Asia. See Vivian S. Louie, "Parent's Aspirations and Investment: The Role of Social Class in the Educational Aspirations of 1.5- and Second-Generation Chinese Americans," *Harvard Educational Review*, 71, no. 3 (2001).

35. Wendy Luttrell describes how both white and black poor and working-class women define "smartness" in ways that are both gendered and classed. They oppose the notion of being "schoolsmart," which they associate with men and upward mobility, to that of being "motherwise," which they readily incorporate into their own identifications. See Wendy Luttrell, *Schoolsmart and Motherwise: Working-Class Women's Identity and Schooling* (New York: Routledge, 1997); Wendy Luttrell, "Working-Class Women's Ways of Knowing: Effects of Gender, Race, and Class," *Sociology of Education*, 66, no. 1 (1989).

36. Cookson and Persell, *Preparing for Power.*

37. These experiences are quite similar to the experiences of students from working-class backgrounds who attend Harvard Law School (Granfield, *Making Elite Lawyers*). Granfield offers an insightful analysis of the ways in which these students learn to "make it" by "faking it." He draws on Goffman's concept of stigma and the management of spoiled identities to make sense of how these students negotiate the process of becoming elite lawyers. Erving Goffman, *Stigma: Notes on the Management of Spoiled Identity* (New York: Prentice-Hall, 1963).

38. In the PBS documentary *American Dream at Groton,* Johanna Vega, a Puerto Rican student, talks about the challenge of not being "white enough" to be accepted as a student at Groton, yet not being "Puerto Rican enough" to be accepted by her friends and family at home. *American Dream at Groton,* dir. David Grubin (PBS Video, 1991); Johanna Vega, "From the South Bronx to Groton," in Pearl R. Kane, ed., *Independent Schools, Independent Thinkers* (San Francisco: Jossey-Bass, 1992).

39. See Granfield, *Making Elite Lawyers;* Richard Sennett and Jonathan Cobb, *The Hidden Injuries of Class* (New York: Norton, 1972). See also Katherine Newman, *Falling from Grace: Downward Mobility in the Age of Affluence* (Berkeley, Calif.: University of California Press, 1988; rpt. 1999).

40. In contrast to the experiences of working-class students at Harvard Law School, as documented in Granfield, *Making Elite Lawyers,* several students who identified as coming from lower- and working-class backgrounds appeared to be more comfortable claiming the Westonian identification. On the one hand, it may be that they (and their families) considered it an honor and were proud of the accomplishment. In the documentary *American Dream at Groton,* Johanna Vega disagrees with her parents as to whether coming to Groton is good for students like her. It could be that the anxieties provoked by class mobility are less pronounced for students who can recognize class as part of their experience; Jenny Stuber, "Talk of Class: The Discursive Repertoires of White Working- and Upper-Middle-Class College Students," *Journal of Contemporary Ethnography,* 35, no. 2 (2006). Valerie Walkerdine argues that border crossings such as the ones these students experience are fundamentally sites of pain where "the subject [is] ripped from its moorings in the relations of sociality." Valerie Walkerdine, "Workers in the New Economy: Transformation as Border Crossing," *Ethos,* 34, no. 1 (2006): 12.

41. Randall Collins, "Functional and Conflict Theories of Educational Stratification," *American Sociological Review,* 36, no. 6 (1971).

42. Michael's references to Greek culture are an interesting turn in his narrative. Michael is an avid student of Latin and Greek, which (as mentioned in Chapter 3) positions him near the top of the academic hierarchy at Weston. But since he has been at Weston for only two years, he will not receive the

Latin Distinction at graduation and will not get to wear the medal around his neck. Michael expressed resentment about this.

43. Cookson and Persell, *Preparing for Power,* 29. "Part of the socialization for power is learning how to conceal wealth, or at least minimize its importance by never openly referring to it" (28). See also Baltzell, *Philadelphia Gentlemen.*

44. This contradicts Cookson and Persell's conclusion that all students experience a painful separation from home. It is possible that the atmosphere in elite boarding schools has changed since they did their research in the late 1970s and early 1980s. The point I wish to underscore here is that the distance between home and school is experienced differently by different students.

45. In Sittenfeld's novel *Prep,* the main character, Lee, also describes the wealthy popular boys as the "bank boys," "because all their dads work for banks. I mean, not really all of them do, but that's what it seems like" (360).

46. See Penelope Eckert, *Jocks and Burnouts: Social Categories and Identity in the High School* (New York: Teachers College Press, 1989); Milner, *Freaks, Geeks, and Cool Kids.* Milner downplays the role of class differences in his analysis.

47. These patterns are very much in keeping with the work on consumerism and class status. See Juliet Schor, *Born to Buy: The Commercialized Child and the New Consumer Culture* (New York: Scribner, 2004); idem, *The Overspent American: Upscaling, Downshifting, and the New Consumer* (New York: Basic Books, 1998). Note that as a less economically well-off student, Krista is able to "pass" in order to make friends and find entry into this exclusive social space—a kind of assimilation that other analyses of school cultures and cliques would be unable to explain. The activity of shopping serves as a sort of democratic space in which everyone participates, albeit in markedly different ways. In this case, it also has to do with gender and social capital. Being part of the posse implies a particular physical appearance, which Charlene Rodreau in Chapter 4 describes as the Abercrombie and Fitch model. Krista's long brown curls and light-green eyes, her fair skin and slender figure, would fit well in the Abercrombie and Fitch catalogue. As a day student, she is also part of a social network that includes other girls who are considered attractive and with whom she is connected by association.

48. There is also a specific gender formation implied in Krista's description. Indeed, as others have suggested, fashion consumption is part of a classed gender performance. See Bettie, *Women without Class.*

49. This quote is from a collection of essays written by Weston alumni.

50. Sarah Chase, in *Perfectly Prep,* offers a careful and insightful analysis of the more intimate experience of boys and girls within the context of an elite boarding school. As an insider, she was well positioned to gather data about these experiences, and she developed some very clever data-collection strategies for illuminating these relationships. Her analysis reveals how the performance of what she calls "gender extremes" limits the particular versions of both masculinity and femininity available to students in ways that reproduce upper-class traditional gender roles. Her analysis is focused on the social and intimate lives of the students, at the expense of how gender roles are enacted in more widespread though less obvious ways.

51. Similarly, Donna Eder shows that in middle school, boys have a broader range of options for achieving recognition than girls do—a disparity that produces gender differences in how boys and girls become "popular." Donna Eder, *School Talk: Gender and Adolescent Culture* (New Brunswick, N.J.: Rutgers University Press, 1995).

52. As Chloe speaks, I remember having seen her during an English class in which she was the only girl. After my conversation with her, I went back to my fieldnotes. I'd recorded that in the discussion about *Moby-Dick,* some of the boys had rolled their eyes when she spoke, and that the teacher had responded to her comments only at the beginning of the class.

53. In contrast, students—at least publicly—would never laugh at or undermine the idea that multiculturalism is important or that there is such a thing as racism. I found that, in general, sexism was far more explicit and more acceptable than racism or other kinds of oppressive discourse. This is consistent with the descriptions in Chase, *Perfectly Prep.*

54. For some insights on this, see Chase, *Perfectly Prep.*

55. Amy Best, *Prom Night: Youth, Schools, and Popular Culture* (New York: Routledge, 2000). It may be that some girls view these rituals as opportunities to experience sexuality with each other. Jennifer's description of the prom dress fashion show in Chapter 5, however, suggests that students who identify as other than heterosexual don't necessarily see these rituals in sexual terms.

56. Most of the students who lived in large dormitories had a hand-sign they used to express their "dorm pride," as Matthew described earlier.

57. "Homosocial," according to Eve Sedgwick, "is a word occasionally used in history and social sciences, where it describes social bonds between persons of the same sex; it is a neologism, obviously formed by analogy with 'homosexual,' and just as obviously meant to be distinguished from 'homosexual.'" Eve Kosofsky Sedgwick, *Between Men: English Literature and Male Homosocial Desire* (New York: Columbia University Press, 1985), 1. The fact that a ritual or a relationship is homosocial does not imply that it is also homosexual, yet Sedgwick suggests that the two are not very far apart, and that there is an "unbroken continuum" between them. For an analysis of the consequences of homosocial behavior and bonding, see Rosabeth Moss Kanter, *Men and Women of the Corporation* (New York: Basic Books, 1977).

58. See Cookson and Persell, *Preparing for Power;* John Wakeford, *The Cloistered Elite: A Sociological Analysis of the English Public Boarding School* (New York: Praeger, 1969).

59. For a compelling analysis of the way boys and girls talk about sex at an elite boarding school, see Chase, *Perfectly Prep.* Chase draws a clear distinction between the way boys and girls enact their gender through their sexual behavior and the stark differences in the consequences of such behavior. My research confirms her analysis.

60. These differences are well documented in higher education. See Michael Messner, *Taking the Field: Women, Men, and Sports* (Minneapolis: University of Minnesota Press, 2002).

61. For similar analyses from the perspective of relational psychology, see Carol Gilligan, *In a Different Voice: Psychological Theory and Women's Development* (Cambridge, Mass.: Harvard University Press, 1982). Gilligan and a team of researchers also studied the experiences of students at an all-girls elite boarding school. Carol Gilligan, Nona Lyons, and Trudy Hanmer, eds., *Making Connections: The Relational Worlds of Adolescent Girls at Emma Willard School* (Cambridge, Mass.: Harvard University Press, 1990).

62. The theory of the development of racial identity offers a powerful lens through which to understand Scott's emerging awareness of his privilege as rich, white, and male. His statements could be interpreted as expressions of "disintegration" or "pseudo-independence." See Janet Helms, "An Update on Helms's White and People of Color Racial Identity Models," in J. G. Ponterotto, J. M. Casas, L. A. Suzuki, and C. M. Alexander, eds., *Handbook of Multicultural Counseling* (Thousand Oaks, Calif.: Sage, 1995); Janet Helms, ed., *Black and White Racial Identity: Theory, Research, and Practice* (Westport, Conn.: Greenwood, 1990). On white and male privilege, see the important work of Peggy McIntosh, "Understanding Correspondences between White Privilege and Male Privilege through Women's Studies Work," in *National Women's Studies Association Annual Meeting* (Atlanta, Ga.: Spelman College, 1987). See also Benjamin Bowser and Raymond Hunt, eds., *Impacts of Racism on White Americans,* 2nd ed. (Thousand Oaks, Calif.: Sage, 1996); Michelle Fine, Christine Sleeter, and Lois Weis, eds., *Off White: Readings on Race, Power, and Society* (New York: Routledge, 1997).

63. I don't mean to suggest that Cookson and Persell *(Preparing for Power)* are wrong when they assert that students at elite boarding schools learn to become part of the power elite. Rather, I am trying to illustrate that such access is not equally distributed, and that the way elite status is unequally distributed at such schools is a crucial aspect of the way it operates within an inherently unequal social order.

7. ENVISIONING AN ELITE FUTURE

1. On "key informants," see Matthew B. Miles and A. Michael Huberman, *Qualitative Data Analysis: An Expanded Sourcebook,* 2nd ed. (Thousand Oaks, Calif.: Sage, 1994). On exploratory re-

search, see Robert A. Stebbins, *Exploratory Research in the Social Sciences* (Thousand Oaks, Calif.: Sage, 2001).

2. Contrast this view of working at McDonald's with the sense of dignity and pride expressed by low-wage earners about doing work no one else would want; see Katherine Newman, *No Shame in My Game: The Working Poor in the Inner City* (New York: Knopf and Russell Sage, 1999). The trope of McDonald's as a sign of failure is also echoed in the work of Helen Lucey, June Melody, and Valerie Walkerdine, "Uneasy Hybrids: Psychosocial Aspects of Becoming Educationally Successful for Working-Class Young Women," *Gender and Education,* 15, no. 3 (2003). Emily's words confirm the way in which moral claims are attached to economic success and status. The moral character of class dynamics is articulated in the work of several scholars. Michèle Lamont demonstrates that class boundaries are drawn around definitions of success that are tied up in claims about morality; see Lamont, *Money, Morals, and Manners: The Culture of the French and American Upper-Middle Class* (Chicago: University of Chicago Press, 1992); idem, *The Dignity of Working Men: Morality and the Boundaries of Race, Class, and Immigration* (Cambridge, Mass.: Harvard University Press, 2000). See also Katherine Newman, *Falling from Grace: Downward Mobility in the Age of Affluence* (Berkeley, Calif.: University of California Press, 1988; rpt. 1999).

3. Here is another important distinction between elite boarding schools and some other total institutions (such as prisons). At those facilities, the inmates are at the bottom of the status hierarchy; at Weston, it's the custodial staff who have the least status, as marked by the fact that they are the only ones required to wear a uniform. The experiences of such workers are largely undocumented and would be an interesting line of research.

4. While I was at Weston, several student pranks involving cafeteria equipment and the physical facilities made the role of the staff visible in complex ways that highlighted class distinctions.

5. On many occasions, students spoke openly and favorably about the custodial staff. During one dorm meeting, students planned to purchase holiday gifts for their custodian, commenting on the value of his work.

6. Befriending the school staff is likely not a joke for Weston students who are children of staff members. In addition, some of the day students went to middle school with the teenagers who clean tables in the dining halls. Yet when students talk about these relationships, the symbolic boundaries are always underscored, even when a close tie is being described.

7. Wendy Luttrell, "The Two-in-Oneness of Class," in Lois Weis, ed., *The Way Class Works: Readings on School, Family, and the Economy* (New York: Routledge, 2007), 62. See also Lamont, *Money, Morals, and Manners;* idem, *The Dignity of Working Men.*

8. Luttrell, "Two-in-Oneness."

9. W. E. B. DuBois, *The Souls of Black Folk: Essays and Sketches* (New York: Fawcett, 1961), esp. 3–5.

10. See notes 21–25 in Chapter 6.

11. For a powerful critique of the racial politics of physical appearance, see Deborah Britzman, "Narcissism of Minor Differences and the Problem of Anti-Racist Pedagogy," in Britzman, *Lost Subjects, Contested Objects: Toward a Psychoanalytic Inquiry of Learning* (Albany, N.Y.: SUNY Press, 1998). See also Edward Fergus, "Understanding Latino Students' Schooling Experience: The Relevance of Skin Color among Mexican and Puerto Rican High School Students," *Teachers College Record,* 111, no. 2 (2009).

12. See discussion in Chapter 6 (with notes 37 and 39).

13. Paul Willis, *Learning to Labour* (Farnborough, U.K.: Saxon House, 1977). Robert Granfield, *Making Elite Lawyers: Visions of Law at Harvard and Beyond* (New York: Routledge, 1992), arrives at a very similar conclusion regarding working-class students at Harvard Law School.

14. Mitchell Stevens, *Creating a Class: College Admissions and the Education of Elites* (Cambridge, Mass.: Harvard University Press, 2007).

15. If nothing else, this willingness sets her apart from students like Willis' "lads" or MacLeod's

"hallway hangers." At the same time, the outcome of such willingness is starkly unequal for students in other (nonelite) school contexts, such as MacLeod's "brothers" or Luttrell's "teachers' pets," whose willingness to play by the school rules doesn't necessarily yield even a modest shift in upward mobility. Luttrell, *Schoolsmart and Motherwise;* Jay MacLeod, *Ain't No Makin' It: Leveled Aspirations in a Low-Income Neighborhood* (Boulder, Colo.: Westview, 1995); Willis, *Learning to Labour.*

16. This argument parallels the discussion in Laurie Olsen, *Made in America: Immigrant Students in Our Public Schools* (New York: New Press, 1997). According to Olsen, most immigrants find that becoming American means assuming a place in a racial hierarchy in which they can never be at the top.

17. One explanation for their inability to deal consciously and perhaps even critically with the consequences of their status is that they are unaware of it. As Luttrell argues (in "Two-in-Oneness"), they cannot think about what they cannot see.

18. Jean Anyon, in her classic essay "Social Class and School Knowledge," *Curriculum Inquiry,* 11 (1981), points out that "excellence" is likewise one of the overriding themes in the context of the elite public schools she studied.

19. Peter W. Cookson and Caroline Hodges Persell, *Preparing for Power: America's Elite Boarding Schools* (New York: Basic Books, 1985), 21.

20. See James McLachlan, *American Boarding Schools* (New York: Scribner, 1970); Theodore R. Sizer, ed., *The Age of the Academies* (New York: Bureau of Publications, Teachers College, Columbia University, 1964).

21. While today the majority of students do not attend Ivy League schools, these schools and others of the most selective institutions are the ones that admit the largest number of graduating seniors.

22. As Stevens suggests in *Creating a Class,* this generates a great deal of anxiety, especially among middle- and upper-middle-class parents who have high expectations for their children's college prospects and whose own self-worth is bound up with their children's success.

23. The dynamics of this process are much more involved than even students can know, involving complex negotiations between counselors and admissions officers that often have little to do with the students themselves. See Stevens, *Creating a Class.*

24. There are no recent studies of how attending an elite boarding school affects future outcomes. Earlier studies include Beth Mintz, "The President's Cabinet, 1897–1972: A Contribution to the Power Structure Debate," *Insurgent Sociologist,* 5, no. 1 (1975); Michael Useem and Jerome Karabel, "Educational Pathways through Top Corporate Management," *American Sociological Review,* 51, no. 1 (1984). There is considerable and long-standing debate about the effect that attending an elite college may have on future success. The evidence is mixed, and mostly suggests that the quality or stature of a college has the most effect on the future lives of those with the most to gain. See Jennie Brand and Charles Halaby, "Regression and Matching Estimates of the Effects of Elite College Attendance on Educational and Career Achievement," *Social Science Research,* 35, no. 3 (2006); Dominic Brewer, Susan Gates, and Charles Goldman, *In Pursuit of Prestige: Strategy and Competition in U.S. Higher Education* (New Brunswick, N.J.: Transaction, 2002); Stacy Berg Dale and Alan B. Krueger, "Estimating the Payoff to Attending a More Selective College: An Application of Selection on Observable and Unobservables," *Quarterly Journal of Economics,* 117, no. 4 (2002).

25. The 1873 Slaughter-House Cases resulted in a narrow reading of the Fourteenth Amendment: to protect those "privileges and immunities" conferred by federal law, rather than state law. At issue was whether the protections granted to freed slaves should also protect the rights of corporations. While shifting from a substantive consideration of due process (whether the amendment protects corporations as citizens) to a procedural consideration (whether the law infringes on Americans' national citizenship, as opposed to their state citizenship), the court also asserted that the amendment was primarily intended to protect former slaves and should not be applied broadly.

26. Cookson and Persell, *Preparing for Power,* 20.

27. Cookson and Persell (ibid.) argue that losses result from the forging of this consciousness. While my work certainly shows that the process of becoming elite entails major psychic investments, the

demands and the rewards of the process are not equally distributed. This is an important addition to their findings, which made few distinctions among the various kinds of elite students.

28. Amy Best, *Prom Night: Youth, Schools, and Popular Culture* (New York: Routledge, 2000). For a description of what happens in the dorms at another elite boarding school prior to prom night, see Sarah A. Chase, *Perfectly Prep: Gender Extremes at a New England Prep School* (New York: Oxford, 2008).

29. Marlene de Laine, *Fieldwork, Participation, and Practice: Ethics and Dilemmas in Qualitative Research* (London: Sage, 2000); Annette Lareau and Jeffrey Shultz, eds., *Journeys through Ethnography: Realistic Accounts of Fieldwork* (Boulder, Colo.: Westview, 1996); Steven Taylor, "Leaving the Field," in William B. Shaffir and Robert A. Stebbins, eds., *Experiencing Fieldwork: An Inside View of Qualitative Research* (Thousand Oaks, Calif.: Sage, 1991).

APPENDIX

1. For a discussion of the idea that ethnographers themselves are the instrument of their research, see David M. Fetterman, *Ethnography: Step by Step*, 2nd ed. (Thousand Oaks, Calif.: Sage, 1998); and Paul Atkinson et al., eds., *Handbook of Ethnography* (Thousand Oaks, Calif.: Sage, 2001; rpt. 2007).

2. Ruth Behar, *The Vulnerable Observer: Anthropology That Breaks Your Heart* (Boston: Beacon, 1996).

3. See Erving Goffman, *The Presentation of Self in Everyday Life* (Garden City, N.Y.: Doubleday Anchor, 1959).

4. Most educational research, in fact, looks "down" upon communities and schools identified as "deficient" or in some way needing "improvement," presumably with the purpose of finding "cures" or ways to improve their predicament. See Howard Becker, "Studying Urban Schools," *Anthropology and Education Quarterly,* 14 (1983); Michelle Fine and Lois Weis, "Writing the 'Wrongs' of Fieldwork: Confronting Our Own Research/Writing Dilemmas in Urban Ethnographies," *Qualitative Inquiry,* 2, no. 3 (1996); Laura Nader, "Up the Anthropologist: Perspectives Gained from Studying Up," in Dell Hymes, ed., *Reinventing Anthropology* (New York: Vintage, 1974).

5. See Rubén A. Gaztambide-Fernández, Heather Harding, and Tere Sordé-Martí, eds., *Cultural Studies and Education: Perspectives on Theory, Methodology, and Practice* (Cambridge, Mass.: Harvard Educational Review, 2004). For a postcolonial perspective, see Linda Tuhiwai Smith, *Decolonizing Methodologies: Research and Indigenous Peoples* (London: Zed, 1999). For a critical perspective, see Jim Thomas, *Doing Critical Ethnography* (Newbury Park, Calif.: Sage, 1993). For a feminist perspective, see Patti Lather, *Getting Smart: Feminist Research and Pedagogy with/in the Postmodern* (New York: Routledge, 1991). See also the essays in Andrew Gitlin, ed., *Power and Method: Political Activism and Educational Research* (New York: Routledge, 1994). Critical researchers have raised questions about the role of "outsiders," particularly those coming from "higher-status" groups and organizations, in pathologizing lower-status communities and often "blaming the victims" for their supposed "deficiencies." In claiming the authority to determine and fix the problems of "others," these "outsiders" assume "a position to give official imprint to versions of reality," and represent communities in ways that reify the very problems they claim to address. Erving Goffman, "The Interaction Order," *American Sociological Review,* 48, no. 1 (1983): 17. See Patti Lather, "Research as Praxis," *Harvard Educational Review,* 56, no. 3 (1986); Edward Said, "Representing the Colonized: Anthropology's Interlocutors," in Said, *Reflections on Exile and Other Essays* (Cambridge, Mass.: Harvard University Press, 2000).

6. Jean Bartunek and Meryl Louis, *Insider/Outsider Team Research* (Thousand Oaks, Calif.: Sage, 1996).

7. Michele Foster, "The Power to Know One Thing Is Never the Power to Know All Things: Methodological Notes on Two Studies of Black American Teachers," in Gitlin, *Power and Method.*

8. Joseph A. Conti and Moira O'Neil, "Studying Power: Qualitative Methods and the Global Elite," *Qualitative Research,* 7, no. 1 (2007).

9. Because adults at an elite boarding school act *in loco parentis,* students initially wondered whether I, as an adult, would be required to report illicit activities that I might witness or that they might share with me. I explained to them that I was ethically required only to report instances in which some-one (whether student or adult) appeared to be in danger or under threat.

10. According to former Harvard dean Henry Rosovsky, "A *true* son or daughter of Harvard is a former undergraduate. A graduate degree bestows at best the status of a cousin, except when fund drives are in progress. At that time we are all one happy family." Henry Rosovsky, *The University: An Owner's Manual* (New York: Norton, 1990), 79.

11. I realize that in belaboring this point I may be working against my own sense of eliteness and privilege. If that's the case, the reader will have to determine its relevance to the present analysis.

12. Foster, "The Power to Know."

13. Joan Eakin Hoffman, "Problems of Access in the Study of Social Elites and Boards of Direc-tors," in William B. Shaffir, Robert A. Stebbins, and Allan Turowetz, eds., *Fieldwork Experience: Quali-tative Approaches to Social Research* (New York: St. Martin's, 1980), 47.

14. Nader, "Up the Anthropologist"; Ian Weinberg, "Some Methodological and Field Problems of Social Research in Elite Secondary Schools," *Sociology of Education,* 41, no. 2 (1968). See also the es-says in Geoffrey Walford, ed., *Researching the Powerful in Education* (London: UCL Press, 1994).

15. Hoffman, "Problems of Access," 46. Hoffman studied the internal dynamics and social organi-zation of the board of directors at a Canadian hospital.

16. Peter W. Cookson and Caroline Hodges Persell, *Preparing for Power: America's Elite Boarding Schools* (New York: Basic Books, 1985), 6.

17. Weinberg, "Some Methodological Problems." Weinberg studied British "public" schools, which are the equivalent of elite boarding schools in the United States. Ian Weinberg, *The English Public Schools: The Sociology of Elite Education* (New York: Atherton, 1967). In his 1968 article, he described the various challenges he encountered, as well as strategies for dealing with such challenges in future re-search, highlighting the importance of studying elite schools in order to develop a full understanding of schooling in any society.

18. Hoffman ("Problems of Access") describes how disclosing family friendships and ties sud-denly shifted the kind of information her participants would disclose with regard to the internal work-ings of a board of directors.

19. Wendy Luttrell argues that coming to terms with these choices is necessary for developing a "good enough" methodology for ethnographic research, and she describes her own decisions. Wendy Luttrell, "'Good Enough' Methods for Ethnographic Research," *Harvard Educational Review,* 70, no. 4 (2000). Michèle Lamont agrees, maintaining "that social life cannot be studied 'whole,' and that knowl-edge production sometimes requires cutting into it with a scalpel that often does violence to it." Michèle Lamont, "A Life of Sad, but Justified, Choices: Interviewing across (Too) Many Divides," in Martin Bul-mer and John Solomos, eds., *Researching Race and Racism* (London: Routledge, 2004), 171. Some members of the Weston School community may disagree and perhaps even take offense at the represen-tations I put forth here. This is, in some sense, an inevitable outcome of the ethnographic process, through which experience is reduced to a glimpse—or, as Paul Willis puts it, "a supremely ex post facto product of the actual uncertainty of life, [a product in which] the subjects stand too square in their self-referenced world." Yet as Willis insists, "The ethnographic account, for all its faults, records a crucial level of experience and through its very biases insists upon a level of human agency which is persistently overlooked or denied but which increases in importance all the time for other levels of the social whole." Paul Willis, *Learning to Labour: How Working Class Lads Get Working Class Jobs* (Farnborough, U.K.: Saxon House, 1977), 194.

20. There were only two one-year seniors in the class, and they were both Canadian—a fact that excluded them from the research, since they were "international" students. There were also thirty-nine postgraduates (or PGs): students who had finished high school and who had come to Weston for an ad-ditional year. As newcomers, these students had an interesting perspective on the school. But they did not identify as Westonians, and were not identified as such by others. I chose to exclude PGs from the re-

search so that I could focus on the construction of elite identifications. I did interview several PGs during the first year of research, and I interviewed one female PG (whose brother had been a PG before her) during the in-depth interview phase the second year, mostly to use her perspective as a point of reference. Much of what I learned from her confirmed my suspicions about the roles available to PGs in the school.

21. Robert M. Emerson, Rachel I. Fretz, and Linda L. Shaw, *Writing Ethnographic Fieldnotes* (Chicago: Chicago University Press, 1995); Stephen L. Schensul, Jean J. Schensul, and Margaret D. LeCompte, *Essential Ethnographic Methods: Observations, Interviews, and Questionnaires,* vol. 2 (Walnut Creek, Calif.: Altamira, 1999).

22. On "deep hanging out," see note 11 in the Introduction.

23. It could be argued that full immersion in campus life, whether as an official member of the community or as a guest, would have been a better way to conduct this research. For personal as well as professional reasons, I chose not to move to the school. The decision had advantages and disadvantages. I am confident that the validity and reliability of my research were not compromised by my decision to reside off-campus. For ethnographic studies involving complete immersion in the context of elite boarding schools, see Sarah A. Chase, *Perfectly Prep: Gender Extremes at a New England Prep School* (New York: Oxford University Press, 2008); Shamus Khan, "The Production of Privilege" (diss., University of Wisconsin, 2008).

24. Matthew B. Miles and A. Michael Huberman, *Qualitative Data Analysis: An Expanded Sourcebook,* 2nd ed. (Thousand Oaks, Calif.: Sage, 1994).

25. David Barton and Mary Hamilton, *Local Literacies: Reading and Writing in One Community* (New York: Routledge, 1998); Wendy Luttrell and C. Parker, "High School Students' Literacy Practices and Identities, and the Figured World of School," *Journal of Research and Reading,* 24, no. 3 (2001).

26. One possible clue to this puzzle is the fact that all four of the students who identified as Asian Americans were ambivalent about this label, and three of them explicitly stated that they did not entirely embrace the identification. It is possible that students who identified strongly as Asian Americans felt that this study, which explicitly focused on being Westonian, was not really about them, or at least not about something they wanted to share with someone they saw as non-Asian.

27. Miles and Huberman, *Qualitative Data Analysis,* 28.

28. Joseph A. Maxwell, *Qualitative Research Design: An Interactive Approach,* 2nd ed. (Thousand Oaks, Calif.: Sage, 2005).

29. Miles and Huberman, *Qualitative Data Analysis.*

30. Ibid.

31. Schensul, Schensul, and LeCompte, *Essential Ethnographic Methods.* If this process sounds mysterious, that's because it often is. Paul Rock reflects on this and describes how at some point early in the research "someone will emerge, *deus ex machina,* like a fairy godmother, to help the forlorn ethnographer." Paul Rock, "Symbolic Interactionism and Ethnography," in Atkinson et al., *Handbook of Ethnography,* 34. For a compelling description of how one ethnographer engaged the "services" of a key informant, see Ann Arnett Ferguson, *Bad Boys: Public Schools in the Making of Black Masculinity* (Ann Arbor: University of Michigan Press, 2000).

32. On girls, see Amira Proweller, *Constructing Female Identities: Meaning Making in an Upper Middle Class Youth Culture* (Albany, N.Y.: SUNY Press, 1998). On the experiences of boys, see Peter Kuriloff and Michael Reichert, "Boys of Class, Boys of Color: Negotiating the Academic and Social Geography of an Elite Independent School," *Journal of Social Issues,* 59, no. 4 (2003); Michael Reichert, "Disturbances of Difference: Lessons from a Boy's School," in Lois Weis and Michelle Fine, eds., *Construction Sites: Excavating Race, Class, and Gender among Urban Youth* (New York: Teachers College Press, 2000). For a focus on gender that relates to both girls and boys, see Chase, *Perfectly Prep.* On black students, see Richard L. Zweigenhaft and G. William Domhoff, *Blacks in the White Establishment? A Study of Race and Class in America* (New Haven, Conn.: Yale University Press, 1991).

33. The research literature is too extensive to cite here; recent examples are as follows. On race,

see Prudence Carter, *Keepin' It Real: School Success beyond Black and White* (Oxford: Oxford University Press, 2005); Signithia Fordham, *Blacked Out: Dilemmas of Race, Identity, and Success at Capital High* (Chicago: University of Chicago Press, 1996). On gender, see Donna Eder, *School Talk: Gender and Adolescent Culture* (New Brunswick, N.J.: Rutgers University Press, 1995); Wendy Luttrell, *Pregnant Bodies, Fertile Minds: Gender, Race, and the Schooling of Pregnant Teens* (New York: Routledge, 2003). On class, see Julie Bettie, *Women without Class: Girls, Race, and Identity* (Berkeley, Calif.: University of California Press, 2003); Adam Howard, *Learning Privilege: Lessons of Power and Identity in Affluent Schooling* (New York: Routledge, 2007). See also Lois Weis and Michelle Fine, eds., *Beyond Silenced Voices: Class, Race, and Gender in United States Schools* (Albany, N.Y.: SUNY Press, 1993); Lois Weis and Michelle Fine, eds., *Construction Sites: Excavating Race, Class, and Gender among Urban Youth* (New York: Teachers College Press, 2000).

34. It was clear to me from the little time I spent with some international students that they did not share the experiences of immigrant students in public schools, as described in Laurie Olsen, *Made in America: Immigrant Students in Our Public Schools* (New York: New Press, 1997). See also Carola Suárez-Orozco and Marcelo Suárez-Orozco, *Children of Immigration* (Cambridge, Mass.: Harvard University Press, 2001). These students not only retained their international status, but most of them returned home during school vacations. Additionally, most if not all of these students came from very wealthy families in their respective countries, where attending elite U.S. boarding schools is seen as a symbol of high status. I am not aware of any study of the experiences of international students at elite U.S. schools. Chase, *Perfectly Prep,* is likewise sparse on the experiences of international students.

35. All students in the senior class were notified by the school about my study and received subsequent emails from me (through the school) regarding my study. Parents received notification as well, and were given an opportunity to exclude their children from participation.

36. Catherine Riessman, "Analysis of Personal Narratives," in Jaber F. Gubrium and James A. Holstein, eds., *Handbook of Interview Research* (Thousand Oaks, Calif.: Sage, 2002).

37. Elliot G. Mishler, *Research Interviewing: Context and Narrative* (Cambridge, Mass.: Harvard University Press, 1986); idem, *Storylines: Craftartists' Narratives of Identity* (Cambridge, Mass.: Harvard University Press, 1999).

38. Charles Briggs, *Learning How to Ask: A Sociolinguistic Appraisal of the Role of the Interview in Social Science Research* (Cambridge: Cambridge University Press, 1986); I. E. Seidman, *Interviewing as Qualitative Research: A Guide for Researchers in Education and the Social Sciences* (New York: Teachers College Press, 1991).

39. I piloted the focus group activities with a group of students who volunteered to help me refine the tasks, but whom I had not interviewed. The activities I planned changed significantly in response to the students' feedback and suggestions, which enabled me to make better choices about how to use the focus groups more effectively.

40. David L. Morgan, *Focus Groups as Qualitative Research,* 2nd ed. (London: Sage, 1997).

41. Sarah Pink, *Visual Ethnography: Images, Media, and Representation in Research* (Thousand Oaks, Calif.: Sage, 2001).

42. Helen Lomax and Neil Casey, "Recording Social Life: Reflexivity and Video Methodology," *Sociological Research Online,* 3, no. 2 (1998), cited in Pink, *Visual Ethnography,* 88.

43. Pink, *Visual Ethnography,* 88.

44. Edward F. Fern, *Advanced Focus Group Research* (Thousand Oaks, Calif.: Sage, 2001).

45. Morgan, *Focus Groups.*

46. Sara Delamont, *Fieldwork in Educational Settings: Methods, Pitfalls, and Perspectives* (London: Falmer, 1991), 158.

47. This kind of engagement with participants is quite common in participatory action research; see Reason and Bradbury, *Handbook of Action Research.* Dolores Delgado Bernal, "Using a Chicana Feminist Epistemology in Educational Research," *Harvard Educational Review,* 68, no. 4 (1998), offers a compelling discussion of this process with her participants.

48. Miles and Huberman, *Qualitative Data Analysis.*

49. Emerson, Fretz, and Shaw, *Writing Ethnographic Fieldnotes.* See also the essays in Roger Sanjek, ed., *Fieldnotes: The Makings of Anthropology* (Ithaca, N.Y.: Cornell University Press, 1990).

50. Emerson, Fretz, and Shaw, *Writing Ethnographic Fieldnotes,* 11, emphasis in original.

51. Other authors have used this metaphor to describe their ethnographic data. See Rafael Ávila Peñagos and Marina Camargo Abello, "The Role of Institutional Education Projects in the Reconstruction of the School Labyrinth," in Bradley A. Levinson et al., eds., *Ethnography and Education Policy across the Americas* (Westport, Conn.: Praeger, 2002); Eve Gregory, "Taking Decisions: Introduction to Part Three (The Turning Point: Methodology)," in Jean Conteh et al., eds., *On Writing Educational Ethnographies: The Art of Collusion* (Stoke-on-Trent, U.K.: Trentham, 2005).

52. Briggs, *Learning How to Ask;* Mishler, *Research Interviewing.*

53. Clive F. Seale, "Computer-Assisted Analysis of Qualitative Interview Data," in Gubrium and Holstein, *Handbook of Interview Research.*

54. Miles and Huberman, *Qualitative Data Analysis.*

55. William Labov, "Speech Actions and Reactions in Personal Narrative," in Deborah Tannen, ed., *Analyzing Discourse: Text and Talk* (Washington, D.C.: Georgetown University Press, 1981); William Labov and Joshua Waletzky, "Narrative Analysis: Oral Versions of Personal Experience," in June Helm, ed., *Essays on the Verbal and Visual Arts* (Seattle: University of Washington Press, 1967); Mishler, *Research Interviewing;* idem., *Storylines;* Riessman, "Analysis of Personal Narratives"; Catherine Riessman, "Narrative Analysis," in Michael S. Lewis-Beck, Alan Bryman, and Tim Futing Liao, eds., *The Sage Encyclopedia of Social Science Research Methods* (Thousand Oaks, Calif.: Sage, 2004).

56. These coding strategies parallel those presented in various guides for qualitative data analysis. See Miles and Huberman, *Qualitative Data Analysis;* Anselm L. Strauss, *Qualitative Analysis for Social Scientists* (Cambridge: Cambridge University Press, 1987); Anselm L. Strauss and Juliet Corbin, *Basics of Qualitative Research: Techniques and Procedures for Developing Grounded Theory* (Thousand Oaks, Calif.: Sage, 1998). Yet the specific choices I made in developing coding strategies at various levels of analysis were grounded on my emerging understanding of the data.

57. Emerson, Fretz, and Shaw, *Writing Ethnographic Fieldnotes.*

58. Strauss, *Qualitative Analysis.*

59. Strauss and Corbin, *Basics of Qualitative Research.*

60. Nigel G. Fielding and Raymond M. Lee, *Computer Analysis and Qualitative Research* (London: Sage, 1998). For more on the use of Computer Assisted Qualitative Data Analysis (CAQDAS), see the many resources of the CAQDAS Networking Project at caqdas.soc.surrey.ac.uk/ (accessed March 28, 2009).

61. Strauss and Corbin, *Basics of Qualitative Research,* 124.

62. Howard Becker, "The Epistemology of Qualitative Research," in Richard Jessor, Anne Colby, and Richard A. Shweder, eds., *Ethnography and Human Development: Context and Meaning in Social Inquiry* (Chicago: University of Chicago Press, 1996); Conteh et al., *On Writing Educational Ethnographies.*

63. Sherryl Kleinman and Martha A. Copp, *Emotions and Fieldwork* (Newbury Park, Calif.: Sage, 1993); Annette Lareau and Jeffrey Shultz, eds., *Journeys through Ethnography* (Boulder, Colo.: Westview, 1996); Luttrell, "Good Enough"; Maxwell, *Qualitative Research Design;* Geoffrey Shacklock and John Smyth, *Being Reflexive in Critical Educational and Social Research* (London: Falmer, 1998); Paul Willis, *The Ethnographic Imagination* (Cambridge: Polity, 2000).

64. Kleinman and Copp, *Emotions and Fieldwork.*

65. Vincent A. Anfara, Kathleen M. Brown, and Terri L. Mangione, "Qualitative Analysis on Stage: Making the Research Process More Public," *Educational Researcher,* 31, no. 7 (2002).

66. Only two participants communicated with me about their transcripts, and only one of them offered a brief clarification about what he said. He asked me not to cite him directly.

67. Maxwell, *Qualitative Research.*

68. Behar, *The Vulnerable Observer;* Kleinman and Copp, *Emotions and Fieldwork.*

69. Christopher Shea, "Don't Talk to the Humans," *Lingua Franca,* 10, no. 6 (2000).

70. Reason and Bradbury, *Handbook of Action Research.*

71. James Clifford and George E. Marcus, eds., *Writing Culture: The Poetics and Politics of Eth-nography* (Berkeley, Calif.: University of California Press, 1986); Fine and Weis, "Writing the 'Wrongs.'"

72. Clifford and Marcus, *Writing Culture;* Luttrell, "Good Enough."

73. Clifford Geertz, *The Interpretation of Cultures* (New York: Basic Books, 1973), 29.

ACKNOWLEDGMENTS

It is a cliché to acknowledge that all scholarly work is the product of collaborations and contributions by many hands. But it can hardly be repeated enough, particularly since the trope of the lone scholar persists despite all evidence to the contrary. Many have imprinted their thoughts, their hands, and their feelings on this work—and although I cannot possibly mention them all, there are some to whom I owe particular gratitude.

The research presented in this book could not even have begun without the assistance and support of various individuals at the "Weston School," who unfortunately must remain nameless. Several members of the administration kept inviting me to continue the research I had started on their behalf. Several members of the faculty were particularly supportive, including the Assistant Head, whose family welcomed me into their guest quarters week after week during the second year of research. Other teachers helped me to navigate the school space, allowed me to sit in on their classes, and joined me in extended conversations that greatly informed the analysis. Several members of the faculty were particularly interested in my work and willingly served as sounding boards for emerging ideas. They offered sharp criticisms whenever they thought I was jumping to conclusions, and generously granted me access to their classrooms, their dormitories, and even their personal spaces. On some evenings, after a long day of fieldwork, I would go to their homes for dinner, turn on the tape recorder, and converse with them about what I had seen that day. They offered their unique perspective as teachers, and suggested leads that I might follow, students I should talk with, events I should observe. I trust that these teachers will recognize the ways in which I try to honor their insights in this book.

The thirty-six students who allowed me into their lives and considered my questions deserve more than an acknowledgment—yet they, too, must remain anonymous. Their curiosity and their willingness to subject their experiences to my—as well as their—sociological scrutiny filled my time at Weston with surprises and discoveries. There were also a number of students who were not part of the in-depth interviews but who became deeply interested in the work and with whom I had many late-night conversations. They offered critiques as well as reassurances, and taught me a great deal about the social and physical landscape of the Weston School. I owe them much more than I can say.

Throughout this research, Sara Lawrence-Lightfoot, Wendy Luttrell, and Michèle Lamont have been masterly mentors, incisive readers, and demanding critics without whose expertise and dedication this book would never have taken shape. Others whose guidance was indispensable were Jessica Davis, who believed in me from the beginning; Eileen de los Reyes, who introduced me to the world of critical educational theory; and James T. Sears, who was the first to encourage me to turn my research into a book. Conversations with Ellen Brantlinger, Josh Guetzkow, Adam Howard, Jerry Karabel, Shamus Khan, Mitchell Stevens, and many others shaped my thinking as the work evolved.

I have been fortunate to be part of an interpretive community whose members are a tremendous source of support, intellectually, personally, and politically. Heather Harding and Eric Toshalis have become more than colleagues; they are my siblings, and we have shared the headaches and the heartaches as well as the joys and illuminations of academic work. I owe the two of them my integrity. At various times, other colleagues joined our study group and offered insights and critical perspectives. Elis Kanner, Victor Milner, Tere Sordé-Martí, Erin Murphy-Graham, and Abdi Ali supported the early stages of this work. Adriana Katzew and Anju Saigal assisted me in the process of reviewing questionnaires and selecting participants, and offered their perspectives in the early stages of analysis. In the last two years of writing, Polly Attwood read drafts of chapters with a painstakingly critical eye and dedication. My one and only Puerto Rican brother throughout this process, James Seale-Collazo, keeps me honest, and alert to my own "elite subjectivities," with relentless kindness. ¡Gracias, hermano! Since my arrival in Toronto, Lance McCready, Indigo Esmonde, Joseph Flessa, and Roland Coloma have read drafts of various chapters and offered critical feedback. Dennis Thiessen and Tara Goldstein offered assistance and support throughout the publication process.

Elizabeth Knoll at Harvard University Press has been a patient, supportive, and keen editor. She selected three magnificent reviewers who offered sharp criticism and excellent suggestions. With their feedback, Elizabeth skillfully shepherded me through the challenging process of transforming the manuscript into a book. Maria Ascher's dedication to the editorial work and Dody Rigg's sharp and discerning eyes brought luster to the final product.

Last, I wish to thank my family: my mother, who first taught me that all of our lives are interconnected and that each of our actions has consequences for the lives of others; my two fathers, whom I cannot list or describe because I cannot decide in what order to list or describe them. ¡Gracias! Jean and Walter Spillane welcomed me into their family one Easter Sunday thirteen years ago and have been staunch in their support. For almost twenty years my Boston moms—whom my children know as Grand-C and Grand-D—have been the best adoptive moms a Puerto Rican boy can have 1,677 miles from home.

This book would not have been possible without the patience, kindness, love, and dedication of my wife, Bonnie Jean Spillane-Gaztambide. When I doubted, she lifted my hopes. When I wavered, she was my compass. When I fell, she lent me her hands. And I thank my children, Mercedes Irene and Alejandro Tomás Gaztambide-Spillane, for making me laugh, dancing with me, and always keeping my feet on the ground. Every word, punctuation mark, and empty space in these pages belongs to them. Los amo.

INDEX